Court Government and the Collapse of Accountability in Canada and the United Kingdom

Throughout much of the Western world there is growing conviction among politicians, the media, students of government, and civil servants themselves that the public sector is in urgent need of fundamental reform. Public trust in political institutions, politicians, and civil servants has fallen sharply in recent years. Some critics have argued that our inherited systems of bureaucracy are ill-equipped to meet the challenges of governance today.

By looking at changes in values both in society and inside government, and the shifting relationships and tensions between politicians, civil servants, and citizens, this study seeks to understand the apparent dysfunction in the public sector. Comparing developments in Canada and the United Kingdom, Donald Savoie contends that both countries now operate under a system of court government, in which power essentially rests with the prime minister and a small group of selected advisers, or 'courtiers.' In contrast to cabinet government, in which decision making is relatively formal and democratic, court government is more centralized and arbitrary. Only in matters that are of less importance to the main players is decision making allowed to devolve into a more horizontal and consultative, albeit often cumbersome, process, involving actors from different government departments and agencies as well as individuals operating outside government.

In this timely and controversial work, Savoie argues that the civil service, beset by many conflicting and impossible demands and pressures, has lost its way. Court government undermines both the traditional bureaucratic model and basic principles of accountability that have guided the development of our Westminster-Whitehall parliamentary system. Many of the conventions that Canada and the United Kingdom cling to have outgrown their usefulness, and there are sure signs that the civil service is shedding some of the characteristics of the traditional model – notably, the old emphasis on political hierarchy and loyalty. However, a new model has yet to fully emerge. Through a critical re-examination of both the operation of and assumptions about the civil service, this comprehensive comparative analysis demonstrates the need for new approaches in the effort to strengthen accountability in our political and administrative institutions while suggesting directions for change.

DONALD J. SAVOIE holds the Canada Research Chair in Public Administration and Governance at l'Université de Moncton.

D1003122

IPAC **IAPC**

The Institute of Public Administration of Canada Series in Public Management and Governance

Editor: Luc Bernier

This series is sponsored by the Institute of Public Administration of Canada as part of its commitment to encourage research on issues in Canadian public administration, public sector management, and public policy. It also seeks to foster wider knowledge and understanding among practitioners, academics, and the general public.

For a list of books published in the series, see page 443.

DONALD J. SAVOIE

Court Government and the Collapse of Accountability in Canada and the United Kingdom

UNIVERSITY OF TORONTO PRESS
Toronto Buffalo London

© University of Toronto Press Incorporated 2008
Toronto Buffalo London
Printed in Canada
www.utppublishing.com

Reprinted 2008

ISBN 978-0-8020–9870-2 (cloth)
ISBN 978-0-8020–9579-4 (paper)

Printed on acid-free paper

Library and Archives Canada Cataloguing in Publication

Savoie, Donald J., 1947–
Court government and the collapse of accountability in Canada
and the United Kingdom / Donald J. Savoie.

(Institute of Public Administration in Canada series in public management
and governance)
Includes bibliographical references and index.
ISBN 978-0-8020-9870-2 (bound).   ISBN 978-0-8020-9579-4 (pbk.)

1. Public administration – Canada.   2. Public administration – Great Britain.
3. Administrative responsibility – Canada.   4. Administrative responsibility –
Great Britain.   I. Title.   II. Series.

JF51.S29 2008   351.71   C2007-907631-9

Financial support from the Canada School of Public Service for this book is
gratefully acknowledged. The views expressed herein are not necessarily
those of the Canada School of Public Service or of the Government of
Canada.

University of Toronto Press acknowledges the financial assistance to its publishing
program of the Canada Council for the Arts and the Ontario Arts Council.

University of Toronto Press acknowledges the financial support for its publishing
activities of the Government of Canada through the Book Publishing Industry
Development Program (BPIDP).

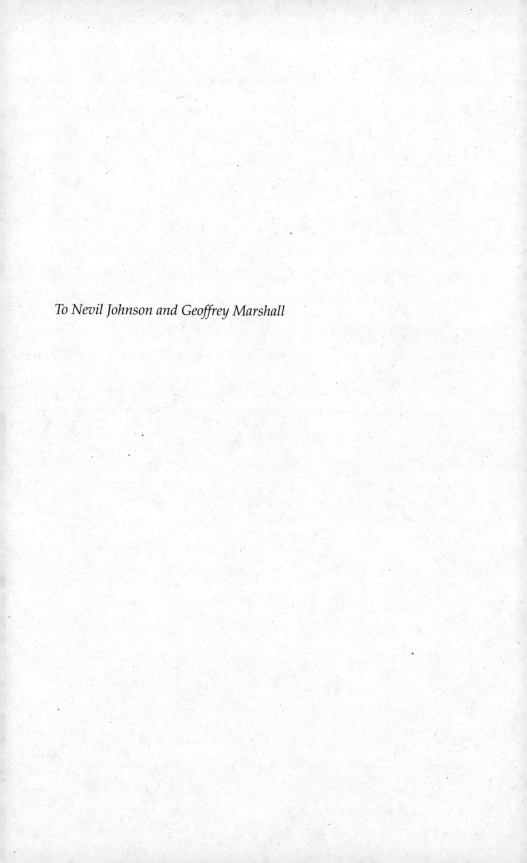

To Nevil Johnson and Geoffrey Marshall

Contents

Preface

Prize fellows at All Souls College, Oxford, are special; they are *la crème de la crème*. Every year All Souls invites about fifty of the best of Oxford's graduating class to compete for two prize fellowships. The winners enjoy a seven-year appointment and are free to pursue whatever interest they may wish.

In January 2006 I had lunch with a prize fellow. He was torn between a career in academe or as an entrepreneur. Both offer promise, I responded. But, I asked, why not contemplate a career in the civil service? Thirty years ago, I added, prize fellows would certainly have considered the civil service to be as attractive as academe or business as a career choice. With no hesitation, he replied, 'Well, not me. It is either academe or business.' He explained: 'I want to look back at some point in my career and see that I have built something, that I have built a business or written a book. It is really not about accumulating money.' In government, he added, 'you are part of a maze, a process, and you never know if in the end you have contributed to the success or failure of anything.' I asked around All Souls, and sure enough I learned that the civil service holds far less appeal for prize fellows than it did thirty or forty years ago. And yet, Oxford and Cambridge have been the prime training ground for British politicians, including prime ministers and senior civil servants, since the Northcote-Trevelyan report was tabled in 1854.

The decision by the All Souls prize fellow to forgo a career in the civil service is hardly unique to Britain. At the Université de Moncton I teach public administration, a subject that one would assume would attract students wishing to pursue a career in government. But that is not always the case. A good number of my students would prefer a career as a consultant or to work in such areas as the environment or promoting foreign aid than for a government department.

In the spring of 2006, I met with a recent graduate in computer science from one of Canada's leading universities. He had joined the federal government shortly after graduation, but stayed only a few months. He quit to join a much smaller organization, explaining, 'I could see that if I stayed, it would get to my soul. Excellent salaries, pension plan and benefits, but little job satisfaction. We could have done the work with half the staff. Worse, whenever there was something new or different to do, we would hire outside consultants. There were too many people chasing too little real work, which consisted of managing consulting contracts. The toughest part of my job was to find ways to look busy. Now, where I am, we need twice as many people to get the job done and there is little contracting out. Less salary and a less attractive pension plan, but I have plenty of real work and a sense that I am making a contribution. I would much rather be here.'

I participated in a conference in June 2006 at which Professor Janice Stein, arguably Canada's pre-eminent scholar in the field of international relations, declared, 'If asked, I would not support increasing Canada's foreign aid budget. The Canadian International Development Agency [CIDA] is incapable of doing anything right these days. It would be like pouring money down the drain.' Her commitment to foreign aid was undiminished, but she had simply given up on the ability of Canada's civil service to get the job done.

I was very often in contact with federal civil servants in Ottawa throughout 2005 in my capacity as director of research for the Commission of Inquiry into the Sponsorship Program and Advertising Activities, and I heard, time and again, references to the 'serious morale problem' within the Canadian civil service. A few months later, I heard the very same phrase while meeting with civil servants in Britain in my research for this book.

So, what happened – why is it that the civil service no longer holds the kind of appeal that it once did for the keenest minds? Why is it that politicians are now held in such low esteem, that political parties have essentially been turned into election-day organizations, that voter turnout is down virtually everywhere in the Western world, and that civil service morale in Canada and Britain is low, despite job security, attractive pay, and excellent fringe benefits? The purpose of this book is to explore these questions.

My former Oxford tutor, Nevil Johnson, would often ask, Why do people insist on going around trying to fix government? Government is government, he would argue, and there are many things about it that can never be fixed. Some problems, he insisted, have no solution, only perspectives, and government is a classic case. I accepted this view, as my work on New Public Management (NPM) makes clear. I no longer do. I have come to the conclusion that our national, political, and administrative institutions are in urgent need of some rethinking. They are beyond repair. For anyone interested in seeing government play a positive role in society, things can no longer go on as they are. We need to begin by diagnosing the patient before we can offer prescriptions on how to fix government. Nevil Johnson, towards the end of his career, also came to accept that our institutions needed a serious overhaul, as his last book, *Reshaping the British Constitution*, makes clear.

This book starts from a broad perspective in search of answers. There is, of course, a price to pay for this approach. The specialists will invariably be more familiar with some of the points made, but the price is well worth paying if it generates research and interest in the state of our political and administrative institutions and in the state of our civil service and its relations with politicians and citizens.

I incurred many debts in writing this book. I started the research at All Souls College, Oxford, where I was visiting fellow in 2006. It was the best of times. I had no other responsibility than working on this book. I had the run of one of the world's greatest libraries, and I enjoyed many stimulating conversations at dinner where I met a number of former senior British civil servants attached to various Oxford colleges and current senior civil servants attending conferences or seminars at the university. I learned a great deal from them, and I owe a deeply felt thank you to All Souls, its fellows and staff, and to many current and former civil servants. In the winter of 2007, I returned to Britain, this time as visiting professor at the London School of Economics (LSE). This gave me the opportunity to interview senior British government officials, to consult government documents, and to test my thinking with leading students of government. I also want to express my gratitude to the LSE and to its faculty in the Department of Government. The Trudeau Foundation made this book possible when it awarded me the Trudeau prize in 2004. It enabled me to carry out a number of interviews in Ottawa and London and to purchase data and research material that were essential to the completion of this book.

All authors are more in debt to those who travelled the road before them than is commonly known, and I acknowledge many intellectual debts in the notes. Others, however, are not so formally acknowledged. I must first thank present and former government officials in both Canada and Britain who gave generously of their time and dealt with all my questions. No doubt it would have been entertaining to attribute points and quotations directly to those I consulted. It would have been inappropriate to do so because many specifically requested anonymity. I also want to thank Professor Christopher Hood at All Souls College and Professor Patrick Dunleavy at the LSE for insightful conversations and for making me feel at home in their institutions. Professors B. Guy Peters, Peter Aucoin, and Ned Franks read the manuscript and made extremely helpful suggestions for improving it. They saved me from a number of errors and led me to explore new avenues and to rewrite parts of the manuscript. The University of Toronto Press once again provided its reliable services, including anonymous reviewers and a sharp-eyed editor.

I also would like to single out several practitioners in Britain for their assistance. Sir Robin Butler was very generous with his time on two separate occasions, and there was no one more knowledgable with whom I could test my thinking. Robert Key, the member of Parliament from Salisbury since 1983, patiently explained how and why the role and duties of MPs have changed over the years and made important data and information available. Mark Etherton, clerk of the public accounts committee, gave freely of his time to explain the workings of Westminster and its committees. The reader will appreciate why I would like to stress, with more than usual emphasis, that the conclusions of this study are mine alone and that I take full responsibility for them.

I decided to dedicate this book to Nevil Johnson and Geoffrey Marshall. Both were my Oxford tutors, Nevil at Nuffield, and Geoffrey at Queen's, and both became friends. Both had a profound influence on my work, as this book can attest, and both had a marked influence on the literature on parliamentary government and the doctrine of ministerial responsibility. Sadly, both passed away much too early, and this book is my way of saying thanks to two excellent scholars of government and the British constitution.

I once again want to thank three women who have always been there for me – Ginette Benoit for her good cheer, her competence and professionalism, and her ability to read my handwriting; Joan Harcourt for her ability to make my sentences read better; and my wife, Linda, for her incredible patience.

I would like to stress with more than usual emphasis that I am responsible, answerable, and accountable for any errors and deficiencies.

Donald J. Savoie
Canada Research Chair in Public Administration and Governance
Université de Moncton

Court Government and the Collapse
of Accountability in Canada
and the United Kingdom

1 Introduction

If there is a consensus among politicians, many civil servants, the media, and students of government, it is that the public sector, broadly defined, is in urgent need of review, if not a fundamental overhaul. Political institutions, politicians, and civil servants have all fallen sharply in recent years on the public trust scale. We have seen a spate of books over the years documenting the decline of confidence in government. Several years ago, for example, three well-known scholars set out to explain why 'people no longer trust government.'[1] One leading student of government in Britain insists that 'nineteenth century bureaucracy is ill suited to any of the problems likely to be thrown at governments in the future.'[2] Another recently argued that the 'public domain' itself needs to be reinvented. He added that it is necessary to ensure that the failings which gave the public sector a bad reputation do not reappear.[3]

This book seeks to shed light on some of these failings by focusing on the relationship between elected politicians, bureaucracy, and citizens. We look to two areas to understand why people no longer trust government: the relationships between politicians and civil servants at the top and between civil servants and citizens at the bottom. The book argues that these relationships are under considerable stress. A new model has yet to emerge fully, but there are sure signs that it is shedding some of the characteristics of the traditional model, notably hierarchy and loyalty.

The relationship between politicians, bureaucrats, and citizens is essentially about organizing political and administrative power and putting in place structures under which people live. In his exhaustive history of government, S.E. Finer identified several recurrent themes in successive forms of government from the earliest times.[4] Regime and government stability, he pointed out, required and still require a basis for legitimacy, a political process in whatever form, from an autocracy to representative democracy, a community in arms or a military capacity, and a bureaucracy. The latter two go hand in hand since, whenever there is a regular standing army, 'even relatively small ones, we find a bureaucracy that is also strong and well organized.'[5] In turn, the bureaucracy, again according to Finer, will have a number of defining characteristics. It will be 'hierarchical, permanently in function, specialized into its various forms, educationally qualified, paid, and full time and rule governed.'[6] Undoubtedly, the military model influenced how bureaucracies worldwide took shape: witness its defining characteristics – notably, hierarchy, command, and control, and clear lines of responsibility. Political leaders from monarchs to elected presidents and prime ministers have always expected loyalty, responsiveness, ease of command, and a high level of efficiency and effectiveness from both the military and the bureaucracy.

The broad outline of the traditional bureaucratic model was evident long before Max Weber set out to describe an 'ideal type bureaucracy.' Leaving aside Weber's point that bureaucrats should be qualified in law, one can see many characteristics of the traditional bureaucratic model in ancient Egypt, the Roman Empire, and imperial China. The word *bureaucracy* itself came into existence before the French Revolution, about seventy-five years before Weber was born. Long before Weber, monarchs and autocrats organized responsibilities and placed them in compartments, so that one group was responsible for collecting taxes, another for receiving correspondence, yet another for answering correspondence, and so on, but all of them were expected to be loyal to the political rulers. Civil servants throughout history have accepted the necessity for hierarchy and specialization and also, for the most part, for loyalty to the government of the day.

Some 100 years before Weber, Hegel saw bureaucracy as the main governing organization of the modern state and described it as a neutral agent implementing, with impartiality, policies that would emerge from the 'battleground of political struggle.' Hegel described bureaucracy's organizational characteristics – 'divided branches are articulated by the principle of hierarchy ... talent becomes the main criterion of recruitment ... bureaucrats live off fixed salaries remunerated by the state in order to be independent from external influences ... the main advantages of a centralized bureaucratic organization are maximum simplification, speed and efficiency in handling state affairs.' He describes 'civil officials' as the 'pillars of the state because they are endowed with the highest political consciousness and knowledge about public affairs.'[7]

All of these ideas found their way to Max Weber, who refined them to outline the traditional bureaucratic model. That the traditional model has survived so long is remarkable and speaks both to its merits and to our inability to come up with a better one. In the absence of a better model, the Weberian model and variations of it have served many different representative democracies over the years.

Weber's traditional model called for civil servants to deal with citizens equally, having no regard for their position in society or their wealth. It is in part for this reason that he insisted that officials be subject to strict and systematic discipline and control in the conduct of the office they occupy and that they be subject to authority only with respect to their impersonal official obligations. Civil servants should be governed by 'calculable rules and without regards for persons.' He added, 'the more perfectly the bureaucracy is dehumanized the more completely it succeeds in eliminating from official business love, hatred and all purely personal, irrational, and emotional elements which escape calculation. This is the specific nature of bureaucracy and it is appraised as its special virtue.'[8]

The traditional model enabled politicians to give policy direction to civil servants while, in turn, enabling civil servants to deal with all citizens through calculable rules. This would instil distinct values within government, values that would guide how civil servants dealt with citizens, with one another, and with public funds. The traditional model also promoted a sense of loyalty between civil servants and politicians and between civil servants and citizens. Citizens would come to expect several things from civil servants – impartiality and decisions without regard to persons, as well as an orderly formal process to get things done and programs implemented.

It is important to bear in mind that, though he insisted that the traditional bureaucratic model was highly efficient, Weber himself also expressed reservations about its application. He worried about the ability of at least some politicians to direct and control it. He wrote that 'the power position of the bureaucracy is always overtowering. The political master finds himself in the position of "dilettante" who stands opposite the expert, facing the trained official who stands within the management of administration.'[9]

It is also important to note that Weber wrote this when democratic institutions operated under different rules than they do today and when government was considerably smaller. Still, Weber, in his discussion of bureaucracy as an ideal type, stressed the need for a 'strong Parliament.' A strong Parliament and an ideal type bureaucracy have distinct roles and responsibilities and require vastly different skills. As he explains, 'Our officialdom has been brilliant whenever it had to prove its sense of duty, its impartiality and mastery of organizational problems in the face of official, clearly formulated tasks of a specialized nature ... But here we are concerned with political, not bureaucratic achievements, and the facts themselves provoke the recognition which nobody can truthfully deny: that bureaucracy failed completely whenever it was expected to deal with political problems. This is no accident; rather it would be astonishing if capabilities inherently so alien to one another would emerge within the same political structure.'[10] Thus politicians and civil servants would occupy two relatively distinct spaces – one political and the other administrative – only because both required distinct skills. Weber's purpose in establishing distinct responsibilities was designed to keep civil servants out of politics to 'protect, not destroy, the autonomous and morally responsible individual.'[11] In terms of responsibility and accountability, elected political leaders would control bureaucracy, and in turn Parliament would control political leaders.

A strong working Parliament has three important responsibilities: it provides the means for controlling the unrestrained power of the bureaucracy, generates the necessary political leadership, and holds officials and politicians to account. A strong Parliament is also needed to attract talented political leadership since, according to Weber, a powerless Parliament makes 'a political career uninviting.' The natural selection of struggle for political office will push the more talented and competent leaders to the top positions. Here, Weber insists, political parties play 'an absolutely key role.' Politicians become effective leaders not because they have better personal qualities than bureaucrats but because they operate in an institution that develops political talents.[12] In short, politicians and bureaucrats occupy distinct spheres of responsibility. Formal processes guide the work of bureaucrats, and formal relations guide dealings between ministers and civil servants and between Parliament and bureaucracy.

Today, the Weberian model is being challenged as never before. Though it is widely acknowledged that the model worked well in its time, there are now many criticisms. David Osborne and Peter Plastrick write that, 'As long as the tasks were relatively simple and straightforward and the environment stable, it worked. But for the last twenty years, it has been coming apart. In a world of rapid change, technological revolution, global economic competition, demassified markets, an educated work force, demanding customers, and severe fiscal constraint, centralized top-down monopolies are simply too slow, too unresponsive, and too incapable of change and innovation.'[13] Many politicians buy into this line of argument, insisting that citizen participation has increased in recent years, thus changing the dynamics inside government, and that greater flexibility is required to recruit more politically responsive civil servants, given the rapid pace of change in society. Weber's emphasis on the merits of 'calculable rules, without regard for persons' and of a dehumanized bureaucracy hardly squares with the emphasis on the need of present-day government to respond, much as the private sector does, to 'customers.' It is difficult to imagine that one could promote such a shift without significant implications for the traditional values found in government.

Though the traditional model has served to promote a sense of loyalty between politicians and civil servants, these two groups have also had an uneasy alliance, a kind of love-hate relationship, from the very beginning. History records numerous instances when emperors and monarchs had civil servants tortured, beheaded, and flogged. One emperor, to discourage corruption, ordered that the skins of executed officials be stuffed with straw and hung up in full public view.[14] But political rulers also recognized that they could not rule without civil servants. The Ottoman Empire, for example, survived because a professional bureaucracy was firmly entrenched and kept things going 'despite degenerate sultans, incompetent ministers, harem intrigues and military mutinies.'[15] We need not look that far back in history to see that the work of civil servants sustained systems in desperate shape – witness, for example, the role of civil servants in France during the Fourth Republic.[16]

Modern bureaucracy, as Finer points out, emerged as feudalism faded into history. In the modern state, bureaucracy became more impersonal and institutionalized, in contrast to feudalism, when aristocrats regarded administrative positions as their own and incumbents as their own resources. Despite the shift to the modern state, this uneasy relationship between political rulers and their civil servants has remained. If anything, it appears to have taken a downturn in recent years. Political leaders no longer behead or flog their civil servants, but many have had less than kind things to say about them.

Modern political leaders have indeed made clear their deeply felt reservations about civil servants on many occasions. U.S. President Ronald Reagan said that he had come to Washington to drain the swamp; British prime minister Thatcher said that she disliked bureaucrats as a breed; and Canadian prime minister Brian Mulroney pledged to give bureaucrats 'pink slips and running shoes' if elected to power.[17] Under former British prime minister Tony Blair, we were told that civil servants and ministers no longer work in partnership and, further, that civil servants are 'for the first time treated as simple subordinates.'[18] Presidents and prime ministers have launched one reform measure after another for the past thirty years in an attempt to reinvent government, to strengthen their hand in shaping policy, to make civil service managers more effective, to streamline government, to consult citizens and interest groups in striking major policy initiatives, to make government more transparent, and to deliver programs and services more efficiently. However, although politicians on both the political right and left have, over the past forty years or so, laid down ambitious plans to reinvent bureaucracy, they have been very reluctant to take a critical look at their own offices, Parliament or Congress.

As for reforming bureaucracy, there are precious few signs to suggest that the reforms have had much of a positive impact, if any. Indeed, there are signs that things may be worse today than they were forty years ago. Was the patient misdiagnosed, or was the wrong medicine applied? Public opinion surveys reveal that citizens increasingly hold a dim view of both politicians and civil servants. One such survey of Canadians conducted for the Trudeau Foundation revealed that 'trust in government has plummeted' and 'cynicism towards politicians has increased.' The survey also revealed that political engagement in Canada, already low, is 'declining' further. In only five years (from 2000 to 2005), the number of Canadians who report that they have never been members of a political party or worked for a party in the past three years has risen substantially.[19] A major study, based in part on a public opinion survey of both Canadians and civil servants and on focus groups sponsored by the federal government, recently delivered a harsh verdict of the state of the Canadian civil service. It concluded that Canadians see civil servants as 'disconnected, lazy and overpaid.'[20]

Data paint a similar picture in Britain. Indeed, Prime Minister Tony Blair warned that 'cynicism' in Britain towards politicians and government represents a 'corrosive danger to democracy itself.'[21] A recent report on the state of democracy in Britain reveals that 'the level of alienation felt towards politicians, the main political parties and the key institutions of the political system is extremely high and widespread.'[22] A former senior civil servant writes about the 'denigration' of civil servants by both ministers and citizens and concludes that the British government is now in a state of crisis.[23] In virtually the entire Western world, over the past twenty years or so, cynicism towards the state has become rampant and, in the process, bureaucracy has 'served as the punching bag.'[24]

What is it about bureaucracy that causes political leaders such unease? Civil servants are their 'loyal servants,' there to advise or implement policies established by them. Bureaucracy, the traditional model suggests, is governed by specific principles, all of which are designed to produce efficient administration and to serve political masters. Official business is conducted in strict accordance with the prescribed rules; every official's responsibilities and authority are part of a vertical hierarchy, with respective rights of supervision and appeal; officials do not own the resources necessary for the performance of their assigned functions but are accountable for their use of these resources; official and private business and income are strictly separated; and official business is conducted on the basis of written documents.

On the face of it, at least, political leaders should be well served by these principles and, indeed, by all civil servants. Civil servants should be their natural allies. However, the never-ending reforms introduced in Western democracies during the past forty years, all designed to improve government operations and to strengthen the ability of politicians to shape new policy initiatives, suggest that all is not well in the relationship between politicians and civil servants.

We elect politicians to represent us and to manage the affairs of state and, if we are not happy with their performance, we are free to turf them out every four years, or even sooner in certain circumstances. We elect politicians in the same fashion that we elected them forty years ago. So why our discontent? This book seeks to provide some answers.

Was there ever a golden age when politicians and civil servants worked hand in hand? Was there a time when political and administrative institutions enjoyed widespread support from citizens? If there is a consensus in the literature, the heyday for the parliamentary system was in the nineteenth century before the advent of disciplined political parties. Meanwhile, the heyday for cabinet government in both Britain and Canada was between 1945 and the mid-1960s and that for bureaucracy in both presidential and parliamentary systems was from the 1940s to the late 1960s/early 1970s. It is more than a coincidence that this period encompassed what has been described as 'the triumph of collectivism' in the aftermath of the Second World War.[25]

It will be recalled that the Keynesian revolution captured departments of Finance and the Treasury throughout the Western world. By war's end, the public's belief in the ability of government to intervene and to manage the economy was high. Large latent demand and rapid population increase combined with the realization that the government management of activity related to the war effort, at least in Anglo-American democracies, had been successful gave governments carte blanche to expand. Canadians had learned during the war 'that governments were able, in moments of crisis, and when moved by an all-consuming goal, to lead the country to high levels of economic activity and employment.'[26] Not only did the Allies win the war, but the government had run the war economy well. Unemployment had fallen to zero, and yet prices had been held down. Growth of productivity and real gross national product (GNP) was accelerated, inequalities among social groups were diminished, civilian consumption actually increased, there were no balance of payment crises, and foreign exchange rates remained relatively stable.

Civil servants played a key role in the triumph of collectivism in the aftermath of the Second World War. Writing about the British civil service, Peter Hennessy notes 'the widespread, if not wholesale, usurpation of individual greed by collective good.' He quotes a British civil servant in claiming that the Second World War was bureaucracy's 'finest hour.' He adds that private sector people 'were never a large number' and that there were, at the time, limited opportunities for university graduates.[27] But things have taken a dramatic turn. The private sector has been in the ascendancy for the past thirty years, while bureaucracy has been under attack from several quarters.

Looking to history, the relationship between citizens and civil servants, meanwhile, has not fared much better than that between civil servants and politicians. Tax collectors and citizens have hardly had a happy relationship down through the ages, and history books have not been kind to bureaucrats. Citizens' groups have complained in recent years about the growing cost of 'bureaucracy,' the quality of public services, and their ability to influence public policies and decision making.[28] As B. Guy Peters and Jon Pierre point out, there is now 'a large scholarly and popular literature arguing that bureaucracies are major problems limiting the capacity of democratic institutions to effectively respond to their citizens.'[29]

A good number of academics have also recently taken a dim view of 'bureaucrats.' Some have written about the inherent disconnect that bureaucratic influence creates between citizens and politicians.[30] Others have made the case that the civil service reduces the state's ability to produce innovative policies.[31] Bertrand Russell insisted that the power of bureaucrats could well be a kind of 'irresponsible, behind-the-scenes power, like that of Emperors' eunuchs and kings' mistresses in former times.'[32] Patrick Weller and R.A.W. Rhodes sum up the decline of the senior mandarins in this fashion: 'Heads of government departments used to be regarded with some awe. They were people of weighty experience, wise and powerful, if deliberately remote and at least partially anonymous. They worked in the shadows, advising, managing and influencing the direction of their respective countries. They were the mandarins, recognized as the real rulers, the providers of continuity. Their reputation is now far more mixed.'[33]

To be sure, not all academics have been critical of bureaucracy. Woodrow Wilson, writing in 1887, praised the work of a professional bureaucracy and was one of the first to write about the importance of separating administration from politics. Others have approved the bureaucracy's capacity to provide 'neutral competence' and thus promote an objective and superior outcome to any decision.[34] Still others, from Luther Gulick to Hugh Heclo and Joseph Lapalombara, have been positive on the role of a professional, non-partisan public service.[35] It is interesting to note, however, that many of these scholars wrote about bureaucracy (mid-1930s to the early 1970s) during the period that we described earlier as the golden age for bureaucracy.

Again, things appear to have taken a turn for the worse. The rise of the public choice theory and the absence of an equally convincing counter-theory, on the one hand, and an inability to discredit public choice, on the other, have cast bureaucracy in a negative light. Public choice theorists, as is well known, maintain that bureaucrats occupy a privileged position in the government's policy and decision-making process and will implement policies that favour their own interests.[36] To be sure, the public choice literature has had a substantial impact on bureaucracy, particularly in the Anglo-American democracies.[37] Not only has it put civil servants on the defensive in terms of their policy advisory role, but it has also led politicians to search for ways to constrain their bureaucrats. In addition, the literature has spawned a number of studies on the inability of political institutions to control bureaucracy. We now have reached the point where no discussion of democratic governance can be divorced from a discussion of bureaucracy.[38]

Practitioners and the literature have also focused on developments in the relationship between bureaucracy and citizens. Governments, again in Anglo-American democracies, have made various attempts to strengthen the relationship between government and citizen. Britain, for example, introduced a citizen's charter to ensure that its citizens would receive quality public service in a timely fashion. Former prime minister John Major pointed out that 'failing public service providers will be forced to offer customers cash refunds or face government budget cuts.'[39] Subjects became citizens in Britain, but no one has been able to pinpoint when or precisely for what reasons. Still, the shift is now complete, and British passports employ the term 'citizen' rather than 'subject.' More recently still, citizens have become 'customers' in relation to a number of government activities.

To make matters worse, the discontent with bureaucracy is not limited to politicians and citizens. There is plenty of evidence to suggest that civil servants themselves are not happy with their lot in life. Surveys throughout Anglo-American democracies reveal a serious morale problem in their ranks.[40]

Ezra Suleiman writes that the study of bureaucracy, much like the study of political science itself, is confronting both methodological and substantive challenges. He adds that the 'primary issue should always be the importance or pertinence of questions asked, an issue about which a certain degree of subjectivity will be inevitable.'[41] A number of questions are explored in this book: Accepting that bureaucracy has rarely been popular down through the ages, does the level of discontent suggest that we are dealing with a new phenomenon? What are the causes of our discontent with government? Are we witnessing the emergence of new relationships between politicians, public servants, and citizens?

In its search for answers, this book looks largely to Canada and Britain, both of which offer excellent opportunities for investigation. I have long held that we can learn more by comparing the experiences of two countries operating under a similar system of government than by focusing exclusively on one. As one student of government observed, 'he who knows only one country knows none.'[42] There are strong similarities between the two systems of government, and both, but particularly Britain, have been key players in the old Commonwealth or Westminster democracies. The two countries are reasonably homogeneous for comparative purposes, given their heritage. In addition, both are electoral democracies in that the key positions of political power are filled through regular, free, and fair elections among competing parties.[43] Both countries have resisted a shift to proportional representation and continue to rely on a first-past-the-post electoral system. Both countries are home to a free press with no limitation on its ability to criticize the government, its policies, and its activities. Both countries also have state-owned national television and radio services, and both have witnessed a rise in voter alienation towards politicians and government. Yet the role of government still looms large in both countries – governments in Canada and Britain take in an identical share of gross domestic product (GDP) in revenues (40.7 per cent), which is higher than the United States (31.7 per cent) but lower than France (50 per cent).[44]

Canada borrowed heavily from Britain in establishing its political institutions. Indeed, the very first part of Canada's Constitution Act, 1867, states that the new Dominion shall have a 'constitution similar in Principle to that of the United Kingdom.' Accordingly, given that both countries operate under the Westminster-type parliamentary system, the incentives and constraints in terms of accountability should roughly be the same. In addition, Canada has continued, over the years, to look to Britain for inspiration to update its machinery of government. For example, Canada's Privy Council Office was modelled on Whitehall's Cabinet Office.[45] Both governments have central agencies, line departments and agencies, and a non-partisan professional civil service. It is perhaps more than ironic that Canada was born in 1867, the year Walter Bagehot's famous essay *The English Constitution* was first published. But there are also sharp differences between the two countries. One has been a federation for about 140 years, while the other is just now taking tentative steps towards a federal system. Britain has been much more aggressive than Canada in recent years in experimenting with new approaches to program and service delivery mechanisms, though Canada has not sat idle in this area.

Both countries have also witnessed profound changes in their socioeconomic environment. Britain joined the European Commission (EC), and Canada signed on to the North American Free Trade Agreement (NAFTA). Globalization continues to have a profound impact on the economies of both countries. These developments, at a minimum, suggest that the two national governments have ceded some of their power to regional or supranational organizations. Further, in part because globalization is enabling firms to move production capacities to lower-wage regions or countries, the case has been made that it has reduced solidarity and trust within society.[46]

Ronald Wintrobe maintains that solidarity within society is built in several ways, including mechanisms that ensure equality among the group (e.g., common pensions and medical insurance) and that globalization is having an impact on this front. Britain and Canada have both over the years promoted solidarity through programs associated with the welfare state. The United States, meanwhile, has had fewer such programs, and globalization is serving to spread American values to other countries.[47] A former Canadian foreign affairs minister, Pierre Pettigrew, explains that globalization means 'corporations can decide to carry out a given industrial function in a given geographic region for economic reasons, notwithstanding any political considerations.' He adds that 'globalization ignores political borders and merges economic spaces. And thus, on the margin of the state's areas of responsibility, there emerges a new anonymous and stateless power, a power that is at once intoxicating and fearsome. In this time of globalization, then, the vertical power of the state is gradually replaced with the horizontal power of the marketplace.'[48] None of this, he insists, springs from decisions 'that we made in Cabinet.'[49] Accordingly, some of our discontent with our government may well relate to the perceived, if not actual, inability of our national government to protect the economic interest of citizens.

Politics and public administration depend on society to assess how well they are doing, and both have felt the rise of individualism.[50] The study on the state of the Canadian civil service referred to earlier reported that civil servants, including senior executives, expressed a profound sense of demoralization because 'they know that they are held in relatively low esteem by the public and feel that they don't have the support of the public, politicians or opinion makers. Their comments suggest that they react to public cynicism with resignation.'[51] As market liberalism began to flourish, the attitude towards the role of government also began to change. Henry Mintzberg explains that the collapse of communism led many to declare that capitalism had triumphed and public bureaucracies had failed. The push was on for government to emulate the private sector and to operate more like a business.[52]

A former Canadian senior government official suggests that recently things have got out of hand and that the civil service has simply lost its way. He writes that, 'Without blushing or even without a second thought, we now talk about our "customers" or "clients" in a way that would not have occurred to public servants three or four decades ago. And this is just the tip of the iceberg.' He adds, 'Sometimes the results of this attempt to reinvent the public sector into the private sector are quite bizarre. I recently visited a well-meaning colleague who proudly presented to me the organizational renewal efforts of a high-priced foreign consultant that consisted in, among other things, the translation of all terms of public administration and parliamentary democracy into private sector equivalents, including the reinvention of members of Parliament as the shareholders of the corporation and Cabinet as the Board of Directors.' In the early 1990s, when the New Public Management approach was in vogue, a deputy minister had waxed expansive about what he believed to be the renewal and transformation of his own department. 'This is really serious stuff,' he exclaimed proudly. 'It's just like the private sector.'[53]

Vernon Bogdanor also reports on the decline of influence of the mandarins in Whitehall as the private sector came into fashion as the model to emulate. He writes that the 'claims of the market are now held to trump the claims of the public domain and the state has been a widely acknowledged disappointment.'[54] The public sector in Britain, he adds, has become a new kind of marketplace, where citizens are being transformed into consumers.

The public sector can no longer look to its traditional allies in the academic community, as they have been hard pressed to challenge the findings of public choice and rational choice theorists. The roots of political science, as B. Guy Peters explains, were closely tied to the study of public institutions. But all of that had changed by the 1980s. The discipline is now dominated by the rational choice school. The fundamental assumption of rational choice is that individuals in government act to promote and maximize self-interest.[55] Given that the discipline and its literature are a product of their time, does this suggest that we should be searching for answers in society and in the behaviour of individuals rather than in the machinery of government?

It takes only a moment's reflection to appreciate that all these developments have far-reaching implications for the relationship between politicians and civil servants on the one hand and between civil servants and citizens on the other. This book argues that these relationships are now broken. The civil service itself needs to rethink how it relates to political authority. The reasons for this are to be found both inside and outside of government. Government is no longer able to establish policy and manage programs on the basis of the traditional model. Some of the difficulty is self-inflicted, but the multiple voices now at play, both inside and outside of government, not only are redefining the concept of loyalty, but also are calling for a fundamental rethinking of how our political and administrative institutions should work.

These and other forces have given rise to court government. By *court government* I do not mean the rise of judicial power. Rather, I mean that effective political power now rests with the prime minister and a small group of carefully selected courtiers. I also mean a shift from formal decision-making processes in cabinet and, as a consequence, in the civil service, to informal processes involving only a handful of key actors. We now make policy by announcements, and we manage government operations by adjusting administrative and financial requirements to the circumstances of the day. Court government has its advantages but also its drawbacks, and this study explores both. Decisions over coffee and a willingness to pick and choose initiatives to deal with the political pressure of the day and to respond to the media invariably promote an undisciplined process. It means that the capabilities of politicians and senior civil servants are no longer 'alien to one another.' Unlike in Weber's world, civil servants, at least at the senior levels, are now expected to deal with political problems. In brief, as formal processes, hierarchy, and structures lose their importance under court government, the skills of politicians and senior civil servants begin to look alike.

In addition, the importing of private sector management practices to government and other forces have contributed to a muddling of voices, values, and loyalty in government. They have made the relationship between politicians and civil servants and between civil servants and citizens more complex and have played a role in the rise of court government. They have also undermined traditional bureaucracy and produced far-reaching implications for how we hold elected politicians and civil servants accountable for their decisions and activities.

Court government is different from cabinet government in other ways. Authority is highly concentrated in the hands of prime ministers and their courtiers. Courtiers are drawn from the cabinet, from partisan political staffers, from the bureaucracy, and from outside, including selected lobbyists and think tanks. Policy making and decision making take various forms – when prime ministers and their courtiers want something, funding is easily secured and decisions are quickly struck. However, when prime ministers and their courts have limited interest in a proposal, the decision-making process is elaborate (it can involve other governments, a number of government departments and agencies, and outsiders), slow, porous, and consultative.

Career patterns are also different. Senior civil servants now look to the prime minister's court for making it to the top. Gone are the days when civil servants climbed up their department's ladders to become its administrative head. Today, more often than not, administrative heads are appointed from outside the department, frequently from central agencies where their work is visible to prime ministers and their courtiers, including the cabinet secretary.

This study makes the case that parliamentary governments in both Canada and Britain remain responsive but respond more and more to demands for a certain output from people or groups rather than from the electorate. A whole matrix of demands and a host of new policy actors now operate both inside and outside government, including constant pressure from the media. All of this has altered substantially how parliamentary government operates, particularly how the civil service goes about its work. The study argues that the civil service in both Canada and Britain has lost its way, that it is now beset by many conflicting and impossible demands and pressures, and that it has failed to respond in a serious and sustained fashion to fundamental changes now taking place between politicians and the media, between politicians and civil servants, and between politicians and citizens.[56] It is important to underline that the focus of this study is on the Canadian and British Parliaments and governments and does not deal with developments in public administration in Canada's provinces.

Outline of the Study

The study goes back to the very beginning to understand how our national political administrative institutions took form. Chapter 2 presents an overview, albeit brief, of the development of democratic institutions from the Greek polis to the birth of the Westminster-Whitehall model. I have become deeply concerned with the historical amnesia of both students of public administration and practitioners, particularly in Canada. A good number of practitioners, trained in a variety of disciplines, have a very limited understanding of how the political and administrative institutions they serve took shape. My hope is that, apart from providing the necessary backdrop for this study to make its case, this chapter will help the reader to gain an appreciation of the historical events and forces that shaped their institutions.

Chapter 3 asks if there really was a golden era for national political administrative institutions. It explores the question from different perspectives: Parliament, cabinet government, and the civil service. Chapter 4 argues that the public sector in Anglo-American democracies began to lose its way during the 1970s. Stagflation, the government overload problem, bureaucracy bashing, and failed attempts to reform the public sector all contributed to give the public sector a bad reputation.

Chapter 5 looks at cultural and sociological changes in society over the past forty years or so. It explores the role of social capital in shaping values and considers the implications for government and the civil service. We know that governments throughout the Western world have sought to strengthen values and ethics to guide elected politicians and civil servants. Chapter 6 compares the exercises in values and ethics undertaken in Canada and Britain. It explores both the similarities and differences in the two approaches and makes the point that the various values and ethics exercises have left virtually intact the accountability relationships between ministers and civil servants.

Chapter 7 explores the role of 'voices' in shaping government policies and decisions and the substantial increase in their number in recent years. Think tanks, research institutes, consultants, and lobbyists have been added to the panoply of voices that governments have had to learn to deal with in recent years. Loyalty has, over the years, played a pivotal role in government. Prime ministers look for loyalty from their cabinet colleagues and members of their political parties. Cabinet ministers attach a great deal of importance to loyalty from the civil service, and senior civil servants expect loyalty from front-line managers and employees, who, in turn, look for loyalty from their departments and agencies. Chapter 8 makes the case that loyalty has taken on a new meaning and that the emphasis is now on the individual rather than the collective. Loyalty to self has been on the ascendancy, and the implications for the public sector are far-reaching.

Chapter 9 looks at government from the bottom up, from the perspective of those who work on the front line, dealing with citizens and delivering public services. It makes the case that front-line managers now have to deal with new oversight bodies and constraints that are making it more difficult for them to get things done. Chapter 10 looks at government from the top down, from the perspective of those occupying senior positions in government. Here, too, their job has been made more difficult, but for different reasons. Media relations and the need to protect prime ministers and ministers have become very important to their day-to-day activities. The result is that we have witnessed a degree of convergence in the skills of elected politicians and senior civil servants. These and other changes have had a profound impact on accountability.

Chapter 11 revisits the doctrine of ministerial responsibility. The public sector, in both Canada and Britain, has changed considerably over the past forty years, changes that have made accountability requirements more demanding. Chapter 12 takes stock of recent developments in our political and administrative institutions from a comparative perspective. It looks at the role individuals play in government and how traditional accountability mechanisms function in today's environment.

Chapter 13 concludes that our unwritten constitution has been dismantled and our machinery of government can no longer cope with the political environment that has evolved over the past forty years. The chapter argues that the personalization of public administration calls for new approaches in our efforts to strengthen accountability in our political and administrative institutions.

2 How Did We Get Here?

We inherited our constitutional arrangements, our political institutions, and our bureaucracy. We did not create them, though we may, on occasion, be witness or even party to important changes to their operations. They are a product of history, of accidents of history, of ideas, of previous generations, and of precedents. If every generation were able to create its own constitutional arrangements and political institutions, one can hardly imagine that the House of Lords in Britain and the Senate in Canada would have survived for as long as they have. This chapter provides a broad review of how we got here, how previous generations of political leaders and civil servants learned to make democratic institutions work, and how they learned to deal with citizens. Institutions, no less than public policies, are 'path dependent'; once launched on a particular path, they will stick to it until a substantial force intervenes to divert them to a new direction.[1] There are several important forces today trying to push and pull our political and administrative institutions onto a new path. However, before we consider these forces, it is important to understand those that shaped the institutions we inherited.

This brief overview makes no claims to being an historical study. However, it is important for us to gain an appreciation, however cursory, of how our systems of government took shape and to identify the sharp breaks that took place over the years with the established order. There is a rich body of literature readily available on the history of government that the reader may wish to consult.[2] Our present purpose is to examine how and where our political institutions took root.

Getting There

Political and administrative powers have, throughout history, rested in the hands of a small group. When communities first took form, power was concentrated in the hands of tribal leaders, rulers, or kings, who were all free to rule as they wished. Their *raison d'être* was essentially to wage war, and to this end their authority was absolute. As Sam Finer writes, in some societies the ruler was 'the manifestation of a god and in principle the entire land was his.'[3] The state, to the extent that it had an administrative apparatus, existed solely to serve the ruler and his interests.

The Greek polis (essentially, small, independent city states) introduced innovative and important changes to government. It gave the word *democracy* to the world and a democratic process that involved all citizens (narrowly defined) – no small contribution, to be sure. It experimented with direct democracy through an association of citizens that would, if nothing else, do away with kings, politicians, and even, to some extent, bureaucrats. Some administrative responsibilities were delegated to boards, but officials had to account directly to the assembly for their decisions and their spending.[4] It is important to underline the fact that the polis was small, both in geography and in population – Plato, it will be recalled, maintained that the ideal size for a polis was 5,040 citizens. Ancient Greece saw no need for representative democracy, partly because of the small size of the polis, but also because it simply did not square with what it understood democracy to be. Decisions were made by citizens in an open forum, and so there was no need to elect politicians. Citizens would cast lots every day to determine who would chair the meetings. Any citizen present could propose an amendment to any proposal, all citizens were free to speak on all matters, and a vote was taken by a show of hands. The power of the assembly was far-reaching, and it had the final say on 'war and peace, alliances, the size of the armed forces, finance, currency and custom duties ... elected magistrates ... and even to depose generals.'[5] If blame were to be assigned, then it would belong to all citizens.

The Greek polis, however, is not without its critics, with some insisting that it was not democratic at all, since political power remained concentrated in the hands of the minority. Male citizens only could participate in decision making. Slaves formed a majority of the residents, the ratio of slaves to citizens being about three to one.

Slaves, of course, did the manual work, thus freeing up time for citizens to become full participants in Athenian democracy.[6]

The reasons for the decline of the Greek polis has been a subject of debate over the centuries. Military conquest was, of course, one reason. Had conflicts among Macedonia, Carthage, and Rome and constant warfare between the polis not existed, the Greek polis might well have survived longer than it did. But there were structural deficiencies as well, deficiencies that would not only spell the end of direct democracy but also give democracy itself a bad reputation that would last for centuries. Some argue that the Greek polis should have come together under a national state; others maintain that demagogues had a field day, giving rise to mob rule (witness the trial and death of Socrates for 'corrupting the youth'), that direct democracy soaked the rich, and that the polis made no distinction between state and society so that the state was in total command and citizens had no inherent rights.[7]

Still, the Greek polis did provide important lessons for all those charged with designing political institutions. One was that a society did not have to be ruled by kings – that alternative forms of government could exist. Another, however, left a deep suspicion of direct democracy, even of democracy itself. As recently as the eighteenth century, James Madison, in the *Federalist Papers*, issued a strong warning against pure democracy, writing that 'such democracies have ever been spectacles of turbulence and contention, have ever been found incompatible with personal security or the rights of property, and have in general been as short in their lives as they have been violent in their deaths.'[8] The architects of the American system of government concluded that the will of the people needed to be 'tempered by an acute awareness of the potentially negative effects of citizen power, particularly citizens who were not of the chosen body.'[9] They were concerned that the 'masses' would simply 'vote themselves free beer and pull down the churches and country houses.' Democracy, for a long time, was a pejorative word and only became 'an affirmative term of pride' when Thomas Paine took it up in his first volume of the *Rights of Man*.[10] The crucial lesson learned, then, was that democracy needed checks and balances if it were to serve citizens well.

Rome, in its turn, was ruled by aristocrats and could not claim to be a democracy. That said, the Romans did introduce checks and balances in their system of government. For this and other reasons, there were sharp differences between Rome and ancient Greece. In the Greek democracy, all male citizens could vote, while in Rome, only men with money and property could do so. Though it never produced a written constitution, the Roman Republic form of government, unlike that of ancient Greece, provided for the three branches of government (circa 287 BC) that we still see today: the legislative, the executive, and the judicial branches.

The republic evolved into an empire and, as the empire grew, political power was concentrated in the hands of the emperor. The emperor played multiple roles, including commander-in-chief, high priest, head of government and the bureaucracy, and even the source of all laws.[11] In the provinces, he was 'God.'[12] Yet, he was not the vicar of the gods, but a man on whom the Senate had conferred political power, and so his power flowed from men rather than from God, or gods, an important distinction.[13] Rulers who claimed that their authority flowed directly from God would also claim that they answered only to God for their decisions.

Still, the emperor dominated political and administrative life in Rome. All major decisions and even a number of minor ones flowed from him. But there were some constraints. Roman emperors, for example, ignored the Senate at their peril. As Finer writes, 'experience ought to have shown this (i.e., confronting the Senate) to be unwise: the four emperors who openly terrorized the Senate – Caligula, Nero, Dominitian [sic], and Commodus – all came to bad ends; not so the Antonines, who made it their business to co-operate.'[14] The point is that although the legislative branch may have been weak in relation to the emperor and his political power, it did exist, and emperors had to learn to deal with it or pay a steep price.

There are two other relevant developments that we need to highlight: Rome's code of laws, and the role of the bureaucracy. The Emperor Justinian drew on a long history of law making in Rome to prepare his 'Justinian code.' Not only did the code preserve for posterity a unique experience in Roman government, but it also transmitted to Europe and beyond the basis for legal systems now found throughout the Western world. The existence of a body of laws meant that all the power could not, or at least should not, rest in the hands of an absolute ruler. This was in sharp contrast to systems of government where power rested with an absolute monarch who enacted laws that applied to everyone except himself. Since he was the source of all laws, he was thus above them.[15]

Unlike ancient Greece, Rome also developed a bureaucracy, in order to manage its empire. Still, the imperial bureaucracy grew very slowly, reaching only 30,000 by the fourth century. It is important to stress that, although the civil service had an identity separate from the military, at the same time it adopted the military model. It too had a chain of command, hierarchy, and a graded salary scale. It also divided responsibilities by function, with some looking after the emperor's household, others responsible for drafting legislation, and still others responsible for handling financial transactions. The civil service was made up of two grades – high posts and lower grades. The high posts were short-term appointments and were the preserve of the aristocracy. These positions were viewed as 'distinctions to be won,' the motive being neither to make money nor to gain political influence, since aristocrats already had both. Rather, their motive was to gain the 'honour' that the posts entailed. The lower posts were held by career officials whose salaries were quite modest. However, they could augment their salaries by charging fees for the services they provided.[16]

The Byzantine empire and China, much more than Rome, would pave the way for our modern-day bureaucracy. The Byzantine state had a palace-type government with a highly structured bureaucracy. The emperor dominated all aspects of the political process, the government, and the military, and his palace was sacred. He held all the power in his own hands, concentrated the operation of government in his palace, and dominated the state's bureaucracy – there were no civil servants, just servants of the emperor.[17] Unlike in Rome, the Byzantine emperor organized the bureaucracy into approximately sixty units, all of which reported directly to him. Thus, many of the decisions were taken by the emperor inside the palace. As in Rome, however, the emperor drew a line between the military and the bureaucracy, and though both were loyal to him, each operated with some degree of independence from the other.

China, most specifically the T'ang dynasty (circa 618 to 901), gave the world an important innovation in bureaucracy when it introduced specialization in administration. It then produced a detailed account of this specialization in shaping functions and departments, even down to individual jobs. Along the lines Weber would promote more than 1,000 years later, it established a recruitment process for bureaucrats, a job description for individual positions, a full-time appointment for the incumbent, and a reporting relationship based on hierarchy.

All departments were loyal to only one person – the emperor – and they all reported to him. That said, they did not report through one person, a kind of superbureaucrat charged with overseeing the administration. Rather, the emperor, like the emperor in the Byzantine empire, had for long periods several departments reporting directly to him, ensuring some checks and balances in the system.[18]

The dynasty's more important and lasting contribution to government was in designing the 'definitive hierarchical organization of the bureaucracy – the mandarinate'[19] and in introducing an examination competition to gain entry to the bureaucracy. The system was designed to select the best talents to be turned into a cadre of scholar-officials to serve in government. The bureaucracy was therefore merit-based and consisted of a body of career officials with no independent power base of its own. However, it did act as a counterweight to the aristocracy and the military. Though the mandarinate did not wield power separately from the emperor, its influence on society was substantial, prompting scholars to write that 'the nobility of the pen extruded the nobility of blood.'[20] The important point here is that bureaucracy was taking its place as a centre of influence, if not power, in society.

The Westminster Model

The history of the Westminster parliamentary system is a story of the struggle for power between the king and Parliament, then between Parliament and the executive. Some would argue that the struggle has recently been extended to ministers and public servants. Adam Tomkins sums up the earlier struggle well when he writes that 'power resides in the authority of the Crown, save for that which has been specifically forced from it by Parliament.'[21]

English kings, like their European counterparts, enjoyed a divine right to rule, and they could make the case that they were accountable only to God until 1701.[22] European monarchs, at least those who remained in power, were able to cling to this notion much longer – until the early years of the twentieth century, in some cases. Kings and queens throughout Europe had unique authority, made evident by the fact that it was from the pope or bishop that they received their crowns. The message was clear – their mandates, as already noted, were from God, not the people. In brief, they were chosen by God in accordance with the doctrine of the 'Divine Right of Kings.' For a long period in Europe – from the Middle Ages to the early twentieth century, in some instances – the power of rulers, emperors, and kings was viewed as being derived from God. Thus, no man could punish them if they broke the law, only God.[23] Yet they were also head of 'their' people, and all political power flowed to and from their hands. The crown had the authority to call upon its subjects for support in times of war or in raising revenues. King Charles I, though with no success, reminded his accusers that they should remember that they were 'born his subjects and born subject to those laws which determined that the king can do no wrong.'[24]

The Magna Carta, the Bill of Rights, and the Act of Settlement, in the case of England, served to limit the power of the crown and then to hold it to account. As is well known, the barons revolted against tax increases and took London by force in 1215. They forced the hand of King John to agree to a document limiting his power, and in return they renewed their oaths of allegiance to him. King John was later to renege on the document, but King Henry II reissued a shorter version of the Magna Carta later. The document contains a number of provisions, including freedom for the church, new feudal rights, judicial rights, and the establishment of a council consisting of the most powerful men of the country working for the benefit of the state and not simply for the king. This council, though subservient to the monarch, would in time form the basis for Parliament. Thus began the long struggle that would establish Parliament – or rather the king in Parliament – to become a completely sovereign authority, at least in theory. As a result, the Magna Carta set in motion a number of reforms to strip away some of the power that had been concentrated in one individual. For this and other related reasons, it has been described as 'perhaps the most important legal document in the history of democracy.'[25]

It was during the reign of Edward III (circa 1216–72) that the council was actually transformed into Parliament. Though monarchs would learn ways to get around it, the precedent was set then that no law could be made and no tax could be imposed without the consent of Parliament. Parliament, however, was hardly a representative body – it was divided into two houses, one for the nobility and the higher clergy and the other for knights and landowners. But again this hardly settled the matter. Parliament still functioned as a kind of temporary committee to be summoned or dismissed by the king to serve his interest. He would summon Parliament whenever he needed new tax revenues, and Parliament, apart from withholding financial resources, had no means to force its will on the monarch. But even here monarchs had ways to raise money outside of Parliament if they had to, and they would exercise this option from time to time.

Monarchs, as history has shown time and again, in England and else-where, would not easily part with their levers of power.

Some 400 years later England was plunged into a civil war that would once again pit the crown on one side and Parliament on the other. There were many grievances that led to civil war in England, but the one most relevant to our purpose was the king's desire to rule without Parliament. Charles I was successful, at least for a period, deciding not to summon Parliament for ten years. Matters came to a head, however, when he needed new money to deal with a northern rebellion. Parliament responded by drawing up a list of grievances, which the king simply dismissed out of hand. He then dissolved Parliament. Without parliamentary consent, he had his forces attack Scotland and decided to raise funds by means that lay outside Parliament's authority. His forces went down to defeat. The king then had no choice but to summon Parliament again, and once again Parliament drew up a list of grievances. This time parliamentarians simply refused to be dismissed and were able to extract a number of concessions. Parliament became a permanent body and no longer a temporary or an intermittent feature of the country's constitution. Parliament was also able to block non-parliamentary means of taxation.

Parliament went farther than it ever had in its dealings with the monarch when it refused a request from Charles I for new funding for the army and then asked to transfer control of the army to itself from the king. Charles I refused, and civil war broke out. Parliament, with this step, sent out the message that the king's divine right to rule no longer held and that it was taking in its own hands key decisions of government. The king and his troops went to Parliament to arrest five of its members and directed the Speaker of the Commons to reveal where they were. The Speaker refused, stating that he was above all a servant of Parliament, not the king, thus establishing his loyalty to Parliament rather than to the king.

A number of new constitutional experiments were tried and abandoned between 1648 and 1660. After Oliver Cromwell's death, numerous proposals were put forward to define a republican constitution. Nothing came of it, the monarchy was restored, and 'with it the law-making authority of the king in Parliament.' It also, however, left a bad taste in Britain for constitutional innovations and a written constitution, and it instilled a strong bias for 'pragmatic, incremental adaptation of customary institutions.'[26] While it is true that when the monarchy was restored legislation passed during the interregnum was declared null, the interregnum nonetheless had a lasting impact: the prerogative courts were never restored, and laws precluding the monarch from raising taxation and enacting legislation except through Parliament were left intact.[27] The other legacy that is still being felt today in both Britain and Canada is the inherent bias for incremental change in shaping our political and administrative institutions.

Less than thirty years after the Restoration, the king and Parliament were again in conflict, a conflict that would once more give rise to important constitutional developments. Fearing that King James II would try to promote Roman Catholicism in British institutions, a group of notables asked Protestant Prince William of Orange and Mary to intervene on their behalf. A number of officers from the king's army decided to defect to Prince William as he landed in England, and the king fled the country. Parliament simply declared that James II had abdicated and recognized William and Mary as monarchs.

Parliament passed the Bill of Rights, which was read to William and Mary during the ceremony when they were offered the crown. The 'rights' are those enjoyed by Parliament, and the central provisions of the bill remain in force to this day. The legislation essentially laid the foundations for affirming the ultimate sovereignty of Parliament.[28] It restricted many royal prerogatives, placed some power under the direct control of Parliament, and declared that raising money for the use of the crown 'by pretence of prerogative, without grant of Parliament' was illegal. It also gave Parliament the ability to control the identity of the monarch by altering the line of succession (so much for the divine right to rule) and made Parliament master of its own affairs. One student of British politics sums up these developments very well: 'Power started with the Crown, but it continues to be vested in the Crown only because, and for only as long as Parliament continues to wish it.'[29] In brief, the Bill of Rights saw to it that sovereignty was vested in the king or queen in Parliament and not in the king or queen alone, a seminal moment in the development of the Westminster model.

By the end of the nineteenth century, Parliament had forced from the crown virtually all the power it wanted. It would have been hard to find anyone by then claiming that Parliament did not in practice possess unlimited legislative authority. Walter Bagehot, the most celebrated student of government in Victorian Britain, maintained that Parliament, and more specifically the House of Commons, now firmly held the upper hand. He wrote that 'no matter whether it concerns high matters of the essential constitution or small matters of daily detail, the House of Commons can despotically and finally resolve it ... it is absolute, it can rule as it likes and decides as it likes.'[30] With respect to the role of Parliament and its relations with the monarch, Walter Bagehot wrote that the 'Queen must sign her own death warrant if the two Houses unanimously sent it up to her.'[31] Bagehot very likely employed the word 'rule' to signify laying down the rules, since Parliament does not rule in the sense of governing or managing the government.

There was also at the time a widely held consensus that the country required a 'final, unchallengeable decision maker, entrusted with unchallengeable authority to make laws, and declare laws.'[32] This would promote stability, efficiency, and decisiveness, important considerations at a time when the role of government centred on military issues. There was also a consensus that 'the people' should have only an 'indirect' and a 'strictly limited role in public decision-making.'[33] The indirect role would be through Parliament and cabinet. As Sir Ivor Jennings explains, 'the House of Commons and the Cabinet are the instruments of democracy so that the prerogative of the Crown, and, to a lesser degree, the powers of the aristocracy, have been subordinated to public opinion.'[34] Public opinion was important, but no one was suggesting that direct democracy was an option. Rather, citizens would elect representatives to establish policies and strike decisions on their behalf.

Historians regard Sir Robert Walpole (1676–1745) as Britain's first prime minister, although the title was first used in an official document only in 1878, when Benjamin Disraeli signed the final instrument of the Congress of Berlin. Walpole established the precedent that a minister needed the confidence of Parliament, no less than of the sovereign, to continue in office. Before Walpole, and arguably for some years after him, the government was really the sovereign's government and the ministers were his or her ministers, in the sense that both the first lord of the treasury and the prime minister were servants of the sovereign. But when Walpole resigned in 1742 after he lost the confidence of the Commons, he set in motion a series of events that would give rise to a minister who would stand 'primus inter pares.' Walpole also, according to Harold Wilson, created for the premiership what Walter Bagehot would later attribute to cabinet – 'a position of a hyphen which joins, a buckle which fastens the Legislative part of the Executive to the Executive part of the State.'[35]

Walpole resigned office under pressure from the House, including some of his own cabinet colleagues. He left, but his colleagues remained in office. Thus the Commons had removed a prime minister but not the ministry. Some forty years later, in 1782, King George III invited Lord North to form a government after the opposition had successfully attacked the whole ministry and its policies. North told the king that the whole cabinet, except for the lord chancellor, would have to resign before he would form a new government. The king agreed, and those who were removed stayed together 'in a nascent opposition and the nineteenth-century party system began to emerge.'[36] This development ended the legislature's ability to pick and choose policy by overthrowing a combination of parliamentary groups. It also signalled ministerial responsibility – the collective responsibility of the cabinet to the House. It should be noted that the evolution of individual ministerial responsibilities was different and preceded the evolution of collective ministerial responsibility.

Historians credit William Pitt with creating the office of the prime minister, since he was the first to hold the position (from 1766 to 1768) in a sense that it would be recognized today. He became the effective head of cabinet, picked its members in consultation with the sovereign, and ensured that government policies were accepted by his cabinet colleagues and were collectively recommended to Parliament.[37] Thus, Pitt's ministers became his ministers rather than the king's. It was only natural that anyone invited to become the sovereign's chief minister would want a say in deciding which member of Parliament was to be invited to hold a cabinet position. The need to hold a collective front in Parliament, and at times against strong public criticism, meant that the chief minister would wish to pick ministers with similar political views and policy preferences. For this reason, political parties grew and were able to secure an increasingly important role throughout the nineteenth century, both in Britain and later in Canada.

It became widely accepted that parliamentary government and indeed democracy itself would function best if there were both a minority and a majority in Parliament. Further, groups of MPs ideally should have shared objectives and expectations. Thus parties competing for power would become a central feature of parliamentary government. Jennings explains that 'the democratic system implies an appeal to the people by contending parties supporting different policies ... and if there be no Opposition there is no democracy.'[38] Thus citizens would now select their representatives from candidates able to secure the nomination of their political parties.

Political parties and party government became necessary when the government required parliamentary majorities to survive rather than relying on the support of the crown. In Britain, the process began in the mid-eighteenth century and became fully developed between 1832 and 1867, while in British North America it emerged in the 1840s. Thus there is a direct link between the rise of party politics and the principle of ministerial responsibility in Britain and the development of responsible government in British North America.

Responsible government was a product of its time, and it took form during the gradual shift of power from sovereign to Parliament. Ministers became part of a team, no longer the personal choice of the monarch. No matter how competent a minister, and regardless of the sovereign's confidence, he had to resign along with the rest of the cabinet when his party lost power or the confidence of the Commons. This development transformed the struggle for power. And, leaving aside legal and technical niceties, the fact that the monarch no longer constituted the executive required new relationships and processes. Earl Grey explained that parliamentary government necessitated that 'the powers belonging to the Crown ... be exercised through Ministers who are held responsible for the manner in which they are used ... and who are entitled to hold their offices only while they possess the confidence of Parliament and more especially of the House of Commons.'[39]

In parliamentary government, 'the people' are represented in and by the House of Commons. The government and its general policy require the confidence and approval of the House, and, in the final analysis, the sovereign and cabinet must give way to the Commons. Political parties appeal to the electorate, and election outcomes decide the composition of the House, which determines the party origin of the cabinet.[40] The difficulty lies in applying what Grey describes as 'the first principle of our system of government – the control of all branches of the administration by Parliament.'[41]

Democratic control within a parliamentary system is mainly conventional. The key convention is the concept of ministerial responsibility: in Grey's words, 'all holders of permanent offices must be subordinate to some minister responsible to Parliament.' Are ministers responsible *to* someone or somebody, or *for* decisions or activities, or both? What is collective cabinet responsibility as opposed to individual ministerial responsibility? What is the origin of the doctrine? Where does the civil service fit in?

While the supremacy of Parliament remains a 'given,' there are three basic components to the doctrine – the collective responsibility of the cabinet, the individual responsibility of ministers, and the anonymity of civil servants. Most students of public administration believe that the doctrine must come as a package, that it is not possible to favour one of the three components and discard the other two to suit a particular circumstance or issue.

As Henry Parris observes, 'A person is responsible to someone for something and ministerial responsibility is an ancient feature of English government and this sometimes obscures the fact that neither the someone nor the something have remained constant.'[42] Parris explains that ministers became responsible to the crown and to the political nation in medieval times and to the law courts in Tudor times.[43] But the doctrine evolved again during the Victorian era to become a central feature of government. By then it had come to signify 'in ordinary parlance the responsibility of ministers to parliament, or, the liability of ministers to lose their offices if they cannot retain the confidence of the House of Commons.'[44] The doctrine should leave no doubt that the government is subordinate to Parliament and that ministers are accountable to Parliament.

In turn, however, Parliament does not give specific orders or directions to permanent officials, and it has no direct control over any department. Or, to put it another way, MPs should not attempt to govern unless they are members of the cabinet. There are several reasons for this, including the fact that, traditionally, acts of the executive properly belonged to the monarch or the executive. In any event, it is difficult to imagine how a body such as the House of Commons, with hundreds of members representing several political parties, could possibly establish policy priorities and make decisions on a day-to-day basis. The proper role of the House of Commons, then, is not to govern but to act as a public forum, to be the country's leading deliberative body, to focus opinion, to criticize government, and to hold ministers accountable.

Geoffrey Marshall and Graeme C. Moodie explain that the government's collective responsibility means that it has to 'submit its policy and defend its policy before the House of Commons and to resign if defeated on an issue of confidence. The defeat of any substantial bill should be regarded as a loss of confidence.'[45] However, in more recent years it has been unclear what constitutes a vote of confidence.[46] One can speculate on what prompted Lord North in 1782 to ask King George III to remove all ministers except the chancellor when invited to form a new cabinet. It may be that he wanted a fresh start and that he truly felt that the Commons had lost confidence in the whole ministry, not just in one or two ministers. But some historians suggest that early cabinets favoured the collective element mainly because it protected them against the monarch, who otherwise could pick ministers off one by one to produce a more pliant group of advisers. However, cabinet solidarity has, in more recent times, strengthened the prime minister's position, enabling him or her to force the hand of a recalcitrant minister – to accept a policy or to resign. The flip side, of course, is that the doctrine enables a government to function. Still, it is ironic that the collective element of ministerial responsibility was established some 200 years ago to attenuate the king's power, while today it strengthens that of the prime minister.

Jennings sums up the individual responsibility of ministers as follows: 'Each minister is responsible to Parliament for the conduct of his department. The act of every civil servant is by convention regarded as the act of his minister.'[47] Marshall and Moodie elaborated by pointing out that the minister is the 'constitutional mouthpiece through which departmental actions will be defended or repudiated and from whom information is to be sought.'[48] Only the minister can speak for the department to the House, which in turn must look to the minister to secure answers about departmental policies and activities. This element of ministerial responsibility is particularly relevant to our purpose because it links the political and the administrative. It is also important to recognize that this view of individual ministerial responsibility has been severely qualified in more recent years.

Representative Democracy

There has not been much of an appetite for direct democracy since the days of ancient Greece. Oliver Cromwell and the Levellers knew what they wanted – to do away with an absolute monarch with a divine right to rule – but it was not all that clear what system they had in mind to replace it. The search was on for a republican alternative throughout the interregnum, but Cromwell was not successful in laying the groundwork for such a system – his regime collapsed when he died. In the end,

Cromwell simply replaced an absolutist government with another one, one that did not have the political legitimacy to carry on.

The march towards representative democracy was uncertain and slow. Indeed, it was monarchs in the Middle Ages who first turned to representatives of certain segments of the population to gain some political legitimacy. As we have seen, it was only over time and with considerable effort that the House of Commons gained the upper hand in Britain. Parliament, for a long period, represented many segments of the population in relative isolation rather than the population as a whole. It represented the aristocracy and the church, if only because both the church and the wider community were regarded as one and the same.[49] The House of Lords was unelected, and its purpose was to prevent the potential excesses of unchecked democracy.

Notwithstanding hesitant steps towards representative democracy, R.H. Lord described its development and that of Parliament as one of 'the greatest achievements of the Middle Ages.'[50] To be sure, the principle of representation has stood the test of time. David Held explains that representative government solves the problem that a large citizenry imposes on democracy: 'representative democracy could be celebrated as both accountable and feasible government, potentially stable over great territories and time spans.'[51] By the early twentieth century, representative government had won the day as the most promising democratic model. As Joseph Schumpeter explains, 'democracy does not mean and cannot mean that the people actually rule in any obvious sense of the terms "people" and "rule." Democracy means only that the people have the opportunity of accepting or refusing the men who are to rule them. But since they might decide this also in entirely undemocratic ways, we have had to narrow our definition by adding a further criterion identifying the democratic method, viz., free competition among would-be leaders for the vote of the electorate.'[52]

Representative democracy has come to encompass many things. It now means the supremacy of the lower house, competitive political parties, a widely held right to vote, free speech, and a free press. Representative democracy and accompanying liberal instruments speak to controlling government rather than to running it. John Stuart Mill wrote about the 'radical' distinction 'between controlling the business of government and actually doing it.'[53] Western representative democracies, particularly in more recent years, have been trying 'this' and 'that' to come up with the best possible means to control the business of government and to hold governments to account for their policies and decisions.

Two theories emerged on the role elected representatives should play: delegate and representative theories. The delegate theory calls on the elected member to be the voice of his or her constituency and to promote its interests. The representative theory, meanwhile, calls on the elected member to take the views of his or her constituency as one of several considerations in shaping his or her position on issues. It will be recalled that Edmund Burke brought life to this debate in his address to the electors of Bristol in which he attacked the delegate model of representative democracy.

Though one obviously needs to review the work of individual members of Parliament to determine in which camp they sit, the literature in both Britain and Canada suggests a bias towards the representative theory. Jennifer Smith maintains that Burke's attack on the delegate theory has 'stuck' over the years.[54] More than forty years ago, R. MacGregor Dawson, the dean of students of Canada's political institutions, wrote that, 'so far as any generalization on such a matter is possible, the bulk of the Canadian constituencies and of the members who sit for them favour the representative rather than the delegate idea, although in most instances a substantial dependence on the constituency is apparent.'[55]

Both representative and delegate theories come up against political parties and the electoral process. To win election to the Commons, one nearly always needs to be a member of a political party. Traditionally, loyalty to the party, its policies, and the party leader are very important factors determining a member's position on virtually all issues. Surveys of MPs reveal that they believe that loyalty to the party leader matters more than expertise or merit in deciding who makes it to cabinet.[56]

Importing the Westminster Model

The ties between Canada and Britain at the time Canada was born were extremely strong – witness, for example, the cry of Canada's first prime minister, Sir John A. Macdonald: 'A British subject I was born, a British subject I will die.' British influence informed virtually every major development in the rise of Canada's political and administrative institutions. Westminster and Whitehall provided the model for Canada to emulate in developing its basic government structure. Indeed, the preamble to Canada's written constitution declares that 'whereas the Provinces of Canada, Nova Scotia and New Brunswick have expressed their desire to be federally united into one Dominion under the Crown of the United Kingdom of Great Britain and Ireland, with a Constitution similar in principle to that of the United Kingdom ...' In brief, the Fathers of Confederation embraced the British constitution as the model to guide Canada's development, and the British North America (BNA) Act of 1867 was British in both spirit and design. The goal then was to write as little as possible in the constitution and to establish representative democracies for the national and provincial governments based on parliamentary principles developed over the years at Westminster. As in Britain, the Canadian Parliament was designed to stand unchallenged to create laws for all aspects of collective life and constitute the one polity to provide, at the national level, the continuing source for authoritative action for society. This explains why the Fathers of Confederation, for example, gave the national government the power to disallow provincial government initiatives. That said, the division of powers between the federal and provincial governments imposes important constraints on the role of the Canadian Parliament.

Still, the North American colonies had to deal with something the British did not – vast geography and linguistic tensions. Thus, Canada would go as far as it could in embracing the British model, but there were limits. The Fathers of Confederation, however reluctantly, also looked for guidance to the United States – another nation that grew out of British colonial status. Several reasons accounted for their reluctance, including the widely held view in Britain that the United States was too democratic and too republican.[57] The limits on the British model were significant, including the need to design a federal system like that of the Americans. Thus, the BNA Act provided for both parliamentary government at the national level and a division of powers between the two levels of government, thereby limiting in time, at least, the supremacy of Parliament. Other developments have further shifted Canada away from the British model. The Constitution Act of 1982 and its Charter of Rights and Freedoms have moved many issues to the courts, where Canadians can test legislation for its constitutionality. The desire to borrow from both the British and American models prompted noted Canadian historian Kenneth McNaught to observe that Canada has 'produced a unique sense of ideas, structure and custom that defies the model maker.' He added that the resulting potpourri of 'ideas and customs' could make a contemporary analyst 'about as secure as a goose on shell ice.'[58]

It is important to stress, however, that the American federalist model was adopted because it was the only way to unite the colonies. In every other way, the inspiration was British. Consider, for example, that the House of Lords and members of the Canadian Senate are not elected. The role of the Canadian Senate, as defined in 1867, is to provide a 'sober second thought' to the work of the House of Commons – hence the fact that it is unelected. This is a clear signal that in the latter half of the nineteenth century, the merits of democracy were considered to have their limits. Unlike those of the United States, Canada's political institutions are relatively free of checks and balances. The idea in Canada, as in Britain, was to have a 'final, unchallengeable decision maker, entrusted with unchallengeable authority to make laws and declare laws,' in part because that is the way the mother country operated, but also because, as Roger Gibbins explains, a strong central government was seen as a necessary condition for economic and political survival.[59] The challenge was to unite British colonies that would remain loyal to the British crown and forge a national economy that would withstand the economic pull of the United States to the south.

Bureaucracy

S.E. Finer does not spend a great deal of time discussing the work of bureaucracy in his three volumes on the history of government. J.M. Roberts hardly mentions bureaucracy in his *History of the World*.[60] The reason, at least in part, is that civil servants, if only in the interest of survival, have much preferred working away from the limelight. In addition, it is only recently that scholars have taken a strong interest in bureaucracy. The role of bureaucracy, until the latter part of the nineteenth century, was to play a supporting role to monarchs, to manage an empire (in the case of Britain), and to support the military. Its work was taken for granted, and there was little need to spend much time and effort reviewing its operations.

When modern bureaucracy first started to take form during the Victorian era, the role of the civil service was relatively straightforward. It was to have no constitutional persona, it was to be loyal to the government of the day, and it was to take no public credit or blame for policies or even for administrative decisions. The flip side of this, of course, is that ministers, in theory at least, were responsible to Parliament for everything done in and by their departments. A selection of quotations to explain how it works might include the following: 'ministers are responsible for the misdeeds of civil servants'; 'the minister is responsible for every stamp stuck on an envelope'; 'when things go right ministers take the credit, when things go wrong they take the blame, if necessary they offer their resignation'; and 'civil servants are anonymous and their personal failures are not a matter of knowledge or debate.'[61]

Again, the Victorian civil service was a product of its time, a time when ministers could readily accept responsibility for policy decisions, which were clearly *their* decisions and *their* policies. Similarly, they could, if they so wished, dominate the administration of their departments. Henry Parris writes that 'the early nineteenth-century minister, if he was also a man of business, bestrode his department like a colossus. His duties were both political and administrative, but he worked within a system which enabled him to give much time to the latter.'[62] For example, Lord Palmerston was secretary of war from 1809 to 1828, and during those nineteen years there was no issue too small to escape his attention, including 'the disposal of one unserviceable horse.'[63] He retained this devotion to detail when he went to the Foreign Office in the 1830s, where he 'read every report, every letter and every despatch received ... down to the least important letter of the lowest vice-consul. What is more, he answered them.'[64] It is well known that Prime Minister Gladstone drafted legislation himself to present to Parliament. Little wonder, then, that the doctrine of ministerial responsibility made eminent sense when it first took root.

Things were no different in Canada. Sir John A. Macdonald was asked as minister of the militia in July 1862 to explain the absence of three officials in the department – one who suffered from epilepsy, another who had lost his eyesight, and a third whose delicate health made attendance impossible.[65] In Canada, in 1867, there were about ten civil servants for every member of Parliament. Today, there are about 1,000, and this figure does not include crown corporations.[66]

The Murray report, tabled in 1922, observed that ministers 'have too much to do and do too much ... and Cabinet business ranged from questions of the highest importance ... down to the acceptance of a tender for the erection of a pump.' Murray concurred with the Wilsonian view that 'the business of a minister is not to administer, but to direct policy ... the carrying out of this policy ... should be left to his subordinates.'[67]

The simplicity of government operations allowed ministers this picayune attention to detail. As already noted, the civil service borrowed heavily from the structure of the army and the navy in building its organization. Government departments had a 'series of levels of authority and command, each answerable to those at a higher level and able to give orders to those at a level below them.'[68] An era of limited government and a pyramid chain of command made it easy for a department to speak with one voice to its minister and hence through him with one voice to Parliament, the public, and other departments.

Nor did nineteenth-century ministers have to spend much time dealing with the media. There were only a few newspapers, and the era of the twenty-four-hour-a-day electronic media was still 100 years away. There were no paid lobbyists and precious few interest groups demanding access to ministers. The time was ideal for the development of cabinet government, ministerial responsibility, and anonymous civil servants.

The nineteenth century gave birth to another significant development for the relationship between ministers and civil servants: the rise of political parties and the belief that the best government would emerge from a conflict between parties – one in government and at least one other in opposition. The party in power would constitute the government, and the opposition would question, criticize, and be available to assume power. Sir Norman Chester points to a significant related development: the conflict over power 'placed emphasis on government secrecy, not disclosing any information that might be of use to the opposition.'[69] The notion of anonymity and the loyalty of civil servants would take on added importance for the party in power, and it would not die easily, even with the arrival of more activist governments. As Clement Attlee, Britain's Labour prime minister from 1945 to 1951, stated bluntly, 'No Government can be successful which cannot keep its secrets.'[70] Attlee's views still resonate in Canada in senior government circles. Prime Minister Jean Chrétien echoed them when he chaired his first cabinet meeting in 1993.[71] Gordon Robertson, former clerk of the privy council and secretary to the cabinet, writes that 'the whole basis of cabinet government rests on privacy or full discussions will not be possible.'[72] Thus the doctrine of ministerial responsibility in the Westminster model places a premium on secrecy and managing confidential information.

In line with British experience and the development of parliamentary government, no single event defined the role of civil servants, which adjusted and evolved to deal with changing circumstances. Permanence is a case in point. It became a central feature in Canada only in 1918, when nearly the entire civil service and virtually all appointments were placed under the Civil Service Commission. And, as in

Britain, it was in the nineteenth century that Canada made the transition from a civil service based on office to one based on salary. Civil servants had previously performed services that provided opportunities to increase fees or levels of services in order to generate more revenue for themselves and, at times, for their staff.[73] A new culture emerged when salaries were introduced – remuneration was relatively modest compared to the commercial world, and no profit was permitted from areas of responsibility. The public 'ought unquestionably to be served as cheaply as is consistent with being served with integrity and ability.'[74] Indeed, for a long time the moral authority of the civil service was based on its ability to be parsimonious with public funds. One of the basic goals of the civil service was to do things as cheaply as possible and, if at all possible, to avoid spending. Demanding administrative and financial rules in all government departments ingrained this approach.[75]

Permanence of employment for civil servants, as we saw above, also developed over time in both Britain and Canada. It arose because of the increasing complexity and volume of work in government and the need to do away with political patronage in staffing.[76] Permanence does not mean simply holding on to a job for a long time. Rather, it means keeping a position through change of government, a concept that appeared with the arrival of responsible government.

The rationale for a permanent civil service appears in the opening pages of the Northcote-Trevelyan report: 'It may safely be asserted that, as matters now stand, the Government of the country could not be carried on without the aid of an efficient body of permanent officers, occupying a position duly subordinate to that of the ministers who are directly responsible to the Crown and to Parliament, yet possessing sufficient independence, character, ability and experience to be able to advise, assist, and to some extent, influence those who are from time to time set over them.'[77] The report was tabled in Britain in the 1850s, at a time when political leaders came and went quickly; thus a permanent civil service was seen as a counterbalance to the impermanence of politicians. It also constituted the key that enabled civil servants to advise ministers as they saw fit. Permanence would thus entail a higher standard of conduct, forthrightness, discretion, and loyalty to whatever government was in power.

To ensure that career officials could advise ministers without fear or favour, they also had to be shielded from attack – and hence to forego public praise. An institutional culture developed in which civil servants avoided the limelight and public praise to the same extent that ministers pursued them. Thus separate arenas emerged for the politicians and for the civil service. Politicians would need approval every four years or so to provide political legitimacy to the public policy process. The public service would be permanent and show loyalty to the government of the day.

Permanence finally triumphed in Canada for good with the implementation of the Murray report of 1912 and revisions to the Civil Service Act in 1918. There was one question left to resolve – how far up the hierarchy was permanence to go? Canada again borrowed from Britain and extended permanent status to the deputy minister level (permanent secretary in the case of Britain), the level just below the minister.

Looking Back

This *mise en scène*, however brief, reviews how political-bureaucratic institutions took form. It is a story about the struggle for power. It begins with the Greek polis, where power rested in the hands of citizens, narrowly defined, and ends with representative democracies in which very little power is in the hands of the people, who have to rely almost entirely on politicians and civil servants. There was a distrust of 'citizen power' at the time our representative democratic institutions were being developed. Today, it is the opposite, as distrust is now directed at the political and bureaucratic elites.

Political institutions in the case of Britain, and by ricochet in Canada, took shape as the monarch and Parliament struggled to have the upper hand. The shift of power from monarch to Parliament was gradual, not the result of a single conflict, one event, or even one revolution, and the same can be said about the shift of power or influence from Parliament to the executive and more recently still from cabinet to the prime minister. The enormous centralized power now in the hands of the prime minister is also part of the monarchical heritage. This may well explain why Britain was reluctant to cast into law or into a written constitution how politicians should relate to citizens and to civil servants and how the machinery of government should work. For example, it is a matter of convention, not law, that the prime minister is a member of the House of Commons. It is a matter of convention, not law, that cabinet exists, that its deliberations are held in secrecy, and that a minister must not knowingly mislead Parliament. The doctrine of ministerial responsibility is also a matter of convention, not law, and the list goes on. Adam Tomkins explains that 'the complex relations between civil servants, ministers, Parliament, and the public have developed without and despite the law rather than under the authority and within the framework of the law.'[78] One should bear in mind that things are somewhat different in Canada where the panoply of laws governing the civil service and the powers of ministers and civil servants is much more extensive than in Britain.

The doctrine of ministerial responsibility has long been held as the cornerstone that guides the relationship between Parliament, ministers, and public servants. However, as Geoffrey Marshall states in his seminal work on the British constitution, it is exceedingly difficult to provide 'a clear and succinct account of the principle or convention of ministerial responsibility.'[79] He writes that the convention 'like most British conventions, ... [is] somewhat vague and slippery ... and that collective and individual responsibility are two doctrines, not one, and each divides in turn into a series of disparate topics.'[80] The slipperiness is evident in many ways.

Bureaucracy also grew gradually. It first emerged to serve tribal chiefs, monarchs, and emperors and existed solely as an appendage to their interests. It was imperial China that introduced specialization and a competitive process to gain entry into the bureaucracy.

Loyalty was central to the ability of bureaucracy to serve monarchs and emperors, whether in China, in the Byzantine empire, or in Europe. Bureaucracy, in many ways, existed to serve the monarch's immediate needs and the affairs of state as he saw them. In the case of Britain, when the time came the bureaucracy simply shifted its loyalty from the monarch to the government of the day. Given its strong bias for 'pragmatic, incremental adaptation, [of] customary institutions' Britain refrained from putting into law how the civil service would work with politicians and deal with citizens. Loyalty did not require legislation or a place in the constitution: it was a matter that could be easily understood.

The British civil service would not have a constitutional, legal, or statutory persona distinct from the government of the day. Ministers would accept responsibility for everything done in their departments, down to 'every stamp stuck on an envelope.' Ministers and civil servants were to speak to Parliament and the public with one voice, that of the minister. At the same time, however, the civil service would develop a non-partisan persona that enabled it to serve through a change of government. A permanent status for civil servants would act as a counterbalance to the impermanence of politicians. No one saw this in terms of a power struggle or doubted that the civil service would be less loyal to the government of the day if it enjoyed a permanent status. Rather, permanence was deemed necessary to attract strong candidates to manage the affairs of state in an increasingly complex environment. Things were simple and straightforward. Does this suggest that there was once a golden era for the relationship between politicians and the civil service and between civil servants and citizens and that over the years we have lost our way? The next chapter explores this question.

3 Was There Ever a Golden Era?

Some students of government believe that, in fact, things are not much different today from what they were fifty or seventy years ago and that any present discontent stems from a tendency to view the past through rose-coloured glasses. They dismiss those who believe otherwise as suffering from a case of 'golden ageism.' More, they maintain that we are now actually better governed than we were, for example, during the 1960s and assert that to see the current era as in decline has been a common complaint down through the ages. T.S. Eliot believed that of his time, as did Matthew Arnold and Shakespeare before him. They claim that this human trait accounts for the dismay as well as the widespread 'revulsion against the ugliness of our time.'[1]

Whether or not we are better governed today than we were twenty-five, fifty, or seventy years ago is an important question, and there are a number of ways to address this question. The issue for us is whether the current discontent with politicians and civil servants is a passing phenomenon or whether it relates to a more fundamental problem with the working of our political and administrative institutions. This study takes the latter position. That said, it is important to recognize that it is impossible to compare, with any degree of precision, one era with another. Indeed, recent experience shows that it is extremely difficult even to evaluate the impact of a current government program because so many variables come into play to influence its outcome or to explain its success or failure. How then can anyone possibly compare the state of government and public administration from one era to another?

To be sure, Western nations are much richer today than they were forty years ago, and it is to be expected that the quality of front-line public services will have improved, if only because more resources are committed to them. This study is concerned less about the level of program spending or the quality of public services today compared with forty years ago than about the comparative state of our political and administrative institutions. In addition, change can be seen as positive or negative, depending on the eye of the beholder. Some citizens, for example, welcome access to information legislation, while civil servants do not. Civil servants may well see growth in the bureaucracy in a positive light, while citizens do not, and the list goes on. A former British cabinet secretary, Lord Wilson, sums it up well when he writes that, though 'it would be wrong to glorify the mandarin period ... their heyday was in the postwar years when the performance of the service was strong.'[2] His point is that the British civil service has changed and will continue to change to accommodate the different circumstances of different eras. The mandarin period, with all its strengths, was appropriate for the postwar years but may not be suited to today's political and economic circumstances.

As noted in the introduction, if there is a consensus in Western society among politicians, civil servants, the media, and academics, it is that the public sector is in urgent need of repair. There is now wide agreement among British academics that the country is confronting a 'crisis of constitutional legitimacy.'[3] Tom Bentley writes that British democracy 'is in crisis. Party membership is falling; electoral turnout in the United Kingdom appears to have bottomed out at a new low and, when asked, we say we distrust governments like never before.'[4] Sir Robin Butler, former cabinet secretary under Prime Ministers Major and Blair, told MPs that not 'everything about government is bad, but it is deteriorating.'[5]

Similar comments have been made in Canada by both practitioners and scholars. Senator Lowell Murray, a widely respected senior minister in the Mulroney government, writes that 'anyone interested in democracy and in public policy in Canada cannot help but be concerned about the steep decline of confidence in public institutions, notably Parliament, and in political parties, candidates and representatives that has been captured by survey after survey.'[6]

What is remarkable is that the belief that the public sector is in a perilous state transcends jurisdictions and systems of government throughout the Western world. Why is this so? Is the machinery of government not operating as efficiently as it once did? Has society itself changed so that its expectations of government are higher today than they were, say, forty years ago? Are key policy and administrative actors playing a different role today? Are the media to blame? It is important to ponder these questions to ensure that we do not misdiagnose the patient.

The Westminster-Whitehall Model

A former senior British civil servant blames the decline in the British public sector on the fact that the institutions at the heart of our democracy – cabinet, Parliament, secretaries of state, the civil service – no longer work well.[7] The same has been said of Canada, where the cabinet has recently been described as a 'focus group' in which the prime minister tests his ideas or briefs ministers on what he proposes to do.[8] The consequent decline of the role of Parliament in the nation's business has given rise to a number of studies and reports of task forces in recent years on ways to make Parliament more relevant to citizens in both Britain and Canada.[9] As for the numerous efforts to reform the civil service in Britain and Canada, they can scarcely be described as successful. A prominent Canadian practitioner had this to say about the state of the civil service, and it is worth quoting him at length:

> The existential crisis of public administration had several sources. One was fiscal ... Another related and even more important source of the existential crisis was the crisis of legitimacy. In the 1980s and the 1990s the public service was experiencing the second and third decades of what I have elsewhere called the second 'long wave' of legitimacy since the Second World War. In the first wave, with some exaggeration, the public sector could do no wrong, the private sector could do no right. In the second, beginning, in the 1970s, the roles were reversed. By the beginning of the 1990s this second wave was reaching its peak, bringing with it attacks on the foundations of public service from without *and* from within.[10]

It was not always thus. There was a time when the civil service was much more confident in its role and when Parliament occupied a more central and prominent role in society. First, Parliament. In the second half of the nineteenth century, virtually all key public policy actors in Britain agreed that Parliament 'possessed a legally unlimited legislative authority.'[11] Politicians, political theorists, and lawyers made the case that, while the Americans divided power by nesting it in different branches, the English constitution provided for only one authority to deal with 'all sorts of matters.'[12] Walter Bagehot writes that 'no matter whether it concerns high matters of the essential constitution or small matters ... a new House of Commons can despotically and finally resolve it ... when freshly elected, it is absolute, it can rule as it likes and decides as it likes.'[13]

Bagehot was not alone in this view. C.D. Yonge observed in 1868 that the first principle of the constitution was 'the omnipotence of Parliament.' Justice Willes asserted in 1871 that 'Acts of Parliament ... are the law of the land; and we do not sit here as a court of appeal from parliament ... We sit here as servants of the Queen and the legislature ... The proceedings here are judicial, not autocratic, which they would be if we could make laws instead of administering them.'[14] In 1872, Chief Justice Cockburn and Justice Blackburn wrote, 'There is no judicial body in the country by which the validity of an act of parliament can be questioned. An act of the legislature is superior in authority to any court of law ... and no court could pronounce a judgment as to the validity of an act of parliament.'[15] A few years later, Sheldon Amos claimed that 'in one sense Parliament can do anything, because it can pass a law which by the existing Constitution must be recognised in every Court of Justice in the land.'[16] One would be hard pressed to find many judges, if any at all, in either Britain or Canada, making the same observation today. In brief, in nineteenth-century Britain, members of the judiciary knew their place in the pecking order, and Parliament was on top.

During the nineteenth century, the franchise was extended in Britain, first in 1832 on a property basis and then in 1867 to include most of the artisan class. This strengthened the hand of Parliament in relation to the crown. It will be recalled that in 1834 the king turfed out the Whigs and invited the Tories, led by the Duke of Wellington, to take power. Parliament was dissolved; however, in the subsequent election the Whigs won again. The electorate had spoken and chosen a government without regard to the king's preference. The relationship between king and Parliament had been turned on its head: 'the system which had been devised so that the king might control the Commons became the means by which the House of Commons through its leaders, controlled the king.'[17]

Adam Tomkins describes the period between 1832 and 1870 as 'the golden age of genuinely parliamentary government.' This was the era that followed government by the crown but before government by parties.[18] Between the two reform acts of 1832 and 1872, no less than ten governments lost power because they lost the confidence of the House of Commons. Tomkins adds, however, that with the arrival of the modern, centralized organization of the political party came the 'greatest single challenge that the system of political accountability had yet to face.'[19] Another major challenge described below is the growth of government. It only takes a moment's reflection to appreciate that accountability would become considerably more difficult as government assumed a greater role in society. It is not too much of an exaggeration to suggest that the role of government in nineteenth-century Britain was limited to managing the empire, wars, maintaining law and order, and taxation. This held for Canada as well, although here we can substitute managing an empire with building a vast physical infrastructure.

It also takes only a moment's reflection to appreciate that it was easier for Parliament to perform its role in simpler times and with a smaller government. Parliament traditionally has played a variety of roles: it represents the country's leading and legitimate deliberative body, it establishes a legitimate government, makes government work by allocating resources and adopting legislation, makes government behave and holds it accountable, and provides for an alternative government. It also functions to express the 'mind of the people, teach society and inform both government and citizens of grievances and problems.'[20] There are any number of reasons why it is increasingly difficult for Parliament to perform these roles today, ranging from the size and complexity of government departments and agencies to a better informed public and the role of the new media.

However, it was the rise of political parties that transformed parliamentary politics into party politics.[21] Political parties were the vehicle by which political power was secured, and as these parties grew, the party leader and professional party officials began to exert considerable influence on them. The House of Commons divided and remains divided between the government party and opposition parties or between 'them' and 'us,' making the institution partisan and adversarial.

Party discipline became the key to survival for the governing party but also for the opposition parties, if only to present a united front leading up to the next general election campaign. There are any number of carrots that party leaders have in hand to induce party discipline: a cabinet appointment, a patronage appointment, and strong party support, including that of the leader, at election time. It is this that prompted Tomkins to write about 'the golden age of genuinely parliamentary government before the arrival of disciplined political parties.' Before parties came to dominate the House of Commons, the prime minister and ministers were accountable to Parliament but could not yet control it. Now, though they remain accountable to Parliament, they can and do control it whenever they have a majority mandate.

In both Britain and Canada, when there is a Conservative, Liberal, or Labour majority in the House of Commons, there is a Conservative, Liberal, or Labour government. Accordingly, as Tomkins explains, 'what we have come to mean when we say that the government is accountable to Parliament is that the government is accountable to a group of politicians, the majority of whom are members of the same political party as that which forms the government.'[22] The result is that disciplined political parties have undermined the independence of MPs so that ministers no longer regard themselves as accountable to the House of Commons, as was the case between 1832 and the 1870s in Britain when responsible government took form.

The above is not to suggest that the rise of political parties has been a completely negative force in parliamentary politics. As we saw in the previous chapter, disciplined parties are necessary in the search for reliable legislative majorities. Question Period, consideration of legislative proposals, review of the expenditure budget, and parliamentary business in general are better suited to disciplined political parties than undisciplined ones or independents. Jennifer Smith writes that 'while responsible government does not necessarily require party government in theory, it has become party government in practice.'[23]

Still, there are few voices today claiming that sovereignty belongs with Parliament or with the Queen in Parliament. Its sovereignty is now relegated to a legal concept and is no longer a political reality, in that whenever there is a majority government practical sovereignty belongs to the prime minister and to his cabinet.[24] Lord Hailsham declared, as far back as 1978, that Britain had an elected dictatorship.[25] The very same has been said of Canada. In fact, Jeffrey Simpson, a columnist with Canada's *Globe and Mail* newspaper, published a book in 2001 describing the Canadian prime minister as a 'friendly dictator.'[26]

Peter Hennessy reports that Aneurin Bevan sought election to municipal council because his father told him that it was a very important place, with powerful men. However, when he made it to council, he discovered that, though power had once been there, it had since gone elsewhere. Hennessy adds that, though Bevan never recorded his thoughts on the matter, when he made it to the House of Commons in 1929 and to cabinet in 1945, he speculates that Bevan also saw power slip out of the door each time.[27] Practitioners and observers of British politics have hardly been more positive than Hennessy of late on the role of Parliament. Sir Frank Cooper, for example, writes that 'One has only to enter the Houses of Parliament to sense the magic and past glory of our parliamentary history. One has only to watch the proceedings on the floor of the Lower House often to feel ashamed by the behaviour of its members, by the inability of the Opposition to influence the government.'[28] Sir Christopher Foster goes even farther and writes about the 'catastrophic decline' of Parliament 'brought about by the media.' He adds that the point was brought home when the editor of *The Times* decided to do away with its dedicated parliamentary page because 'it was only read by MPs. It was a symptom of both rapid decline in media attention to Parliament and of media takeover of the Commons' function of accountability.'[29]

The report *Power to the People*, the centenary project of the Rowntree Trust, echoes these comments, stating that 'accountability and scrutiny' by Parliament have weakened in recent years.[30] The authors of the report consulted members of the House of Commons, and here again the observations are hardly positive. Gwyneth Dunwoody maintains that 'Parliament has run away from its responsibilities in the sense that it should not allow its programme to be decided by the executive,' while John Bercow argues that 'my impression is that for at least two decades and possibly quite a lot longer, government control of parliament has been increasing.'[31]

Again, things are no different in Canada. C.E.S. Franks, arguably Canada's leading student of Parliament, claims that the decline of Parliament can be viewed from two perspectives: actual measures that indicate its decline, and the growing complexity of modern politics and government, which has made it much more difficult for Parliament to perform its role.[32] The first wound is largely self-inflicted, and the second includes forces that are beyond its immediate control.

There is ample evidence to document the substantial decline in the quality of parliamentary debates and in their significance to Canadians and to the government.[33] The prime minister and ministers increasingly make major announcements outside the House. Interest groups or special gatherings of one kind or another provide an ideal backdrop and also guarantee favourable reactions on the national evening news. Representatives of opposition parties are often not in attendance to add a negative spin. Contrast this development with the days when announcements were made in the Commons, giving opposition parties the opportunity to react immediately and point to flaws, real or contrived.

The Ontario government took this new practice to extraordinary lengths when it made its 2003 budget public in a television broadcast from the headquarters of auto parts manufacturer Magna International. This was a first in Canadian history. No government budget had previously been presented to television cameras rather than to Parliament or to a legislative assembly. The move ensured a wider TV audience for the government, but it also met a storm of protest, from the Speaker and members of the Legislature.[34]

Former Prime Minister Pierre Trudeau spoke to the decline of the role of Parliament when he declared that 'MPs are nobodies' beyond fifty yards from Parliament Hill. A good number of MPs responded that the opposite was true, that they were important in their communities but were nobodies in the nation's capital.

There are a number of forces contributing to the decline of Parliament in the political life of both Britain and Canada. For instance, Parliament is no longer the source of all laws. As Britain gets further integrated into the European Union, it is of course more and more difficult to write about the supremacy of Parliament at home. Policies struck by the European Community and rulings from the European court and decisions from the European Community have had and continue to have a profound impact on public policy in Britain. This prompted Geoffrey Marshall to ask if the sovereignty of Parliament had been abandoned. His answer is that 'parliamentary sovereignty is alive but unwell, some violence having been offered to it.'[35]

The incorporation of the European Convention of Human Rights into Britain's domestic law has also had considerable impact – the courts are playing an increasingly important role in reviewing the constitutionality of parliamentary statutes. Section 6 of the 1998 act provides that it is 'unlawful for a public authority to act in a way which is incompatible with a convention right' and defines 'public authority' as 'any person certain of whose functions are functions of a public nature.'[36]

In Canada, the Charter of Rights and Freedoms has had and continues to have a profound impact on Canadian politics. Those who put forward claims under the charter in Canada are in no mood for compromise. They seek a straight answer to their grievances, the kind of answer that is not always forthcoming in the less than clear-cut political-bureaucratic world. There is also every indication that Canadians are turning to the courts in search of a straight answer. Canada's federal government published a performance report on the Supreme Court in early 2002 revealing that the court received 686 leave applications in 2001, up from 445 in 1991. The Supreme Court attributes this change to an assertive population that is 'more willing to challenge the perceived wisdom of its leaders – often in court.'[37]

The Supreme Court has a case. Civil servants point to the courts as an important factor that has reshaped their work over the past twenty or thirty years. A senior official at the Department of Fisheries and Oceans (DFO) reports that thirty years ago civil servants rarely thought about the courts as they went about their work. Today, he maintains, the courts are never far from people's minds when planning departmental activities. As he explains, 'When you launch a new activity or unveil an important decision, you should always make provision for a court injunction to stop the department from moving forward.'[38] He adds, 'In 1979 there were three lawyers handling DFO legal issues. Today [May 2002], there are twenty-six lawyers handling our cases. That in itself tells you what has happened inside government.'[39] Another senior line-department official reports that he and his staff are very careful about putting things down on paper for fear that the information will be employed against the department in a future court case.[40] Civil servants in the Department of Justice confirm these developments. One senior official there reveals that, despite the program review of the mid-1990s, the number of lawyers in the department responsible for 'litigation' and 'litigation avoidance' has more than doubled over the past ten years.[41]

The courts have also been drawn even into management issues. A senior manager with Corrections Canada reports that both employees and their unions now turn to the courts about issues that thirty years ago were quietly handled internally. It has never been easy to deal with non-performers in government. It is still more difficult today, as employees and their union representatives go to court if management initiates any action to remove anyone for non-performance. Again, senior officials at Justice reveal that the number of lawyers working on behalf of the employer in personnel-related cases has increased substantially in recent years.[42]

Since the Charter of Rights and Freedoms was made part of Canada's constitution, a debate has raged on the role of the courts in Canadian society – on how it squares or, more to the point, how it no longer squares with the British model on which the country's judiciary is based. The point has been made time and again that Canadian courts no longer follow judicial self-restraint. Canada's chief justice recently made clear her views on the role of the judiciary. She wrote, 'I believe that judges have the duty to insist that the legislative and executive branches of government conform to certain established and fundamental norms, even in times of trouble.' She adds that the 'debate is not about whether judges should ever use unwritten constitutional norms to invalidate laws, but rather about what norms may justify such action.'[43] One can hardly imagine a nineteenth-century judge in Canada or Britain making a similar observation. Judicial power has grown substantially in Canada in recent years to the point that policy makers must now 'govern with judges.'[44]

The theory of parliamentary-cabinet government envisages two systems, a Parliament and a government, with cabinet being the link between them.[45] In addition to the division of powers between Ottawa and the provinces, there are now several systems at play in addition to Parliament and government – the courts, the bureaucracy, interest groups, and the media.

Bureaucracy

A good number of civil servants in both Britain and Canada regard the post-Second World War period (circa 1945 to the early 1970s) as the golden age for bureaucracy. Peter Hennessy, as mentioned earlier, quotes a senior British civil servant as saying, 'it seems to me that the most remarkable of the many remarkable things about the Second World War is that it really was our *finest hour*.'[46] Julian LeGrand, in his much acclaimed book *Motivation, Agency and Public Policy*, describes the period as a 'triumph of collectivism,' and there is a link, of course, between collectivism and the civil service.[47] Vernon Bogdanor writes that the 'philosophy of state action reached its apogee in the years following the Second World War when the post-war settlement legitimised the role of government.'[48] The goal of many young university graduates in the immediate postwar years was to work for the common good, and the state provided the most promising avenue to do so. Government had little difficulty in attracting its share of the best and brightest that came out of the universities.

Bogdanor and others also see a link between religion and public service. They look back to the work of T.H. Green and efforts to 'redefine Christianity as an ethical doctrine whose fundamental notions were those of duty and service' and to Beatrice Webb, who wrote that 'during the middle decades of the nineteenth century in England, the impulse of self-subordinating service was transferred, consciously and overtly, from God to man.'[49] In Canada, the role of the civil service expanded as that of organized religion began to wane. By 1961, for example, 47,000 Roman Catholic nuns in Quebec assumed responsibility for education, health care, and social services. Today there are only 13,450 nuns in Quebec, the great majority of whom are retired, and the responsibilities once assumed by the clergy now account for 60 per cent of the province's budget.[50]

In the immediate postwar period, the civil service did not lack for self-confidence or certainty of purpose. Senior civil servants in both Britain and Canada spoke of the 'vocation of a civil servant,' a vocation 'imbued by the feeling that they [i.e., civil servants] alone possess all the answers.'[51] One former senior British civil servant observed that when he left Oxford in the 1950s, he was interested in a career only in the civil service because that was where one went if one hoped to make a difference and because at the time the private sector was simply 'not on.' It was, in his words, 'beneath us, it was getting one's hands dirty to join a private firm.'[52] Simply put, role models for university graduates were to be found in the public sector, not the private sector.

In Canada, a government task force report on values and ethics in the civil service stressed in 1996 the 'publicness of public organizations' and essentially described a career in the civil service as a vocation or a special calling.[53] As one senior Canadian civil servant explains, 'Public service values are the means, or part of it, by which we articulate this vision of the good, as far as the public service is concerned. Taken as a whole, they describe not just what it is right to *do* but – which is prior to that – what we want to *be*. They are the "higher goods" inherent in our vision of the good life – the good public service life – to which we can give our loyalty, and our love. To which, in specific circumstances, we are prepared to sacrifice our own personal interest, possibly our careers, possibly even our lives.'[54]

As already noted, this calling was to be carried out without a distinct constitutional persona from the government of the day. In 1985, Robert Armstrong, then secretary to the cabinet in Britain, in a carefully worded statement, wrote that 'Civil servants are servants of the Crown. For all practical purposes the Crown in this context ... is represented by the Government of the day ... The Civil Service has no constitutional personality or responsibility separate from the duly elected government of the day.'[55] Armstrong has been quoted time and again in the literature, and his view has long been an important part of the bargain guiding the relationship between ministers and civil servants in Westminster-style parliamentary systems. It has, however, been recently challenged both in Britain and Canada, and there is now some doubt that this claim can any longer be considered valid. Christopher Hood, for example, maintains that this assumption is 'today certainly viewed as being at the far end of the spectrum.'[56] Subsequently, two secretaries to the cabinet, Richard Wilson and Robin Butler, sought to modify Armstrong's position. Robert Armstrong himself, now retired from the civil service, has also recently changed his tune somewhat, suggesting that the need for a Civil Service Act that would in effect gave a public personality to the civil service 'stems from a gradually increasing lack of trust in government.'[57] That said, the British government continues to insist through its official publications that 'the Civil Service has no separate constitutional personality or responsibility.'[58]

The government of Canada continues to adhere to the Armstrong view, though recent developments have raised a number of questions regarding its current relevance. The Privy Council Office (PCO) – the equivalent to the Cabinet Office in Britain – has maintained over the years that 'the deputy ministers' accountability cannot be exercised without reference to the responsibility of ministers to Parliament. Deputies act on behalf of their ministers.' The document adds, 'Administration and management of programs consist of carrying out policies based on political decisions … The attempt to identify discrete areas of official accountability to Parliament would likely result in the further blurring of lines of accountability, weakening the ability of the House to hold the minister responsible when it chooses for matters falling under his or her authority.'[59]

Things took a different turn when Stephen Harper, within months of coming to power in 2006, unveiled a legislative package designed to strengthen accountability. The package provided for the introduction of the accounting officer concept (already in effect in Britain) to Canada 'within the framework of ministerial responsibility.'[60] Accounting officers occupy a key position in the system of financial control and accountability in Britain; they hold responsibility in their own right and are the responsible witnesses before the Public Accounts Committee. As the Treasury explains, 'The essence of an Accounting Officer's role is a personal responsibility for the propriety and regularity of the public finances for which he or she is answerable. The responsibilities of an Accounting Officer are laid down in a memorandum which is sent to every new Accounting Officer on appointment. The memorandum establishes the procedure to be followed when a minister overrules an Accounting Officer's advice on an issue of propriety and regularity. It also makes it clear that the Accounting Officer is responsible for delivering departmental objectives in the most economic, efficient, and effective manner.'[61] This should go some distance towards acknowledging that the public service has a distinct persona. That said, as we shall see, Harper later watered down his proposal on the accounting officer concept from what he had to say in his 2006 election campaign platform. It is also interesting to note that he endorsed the traditional PCO review in his *Accountable Government: A Guide for Ministers*, a document that he issued as his government assumed office.[62]

There is every indication that the Privy Council Office had serious reservations about Harper's proposal, and this may well explain his decision to change his position once in power. For instance, the PCO produced a document for the use of deputy ministers that did not square with Harper's original position. The document, *Guidance for Deputy Ministers*, which is still on the PCO's website, goes beyond the argument that the public service has no 'constitutional personality' to argue that civil servants 'do not have a public voice, or identity, distinct from that of their Minister, nor do they share in their Minister's political accountability.' It adds, 'in supporting the Minister's accountability, a Deputy Minister may find himself or herself before a parliamentary committee to explain what went wrong. He or she might say, for example, yes, an error was made. I am accountable to the Minister of the department and, with the support of the Minister, I have fixed the problem – this could include informing a committee that disciplinary action has been taken, but it would not extend to naming those concerned even if their identity had somehow been disclosed through the media or otherwise.'[63]

The Privy Council Office did not revise this document after Harper's accountability package made it through Parliament. It did produce in March 2007 a document, *Guidance for Accounting Officers*, that further attenuates the concept. It argues that accountability before parliamentary committees for accounting officers means supporting the accountability of their ministers before Parliament. This suggests that accounting officers are not accountable in their own right, independent of their departmental ministers.[64] It does not deal with the fact that deputy ministers are delegated authority directly by Parliament under various statutes, including, among others, the Public Service Employment Act and the Financial Administration Act. In addition, these acts do not allow powers to be delegated to ministers. Parliament turned specific powers over to deputy ministers to protect the neutrality of the civil service and the public purse from abuse by politicians.

The Public Accounts Committee of Canada's House of Commons, meanwhile, spent months developing a protocol to spell out the roles and responsibilities of MPs, how they should behave, and what types of questions they should and should not ask of the accounting officers, so that the proceedings of the committee should be directed towards affirming and strengthening the responsibilities and accountability of accounting officers. The draft version of the committee's protocol was forwarded to the Treasury Board and the PCO with a request that they work with the committee to produce a protocol, but the two central agencies chose not to cooperate. Instead, the PCO, without consulting with the Public Accounts Committee, posted its own document on its website.[65] The Public Accounts Committee nevertheless adopted its own protocol. The House of Commons subsequently voted concurrence in the Public Accounts Committee's protocol, against the desires of the minority Conservative Harper government, most of whose members voted against this implementation of their own election platform commitment.

The PCO insists that ministers alone are accountable to Parliament for all actions of the executive, including management, and that accounting officers appear before parliamentary committees only to answer questions on behalf of their minister, to provide information, and to support their minister's accountability to Parliament. The PCO insists that this holds even when the deputy minister, not the minister, possesses the statutory or delegated responsibility. The clerk of the Privy Council Office quoted from an open letter signed by Prime Minister Harper on the accounting officer initiative to say that 'the fundamental accountability between a minister and Parliament and between a minister and his or her deputy minister has not been altered in any way.' While the Public Accounts Committee agreed with this proposition, it maintained that the accountability of accounting officers before a parliamentary committee means a great deal more than simply answering questions on behalf of their ministers. It means that they are personally accountable before the committee for the management responsibilities they hold in their own right and that ministers cannot be accountable for matters for which deputy ministers, not ministers, hold the responsibility.

The chair of the Public Accounts Committee, Liberal MP Shawn Murphy, wrote to all accounting officers (well over 100 of them are

identified in the Federal Accountability Act) to outline the position of
the Public Accounts Committee and Parliament. He explained that the
protocol was adopted by the Public Accounts Committee on 26 March
2007. Once the House of Commons concurred with the report, the protocol acquired the same force as Standing Orders and forms part of the
law of Parliament. He told the accounting officers that 'it is for Parliament and Parliament alone to dictate how it will hold the government
to account for its spending of public funds and that future appearances
of accounting officers before the Public Accounts Committee will be
therefore governed by the enclosed protocol regardless of any other
directives.'[66] The result is that accounting officers in Canada will have
to deal with two competing sets of rules governing their role and
accountability, one established by Parliament and the other by the
Privy Council Office.

It is unfortunate that, while the accounting officer concept was
designed to eliminate confusion over responsibility and accountability,
it now appears to have made matters worse. Parliament has the constitutional right to dictate how it conducts its business, including the
terms and conditions for the attendance of witnesses before its committees. The Privy Council Office, in its enthusiasm for the status quo
and the doctrine of ministerial responsibility, appears to have forgotten
this other fundamental constitutional principle. No other Westminster-
style parliamentary doctrine maintains the same absolutist primacy of
ministerial responsibility as the Privy Council Office. The British Treasury, for example, states that, 'Under the minister, the head of the
department, as its Accounting Officer, is also personally responsible
and accountable to Parliament for the management and organisation
of the department, including the use of public money and the steward-
ship of its assets.'[67]

In yet another document, the Privy Council Office explains that civil
servants 'should and do of course appear before Parliamentary committees on behalf of their Ministers to answer questions or to provide
other sorts of information that Ministers obviously could not be
expected to provide personally ... while Parliamentary committees are
empowered to examine witnesses on oath, it has not been customary
for public servants to be sworn. This is not because public servants
enjoy privileges which are denied to other citizens, but is rather a
reflection of the fact that they are appearing not as individuals but as
representatives of someone else – the Minister.'[68] It is on this basis only
that parliamentarians are to understand the concept of answerability. It

is important to stress the point that the doctrine of ministerial responsibility and notions of answerability are based on an interpretation of
constitutional conventions, not on law.

In Britain, a good number of students of government have simply
concluded that, despite the accounting officer concept, the doctrine of
ministerial responsibility (or the 'core rules of political accountability')
simply no longer works.[69] Jeffrey Jowell and Dawn Oliver, editors of
the influential book *The Changing Constitution*, decided to remove the
essay on ministerial responsibility from the book, claiming that 'the
doctrine of individual ministerial responsibility has been significantly
weakened over the last ten years or so, so that it can no longer be said,
in our view, that it is a fundamental doctrine of the constitution.'[70]
Christopher Hood maintains that, though the doctrine may still apply,
there is now a great deal of 'cheating' taking place by both ministers
and public servants. Ministers, on the one hand, are no longer willing
to assume responsibility for the actions of their civil servants. But at
the same time, given that the doctrine places responsibility in the
hands of ministers, there is now a greater willingness on their part to
intervene in the running of departments – hence the rise of special
political advisers and the influence of media spin specialists.[71]

Civil servants, however, have not given up so easily on the doctrine,
and some have attempted to update it. Robin Butler, former British
secretary to the cabinet, sought to establish a distinction between ministerial accountability and ministerial responsibility. Appearing before
the Scott inquiry and the House Select Committee on Treasury and the
Civil Service in 1994, he maintained that ministerial accountability
consists of the minister's duty to account to Parliament for the work of
the department. Thus, notwithstanding the accounting officer concept, Butler argued that ministers can be challenged on the action of
civil servants, since civil servants still act on behalf of the government.
Ministerial responsibility, meanwhile, he argued, comes into play
when a minister is directly involved in an action; this suggests that the
minister is responsible or carries personal credit or blame for the
action. The House select committee, however, dismissed Butler's position as 'unconvincing.'[72]

The government decided to clarify its view on the doctrine in
response to the work of the select committee. It maintained that the
minister was accountable for everything in his or her department in
the sense that Parliament can call on the minister to account for it, that
the minister was responsible for the policies of the department, but

that the minister was not responsible for everything that happened in the department in the sense of having either knowledge of or control over every action taken. In addition, the government explained that a minister should not be personally blamed when delegated tasks are carried out incompetently at the bureaucratic level.[73]

The matter did not end there. It will be recalled that, after high-profile prison escapes in Britain (circa 1994–5), the government appointed the Learmont inquiry to review prison security. The inquiry report was critical of both the 'Next Steps' Prison Service agency and the Home Office, the lead department. In response to the report, Home Secretary Michael Howard insisted that he was responsible only for policy issues, that the problems identified in the inquiry report were administrative in nature, and that the head of the Prison Service agency, not he, should resign. Howard had no difficulty in explaining his side of the story and insisted that he was neither constitutionally nor personally responsible for what had transpired.[74] His point was that officials running the Prison Service agency had responsibilities and could speak to the matter themselves rather than through him. Derek Lewis, the administrative head of the Prison Service, did just that. By his account, any shortcomings were largely a consequence of ministerial policies, in that the minister and his department had allowed an increase in total prison population without providing additional resources.[75]

The House committee rejected Michael Howard's distinction between policy and administrative failures. It argued that 'What Ministers must never do is to put the blame onto civil servants for the effects of unworkable policies and their setting of unrealistic targets.'[76] It also argued that a minister should be responsible for broad direction and patterns of incompetence. If an administrative failure was serious enough and could be connected directly to the minister's responsibility, it might well be appropriate for the minister to resign.[77]

The British government has, until recently, held in its own hands full control of the doctrine of ministerial responsibility through its document *Questions of Procedure for Ministers* (QPM), currently known simply as the *Ministerial Code*. The document, a kind of rule book, is issued by the prime minister to newly appointed ministers. The House of Commons Public Service Committee recommended, and Parliament subsequently agreed, that Parliament, not the government, should oversee the rules guiding the doctrine of ministerial responsibility. Parliament passed a resolution in 1997 outlining how ministers should report to Parliament and further stated that 'Ministers should require civil servants who give evidence before parliamentary committees on their behalf and under their direction to be as helpful as possible in providing accurate, truthful and full information in accordance with the duties and responsibilities of civil servants as set out in the Civil Service Code.'[78] When the Blair government came to power, Blair simply reproduced the text of the parliamentary resolution in his *Ministerial Code*, signalling that Parliament, not the government, would henceforth establish the parameters of individual responsibility.[79] In Canada, the government has consistently and firmly resisted any suggestion that Parliament should establish the parameters of individual responsibility. The Harper government's recent decision to ignore Parliament's work on a protocol to guide the implementation of the accounting officer concept continues in this tradition. Time will tell if the work of the Public Accounts Committee will have any appreciable impact on accountability and on the relationships among civil servants, ministers, and Parliament.

Lorne Sossin argues that, while Canada's constitutional texts do not speak directly to the civil service's constitutional status, there is a range of conventions that confer a constitutional status on the public service as 'an organ of government.' He insists that the neutrality and impartiality of the public service 'is not contingent on ministerial responsibility and represents instead a free standing constitutional principle, which owes its modern origins to the rule of law.' He adds that legal and constitutional boundaries between ministers and civil servants have been given life in part through 'common law principles' and 'judges interpreting constitutional conventions.'[80] Sossin reviews a number of court decisions that serve to give the civil service a distinct persona from the government of the day. He cites Justice Dickson, among others, in his judgment in *Fraser v. Public Service Staff Relations Board*, to support this claim. Fraser, an employee of Revenue Canada, was highly critical of the government's decision to introduce metrication. He was sanctioned for his conduct, and he took the matter to court. In his decision, Dickson recognized 'a qualified rather than absolute duty of loyalty owed by public servants,' to the government of the day.[81]

Peter Aucoin and Mark Jarvis in a study for the Canada School of the Public Service, an agency of the federal government, found the doctrine lacking on several fronts. They write, 'In our view, the assumption here illustrates how accountability has come to be viewed as the willingness of ministers or officials to "accept" responsibility. In one sense, it means little for someone to accept responsibility if that merely means acknowledging that one has the statutorily or administratively assigned authority and responsibility for a program and its implementation. Indeed, it is now all too common for elected officials to acknowledge that responsibility rests with them, but then to say that they are not personally responsible for what went wrong. They confess to nothing of any significance.'[82] In some ways Aucoin and Jarvis go farther than the British accounting officer model, recommending that deputy ministers should be held accountable directly by Parliament on certain matters. They explain that 'Deputy minister accountability to Parliament is a logical extension of the ministerial responsibility regime as it has worked in Canada, given the limits on ministerial authority and responsibility.' They add, 'deputy ministers should be held publicly accountable exclusively and solely for the authorities and responsibilities assigned by statute or delegated to them by the Treasury Board and the Public Service Commission and deputy ministers should not expect their ministers to accept responsibility for decisions that fall within the deputy's sphere of authority and responsibility.'[83]

Aucoin and Jarvis state that, given its statutory responsibilities, the Canadian civil service does, indeed, have a personality. They are not alone in this conclusion. C.E.S. (Ned) Franks, in a paper prepared for the Gomery Commission, maintains that 'deputy ministers are accountable in their own right as the holders of responsibility before the Public Accounts Committee. It must be recognized and accepted by all involved that the responsibility of deputy ministers for the use of their statutory and other powers is personal and cannot be delegated.'[84] Justice Gomery became exasperated at one point during phase I testimonies for his Commission of Inquiry and declared, 'Why is it that we have a system of responsible government but no one is prepared to take responsibility for the things that went wrong?'

Practitioners have been divided on the issue. Politicians, for the most part, have been willing to challenge the status quo, while civil servants have not. Former prime minister Jean Chrétien publicly endorsed the accounting officer concept in 2003 and announced his intention to introduce it, but nothing came of it.[85] In May 2005, the Public Accounts Committee recommended that 'deputy ministers be designated as accounting officers with responsibilities similar to those held by accounting officers in the United Kingdom,'[86] but nothing came of this either. Stephen Harper and his Conservative party also made clear their support for the concept during the 2006 election campaign, stating that 'the deputy minister will be responsible to Parliament for the department spending and administrative practices of his or her department.'[87] As already noted, shortly after coming to power, Harper's government introduced legislation to strengthen accountability but watered down considerably the original commitment in drafting the proposal.

In his campaign platform, Harper wrote that his government would require that, 'in the event of a disagreement between a minister and deputy minister on a matter of administration, the minister must provide written instructions to the deputy minister and notify the Auditor General and Comptroller General of the disagreement.'[88] The legislation that was approved in December 2006 has quite a different take, requiring that a process be followed in the 'event that a minister and deputy minister are unable to agree on the interpretation or application of a Treasury Board policy, directive, or standard.' In such cases, the legislation requires that the 'deputy minister seek guidance in writing from the Secretary of the Treasury Board; if the matter remains unresolved, the minister would refer the matter to the Treasury Board for a decision; and a copy of the Treasury Board decision be shared with the Auditor General as a confidence of the Queen's Privy Council.'[89] In addition, the legislation makes it clear that the accounting officer concept in Canada is to be exercised within the framework of ministerial responsibility and accountability to Parliament, which is to remain unchanged. We will return to this point later. Suffice it to note here that civil servants have had a voice distinct from the government, but only up to a point. Though they answer directly to Parliament on some issues, disagreements between civil servants and ministers remain inside government.

A case can be made that the Canadian civil service secured its own persona as far back as 1918, with the enactment of the Civil Service Act. To be sure, the Canadian civil service, by constitutional convention and by law, enjoys a non-partisan status, and employment in its ranks below the deputy and associate deputy minister levels is deliberately placed outside the reach of the prime minister, ministers, and MPs. The British government does not have a Public Service Employment Act, but its civil service also enjoys a non-partisan status.

The Canadian civil service, much as the British civil service did earlier when it embraced the accounting officer concept, gave itself a persona distinct from the government of the day through its own initiative. It has long been a practice in Britain that ministers are not entitled to review the cabinet papers of their predecessors. If a minister makes such a request, then a civil servant has the right to refuse unless the minister is a member of the same political party as his predecessor.[90] In the 1957 Diefenbaker transition to power in Canada, the then clerk of the privy council and secretary to the cabinet decreed that ministers of one government are not entitled to examine the cabinet documents of a former government, other than those that are regarded as being in the public domain. Prime ministers and ministers may well make such a request, but civil servants have the right to deny it. This is now a constitutional convention, one that has been respected since 1957. Gordon Osbaldeston, former cabinet secretary, explained that he had 'a fiduciary role of custodian of the system as a whole in assuring integrity and continuity in the administration of government.'[91] Arnold Heeney, secretary of the cabinet under Mackenzie King, and the man who shaped the modern Privy Council Office after the Cabinet Office in Britain, explains that Diefenbaker and outgoing Prime Minister St Laurent agreed 'that the Secretary to the Cabinet should now be accepted as the custodian of Cabinet papers, responsible for determining what communication should be made thereof to succeeding administrations. With that agreement, the Cabinet Secretariat became a permanent institution of Canadian government.'[92] This suggests that civil servants have a direct and distinct personal responsibility as servants of the crown in addition to serving the government of the day and, further, that the civil service has a constitutional responsibility and personality.

Canadian civil servants hold a number of statutory responsibilities. As already noted, these responsibilities originate from two different sources – from the Interpretation Act and other departmental acts and from powers assigned directly to them in their own right under the Financial Administration Act, the Public Service Employment Act, and the Official Languages Act. Ministers cannot *by law*, and not just because of a constitutional convention, issue specific directions to deputy ministers on matters covered by these statutes. The Government of Canada itself has made clear that 'Deputy ministers are responsible for financial regularity and probity; economy, efficiency and effectiveness; financial management systems for departmental programs and public property.'[93] The above again makes the point that civil servants in Canada have a direct responsibility as servants of the crown and not simply to the government of the day.

The anonymity of civil servants, which ensures that their personal failures are not a matter of public knowledge, has been an important feature in the parliamentary governments of Britain and Canada. It also forms an important part of the argument that civil servants have no constitutional personality or persona distinct from the government of the day. If they are to be loyal to the government of the day and if they are to have no constitutional persona, then civil servants should be anonymous. Gordon Robertson, former secretary to the cabinet, explained in 1983 that 'anonymity ... involves a substantial act of self-denial. It means an unwillingness to hint at influential association with policies or decisions.'[94] However, in Canada at least, civil servants are anonymous no more, partly again through their own doing. Today, the secretary to the cabinet each year reports to Parliament on the state of the civil service. These reports may not be partisan, particularly profound, or newsworthy, but they are political by definition, for they hold clear positions on the health and needs of a national institution, thus speaking publicly to the concerns of an institution that has its own persona. Former prime minister Paul Martin publicly applauded the role Alex Himelfarb, the clerk of the privy council, played in securing a federal-provincial agreement on health care in 2004. Martin said before the television cameras that 'Alex did a tremendous job' in negotiating the agreement with the provincial premiers, thus giving him a public persona.[95]

Senior federal government managers have formed an association, the Association of Professional Executives of the Public Service of Canada (APEX). Established in 1984, with the full support of the Privy Council Office, APEX focuses its efforts on several issues, including public service management reform. The association's executive director does not hesitate to voice publicly the concerns of his association. He made it clear, for example, that the association had every intention of entering the debate on the Harper government's plans to strengthen accountability in government[96] – further evidence that the civil service does indeed have a persona distinct from the government of the day.

Canadian cabinet ministers and the civil service have learned to live with the Access to Information Act, proclaimed in 1985. British ministers and civil servants started this learning process only in 2005 when Britain's Freedom of Information Act came into force.[97] More is said below about the legislation; suffice it to note here that in Canada, the access to information legislation and related developments have enabled the media, the opposition parties, and interested Canadians to pin down what issues particular civil servants are working on, what policy positions they may support, and even with whom they had lunch, if taxpayers paid for it. The only way for senior Canadian civil servants to remain anonymous today is to avoid expense accounts and refrain from putting their views on paper or on their computers, since e-mails are accessible under the act. But even those precautions may not be sufficient to maintain anonymity, since ministers are no longer reluctant to name individual civil servants in order to deflect criticism directed against themselves in Question Period or in the media.[98]

Public inquiries also serve not only to remove the anonymity of civil servants but also to expose their personal failures in full public view. The Gomery inquiry made civil servant Chuck Guité as highly visible and as well known in Canada as any minister in either the Chrétien or Martin cabinet. As experience shows, public inquiries do not limit their investigations to political failures. They delve into failures at the administrative level as well.

The above makes the case that the civil service operates in a vastly different environment today from that of forty years ago in both Canada and Britain. The level of transparency is far greater than it was then, and civil servants are being challenged in public as never before. One can easily appreciate that, for individual civil servants at least, things were better forty years ago than they are today and that their standing in society was also stronger then. Government was far less complicated in the past, and in such circumstances the traditional Westminster-Whitehall model worked well. Civil servants could go about their work while remaining anonymous. Few inside or outside government were critical of the civil service. There was no need for the cabinet secretary to write that the civil service had no constitutional personality or responsibility separate from the duly elected government or to produce an annual report on the state of the civil service, as is now done in Canada. By most accounts, the relationship between senior civil servants and elected politicians was strong and without serious problems. [99]

The Media

Many developments have transformed the media in the past forty years and, as a consequence, the relations between the media and government. They include Watergate, access to information legislation, twenty-four-hour television, and the Internet, to name a few.

Watergate changed journalism in much of the Western world. The media became far more aggressive and less deferential than in the past.

Gone are the days when the media consisted of narrators or independent observers reporting and commenting on political events. Gone also are the days when politicians and journalists would discuss, 'off the record,' major public policy issues. Many politicians have learned, much to their chagrin, that virtually nothing is off the record any more. Gone also are the days when the media were on the outside looking in. John Fraser, one of Canada's leading journalists and former editor of *Saturday Night* magazine, insists that the problem with the media begins with journalism schools, 'which don't just feed into the post-Watergate cynicism and distrust anything or anyone worthy of an investigative report or in-depth profile, they positively foster institutional rumour and disbelieving zealotry with a righteousness no longer to be found even in a fundamentalist divinity school.'[100]

Fraser is not alone in this assessment. The number of leading Canadian journalists with reservations about the current role of the media is worth noting. George Bain, one of Canada's most respected postwar journalists, wrote a book describing the new breed of journalists, who grew up in the heady 1960s. He claims that they 'brought forward certain generational traits including ... a distrust of all things institutional ... a general anti-everything prejudice founded on fond recollections of press clippings from their time as a generation of idealists.'[101] The media are quick to inform, but the information they provide is, much more often than not, trivial and designed to be provocative. As Jeffrey Simpson observes, 'Good news doesn't sell when it comes to government. Trash the government and headlines flow; praise it, however modestly, and get ignored.'[102] Anthony Westell, in his *The Inside Story: A Life in Journalism*, bemoans the 'adversarial and destructive' style of contemporary journalism, wishing that it would start 'from the principle of supporting democratic institutions.'[103]

Canadian politicians have consequently become wary of the media. Prime Minister Stephen Harper decided that he and his ministers would be much less accessible to journalists shortly after coming to power in 2006.[104] To the dismay of many journalists, Canadians did not seem to object. Harper and his office go to great lengths to manage issues so that the media will not be able to obtain information that might place the government in a bad light. A case in point was the silence from the Prime Minister's Office with regard to Canada's apparent inability to remove Canadian citizens from Lebanon in the early days of the Israel-Lebanon conflict in the summer of 2006.[105]

The adversarial nature of government-media relations is now evident in virtually every political and public policy issue. Lowell Murray has this to say about the present role of the media in Canadian politics: 'What passes for political news on TV is the seven-second soundbite that probably distorts more than it reflects the truth about important issues.' He notes that daily newspapers once gave far more prominent and detailed coverage to parliamentary debates than they do now. He asked readers to contrast page one of almost any day's *Globe and Mail* with the page ones of earlier times (which were reproduced by the newspaper in its 'Century of the Millennium' project) to appreciate the difference in substance.[106] Liberal politicians have not been any more positive about current journalistic practices. Former prime minister Jean Chrétien, for example, simply started from the premise that the media were out to get him.[107]

Things are no different in Britain. The memoirs of recently retired British political leaders suggest that the British media are also considerably more aggressive and less deferential than they were forty years ago.[108] Yet the media have come to play a much greater role in British politics than formerly. As Christopher Foster wrote, 'Blair is preoccupied with news management to an extent no previous prime minister was, not even Harold Wilson ... No. 10's working methods are dominated by those appropriate to handling the media 24 hours a day.'[109] A well-known practitioner's explanation of the change in Britain resonates in Canada. He writes, 'post-war journalism in the second half of the twentieth century developed from a straight news-driven agenda, supported by classified advertising and executed by tradesmen, to a polemical profession in the ownership of middle-class graduates; a process that was spurred by improved education and a consequent increase in mass literacy.'[110]

The advent of 'gotcha' journalism has given rise to a new class of political assistants and government employees – spin doctors. Spin doctors are there not only to sell a message but also to contain the political fallout from negative developments or news stories. Politicians now have to be on their guard lest present and past events or incidents are brought up, however small. The London *Times*, for example, ran a front-page story under the headline 'Cameron and the Sex Clinic Mystery.' David Cameron, Conservative party leader, was asked if he had ever been to a particular clinic to check if he had a sexually transmitted disease. He responded that he had once gone there, along with college friends, during his student days at Oxford at the height of the 1980s AIDS scare. The test result was negative.[111] One doubts that *The Times* would have run such a non-story on its front page in the pre-Watergate era.

The search for sleaze in government is never ending and often dominates the media. This is not to suggest for a moment that sleaze in government is new. Indeed, there is a body of evidence to suggest that it was greater in the past than it is today. For example, many parliamentary seats in nineteenth-century Britain were up for sale and, once elected, MPs made money on the side, promoting legislation serving commercial interests. The difference today is that journalists spend a considerable amount of time hunting down unsavoury stories, and the hunting has been made considerably easier.

Access to information legislation has helped the media to become much more aware of how government works and to identify administrative miscues. John Crosbie, a former cabinet minister, writes that the legislation has added to the 'woes of politicians on the government side. It gives the media and other mischief-makers the ability to ferret out snippets of information with which to embarrass political leaders and to titillate the public. In the vast majority of instances, embarrassment and titillation are the only objects of access to information requests.'[112] Journalists have also used the legislation time and time again in pursuit of a story. For example, the *Globe and Mail* reported that documents disclosed under access to information show that the 'monthly charge to the government for cellular phones and services was $874,000 the previous December which translates to at least $10.4 million a year.' The article revealed that 'approximately 280 cell phones were assigned to the Privy Council Office, despite a change of government and promises of cost-cutting.' This particular access to information request had been made after a minister had told an opposition member that it was 'too expensive to find out what cell phones were costing.'[113] In this instance the request was intended to secure information about the government as a whole, not about a department. Several such requests surface every month, necessitating competent spin doctors or political firefighters in Ottawa.

Britain is slowly but surely getting acquainted with access to information legislation and its requirements. The Information Commissioner's Office issued a report in 2006, one year after the British act came into force. The commission had this to say: 'The Freedom of Information Act is making a significant impact and is being taken very seriously by most public authorities. The pendulum is definitely swinging towards disclosure of information unless there is very good reason to do otherwise. Governmental culture is starting to change. There is still a long way to go but I am encouraged by the range and significant number of disclosures we have seen so far.' He added, 'A great deal of important information that is clearly in the public interest has been released over the past 12 months, which would not otherwise have been in the public domain, including details of politicians' expenses, amounts and recipients of farm subsidies under the Common Agricultural Policy and hospital mortality rates.'[114]

Access to information legislation, combined with journalists' sceptical approach to government, have given a new, distinct, and influential voice to the media. In a certain sense, the media are now part of government, given their knowledge of policies as they are being shaped and of administrative decisions, right down to details of expense accounts. Yet the media stand very much apart from the government, always ready to pounce.

Looking Back

Back to the initial question – was there ever a golden era for government? The answer is yes, that there was a time when Parliament was able to hold the government to account (before government by political parties and after government by the crown), and when government was considerably smaller, and when civil servants had no reason to have a distinct persona from the government of the day. This was a time when governments in the Westminster-Whitehall model knew how to keep their secrets, before access to information was introduced, when the judiciary practised self-restraint, and when pursuing the collective good was considered a vocation. It was a time when the great majority of civil servants exemplified the saying 'duty first, self second,' and when the civil service was highly respected by society. A leading student of British political and administrative institutions writes that 'there is little left now of what was once prized as a unified and professional civil service of the Crown, committed to serve ministers of all parties with equal loyalty, yet having a scruple too for the preservation of an enduring public interest.'[115] All of this confirms that there was an era when both Parliament and the civil service enjoyed the respect of citizens. However, such a serendipitous situation could only be obtained in an easier, less complex time for government than is the case today. Whatever the reasons and whether or not one wishes to refer to a golden era, 'some forty years ago,' as Kevin Theakston writes about the British civil service, there was more 'group self confidence within the mandarinate.'[116] The same has been said about the Canadian civil service.[117]

To be sure, neither the media nor citizens would wish to turn back the clock to the days before access to information legislation was introduced. Many ministers and civil servants, however, confess that the legislation has made policy making and decision making much more difficult, if also more transparent. The obvious conclusion is that profound changes have overtaken the public sector. What is perhaps less obvious is that the changes have given rise to new, distinct, and powerful voices. We need to pursue this theme and to consider whether the changes are in response to forces within the public sector or from outside. But before we do, we need to explore further why the public sector and, in particular, the civil service no longer command the respect they once did.

4 Disenchantment Sets In

The public sector began to lose its way in the 1970s in the Anglo-American democracies. The transformation was remarkable, going as it did, from the immediate postwar period, when it could hardly do anything wrong, to the 1970s, when it could hardly do anything right.[1] Citizens pointed their fingers at government writ large, while politicians pointed theirs at bureaucrats. Bureaucrats, meanwhile, had no one to point their fingers at: some even began to point them at themselves.[2]

A slowdown in economic growth coupled with rising inflation gave birth to a new and dreaded word: *stagflation*. The confidence of many of those reared on the merits of Keynesian economics began to sag as they discovered that the scope and cost of government kept growing in good economic times as well as in bad. By the late 1970s, a good number of countries were witnessing double-digit inflation and a growth in the costs of government that outstripped growth in the economy. The standard Keynesian response of increasing government spending to deal with rising unemployment appeared ever more inappropriate in the face of inflationary pressure and growing government deficits. Observers began to write about a crisis of 'governability' and 'governmental overload.' Political parties favouring a greater role for government in society and increased public spending were losing public support everywhere. For instance, in California, a grass-roots movement in 1978 successfully championed Proposition 13, a measure designed to limit taxation and, by extension, government spending.[3]

One concern was related to the apparent inability of governments to deal simultaneously with the issues of unemployment, inflation, balance of payments, and debt. Another extended to the apparatus of government itself, specifically the bureaucracy, which was regarded as a barrier against, rather than a vehicle for, progressive change. Those few who still argued against tampering with the existing machinery of government and its 'armies' of entrenched officials were dismissed by both the political left and right. Even people who had supported the ideas and social welfare programs of leaders such as Franklin Roosevelt, Clement Attlee, Hugh Gaitskell, T.C. Douglas, Lester Pearson, and Adlai Stevenson were now calling for changes to the apparatus of government.[4]

Looking back over forty years, one is struck by the scope and growing intensity of the criticism directed at government and, in particular, at the bureaucracy. It came from virtually all quarters: the political left, the political right, the media, and the academic community. In Britain, a number of journalists and observers by the late 1970s began to write about the scale, cost, and efficiency of the state and 'what was thought to be the privilege of officialdom.'[5] Canadians began to tell public opinion surveys that 'they had less confidence in the public service than in any other institution, save for the trade union movement, politicians and more recently the tobacco industry.'[6] A royal commission on Canada's economic future warned in 1985 that 'The reach of the state has in many ways outrun both our administrative and technical capacities, and our capacity to ensure democratic accountability.'[7] Alan Cairns, one of Canada's leading political scientists of his day, summed it up well when, in the mid-1980s, he observed that 'The binge of post World War II state worship has ended; and a reassessment of state, market and society is underway.'[8]

The political right, starting with Margaret Thatcher, as could be expected, led the charge against bureaucracy. It would be wrong, however, to assume that only right-wing politicians had strong reservations about public bureaucracies. John Kenneth Galbraith, himself a leading proponent in the twentieth century for a greater role for government in society, observed that bureaucracy had given government a bad name. Galbraith argued that 'It's more than the liberal task to defend the system. It is far more important now to improve the operation than enlarge and increase its scope. This must be the direction of our major effort.'[9] British left-wing politicians also contributed to the mounting criticism. Tony Benn argued that 'the power, role, influence and authority of the senior levels of the Civil Service in Britain ... have grown to such an extent as to create the embryo of a corporate state.'[10] Even centrist politicians who had worked well with civil servants while in office became openly critical of them once they were out of power. Shirley Williams, for example, wrote that 'My impression of the British Civil Service is that it is a beautifully designed and effective braking mechanism. It produces a hundred well argued answers against initiative and change.'[11] In Canada there was by the early 1980s a list of senior Liberal cabinet ministers, including Allan J. MacEachen and Lloyd Axworthy, who publicly questioned the work of civil servants.[12]

The most stinging criticism, however, came from British cabinet minister Richard Crossman in his widely read diaries, published in 1975. He took dead aim at the civil service as a powerful bureaucratic machine that had taken on a life of its own. He insisted that 'whenever one relaxes one's guard the Civil Service in one's Department quietly asserts itself … Just as the Cabinet Secretariat constantly transforms the actual proceedings of Cabinet into the form of the Cabinet minutes (i.e. it substitutes what we should have said if we had done as they wished for what we actually did say), so here in my Department the civil servants are always putting in what they think I should have said and not what I actually decided.'[13] The Crossman diaries opened a floodgate of criticism against bureaucracy. Even the Fabian Society, a left-of-centre think tank and a strong advocate of government intervention, joined the debate. It put together a study group in 1979 to look at government operations in the aftermath of Labour's electoral defeat. Its membership included former ministers, political advisers, academics, and even former civil servants. The group reached several conclusions, notably that the civil service has 'distinct ideologies of its own,' that the 'nature of departments limits a minister's capacity to produce a long-term and radical approach,' and that 'civil service advice needs to be augmented by alternative sources of ideas and analysis.'[14]

The Crossman diaries also gave rise to the popular British Broadcasting Corporation (BBC) television series *Yes, Minister*, which attracted some nine million viewers in Britain alone and became the favourite television program of the permanent secretaries. Mrs Thatcher had each episode videotaped and reported that she subscribed to the caricature view of the senior civil service. The series has a lot to answer for. A political satire that was regarded by many as a documentary, it had a profound impact on how the civil service was perceived. Lord Wilson, a former British cabinet secretary, long after the series had come off the air, asked in a public lecture in March 2006, 'Is *Yes, Minister*, accurate?' His answer: 'Yes and no' and that it was a 'most difficult question to answer.'[15]

The television series gained a worldwide audience and became highly popular with many politicians and civil servants in Canada.

Canadian political scientist Sandford Borins writes that it became 'something of a cult program, exceedingly popular with a small following that is intensely interested in public affairs.'[16] The not-so-subtle message of *Yes, Minister* was that civil servants were running the country, their deference to politicians was pure pretence, and the Sir Humphreys of the bureaucratic world wielded not just influence but also considerable power. The series painted a new portrait of the relationship between politicians and career officials. The portrait showed ministers as publicity-seeking dimwits and no match for the highly educated, unprincipled, and Machiavellian career officials. No matter what the issue and however sensible the minister's position, Sir Humphrey, the senior bureaucrat, would have a position at odds with the minister's, and he would invariably have his way. Sir Humphrey's views, however, were not rooted in an ideology that differed from the minister's or, for that matter, that stemmed from profound beliefs. Rather, he could always be counted on to favour the status quo and, more important, to do anything necessary to protect the interest of the department and the civil service. Moreover, Sir Humphrey would not only shape all major policy decisions and run the department, he would also manage political crises on behalf of his minister. Whatever the issue, the minister in the end had to rely on Sir Humphrey's considerable political and bureaucratic skills simply to survive.

Academics, by and large, also became increasingly critical of bureaucracy. One scholar wrote that 'Bureaucracy is a word with a bad reputation.' Another argued that 'Government functionaries work hard and accomplish little. Many people would question the first part of that statement.' Herbert Kaufman concluded in the early 1980s that 'antibureaucratic sentiment has taken hold like an epidemic.'[17] As noted earlier, a new body of literature on public choice and rational choice emerged from the political science community that labelled bureaucrats 'budget maximizers.' The two schools look to the individual as the basic unit of analysis. The individual decision maker is much like the classical economic man and is, as a result, self-interested, rational, and always seeking to maximize his or her own interest. The findings of the two schools hardly paints a positive picture of civil servants. The outpouring of criticism prompted Charles Goodsell to publish a book in defence of public bureaucracies in 1983, a book, as the author readily acknowledged, that was a polemic in response to widespread bureaucrat bashing.[18]

How then does one explain this reversal and rather sudden barrage of criticism directed at government and, in particular, at bureaucracy?

Did society itself and its expectations of government change? Was there a breakdown in the machinery of government? How did the political leadership that came to power in the late 1970s and early 1980s diagnose the patient? It has now been thirty or forty years since the public sector began to lose its way, and there is no sign that it is about to regain the standing it enjoyed in the immediate postwar years through to the 1970s. With *le recul du temps*, we can now explore the reasons for this reversal of fortune. The next two chapters seek to do this by looking at how government diagnosed the patient, the operation of the machinery of government, and society itself.

It's about the Machinery and the Bureaucrats

Margaret Thatcher led the way in the search for solutions, convinced that 'positive government' had not only run its course but in the process had brought Britain low. She knew where she wanted to take the government, and she had, in her own words, 'a bias for action.' She pursued a public sector reform agenda with a sense of urgency. Her view that 'there is no such thing as society, only individuals and families' spoke volumes about her thinking on government. She added that 'I think we have been through a period where too many people have been given to understand that if they have a problem, it's the government's job ... They're casting their problem on society.'[19] She set out to change this.

Thatcher's diagnosis of the problem was straightforward – the state was too interventionist, and the bureaucracy was too privileged.[20] Accordingly, she saw no need to ponder possible solutions for very long: the answer was simply to roll back the state by privatizing state enterprises, to cut government spending or slow down the rate of its growth, and to contract out to the private sector the responsibility for delivering services. A spate of books and articles has been written on the Thatcher reforms, and there is no need to go over the same territory here.[21]

Suffice it to note that the Thatcher reforms gave rise to the New Public Management (NPM) approach, and here again a number of books and articles have been produced detailing its characteristics. NPM carried its own vocabulary, one that was designed to highlight a new approach as opposed to the old, the innovative as opposed to the traditional.[22] NPM's stated purpose was to transform government administrators into managers, to borrow a page from the private sector on how to manage financial and human resources in order to obtain better value for taxpayers and produce the results that citizens wanted. The machinery of government was reformed. A new policy of market testing that had government managers submit their operations to market competition on an annual basis was introduced, and an overhaul of centrally prescribed administrative and financial rules was carried out. In the past, ministers had looked to government-wide administrative and financial policies to ensure that their departmental officials would not get them in political hot water. The political rhetoric, if not the reality, suggested that things would in future be vastly different from the past.

Empowerment became the buzzword of the 1980s. It signalled the search for doers rather than thinkers and emphasized the importance of managers' taking the lead, getting things done, and dealing effectively with customers and their needs. Bureaucracy, red tape, and centrally prescribed rules were to be replaced by a new delegation of authority to managers in line departments, much as in the private sector.

The literature on private sector management is replete with assertions that centrally regulated financial and personnel rules must be kept to a minimum. Henry Mintzberg argues that the central technostructure must be kept lean so that line managers are left unencumbered. In their widely read book *In Search of Excellence*, Thomas Peters and Robert Waterman stressed such issues as the need for simplified forms, for autonomy, and for entrepreneurship, the importance of being close to the customer and of instilling a bias for action among managers. Peter Block wrote that 'empowering managers' was the single most important building block to success in business, insisting that the deepest wish of all employees is to contribute something meaningful to the organization. Employees – and, in particular, managers – can do this only if the organization is prepared to trust them to make decisions.[23] In brief, if government were to be more like the private sector, then it had to adopt its best management practices and let the managers manage.

Although her actions sometimes pointed in an opposite direction, Thatcher spoke the language of Peters and Waterman.[24] She often spoke about 'decentralizing management responsibilities,' and she reformed the machinery of government to give teeth to the measures she introduced. These included a process to review expenditures and a new Financial Management Information system to 'empower budget-holders to make operational management decisions.' Its underlying goal was to encourage middle-rank civil servants to think of themselves as managers first, free to take action whenever circumstances required. Thatcher's target was the mandarins – the cautious careerists who constantly did battle in favour of the status quo. She sought to rid the system of its rigid rules, to place responsibility for decision making squarely on the shoulders of line managers, and to instil in them a 'bias for action.' With an eye to deregulation, her 'coherent and integrated culture of good management' also took dead aim at centrally prescribed rules on financial and human resources, and she launched a thorough review of such rules.[25]

But Thatcher's signature reform measure was the establishment of executive agencies. She divorced ministerial departments from executive agencies, so that departments set policy and program targets and the agencies implemented policies and delivered the services. This move to decouple policy formulation from operations was also designed to empower managers and to make government operations more businesslike, employees more entrepreneurial, and government more customer focused. By 1997, more than three-quarters of civil servants in the Home Civil Service were working in agencies.[26] Executive agencies, however, have fallen out of favour in recent years as the British government seeks to improve control of overhead costs. Hundreds of agencies, each with their own information technology (IT), human resources, and purchasing units are proving to be costly, and efforts are now being made to coordinate common services across government. The Treasury has taken back some of the management authority delegated to the agencies, and there is increasing discussion about integrating some of the agencies back with their home departments.[27]

Thatcher also decided to move some of the bureaucracy into the private sector through privatization. Though she hardly mentioned this intention during the 1979 election campaign, she pursued privatization with enthusiasm once in power. She also gave privatization a new look, a new political support, and a new definition. The term would henceforth mean contracting out, and even deregulation, to signal a return to 'profitable private motivation.'[28] The goal was to transform activities that had become lethargic or in decline as a result of government ownership or regulation. Thatcher sold assets worth billions of dollars during her stay in office, including such high-profile state corporations as British Petroleum, British Aerospace, Jaguar, British Telecom, and British Airways.

Thatcher's influence extended to other Anglo-American democracies, and Canada was certainly no exception. Elected to power in 1984,
Brian Mulroney quickly embraced her approach and echoed her call to
introduce private sector management practices to government. He
arrived in office full of bravado about putting the bureaucrats in their
place. Even towards the end of his second mandate, bureaucrats were
still the butt of many of his jokes, both in caucus and in private.[29]
Mulroney's goals in reforming the civil service were precisely the same
as Thatcher's – to cut down the size of government, to make its operations more efficient, and to reclaim political control over the bureaucracy. He created a new senior-level chief-of-staff position for all
ministerial offices that was designed to act as a counterweight to the
influence of civil servants on policy formulation.

He also imported to the Canadian civil service many of the reforms
Thatcher introduced in Britain. The first was the Increased Ministerial
Authority and Accountability (IMAA) initiative, introduced in 1986 and
designed to remove constraints to good management, to decentralize
decision making, to improve service to the public, and, more generally,
to empower managers to manage. A few years later, a mainly private
sector group devoted to promoting a strong civil service urged the
prime minister to take steps to strengthen the management of people in
government, to eliminate unnecessary bureaucracy, and to modernize
the information and computer capacity of government operations.
Public Service 2000 (PS 2000), like IMAA, was designed to remove many
centrally imposed controls and to emphasize service to the public. Later,
another page was borrowed from Thatcher, and the Special Operating
Agencies (SOAs) came into being. As in Britain, this involved hiving off
activities to be recast as agencies. Again, the underlying purpose was to
free managers to make decisions.

Although Mulroney spoke Thatcher's language, he lacked her conviction. He adopted her agenda, convinced it would get his party back
in power after being frozen out for so long. Mulroney discovered that
one can win votes by running against government and bureaucracy.
But once in office, he was much more at home cutting a deal than
pressing for an ideology or a set agenda. He successfully pursued an
ambitious free trade agreement with the United States but was unsuc-
cessful in securing an equally ambitious constitutional agreement with
the provinces. The result was that Mulroney spent a great deal of time
and energy on major policy initiatives and had little time to pursue

management reform. Those measures he did put in place had only a modest impact. The IMAA efforts simply petered out and have hardly left a trace. The number of SOAs pale in comparison to those in Britain. Canadian SOAs were also given much less autonomy than in Britain and still operate for the most part within the standard departmental accountability structure. PS 2000, meanwhile, was a dismal failure. Peter Aucoin explains why: 'As a public service reform, it could not and did not achieve a sufficient degree of coherence. It tried to maintain traditions while promoting reforms, some of which contradicted one another. The result could not be other than a good deal of inconsistency between the rhetoric and the reality.'[30] The chair of the House Public Accounts Committee went to the heart of the problem when he said that 'over two years after tabling the PS 2000 report, no one is answering how, henceforth, we hold people in government accountable. This is an exceedingly important issue.'[31] It is also an issue that has surfaced time and again and that remains unresolved to this day.

Future prime ministers in both Britain and Canada would leave the management reform measures intact, though in the case of Mulroney there was precious little to undo. In Britain, John Major's most important innovation was the 'Citizen's Charter.' The charter sought to 'find better ways of converting money into better public services.' It would accomplish this by 'increasing competition,' promoting the privatization of public services, and improving standards of services through performance-related pay.[32] The goal was to make government operations more accountable and to increase the rights of citizens in their dealings with government.

Major and his ministers continued in the Thatcher tradition of speaking to the virtues of the private sector with its stronger management practices and in going outside the civil service, to think tanks and academics, for policy advice. As C. Campbell and G. Wilson say in their book *The End of Whitehall*, 'the man from Whitehall no longer knew most, let alone knew best.'[33] Major also began to look outside the civil service to appoint permanent secretaries, a practice that became even more prevalent under Blair. For these and other reasons, civil service morale in Britain plummeted and is still in free fall.[34]

Once out of office, Major reflected on the state of parliamentary government and painted a bleak picture. In his *Erosion of Parliamentary Government*, he wrote that 'we have scarcely noticed that the timbers which support it are creaking and diseased, and are in danger of collapse. The structures remain but many of them are hollowed out. The erosion is evident from top to bottom.'[35] He detected a change in philosophy in the relationship between ministers and career officials, claiming that 'too many Ministers behave as if officials should be committed extensions' of the government's electoral platform and that from the 'Prime Minister downwards, politicians openly blame civil servants for errors that have in the past been accepted as the responsibility of Ministers – and still should be.'[36] The very same concern has also been expressed in Canada.[37]

Notwithstanding the Thatcher revolution and Major's charter, Tony Blair suggested shortly after coming to office that the civil service still operated along the lines defined by the Northcote-Trevelyan report of 150 years ago. In a major address on the state of public services, he declared that 'expectations have risen enormously, yet public services designed for a previous age find it difficult to respond. Unlike 1945, people don't put up with the basics. In a consumer age, they expect quality, choice and standards and too often don't experience them.'[38]

Blair did not introduce fundamental changes to the machinery of government, nor did he tackle constitutional issues in dealing with the civil service. He, much as Thatcher had done nearly twenty years earlier, called for Whitehall to be 'run like the private sector' and for civil servants to strengthen their management skills in delivering public services, but decided to leave basic accountability requirements essentially intact.[39] He moved a great deal of policy work to his own office, went outside the civil service to fill senior-level positions even more than his predecessors had done, and broke with tradition in giving a political staff appointee the unprecedented power to give orders to career officials. By 2004, one in five members of the senior civil service in Britain was recruited from outside the civil service.[40]

In Canada, Jean Chrétien declared that he did not believe in grand schemes, overarching strategies, or ambitious visions. He compared Canada's constitutional challenges, for example, to a car stuck in a snow bank – you simply have to rock the car back and forth and eventually it will be freed.[41] He sought to simplify decision making in government by doing away with cabinet committees, but essentially left the machinery virtually intact. He announced in June 2003 his intention to introduce the British accounting officer concept, but again nothing came of it.[42] He also decided to empower line departments to make management decisions, to improve the quality of public services. He stressed the importance of e-government. He pledged to make the Canadian government the model user of information technology and to be known 'around the world' as the government most connected to its citizens.[43]

Chrétien's most important initiative was a successful program review exercise launched in 1995. The review eliminated or transferred 50,000 positions from the federal civil service. But this was a special initiative to deal with what was perceived as a crisis. In early January 1995, the *Wall Street Journal* described the Canadian dollar as a 'basket case.' It ran an editorial titled 'Bankrupt Canada?' in which it declared that 'Mexico isn't the only U.S. neighbour flirting with the financial abyss.' It argued that 'if dramatic action isn't taken in the next month's federal budget, it's not inconceivable that Canada could hit the debt wall and have to call in the International Monetary Fund to stabilize its falling currency.'[44] The editorial shook ministers reluctant to accept spending cuts. David Dodge, then deputy minister at Finance, labelled the editorial a 'seminal event' in the preparation of the 1995 budget. Line departments were instructed to produce significant spending cuts, and the program review resulted in $29 billion in cuts.[45] Since then, that program review has come to be considered a 'one-off' event. Its impact was felt most keenly at the program level, where some programs were indeed cut and others were restructured into arm's-length organizations (for example, air-traffic controllers and Navcan, which removed spending and person-years from the government's books). Still others – a majority – saw their budgets reduced.

Major political scandals occurred under Jean Chrétien's watch.[46] The Shawinigate and sponsorship scandals dominated the media for months. During his brief tenure as prime minister, Paul Martin established a public inquiry to get to the bottom of Chrétien's sponsorship scandal. The inquiry uncovered a number of unsavoury facts: there had been cash payments to Liberal party organizers, lucrative contracts to Liberal-friendly advertisement agencies, inappropriate political interference in the management of a government program, and senior civil servants all too willing to cooperate.[47] In response to the sponsorship scandal, the Martin government unleashed a veritable pot-pourri of reform measures designed to strengthen management practices. New resources were allocated to upgrade the management skills of civil servants, new investment was earmarked for information technology, and whistle-blowing legislation was introduced, as were stronger comptrollership practices, including having departmental comptrollers report directly to the deputy minister. Martin also appointed a comptroller general 'from outside the public sector.'[48] On the face of it, at least, the problem lay within the civil service, and what needed fixing was the bureaucracy. The best way to fix that was to impose new rules and processes and to hire more auditors.

Stephen Harper rode the sponsorship scandal to power in January 2006 and made greater accountability a central theme of his election platform. Within weeks of assuming office, he brought forward legislation that provided for the introduction of the British accounting officer concept to the government of Canada, established a budget office in Parliament to 'provide objective analysis on the state of the nation's finances,' further strengthened auditing and accountability practices within departments, and enhanced the capacity and independence of the officers of Parliament.[49] However, as we saw earlier, he soon began to back-pedal on some of these commitments, notably the accounting officer concept.

Focusing on the Boiler Room

Prime ministers from Thatcher, Major, and Blair to Mulroney, Chrétien, and Martin all shared one thing in common: they focused on the boiler room of government in their efforts to reform government. The Crossman diaries, the popular television series *Yes, Minister*, the public choice literature, the government overload problem, and the growth in government spending in both good and bad economic times all combined to convince political leaders that they needed to take charge of policy making (after all, presumably that is why they sought elected office) and to force the hand of civil servants to manage government programs and operations more effectively. Senior civil servants were no longer to be fully trusted on policy – thus the strengthening of ministerial offices and the Office of the Prime Minister and the decision to go outside government in search of policy advice.

The accepted wisdom of the political leadership of the past thirty years or so, both right and left, is that private sector management practices are far superior to those found in government. The public service bureaucracy was the villain, and a lack of solid management practices was the problem that needed fixing. But no matter how hard the reformers try and have tried, their expectations of radical improvement have never been met.

Consider, for example, John Major's statement at the time he introduced his Citizen's Charter. After eleven years of Thatcher's dramatic overhaul, he was still able to say that he wanted to release 'the well-spring of talent and energy in our public service.'[50] And consider that Tony Blair, in his first national campaign, pledged to 'modernize Britain's unwieldy state bureaucracy.'[51] Once in power, Blair tabled a major statement on modernizing government, lamenting the fact that 'some parts of the public sector' were not 'as efficient, dynamic and effective' as the private sector. He outlined the reasons, including departments and agencies that 'tend to look after their own interests, inertia, a focus on inputs rather than results, risk aversion, poor management' and low morale stemming from the 'denigration of public servants.'[52] Blair made it clear time and again that the private sector is the key to improving management in government. Consider also this from Paul Martin, coming after twenty years of Mulroney and Chrétien in power. In reply to his government's first Speech from the Throne, he said, 'We will provide transparent, accountable management, treating every tax dollar with respect.'[53] His government then unveiled an ambitious agenda to make the bureaucracy more efficient, accountable, and transparent.

Politicians keep turning to private sector management practices to reform their bureaucracy, *faute de mieux*. In their attempt to introduce a management culture to government operations, they had nowhere else to turn. Senior civil servants were not about to admit that their management practices were lacking. In addition, the introduction of a private sector management culture to government would need the support of senior civil servants – hardly a given. Though the political leadership felt that the policy role of the civil service was 'deeply illegitimate,' one ought not to assume that civil servants also acquiesced in this view. Still, many politicians felt that non-elected officials had become too powerful in shaping policy and that it was important to send them back to a more legitimate role – that of implementing policy decisions and managing government resources more efficiently. The political leadership felt that subscribing firmly to a set of political beliefs, having partisan policy advisers on the public payroll, and enabling pollsters to interact with party strategists would make this possible and render obsolete the 'Sir Humphrey' style of policy making.[54]

Looking back on his experience as an adviser to Thatcher, Derek Rayner wrote that 'the costs of administrating the policies were regarded as the candle-ends of public expenditure.' He went on to report that he found an obsession with policy matters and a general hostility to management in government. The British civil service, he maintained, represents 'a huge slice of the Nation's best talents. It is ironic that, despite the talent, the quality of so much Whitehall management should be so low and that leadership has too often in the past fallen into the hands of those who know nothing of management and despise those who do.'[55] In short, the glamour of government work over the years has been in policy, not in administration. Indeed, senior officials have been happy to live with elaborate rules and regulations so long as they were free to play a policy role. The thinking in some quarters is that the functional units were there to worry about rules dealing with personnel, administration, and financial matters. The senior official's job was to concentrate on politicians and policy issues. Some go so far as to argue that in government in many countries, but particularly in Britain and Canada, the managing of major departmental programs traditionally has been a job for 'junior personnel or *failed* administrative class people who are seen by the mandarins as not being able to make it to the top levels.'[56]

Adjusting to the new role would not be easy for senior civil servants. The road to the top for career public servants has more often than not been through policy rather than administration. 'Have policy experience, will travel' had long been the byword for the ambitious in government. In any event, senior career civil servants are trained as professionals and have, over the years, developed considerable policy expertise in their areas of work.

Arthur Kroeger, a long-serving deputy minister in line departments in Canada, made clear his lack of interest in management, observing that, 'General management, with a capital M, and management theory never interested me very much.'[57] Kroeger was hardly alone in this view. Gordon Robertson, described as the 'gold standard' when he was head of the Canadian civil service from the mid-1960s to the mid-1970s, did not discuss management issues in his memoirs. He did, however, mention that administrative matters frequently left him insufficient time to deal with major policy issues.[58] Al Johnson, a former deputy minister in the 1960s in Ottawa, published an article, 'The Role of the Deputy Minister,' in which he never once employed the word 'management.' He wrote, 'The role of the deputy minister is to make it possible for the minister and the cabinet to provide the best government of which they are capable – even better if either of them happens to be weak.'[59]

So long as there were centrally prescribed rules governing financial and administrative decisions, senior civil servants were free to focus on policy and help cabinet ministers provide the best government of which they were capable. It also promoted a parsimonious culture in government operations: input costs were carefully controlled, and pre-spending comptrollers were in place to ensure that departments had the financial resources before spending commitments could be made. Establishing a new position or reclassifying an existing one required a great deal of paperwork and a hierarchy that was not easily convinced. Government was smaller then, and anything of consequence was brought to the attention of senior officials. Lester Pearson, then a senior official at External Affairs, became exasperated with the kind of details requiring a ministerial signature. He wrote a memorandum in October 1941 to his deputy minister asking how he was 'going to show the Prime Minister how to win the war and make the peace if you have to spend two hours each day talking about the cost of Désy's table linen or the salary of the newest stenographer.'[60]

Civil servants were also not very well paid in the past. Noted Canadian historian J.L. Granatstein documented the kind of civil service that served Canada between 1935 and 1957. On remuneration, Granatstein writes that 'salaries were low ... Robertson was negotiating trade agreements ... wearing suits that were shiny with use.' He adds: 'Of course, they wanted a comfortable salary, but almost all would have remained at their posts without it.'[61] He reports that 'they felt a duty to serve their country and its people. If that sounds trite and pious today, it is only because our age is more cynical.'[62] Senior civil servants believed that they were serving a collective purpose that transcended their own personal interest. The birth of public choice theory was still years away, and one can easily appreciate why these earlier civil servants believed that they were serving a collective purpose in pursuit of the public good.

Things began to change as government grew bigger and as private sector management practices came in to fashion. In Britain, the Fulton report and in Canada the Glassco report were in accord in concluding that management is important. Significantly, both reports appeared in the 1960s. Fulton presented a number of recommendations designed to do away with the cult of the generalist, to strengthen the management capacity of senior civil servants, to increase that of ministers to control their departments, and to abolish the class structure of the public service. The report attached considerable importance to management, suggesting that the service should continually review the tasks it is asked to carry out in order to identify what new skills are required and how to find and train the right people. Fulton called for new management courses for specialists and recommended that, in future, principles of 'accountable management' be applied to the activities of departments. The report called for the 'clear allocation of responsibility and authority to accountable units with defined objectives and a corresponding addition to the system of government accounting.'[63]

Fulton, however, ran up against a problem that would undermine the thrust of many of the report's recommendations. Prime Minister Wilson gave Fulton a sweeping mandate, but he specifically instructed him not to address the 'machinery of government.' Wilson explained that his government's decision to establish the inquiry did not 'imply any intention ... to alter the basic relationship between ministers and civil servants because civil servants, however eminent, remain the confidential advisers of ministers, who alone are answerable to Parliament for policy; and we do not envisage any change in this fundamental feature of our parliamentary system of democracy.'[64]

The Glassco Commission tabled its report in Ottawa in 1962. This commission did address the management issue, stating that the 'ponderous system, virtually unchanged in the past thirty years, is regarded by many as the price that must be paid under democracy in order to hold public servants properly accountable.'[65] However, 'the system in place no longer did the job.' Size appeared to be the key problem. What was a relatively simple government organization in 1939 'has become today a complicated system of departments, boards and commissions engaged in a multitude of different tasks. Obviously, the methods found effective for the management of the relatively compact organization of the prewar days cannot control without extensive alteration, the vast complex which has come into being in the past twenty years.' The government's financial controls were seen as too cumbersome, with a wide variety of 'checks, counterchecks and duplication and blind adherence to regulations.'[66]

The Glassco Commission, too, looked to the private sector for inspiration and recommended sweeping changes. The commission is credited with coining the phrase 'let managers manage.' It argued that management practices in government lagged behind those in the private sector. Glassco strongly urged the government to devolve to departments the authority to make spending decisions free of central controls. Managers, Glassco argued, were not free to make even the most minor of spending decisions without central controllers looking over their shoulders. The commission noted the precedent provided by Britain and the United States in this respect and urged the Canadian government to scrap many of the central financial controls.

In recommending the delegation of spending controls to departments, Glassco was careful to insist that managers be held properly accountable for their decisions. As Glassco explained, 'This re-location of financial powers is in no sense intended to place departmental managers beyond the complete control of the Executive.'[67] Glassco was less than forthcoming when it came to identifying measures to strengthen accountability, probably because the role of Parliament was left out of his mandate. Still, the government accepted the bulk of the Glassco recommendations.

Like Fulton, however, Glassco did not deal with ministerial responsibility, nor did the government in its response. Controls and processes could be scrapped, but the relationship between civil servants, ministers, and Parliament and the rules of accountability, notably the doctrine of ministerial responsibility, were deemed sacred and not to be tampered with.

Political leaders from Thatcher to Brown and from Mulroney to Harper have all echoed the Fulton and Glassco conclusion with regard to changing the bureaucracy: make public sector managers as strong as their private sector counterparts and leave substantial policy issues to prime ministers and ministers. This view, held in common by political leaders, was buttressed by numerous books and journal articles, all of which pointed in a single direction – turn the boiler room of public bureaucracies into private sector clones.[68] But throughout it all, one mantra remained constant: the basic relationship between elected and career officials should remain untouched.

Thatcher, more than anyone, wanted government managers to emulate the private sector. She often talked about improving the 'management of Government business.'[69] But that was as far as she was prepared to go. When the executive agency model was in the planning stages, she was willing to look at different options to hold agencies and their officials accountable. However, when decision time arrived, she baulked. Thatcher told the Commons the day the 'Next Steps' report was released that 'there will be no change in the arrangements for accountability.'[70] Officials interpreted her statement to mean that there would be little difference between agencies and departments – indeed, Sir Robin Butler, head of the Home Civil Service, did not even think 'it would be necessary to revise the rules on civil servants giving evidence to select committees' of Parliament.[71] He wrote, 'No doubt this is because ministers, notably the minister for the civil service, Richard Lace, made it clear that any constitutional changes to redefine ministerial responsibility were out of the question as were any suggestions to end Treasury controls over budgets, manpower and national pay bargaining.'[72]

It is nothing less than a leap of faith on the part of political leaders to think that they can impose a private sector management model on government without revisiting basic arrangements for accountability. Accountability in the private sector is a relatively straightforward affair – leaving aside transparency requirements, it can be summed up in a handful of phrases – profit margin, market forces, market share, return on investment, bottom line, and beating the competition. It only takes a moment's reflection to appreciate that these phrases can never resonate in the government. Thus, although public sector managers have been empowered to manage their operations, there have been only modest developments in strengthening accountability requirements.

To be sure, we have witnessed an explosive growth in the program evaluation industry in Anglo-American democracies in the past forty years. Its track record, however, has been dismal. Departments have learned to cope with program evaluations and a stream of outside consultants, appreciating that one does not bite the hand that feeds without consequences, and they have done very well by it. Departments regard program evaluation more as a 'gotcha' tool for the benefit of everyone but themselves.[73] Why would managers willingly generate information only to provide ammunition for outsiders and the media to point out where they have failed? As one former academic turned practitioner once observed, 'It is a strange dog that willingly carries the stick with which it is beaten.'[74]

The British government has recently invested considerable resources to establish program and management targets, but this has had only limited impact in promoting greater accountability. The efforts have not shed much light on how well programs are managed, but they have given rise to gaming and attempts to distort government priorities.[75] Neither the Canadian nor the British Parliament can be said to have made much use of program and management measurement reports to hold government managers accountable.

Performance pay schemes have also been in vogue in Anglo-American governments since the Thatcher, Reagan, and Mulroney days, but again with precious little success. This brings home the point that public and private sector management are vastly different from one another. Yet governments, no matter what their political persuasion, persist in using monetary rewards as an incentive. The reason they don't work is quite straightforward – it is not easy to assess the performance of government managers. There are too many variables that explain success or failure in government, and there are rarely any clear-cut criteria to determine who is a top performer. The work of the civil service is by nature increasingly collective, which makes it difficult for individuals to shine, on a strictly objective basis, over others. Bureaucrats still operate in hierarchical units, but their work increasingly depends on other government units. There is hardly an issue today that can fit neatly into one policy niche, let alone a single department.

Accordingly, performance, it seems, is in the eye of the beholder – hardly an objective criterion on which to base a performance pay scheme. It may well explain why whatever amount of money is allocated to performance pay schemes is invariably used up and why, in some years, well over 90 per cent of civil service managers in the government of Canada received a performance reward. This prompted the private sector chair of the advisory committee on retention and compensation of senior managers to observe that the committee 'will refrain from recommending further increases ... until the government shows a commitment to ensuring the program does not reward poor performers.'[76]

There have been other developments that suggest that the parsimonious culture that once was an important component of the values that defined the civil service has faded. The removal of centrally prescribed rules has enabled public sector management to emulate the private sector and empower government managers and has turned the civil service and, more specifically, individual departments into self-governing organizations on management matters. We increasingly hear about 'classification creep,' which increases the payroll.[77] Salaries of managers have also increased substantially; there is now no need for senior officials to negotiate trade agreements while wearing suits shiny with use. True to her goal of importing the business-management model to government operations, Thatcher decided that the salaries of senior government officials should be more comparable to those of senior business executives in order to attract outsiders from the private sector to head the Next Steps Agencies. She agreed in 1985 to salary increases of as high as 50 per cent for permanent secretaries: for example, the salary of her secretary to the cabinet, Sir Robert Armstrong, went from £50,000 to £75,000 in one year. Thatcher's decision appeared contradictory to some of her most ardent supporters in the Commons, and it very nearly caused a back-bench revolt.[78]

Senior government managers now look to salaries in the private sector to assess their own remuneration. And why not, given that political leaders have been telling them for some thirty years that they should emulate their private sector counterparts? They are invariably disappointed – Sir Andrew Turnbull, in his valedictory lecture as secretary to the British cabinet in July 2005, spoke about three 'unresolved' issues that he was leaving to his successors. The first – 'civil service pay, particularly at senior levels.' He spoke about a 'two tier pay system' between the public and private sectors that was becoming 'even more pronounced and eventually indefensible.'[79] One can only wonder if senior Canadian civil servants of yesteryear who negotiated trade agreements 'wearing suits that were shiny with use' would have ranked the difference in remuneration between the public and private sectors at the top of their list of unresolved issues as they left the civil service.

Because departments are now self-governing, it is extremely difficult to determine the proper size of the civil service and of government departments. It will be recalled that Thatcher declared a freeze on hiring the day she came to office and scrapped plans to add new positions. She ignored the claim in the civil service briefing books that the 733,000-strong civil service was already stretched to the limit. The books argued that there was no fat in the system and that 'even modest' cuts in staff would inhibit departments from functioning effectively. She announced a series of cuts early in her first mandate, and she directed that the civil service be reduced in size by nearly 15 per cent. By the time she left office, it had been cut by over 22 per cent, down to 569,000. Richard Wilson, former cabinet secretary, pointed out in March 2006 that the size of the civil service had been reduced further in recent years to 460,000.[80] Thatcher imposed cuts by simply outlining targets. It can hardly be described as a sophisticated approach, but it worked. Convinced that more could be done without reduction in services, she said that cuts could be absorbed through superior management practices.[81]

I asked one of the authors of the briefing books if Thatcher had it right when she ignored their claim and imposed cuts by picking a number out of the air? Yes, was the answer. Why, then, I asked, did you attempt to persuade her to hire more civil servants? The answer – permanent secretaries made their claim, and we simply packaged the various requests and made the case for more resources.[82] One can only conclude that, at some point between the late 1960s and the late 1970s, the parsimonious culture in government had indeed lost its appeal.

In Canada, if one wanted to document a lack of management coherence, consistency, and discipline in government, one need look no farther than a Treasury Board initiative of 1989. The secretariat announced with considerable fanfare that it would 'cut executive-level jobs in a bid to improve morale and operations.' It expressed concern that the executive category had grown to 2,562 members and argued that 'if you take a whole layer out of the management pyramid, then the managers below automatically gain greater control over their operations.'[83] Twelve years later this line of thinking was gone, as new management and associate positions emerged in every department and as the executive category had grown by more than 1,200 members. This, after the federal government shifted some of its activities to the provinces between 1995 and 1997.

The political leadership in both Canada and Britain have left unattended two important issues. The removal of a good number of centrally prescribed rules and regulations in the hope that public sector managers would manage like their counterparts in the private sector could never represent the complete solution. That approach also required a means by which to hold government managers accountable for their decisions. However, aside from program evaluation and program and management targets, which have hardly been success stories, nothing was done. The political leadership in both Canada and Britain, from Wilson to Trudeau, Blair, and Harper, on the advice of senior civil servants, decided not 'to alter the basic relationship between ministers and civil servants' or basic accountability requirements and the doctrine of ministerial responsibility. There are probably several reasons for this, but one of the more important is that it serves the interests of both sides by enabling ministers and senior civil servants to serve up a menu of plausible deniability when sensitive issues are raised.

The political leadership, meanwhile, had precious little to offer civil servants on policy. The policy-advisory and policy-making machinery inside the bureaucracy looks like it did in 1970. If anything, the policy-advisory role of civil servants was pushed back so that civil servants could focus more on management. This had the added benefit of making room for partisan advisers, outside consultants, and media specialists.

Managerialism in all its facets did not encourage officials to sit back, to think, to read, to reflect, and to come up with proposals for change to meet the new challenges confronting the nation-state. There was no attempt to get at the reason bureaucracies are uncreative and unable to be self-critical. Program managers, or 'doers,' are too busy to be of much help on this front. And yet, there were facets of government that needed fixing to get at the 'deadly sins' of public administration, including problems on the policy side and, in particular, the inability to adjust to changing circumstances.[84] Political leaders, again from Thatcher to Blair and Brown and Mulroney to Martin and Harper, chose to ignore this area, believing that they needed little help from their civil service to arrive at policy answers, to restructure the policy-advisory function to prepare government to meet the new challenges, or to develop a capacity to challenge the status quo.

Civil servants, in turn, had little to offer to politicians as they set out to reform the civil service. The message they gave politicians was 'all is well,' and 'just add more positions to our ranks.' Politicians, with little to go on, simply embraced private sector management practices as the way ahead. They did not recognize that civil service reform was necessary before public service reform could be successful and that a change in institutional culture was hardly possible without a change in accountability requirements.

Political leaders do not operate in a vacuum. They have, certainly better than most, a sense of what the population thinks and wants. When political leaders ran against government, the message resonated. Disenchantment with government and with bureaucracy became widespread. Elected politicians from both the right and left of the political spectrum, as well as the media and the academic community, began to voice their criticism publicly. Scarcely a voice was heard in defence of the civil service or civil servants. Meanwhile, civil servants were unwilling to engage in a public debate to counter the criticism, on the grounds that it was not their responsibility to do so given their traditional anonymity under the doctrine of ministerial responsibility. An outdated machinery of government may well explain, at least in part, the level of disenchantment with the civil service. But society itself, its values, and the rise of individualism may also be a factor. The next chapter explores this theme.

5 Society Then and Now: From an Obligation to Others to an Obligation to Self

In the movie *Cinderella Man*, James Braddock, a successful American boxer down on his luck during the Depression years, swallowed his pride and filed for government relief to put food on the table for his family. Braddock regained his fighting form a few years later and became the heavyweight champion of the world. He returned to the government relief office to repay the money he had received, insisting that it was the right thing to do and saying that someone else needed the money more than he did. It is difficult to imagine anyone making a similar gesture today. It is, however, easy to imagine that politicians and particularly bureaucrats would welcome dealing with the James Braddocks of the world and that Braddock likely thought of himself as a citizen, not as a customer.

Government and bureaucracy, Ezra Suleiman writes, are as much affected by 'mores in society as by cultural or sociological changes in society.'[1] We have, from the early 1960s, witnessed dramatic changes in technological developments, in education, in political participation, and the list goes on. In 1961, there was no fax machine, let alone e-mail; there was no twenty-four-hour television news; and a politician could still inspire a nation by appealing to the collective instincts of its citizens with the call 'ask not what your country can do for you, ask what you can do for your country.' Yet the role of social capital was hardly mentioned in the political science and public administration literature. It existed, but it was taken for granted. Today, it is described as the 'sine qua non of stable liberal democracy.'[2] There is now a growing interest in many Western countries in documenting and analysing the state of social capital and social cohesion. In Canada, Statistics Canada in 2003 added the 'social engagement' theme to its General Social

Survey (GSS), one of its continuing programs. Both the Office for National Statistics in Britain and the Organization for Economic Co-operation and Development (OECD) have also begun to survey developments in social capital.

Robert Putnam put social capital on the political science and public policy scene and even on the political agenda with his books *Making Democracy Work: Civic Tradition in Modern Italy* and *Bowling Alone*.[3] The later book, as the title suggests, makes the case that social capital has declined substantially in the United States since the 1950s and that this development undermines the kind of civic engagement needed for a strong democratic culture among citizens. Putnam writes about a drop in all forms of civic engagement in the United States since then, including voter turnout and membership in political parties and community organizations. He shows that individuals who came of age during the Depression and the Second World War were far more engaged in their communities than subsequent generations have been.[4] At the risk of oversimplification, *social capital* refers to the attributes of communities, while *human capital* refers to the attributes of individuals. Putnam's work sparked a keen interest in the matter of social capital in many Western countries, and government departments in both Canada and Britain have in recent years commissioned numerous research reports to determine how their countries shape up on the social capital scale.

Peter Hall and others have recently looked at social capital in Britain. Hall reports that Britain is increasingly 'a nation divided between a well-connected and highly active group of citizens with generally prosperous lives and another of citizens whose associational life and involvement in politics are very limited.'[5] That said, Hall maintains that in Britain social capital has not fallen as sharply as it has in the United States. Others in Britain have come to a similar conclusion. The Office for National Statistics, as well as a number of scholars, argue that the decline in social capital in the United States 'is not mirrored' in Britain. They report that membership in some organizations and groups has declined but that other forms of civic engagement are on the rise, notably membership in single-issue groups.[6]

In Canada, Jane Jenson sought to map Canada's social cohesion in 1998, arguing that 'the paradigm shift in economic and social policy towards neo-liberalism has provoked serious social and political strains, and a loss of confidence in public institutions.'[7] She concludes that, though the social capital concept is contested and contestable and though it should not displace other approaches, it does offer some promise in understanding broad developments in Canadian society. Jenson returned to the topic in 2002 with a colleague to produce an extensive review of the Canadian literature and to report on new developments in Canadian social capital. They lamented the lack of an 'adequate theory to provide convincing explanations' underpinning the concept and then went on to describe social cohesion as a 'quasi concept.' But, notwithstanding these reservations, they report that a number of major international and national bodies have embraced social cohesion as a concept to help them plan for the future. They also write that 'after several years of intense discussion, research, and policy development' – and despite the ongoing dialogue about 'what it *really* means' – 'social cohesion is a concept that remains valuable today and is likely to continue to serve us well in the years ahead.'[8] Still, Hall, Jenson, and others have not had the kind of data needed to prepare a thorough comparative review of social capital or social cohesion over time in either Canada or Britain. Most of the data and much of the literature on the topic are relatively recent. There were, for example, only 20 articles in learned journals with *social capital* as a key word before 1981, but the number rose to 109 between 1991 and 1996 and again to 1,003 between 1996 and 1999.[9]

This chapter explores how society has changed. Every effort has been made to go back to 1961 to secure the necessary data to produce a comparative picture but, as the reader will see, with limited success. The data are simply not available. Accordingly, in many instances, data go back only to 1981.

There are many definitions attached to *social capital* and what contributes to it. The literature has looked to a number of indicators to assess the state of social capital at the community, national, and international levels. These include group membership, formal and informal social networks, trust, and civic engagement. Our interest is specific, albeit ambitious, given the need to rely mostly on secondary analysis of existing data sources. This chapter sets out to determine to what extent society has become more or less individualistic, to assess the level of civic engagement, to determine the level of trust citizens have in political and administrative institutions, and to review the level of participation in the country's political life.

Data are from three major sources: Statistics Canada, the Office for National Statistics in Britain, and the World Values Survey (WVS). The WVS has already been conducted in more than eighty societies since its inception by a network of social science researchers at leading universities around the world. It was started in 1981 and grew out of an initiative launched by the European Values Survey, under the direction of Jan Kerkhofs and Ruud de Moor, that covered ten European countries. The survey was very well received, and it was soon replicated in fourteen other countries. It is carried out in waves, of which four have so far been undertaken: 1981, 1990–1, 1995–6, and 1999–2001. The most recent survey was sent out in 2005, and work on it was completed in late 2006. Because of the need to compute all the data and package the material, the results of the next wave were not available before this book was completed. The questions can change slightly, depending on the country and region in question. For example, it makes little sense asking Americans what they think of the European Union, and it makes little sense asking Europeans for their views on NAFTA, but apart from the regional differences, the questionnaires are the same. Though the questionnaires can also change over time, a majority of the questions remain the same in successive versions.

Is Society More Secular?

Leaving aside the Muslim world, it is widely believed that society is much more secular today than it was forty years ago, and for good reason. This development should matter to governments because churches, synagogues, and mosques play a vital role in promoting a nation's social capital. They are not just concerned with the next life; many are deeply embedded in their communities. They provide a community base for doing 'good works,' organizing charity events to help the disadvantaged, and providing a meeting place that, among other things, serves to promote informal social capital building. In brief, they promote the collective interest of communities through various means, and some observers consider them an important indication of a community's social cohesion.

We saw earlier that there are fewer Roman Catholic nuns today (the same is true for priests) and that Roman Catholics no longer attend church services as frequently as they once did. This has important implications for Canada, given its substantial Roman Catholic population. According to the general social survey in Canada (2003), some 40 per cent of Canadians identified themselves as Roman Catholics, while in a similar survey in Great Britain (2001) only 10.1 per cent did so.[10]

Data from the World Values Survey, however, suggest a somewhat different picture from what is generally assumed. The survey reports that church attendance in Canada dropped, but not substantially, between 1982 and 2000 (see table 5.1). However, as is well known, it was during the 1970s that church attendance, including in the Roman Catholic church, witnessed its biggest drop. Canadian surveys carried out in 1965 and 1974 also confirm this – the first survey in 1965 revealed that close to 50 per cent of Canadians attended church 'at least weekly.' The second survey in 1974 saw the number of Canadians attending church drop to 34 per cent. In addition, a close look at table 5.1 reveals that people in the thirty to forty-nine age bracket had a higher church attendance in 1982 than in 2000. This also suggests that church attendance will continue to fall as the population ages.

Statistics Canada has tracked religious affiliation since 1871 and church attendance since 1986, and it paints a different picture from the World Values Survey. In 2001, Statistics Canada reported that attendance at religious services had 'fallen dramatically across the country over the past fifteen years.'[11] The agency reported that only one in five Canadians aged fifteen and over attended religious services on a weekly basis in 2001 compared with 28 per cent in 1986, and that 43 per cent of Canadians had not attended religious services during the previous twelve months prior to the 2001 survey, compared with only 26 per cent in 1986. More revealing, however, prior to 1971, less than 1 per cent of Canadians reported having no religious affiliation, but by 2001 the percentage had jumped to 16 per cent.[12]

Church attendance in Britain, again according to the World Values Survey, is lower than in Canada, as table 5.2 reveals. However, the table also reveals that, as in Canada, the young attend church less often than the older generation.

There may well be another factor at play here, at least in the case of Canada, one that is also particularly evident in the United States. Putnam writes that, while there has been a decline in mainstream church attendance, there has been a significant growth in evangelical and para-churches. Putnam maintains that these new organizations may well require less active participation and that the ties are more to 'common symbols, common leaders and perhaps to common ideals, but not to one another.'[13] The same phenomenon is also evident in Canada. Statistics Canada reports a decline in mainstream church attendance – Presbyterians, Anglicans, and the United Church saw their numbers decline by 36, 7, and 8 per cent, respectively – but notes

Table 5.1
Church attendance by generation: Canada

	1982		1990		2000	
	Once weekly	Never	Once weekly	Never	Once weekly	Never
15–29	14.4	26.8	11.4	31.8	9.4	33.2
30–49	21.8	50.8	16.8	34.2	15.7	29.4
50 and over	36.4	16.0	31.4	22.2	30.2	20.0

Source: World Values Survey

Table 5.2
Church attendance by generation: Britain

	1982		1990		1999	
	Once weekly	Never	Once weekly	Never	Once weekly	Never
15–29	7.9	58.2	6.2	58.5	3.4	59.1
30–49	8.6	45.4	7.5	48.6	8.9	56.2
50 and over	12.5	39.7	14.4	39.2	12.1	49.4

Source: World Values Survey

that in smaller denominations the numbers have increased substantially since 1991, especially among Evangelical Missionaries (up 48 per cent), Hutterites (up 22 per cent), and Adventists (up 20 per cent).[14] The important point here is that the church is much less present in society today than it was forty years ago and that the face of the church, particularly in Canada, has changed with the substantial decline in mainstream church attendance. The argument made by Putnam and others is that an increase in secularism, albeit among other forces, has made society more individualistic.

Disruption of Traditional Family Ties

Students of social capital point to several possible factors, beyond the decline in church attendance and religious affiliation, to explain the drop in social capital. These include the movement of women into the labour force and the disruption of marriage and family ties, without necessarily establishing a link between the two. Putnam writes that

Table 5.3
Workforce participation rates of females (age 15 and older)

Country	1976	1981	1986	1992	2000	2005
U.K.	46.7	48.7	51.2	53.2	55.2	56.1
Canada	44.2	50.0	54.5	56.9	57.9	61.0

Source: Statistics Canada, Labour Force Survey; National Statistics (U.K.), Labour
Force Survey

the 'movement of women out of the home and into the paid labour
force is probably the most portentous social change of the last half century. However welcome and overdue the feminist revolution was, it is
hard to believe that it has had no impact on social connectedness.'[15]
One can appreciate that working mothers would have less time to care
for the family and that they would be more likely to join professional
associations rather than community associations, including parent-
teacher groups. Though Putnam hesitates to rank all the factors
explaining the decline in social capital in the United States in terms of
their importance, it is clear that he regards two-career families to be an
important one.

Whatever the impact on a country's social capital may be, female
participation in the work force has increased substantially in recent
years. Table 5.3 reports that female participation, expressed as a percentage of the total labour force in Canada, went from 44.2 per cent in
1976 to 61 per cent in 2005.

Data from Britain point to a similar trend, though not as pronounced. Table 5.3 reports that female participation as a percentage of
the labour force went from 46.7 per cent in 1976 to 56.1 per cent in 2005.

Barbara Whitehead writes about a divorce revolution that began in
the early 1960s when it moved 'from the margins to the mainstream.'
She explains the change as part of a broader shift 'away from an ethic
of obligation to others and toward an obligation to self.'[16] On the
question of divorce, Putnam maintains that married men and women
rank higher than others on the social capital scale. He explains that,
'controlling for education, age, race, and so on, single people – both
men and women, divorced, separated, and never married – are
significantly less trusting and less engaged civically than married people. Roughly speaking, married men and women are about a third
more trusting and belong to about 15–25 percent more groups than

Table 5.4
Divorces – Canada

Year	Number	% Increase
1971	29,685	–
1981	67,671	127.96
1991	77,020	13.82
2001	71,110	–7.67

Source: Cansim, table 053 0002

Table 5.5
Divorces – Britain

Year	Number	% Increase
1961	27,152	–
1971	79,261	191.92
1981	156,963	98.03
1991	173,454	10.51
1999	158,746	–8.48

Source: Office of National Statistics

comparable single men and women. Widows and widowers are more like married people than single people in this comparison.'[17] Both Canada and Britain have registered sharp increases in their divorce rates, as tables 5.4 and 5.5 reveal.

It is interesting to note that a study of the changing reasons for divorce in Britain divides them into three distinct periods (1949–72, 1973–84, and 1985–96). Violence and adultery broke up many postwar couples, while in more recent times, the 'lack of quality time' a couple spends together is reported to be the key factor.[18]

Voluntary Membership

Canada and Britain, as earlier chapters argue, have many things in common. The two countries have also, over the years, put in place deliberate policies to promote the voluntary sector. Governments in both countries have a long history of spending substantial resources to promote volunteer work. Studies in Britain reveal that government interventions in the twentieth century have served to promote rather than attenuate the tradition of voluntary efforts.[19] In Canada, the federal government has and continues to provide grants and contributions to non-profit organizations engaged in volunteer work.[20] Moreover, the political right and left in both countries have supported and continue to support the voluntary sector. Margaret Thatcher maintained that 'the voluntary movement is at the heart of all of our social welfare provision.'[21] In Canada, Jean Chrétien declared that the voluntary sector was 'one of the strongest fibres in the national fabric.'[22]

Perhaps because of the above, membership in associations has remained relatively strong in Canada and in Britain (although less so in Britain) when compared with the United States. Table 5.6 reports on voluntary membership in both Canada and Britain. Each cell represents the average number of voluntary organizations that a person belongs to.

According to the World Values Survey, the typical person in Canada in 2000 was a member of 1.23 voluntary organizations. It is also possible to break up the responses into age categories (see table 5.7) to see if age has any impact on whether a person belongs to a voluntary organization.

Tables 5.6 and 5.7 reveal that the two countries are diverging, with membership going up in Canada but down in Britain. Tables 5.8 and 5.9 help us to see, for each country, whether the percentage of responses varied from year to year, by how much, and why.

Table 5.8 shows that the percentage of respondents in Canada who belong to a church (since 1982) has remained relatively stable and remains the most cited group. Meanwhile, the groups that have seen the largest increase in voluntary membership are those that include education, arts, music or cultural activities, and professional organizations.

Table 5.9 shows how membership in voluntary organizations has changed in Britain over the three periods. Unlike in Canada, church membership and labour union membership dropped during this period. In fact, the only groups that appear to have experienced an increase in stated affiliation are also those associated with education, arts, music, or cultural activities.

Table 5.10 reproduces the findings of table 5.6 but adds a number of new categories and also presents the data from 1990 and 1999/2000 because the questions asked to the respondents were the same. Thus, starting in 1990, respondents could choose other categories than the ones shown in tables 5.8 and 5.9. As we see in tables 5.11 and 5.12, the categories added were sports, women's groups, health movements, and peace movements.

Table 5.6
Average number of voluntary group memberships per person

Total	1982	1990	2000
Canada	0.964115	1.119653	1.231683
Britain	0.858612	0.762803	0.44

Source: World Values Survey

Table 5.7
Membership according to age

		1982	1990	2000
Canada	15–29	0.736052	0.903226	0.97861
	30–49	1.180974	1.229275	1.345223
	50+	1	1.124324	1.287958
Britain	15–29	0.683652	0.581602	0.362069
	30–49	1.105431	0.895669	0.447837
	50+	0.872063	0.760317	0.421965

Source: World Values Survey

Table 5.8
Change in variables 1983–2000: Canada

Variables	Canada		
	Percentage (%)		
	1982	1990	2000
Belong to social welfare service for elderly	13.0	8.4	13.2
Belong to religious organization	13.28	25.0	29.5
Belong to education, arts, music, or cultural activities	9.7	17.6	21.4
Belong to labour unions	11.3	11.6	14.4
Belong to political parties	5.5	7.2	6.3
Belong to local political actions	0.0	5.1	8.0
Belong to human rights	3.0	4.6	5.1
Belong to conservation, the environment, ecology, animal rights	4.7	0.0	9.1
Belong to conservation, the environment, ecology	0.0	7.5	0.0
Belong to animal rights	0.0	2.6	0.0
Belong to professional associations	11.7	15.9	17.9
Belong to youth work	9.6	9.6	11.2
Belong to consumer groups	0.0	22.7	27.5

Source: World Values Survey

Table 5.9
Change in variables 1981–99: Britain

Variables	Britain Percentage (%)		
	1981	1990	1999
Belong to social welfare service for elderly	8.6	7.3	6.7
Belong to religious organization	21.7	15.9	.05
Belong to education, arts, music, or cultural activities	6.7	0.1	9.7
Belong to labour unions	20.8	13.8	8.2
Belong to political parties	4.6	5.6	2.5
Belong to local political actions	0.0	3.5	3.8
Belong to human rights	1.3	2.3	2.7
Belong to conservation, the environment, ecology, animal rights	4.7	0.0	1.5
Belong to conservation, the environment, ecology	0.0	5.9	0.0
Belong to animal rights	0.0	2.1	0.0
Belong to professional associations	8.9	10.8	1.6
Belong to youth work	6.9	4.3	5.7
Belong to consumer groups	0.0	17.9	.03

Source: World Values Survey

Table 5.10
Average number of voluntary groups, total

Total	1990	2000
Canada	1.696532	1.895391
Britain	1.117251	0.597

Source: World Values Survey

Tables 5.11 and 5.12 report on organizations that gained and lost membership in the decade. Table 5.11 shows a decline in voluntary groups in Britain. The two most prominent groups in 1990 were church and sporting groups, as their numbers dwindled over the decade. On the other hand, the proportion of people citing education, arts, music, or cultural activities and social welfare services for the elderly remained stable or grew over the same period.

Table 5.12 shows that participation in voluntary groups in Canada has increased at many levels, with even church membership increasing

Table 5.11
Total variables: Britain

Variables	Britain Percentage (%)	
	1990	1999
Belong to social welfare service for elderly	7.3	6.7
Belong to religious organization	15.9	5.0
Belong to education, arts, music, or cultural activities	10.0	9.7
Belong to labour unions	13.8	8.2
Belong to political parties	5.6	2.5
Belong to local political actions	3.5	3.8
Belong to human rights	2.3	2.7
Belong to conservation, the environment, ecology, animal rights	0.0	1.5
Belong to conservation, the environment, ecology	5.9	0.0
Belong to animal rights	2.1	0.0
Belong to professional associations	10.8	1.6
Belong to youth work	4.3	5.7
Belong to consumer groups	17.9	3.0
Belong to a women's group	5.2	1.7
Belong to a peace movement	1.3	0.6
Belong to organization concerned with health	3.8	3.0
Belong to other groups	7.9	5.1

Source: World Values Survey

(bear in mind that one can be a member of a church but not attend the services). The second-largest increase was in sporting events or recreation.

It is not always possible to track WVS findings over time because the same question is not always asked. In addition, it is difficult to assess whether associations or groups have an individualistic or a collective bent. Tables 5.13 and 5.14 attempt to provide a breakdown by subjectively dividing the groups along individual-community orientations and tracking the percentage change between 1982 and 2000. The argument is that the top four are more in tune with individual interests and the bottom three more in line with group or community-based interests. The percentage changes are higher for the top four than for the bottom three, suggesting that there has been a tendency towards individual activities and interests instead of group or community-based ones.

Table 5.12
Total variables: Canada

Variables	Canada Percentage (%)	
	1990	2000
Belong to social welfare service for elderly	8.4	13.2
Belong to religious organization	25.0	29.5
Belong to education, arts, music, or cultural activities	17.6	21.4
Belong to labour unions	11.6	14.4
Belong to political parties	7.2	6.3
Belong to local political actions	5.1	8.0
Belong to human rights	4.6	5.1
Belong to conservation, the environment, ecology, animal rights	0.0	9.1
Belong to conservation, the environment, ecology	7.5	0.0
Belong to animal rights	2.6	0.0
Belong to professional associations	15.9	17.9
Belong to youth work	9.6	11.2
Belong to consumer groups	22.7	27.5
Belong to a women's group	6.7	8.1
Belong to a peace movement	2.0	2.1
Belong to organization concerned with health	8.7	11.1
Belong to other groups	12.7	11.2

Source: World Values Survey

Table 5.13
Type of associations: Canada

	1982	2000	% change
Human rights	2.9	4.5	55.17
Conservation, the environment, ecology, animal rights	4.7	8.1	72.34
Professional organization	11.1	15.8	42.34
Educational, arts, music, or cultural activities	9.7	20.1	107.22
Religious	31.6	30.5	−3.48
Services for elderly	11.9	13.1	10.08
Political parties	5.3	6.1	15.09

Source: World Values Survey

Table 5.14
Type of associations: Britain

	1981	1999	% change
Human rights	1.5	2.6	73.33
Conservation, the environment, ecology, animal rights	5.0	1.5	−70.00
Professional organization	10.1	1.6	−84.16
Educational, arts, music, or cultural activities	8.0	10.4	30.00
Religious	21.0	4.8	−77.14
Services for elderly	8.6	6.8	−20.93
Political parties	4.7	2.6	−44.68

Source: World Values Survey

Though hardly sufficient, the findings in tables 5.13 and 5.14 go some way to support the received wisdom that we are witnessing a shift away from collective or community-type associations to single issue and direct action groups addressing topics ranging from globalization to the war in Iraq to fuel prices. A number of scholars have in recent years also written about the rise of individualism in Western society, and the above data tend to support their view.[23] This trend is obviously not without important consequences for both society and government.

Television

Putnam is reluctant to rank factors shaping a country's social capital, but he does not hesitate to point the finger at what he describes as the 'prime suspect.' He insists that he has both 'circumstantial' and 'directly incrementing evidence' that television is the leading culprit. He writes that television today absorbs 40 per cent of the average American's free time, an increase of over 30 per cent since 1965, and that this 'massive change' in the way Americans spend their leisure time occurred precisely during the years of 'civic disengagement.'[24] He maintains that television viewing can account for up to one-half of the total drop in social capital. He contrasts television viewing with newspaper reading and maintains that television is associated with less social trust and less group membership while reading a newspaper is associated with more.[25] Television news, with its fifteen-second clips, stresses style over substance, focuses on party leaders rather than

Graph 5.1
TV watching: Canada, 1982 and 1998

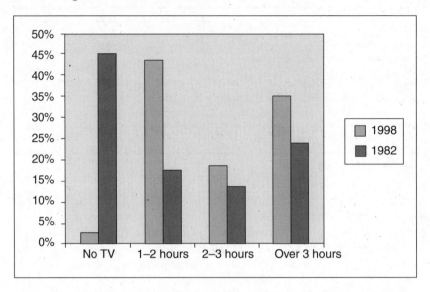

Source: Time Use Survey (Statistics Canada. General Social Survey of Canada [GSS],
1998. Cycle 12: Time use [main file] [machine readable data file]. Ottawa, ON: Statistics
Canada. 9/11/1999); World Values Survey (1982)

members of Parliament, and defines election campaigns around the
performance of party leaders rather than party platforms.

Graphs 5.1 to 5.4 report on television watching and newspaper reading over time in Canada and Britain, starting in 1981 and 1982. The
same questions were not asked in surveys carried out in later waves.
However, the questions were sufficiently similar to make a number of
observations. First, time spent watching television in both Canada and
Britain has not gone down – if anything, the trend line points to still
more hours spent watching television. Second, newspaper readership
is on the decline in both countries.[26]

A study of the Parliamentary Press Gallery membership from 1950
to 2004 in Canada reveals that the structure of the gallery itself has
changed 'significantly' in that the proportion of broadcast journalists
has grown sharply. It explains that 'the erosion of newspaper supremacy in the gallery would be expected to correspond roughly with a

Graph 5.2
TV watching: Britain, 1981 and 2002

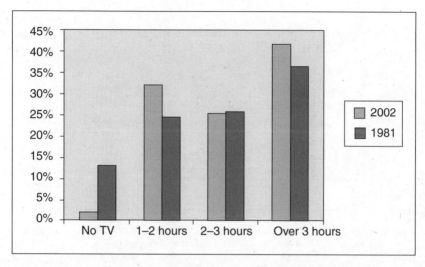

Source: European Social Survey (R. Jowell and the Central Co-ordinating Team,
European Social Survey 2002/2003: Technical Report, London: Centre for Comparative
Social Surveys, City University [2003]); World Values Survey (1981)

shift in Canadians' preferences for broadcast news instead of print
news.' In other words, the study reports that 'the growing proportion
of broadcast journalists in the gallery makes sense because increasingly
Canadians are seeking their news from broadcast media (especially
television) instead of print media (especially newspapers).'[27]

Membership in Political Parties and Voter Turnout

Two factors particularly important for the purpose of our study are
membership in political parties and voter participation. Indeed, voter
participation is held by many to be a key measure of the health of any
representative democracy. If the will of the people is to be established
at election time, then it stands to reason that voter turnout is one of the
most crucial factors shaping it. The majority of Canadians never make
it to Ottawa in their lifetime even for a visit and, if representative
democracy is to have any meaning, they need to participate in choos-
ing who is to represent them in the capital.

Graph 5.3
Regularly read newspaper: Canada, 1982 and 2000

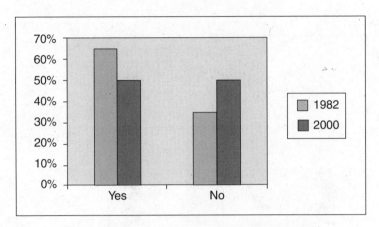

Source: Canadian Election Survey (André Blais, Elisabeth Gidengil,
Richard Nadeau, and Neil Nevitte. Canadian Election Survey, 2000
[Computer file]. ICPSR03969-v1. Toronto, Ontario: York University, Institute
for Social Research [producer], 2000. Ann Arbor, MI: Inter-university
Consortium for Political and Social Research [distributor], 2004); World
Values Survey (1982)

Voter turnout also matters because it gives legitimacy to government
when it claims to speak on behalf of citizens. It matters because, if they
do nothing else in terms of civic engagement, citizens can still participate in periodic elections to choose their representatives through the
mechanism of competitive political parties and thus have a say, however
indirectly, in the running of their country. More to the point, a mandate
from the people requires that people vote. It matters because low voter
turnout could well speak directly to a country's weakening sense of civic
duty. It also matters because it can lead to important differences among
groups in terms of political influence. Arend Lijphart, among others,
argues that 'low voter turnout means unequal and socioeconomically
biased turnout.'[28] In short, unequal voter participation means unequal
influence. It means that election outcomes can less and less be labelled
the 'voice of the people' and more 'the voice of some people,' and the
more privileged ones at that. We have now reached the point where
the number of citizens who do not vote in general elections is larger than
the number of those who voted for the winning party.

Graph 5.4
Regularly read newspaper: Britain, 1981 and 2001

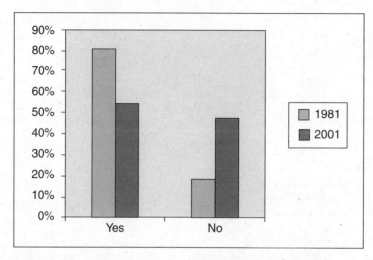

Source: British Social Attitude Survey (National Centre for Social Research.
BRITISH SOCIAL ATTITUDES SURVEY, 2001 [Computer file]. ICPSR
version. London, England: National Centre for Social Research [producer],
2001. Colchester, Essex, England: United Kingdom Data Archive/Ann
Arbor, MI: Inter-university Consortium for Political and Social Research
[distributors], 2004); World Values Survey (1981)

Voter turnout in Canada and Britain recently ranked twenty-fourth
and twenty-sixth, respectively, in a thirty-six-country survey.[29] Both
countries have higher voter turnout than the United States, India, and
Switzerland, but lower than Australia (where the vote is compulsory),
Belgium, Sweden, and New Zealand. That said, there has been a
decline in voter participation in most Western countries, and Canada
and Britain are certainly no exception. Martin Wattenberg, in reference
to the general decline in voter participation in many democratic countries in recent years, writes that 'it is rare in comparative politics to
find a trend that is so widely generalizable.'[30] The decline in voter
turnout is not a recent phenomenon. Indeed, voter turnout in both
Canada and Britain has been on a downward trend since the early
1960s (see tables 5.15 and 5.16), and there is remarkable similarity in
the trend in both countries.

Table 5.15
Voter turnout: Canada

Year	Turnout (%)
1962	79.0
1972	76.7
1980	69.3
1993	69.6
2004	60.9

Source: Elections Canada

Table 5.16
Voter turnout: Britain

Year	Turnout (%)
1964	77.1
1970	72.0
1979	72.0
1987	75.3
1997	71.3
2001	59.4

Source: Library of the House of
Commons, Britain Election Statistics, 1945–2003

Putnam maintains that the decline in voter turnout goes hand in
hand with a general decline in civic participation and in social capital.[31] Low turnout could be the result of many factors. It could mean
that citizens see little point in trudging to the polls on election day.
They may well think that their vote will have no impact on government or on whatever decisions it may strike on any issue and that only
powerful business or political interests can influence governments.
Surveys in Canada suggest that this is one of the main reasons explaining the decline in voter turnout. One survey in the aftermath of the
2000 general election saw seven out of ten Canadians agree with the
statement 'I don't think governments care very much about what
people like me think.' The sponsors of the survey compared the findings of a similar survey asking the very same question some thirty
years earlier and concluded that 'these negative views are much more

pronounced than they were 20 or 30 years ago.' In the 1968 survey, only four out of ten Canadians agreed with the same statement.[32] The 1990 World Values Survey asked Canadians 'Would you say that this country is run by a few big interests looking out for themselves?' Some 70 per cent of respondents said yes, a figure higher than was the case for Britain or the United States.

But that does not tell the whole story. Neil Nevitte, in a widely read book, insists that citizens today tend to be far more assertive and less deferential towards authority. He maintains that, at least in Canada, this is part of a larger phenomenon – the decline of deference in society – and adds that the loss in confidence is greater in political than in non-political institutions.[33] Developing his study around this one central theme, Nevitte draws on a number of sources, notably the World Values Survey, to make a convincing case. He presents many 'indicators' to show that citizens' attitudes towards authority in Canada have changed and continue to change. He acknowledges that the decline of deference is not simply a Canadian phenomenon and that it is evident throughout the Western world.[34]

Canadian and Britain citizens are better educated and better informed than they were forty years.ago. They are also less inclined to accept hierarchies and decisions from above and more anxious to participate directly in decision-making processes that have an impact on their lives. A well-known Canadian pollster, Michael Adams, argues that voter turnout is lower because governments do less and because globalization is moving many policy issues and effective decision making outside the hands of national governments. A good number of citizens today are well educated, prefer to bypass the government's helping hand, and do not defer to traditional figures of authority.[35] The argument goes that if citizens are increasingly able to make it on their own, then why bother voting?

The State of Political Parties

Political parties have also lost ground on the social capital scale. A nineteen-country survey conducted by the British think tank Demos showed that party identification had fallen in seventeen countries between the 1960s and 1990s and that strong attachment to parties had fallen across the board. A series of surveys between 1967 and 1997 reveal that Canadians have also gradually lost confidence in political parties.[36] Yet political parties are or should be the central actors in representative democracies. They are key to election campaigns, they select candidates, they select political or party leaders, and they prepare platforms intended to produce election victories. It is very rare indeed for someone to make it to Parliament without first securing the nomination of a major political party.

Canada has not fared as poorly as Britain in maintaining membership in political parties, as tables 5.17 and 5.18 reveal. The numbers for Canada, however, can be highly misleading. For one thing, as we noted earlier, one 2005 study reported that the number of Canadians who state that they have never been a member of a political party or worked for a party had jumped substantially in the previous three years.[37] Moreover, Canada, as is well known, tends to produce 'instant' Liberals and Conservatives, as potential party candidates descend upon constituencies in the lead-up to an election, signing up as many members as possible to secure their party's nomination. There is also considerable difference in membership rules between provinces. In New Brunswick, for example, there is no membership fee for the Liberal party and members are never removed from the list, so that a party membership can last a lifetime.

Surveys carried out in 1974 and 2000 show a decline among Canadians in their willingness to identify with a political party. In 1974, Canadians were asked if they identified with a political party and 86 per cent said they did. In 2000 in answer to the same question, the percentage dropped to 71 per cent (see table 5.19).

When Canadians were asked in 1979 whether they had 'a great deal, quite a lot, some or very little' respect for and confidence in political parties, 30 per cent answered 'a great deal' and 27 per cent 'very little.' When they were asked the same question in 2001, only 13 per cent answered 'a great deal,' while 39 per cent said 'very little.'[38] In October 2005, Canada's Public Policy Forum teamed up with the Crossing Boundaries National Council, with the support of Elections Canada, to undertake a series of interviews with current and former officials from Canada's political parties to assess the state of political parties. What they heard was not positive. They were told that Canada's political parties are 'not the vehicles for bold new ideas, they do not have strong roots in the community, they have little identity beyond that of their leader, they do not lead on the issues of our time and most parties are trying to dig themselves out of the hole – instant membership, instant leaders, instant democracy.' They also make the point that the capacity

Table 5.17
Membership in political parties:
Canada (percentages)

1982	1990	2000
5.3	7.3	6.1

Source: World Values Survey

Table 5.18
Membership in political parties:
Britain (percentages)

1981	1990	1999
4.7	4.9	2.6

Source: World Values Survey

Table 5.19
Political identification: Canada, 1974 and 2000

	Partisan (%)	Non-Partisan (%)
1974	86	14
2000	71	29

Source: CNES (1974) (Harold Clarke, Jane Jenson, Lawrence
LeDuc, and Jon Pammett. *Canadian National Election Study*,
1974 [Computer file]. Conducted by Harold Clarke et al.,
University of Windsor and Carleton University. ICPSR ed. Ann
Arbor, MI: Inter-university Consortium for Political and Social
Research [producer and distributor], 1977); André Blais,
Elisabeth Gidengil, Richard Nadeau, and Neil Nevitte: CNES
(2000) (Canadian Election Survey, 2000 [Computer file].
ICPSR03969-v1. Toronto, Ontario: York University, Institute
for Social Research [producer], 2000. Ann Arbor, MI: Inter-
university Consortium for Political and Social Research
[distributor], 2004)

of political parties to 'be more than electoral machines has severely declined,' and, referring to national parties, they insist that 'they have constructed a Potemkin village of sorts in the theatre of the nation's capital, but that outside Ottawa, the presence of parties is illusory.'[39] This is hardly a Canadian-only phenomenon. A British think tank went so far as to suggest that the country's main political parties are 'facing oblivion.' Tom Bentley and Paul Miller point out that the combined membership of the three main parties has fallen from 3.5 million in the 1950s to less than 500,000 today and argue that parties are 'failing to convince a younger generation of activists of the value of working through political parties.'[40]

The decline of class-based politics in Canada, but particularly in Britain, means that political parties, whether left or right, now have similar party platforms. The modern media are often far more interested in the personalities of party leaders than in the parties they represent. Election campaigns are also built around party leaders, political war rooms, political gaffes, public opinion surveys, spin, and television ads, including negative ones. This is about party leaders winning and losing, not about political parties and their platforms winning and losing. Money, pollsters, technology, phone banks, and spin doctors have, to some extent, replaced party volunteers.

For the above reasons, if for no other, voters are less loyal to political parties than they were forty years ago. This is the case even in Britain where loyalty to political parties and their programs has traditionally been stronger than in Canada. As is well known, the new Labour party has adopted policy positions that are much closer to those of the Conservatives than in the past. The result is that British voters are now less likely to identify with either party.

Allan Gregg, a highly respected political commentator in the national media in Canada, argues that in the past there was a much greater tendency on the part of Canadians to think of themselves as Liberals, Progressive Conservatives, or New Democrats. They viewed events through selective and partisan filters. This, he insists, is no longer the case. He points out that only weeks before the 2006 election campaign, the Liberals were headed towards one of the largest electoral majorities on record, only to go down to defeat. The work of the Gomery Commission and charges of sleaze directed at the Liberal party dominated the news for several weeks, with the result that the Liberals took a heavy hit. Gregg's point is that voter preference is now linked much more to public reaction to news events than to party loyalty.[41]

Table 5.20
Public interest in national politics in Canada

	Extremely interested (%)
2000	8.3
1988	11.5
1984	14.2
1974	13.8
1964	25.6

Source: Canadian National Elections
Survey

There is also evidence to suggest that interest in national politics is declining. Table 5.20, taken from Canada's national elections survey, speaks to this development in quite convincing terms.

Confidence in Institutions

The World Economic Forum sponsored a 'global public opinion survey' in which 20,000 citizens were interviewed in December 2005 and which reported a significant drop in trust in a range of institutions, to the point where it concluded that it now 'paints an alarming picture of declining levels of trust.'[42] It added that of all the institutions it examined, from the United Nations to large local companies, global corporations, and national governments, the national governments lost the most ground over the two-year period from 2003 to 2005.[43] Neither Canada nor Britain was exempt. Indeed, Canada, along with Brazil, South Korea, and Mexico, witnessed the sharpest drop among national governments.

The World Economic Forum was not the first organization to report a drop in confidence in public institutions. The World Values Survey has been tracking the level of confidence in various institutions since 1982. Tables 5.21 and 5.22 provide a breakdown.

The tables reveal a general decline in public confidence in institutions since the survey began its tracking in 1982. Parliament is not the only institution to lose ground in both Canada and Britain, though there have been only modest changes with respect to the civil service in both Canada and Britain. The media, in particular, have suffered a sharp drop in both countries. The above and other surveys prompted

Table 5.21
Public confidence in selected institutions: Canada (percentages)

	Churches			Press		
	1982	1990	2000	1982	1990	2000
A great deal	28.9	23.2	21.5	6.3	5.5	4.4
Quite a lot	40.1	39.9	40.2	38.9	40.8	31.6
Not very much	25.4	28.8	27.2	46.4	46.6	50.8
None at all	5.6	8.0	11.0	8.4	7.1	13.2
	Labour unions			Parliament		
A great deal	4.9	5.0	6.3	7.1	5.6	5.5
Quite a lot	28.7	29.9	30.8	36.0	31.7	34.1
Not very much	50.8	49.4	44.5	44.3	52.0	45.2
None at all	15.6	15.7	18.5	12.6	10.7	15.3
	Civil service			Major companies		
A great deal	7.4	6.1	7.0	10.6	6.1	6.8
Quite a lot	43.9	43.5	44.6	45.8	45.3	48.7
Not very much	40.2	43.0	39.9	35.0	42.4	37.4
None at all	8.6	7.5	8.5	8.6	6.3	7.1

Source: World Values Survey

Neil Nevitte, among many others, to write about 'a decline in public confidence towards the entire set of governmental institutions.'[44] What is also remarkable is that respondents in both Canada and Britain expressed confidence in major private or publicly traded companies. Canadians, for example, now have more confidence in major private companies than they have in the civil service, Parliament, labour unions, and the media.

In fall 2004, the Association of Professional Executives (APEX), an association of senior Government of Canada managers, commissioned an in-depth study of trust and ethics. The verdict was not positive. It revealed that only 30 per cent of Canadians reported in 2004 that they 'trust just about always, most of the time,' the government's ability to do 'what is right.' The response to the same question in 1964 was 75 per cent. In response to the question 'which of the following groups *have* or *should have* the most influence in defining public policies in

Table 5.22
Public confidence in selected institutions: Britain (percentages)

	Churches			Press		
	1982	1990	1999	1982	1990	1999
A great deal	17.5	18.6	9.4	4.3	3.2	1.2
Quite a lot	28.5	26.6	24.8	24.0	11.7	13.2
Not very much	42.4	42.7	46.6	58.2	56.9	48.3
None at all	11.6	12.1	19.1	13.5	28.3	37.3
	Labour unions			Parliament		
A great deal	4.7	6.5	2.6	8.9	10.2	3.9
Quite a lot	20.7	20.7	25.6	31.2	33.9	32.3
Not very much	52.0	50.3	48.1	48.2	44.4	48.4
None at all	22.6	22.5	23.8	11.7	11.5	15.4
	Civil service			Major companies		
A great deal	8.1	8.4	3.8	9.9	8.2	3.3
Quite a lot	38.8	37.2	42.3	40.6	39.2	36.9
Not very much	45.2	46.1	44.7	41.3	42.5	47.5
None at all	7.9	8.3	9.2	8.2	10.0	12.3

Source: World Values Survey

Canada?' 61 per cent of Canadians reported that senior business leaders *have* the most influence but only 37 per cent felt that they *should have* the most influence (influence gap at +24). Comparable figures for the media were 61 per cent and 25 per cent (influence gap at +24), lobbyists 51 per cent and 36 per cent (influence gap at +15), MPs 46 per cent and 61 per cent (influence gap at –15), senior public servants 43 per cent and 47 per cent (influence gap at –4), and average citizens 22 per cent and 80 per cent (influence gap at –58). When it comes to ethical standards, 78 per cent of Canadians believe that volunteers in non-government organizations have high ethical standards. Similar figures for other groups include 67 per cent for small business people, 49 per cent for civil servants, and 21 per cent for politicians.[45] This finding is all the more remarkable given the sustained efforts over the past twenty years or so to have government managers emulate private sector managers.

Education

Putnam writes that he is mystified by what he calls 'the mysterious disengagement' of the last quarter-century that has 'afflicted all educational strata in society, whether they have had graduate education or did not finish high school.'[46] There is an assumption that, as the population becomes more educated, it should be more engaged in community affairs.[47] More educated individuals should take a stronger interest in their community, join more groups, join political parties, run for political office, or at least make sure to vote. Comparative cross-country analyses reveal a link between higher education and levels of trust in the community.[48] There is solid evidence to suggest that the more politically knowledgable the individual, the more likely that he or she will vote.[49] Peter Hall maintains that exposure to higher education increased community involvement in Britain by 110 per cent over a ten-year period.[50] He concludes, however, that the past fifty years have 'seen subtle changes in the texture of collective life whose full implications we are only beginning to appreciate.'[51] Membership in groups may well be up, but organizations oriented towards the public interest or the collective interest of the community may well have been replaced by ones 'oriented primarily to the provision of services for their members.'[52] On this point Nevitte reports that 'a mountain of evidence demonstrates that the rise of issue-driven movements, movements employing a host of direct-action strategies, has so altered the substance and dynamics of state-society relations across advanced industrial states that conventional interpretations of national political contests no longer apply.'[53]

A more educated population may have higher expectations of government and require higher transparency standards. Thus, a more educated population may well have contributed to the growing lack of deference towards authority that students of politics and government have been witnessing in recent years. Indeed, there is evidence to suggest that individuals with higher levels of education have less confidence in governmental institutions but more in non-governmental institutions.[54]

To be sure, there has been an education revolution in both Canada and Britain over the past forty years. The level of education has jumped dramatically over this period in both countries as tables 5.23 and 5.24 reveal. These tables show over time the percentage of the population in Canada and Britain with a bachelor's degree or higher, and report a truly remarkable jump in education levels in both countries.

Table 5.23
Higher education: Canada

Year	University degree (%)
1961	1.8
1971	3.4
1981	8.0
1991	11.5
2001	15.4

Source: Census of Canada

Table 5.24
Higher education: Britain

Year	University degree (%)
1959	4.8
1991	11.0
2005	18.5

Source: Civic Values Survey and
Labour Force Survey

Society Has Changed

Two students of government write that there is no doubt that 'societal factors, including important shifts in values, play a role, probably the major role, in altering citizen trust and confidence.'[55] To be sure, politicians and civil servants deal with a vastly different society than was the case forty years ago. Richard Wilson, cabinet secretary in Britain between 1998 and 2002, observed in early 2006 that 'the public are no longer patient or deferential.'[56]

A good number of observers have also made the case that economic and social policy has shifted towards neo-liberalism and that Canadian and British social relations have also shifted from collectivist to individualistic in recent years. It takes only a moment's reflection to appreciate that social cohesion in Western countries has eroded over the years – society is, for example, far more urban and, consequently, more impersonal. We know that people who live in rural areas in Canada are more likely to spend time volunteering than those living in urban areas, regardless of their level of education.[57] Urbanization is also not without cost to social capital. Putnam reports that ten minutes of commuting reduces social capital by 10 per cent and that today, compared with twenty-five years ago, we attend fewer club meetings (down 58 per cent), fewer family dinners (down 33 per cent), and have friends over less often (down 45 per cent).[58] But that is not all. Television, the Internet, and video games have all had an isolating influence; large strip malls and department stores have replaced the local corner store; people are less likely to keep the same job throughout their working lives; and the search for better economic opportunities often entails uprooting families.

Study after study has made the case that individuals are much less deferential to authority than in the past, that they are better educated, that traditional family ties are not as strong as previously, and that society is now much more secular. Putnam's work on the decline of social capital resonates in many Western countries, Canada and Britain included. There is strong evidence to suggest that in both countries there has been a marked decline in confidence in public institutions, including Parliament and political parties, in civic engagement, and in voter turnout. Individuals may still be interested in pursuing political objectives, but they are more willing to do so through unconventional forms of political action or by joining single-issue groups rather than those with a collective agenda.[59] Individuals are also considerably less loyal to political parties than was the case forty or even twenty years ago.

The rise of market capitalism, particularly in the Thatcher-Reagan era but continuing to this day, has reinforced liberal values and the tendency of individuals to act in ways that 'reduce our ability to make collective choices.'[60] There is nothing to suggest that the pendulum is swinging away from a focus on the individual. Ten years after Tony Blair's Labour party came to power, a study revealed that a majority of U.K. citizens now believe that life 'is best improved by putting the individual first.' As the head of the research project explains, 'in 1997 ... almost 70 percent of our respondents opted for the community-first approach. Over the decade, we have seen a fast-moving shift towards people feeling more individualistic. Today, 52 percent feel looking after ourselves will best improve the quality of life.'[61]

It stands to reason that the shift favouring the attributes of individuals over those of the community should be felt in every corner of our political and administrative institutions. There is plenty of evidence, as the next chapters document, that this is indeed the reality in both Canada and Britain. Given that government and bureaucracy, as we noted in the opening paragraphs, are affected as much by 'mores in society as by cultural or sociological changes in society,' we now need to explore if values within the civil service have also changed.

6 Searching for Values

In his closing argument in the court case against Charles ('Chuck') Guité, a senior Canadian civil servant charged with five counts of fraud, the crown prosecutor insisted that the important 'message' that should come from the court was that 'public funds are sacred.'[1] Several private sector executives had already been found guilty of fraud in the case, but the crown prosecutor called for harsher penalties for Guité since, he argued, civil servants should be held to a higher standard because they are 'entrusted with public funds.'[2] The judge agreed and sent Guité to jail for forty months. The same judge had before convicted the private sector executives to eighteen and thirty months in jail.[3] The Guité conviction sent out another important message: civil servants appointed on the merit principle, and not just politicians and their political appointees, could be held to account for committing criminal and unethical acts.

Efforts to strengthen values and ethics in government throughout much of the Western world are not new. Indeed, as far back as 1854 the Northcote-Trevelyan report in Britain and, at the turn of the nineteenth century, the establishment of the Civil Service Commission in Canada were designed to promote high standards in government and to get rid of 'corruption.'[4] The goal then was to instil in government employees values that would provide the highest level of public service without discrimination or concern for personal interests or profit.[5]

Now we are back at it. What prompted the more recent efforts? To be sure, the attempted shift to public entrepreneurship by empowering civil servants is not without consequences. Civil servants have been told to contract out many government activities, to practise cost recovery, to think of citizens as customers, and to make performance pay work without clearly establishing what kind of performance is to be rewarded or even how to assess it. All of this implies a high degree of trust in the ethical judgment of individual civil servants. Centrally pre-scribed administrative rules and regulations provided civil servants with one major advantage: the basis on which to deny requests that did not square with specific requirements. The removal of centrally prescribed rules required some kind of accompanying approach to guide civil servants in their work, but politicians like Thatcher and Mulroney paid scant attention to this need.

The search has been on for some time to come up with measures to ensure probity in government operations, and it has given rise to lucra-tive consultant contracts and new career opportunities for civil ser-vants. A former Canadian auditor general summed it up well: 'over time, changes in government have made it clear that ensuring probity will increasingly rest on a strong foundation of values and ethics.'[6] He explained that 'increasing discretion' meant that civil servants now had to balance several 'equally valued courses of action,' hence the need to rely on a greater sense of values and ethics.[7] Britain, mean-while, has been updating a 'civil service code' ever since 1996 when it was first introduced.[8]

By the 1990s, civil servants operating under the Westminster-Whitehall model, if not elsewhere, became concerned that basic elements of the traditional bargain guiding their relations with politicians – political neutrality, loyalty, anonymity, and permanence – were slowly being redefined.[9] Some felt that there was a need to clarify and codify certain basic values and ethical standards to guide civil servants in their day-to-day work. This emphasis on the need for values began not long after central agencies decided to buy further into the notion that managers and front-line employees needed to be 'empowered' in order to make better decisions and to serve customers more effectively. The shift from a rules approach to a values approach required that someone in authority had to make explicit the values to be embraced.

The problem, at least as viewed by civil servants and their advisers, was largely at the political level. Kenneth Kernaghan explains that the 'misconduct of some politicians has not only damaged the public image of politicians in general, it has also damaged the image of public servants, since many citizens do not distinguish the actions of politi-cians from those of public servants.'[10] He adds that 'many of the ethics rules have been ad hoc responses to ethical offences by *politicians*, espe-cially in the conflict-of-interest sphere.'[11] It is interesting to note that governments in Britain, Australia, and New Zealand have all adopted a civil service code of conduct and that both Canada and Britain have produced several major initiatives in recent years to promote values and ethics in government, all with a focus on relations between ministers and civil servants. The thinking on the part of civil servants was that it would be wise somehow to create values that would set them apart from politicians or create their own values and ethics space in order to put some distance between themselves and the misconduct of some politicians.

In Canada, work on values began in earnest with the Public Service (PS) 2000 initiative. It will be recalled that PS 2000 was designed to streamline government decision making, cut red tape, and provide the necessary authority to let managers manage.[12] A committee of deputy ministers produced a report on 'Governing Values,' a report that was later picked up by a high-profile task force chaired by John Tait, a former deputy minister. The purpose of the 1996 task force report (entitled *A Strong Foundation* but commonly known as the Tait report), was 'to help the public service think about and, in some cases, rediscover and understand its basic values and recommit to and act on those values in all its work.'[13] At about the same time in Britain, the Nolan Committee on Standards in Public Life called for a code of public service conduct and ethics to restore 'respect for the ethical values inherent in the idea of public service.'[14] A Civil Service Code was subsequently introduced in 1996 based on a draft prepared by the Treasury and Civil Service Committee, the predecessor to the Select Committee on Public Administration.

Shifting Sands

There is an element of shifting sands in the approach taken to assist the Canadian civil service to 'rediscover and understand its basic values.' To be sure, honesty, probity, and fairness transcend time and remain constant core values. But other values, such as loyalty, impartiality, and anonymity are not so certain. The early reforms, from the Northcote-Trevelyan Commission in Britain and the Templeton Act in the United States to the establishment of a Civil Service Commission in Canada, sought to underpin important values and called for appointment through merit as determined by open competition; administrative neutrality in applying laws; a strong adherence to hierarchy; and deep respect for a chain of command in the decision-making structure.

Reformers of the first half of the last century attached a great deal of importance to establishing a politically neutral civil service. They also sought to protect democracy from the influence of special interests and special interest groups. They, too, embraced hierarchy in government departments and agencies, thus forcing the most important decisions up the chain.[15]

So what values needed to be rediscovered? Better yet, what problems surfaced in the 1980s and 1990s that could be solved or avoided in future by promoting a much stronger sense of values and ethics in government operations? There were several. There was a need to refine accountability requirements as managers gained more authority to manage human and financial resources. Civil servants in both Canada and Britain also became deeply concerned about charges of corruption and cronyism that were directed at the political class, and for good reason. In October 1994, the London *Guardian* reported that two members of Parliament had agreed to ask questions in Parliament in return for payments of cash – demonstrating a willingness to use their public offices to pursue private gain. The election of the Labour government in 1997 did not change things much, although those charges of corruption had been an important factor in the election. Shortly after coming to office, the government was also accused of 'cronyism' because of the appointment of friends and supporters to positions of responsibility. Some of the people appointed to these positions resigned when corrupt behaviour was exposed.[16] Farther into their mandate, Tony Blair and the Labour party were subjected to sustained attacks in the media for selling peerages to help finance election campaign costs. Worse still, the campaign contributions were in the form of loans so that they would not have to be made public.[17] Blair was the first serving prime minister to be questioned by police as part of a criminal investigation, and one of his advisers was arrested over what the media labelled the 'honours cover-up.'[18]

In Canada, a good number of journalists labelled the Mulroney years as the 'sleaze' era in Canadian politics. Few months went by without new charges being directed either at Mulroney himself or at his ministers.[19] Jean Chrétien's Liberals made 'sleaze' a key issue in the 1993 general election campaign and pledged to govern with integrity, insisting that 'if government is to play a positive role in society, as it must, honesty and integrity in our political institutions must be restored.'[20] Despite this promise, the Chrétien years were not much better, marked as they were by the high-profile Shawinigate and sponsorship scandals, both of which could be linked directly to the prime minister or his office.

Below the radar screen, civil servants and their hired consultants were busy packaging core values and ethical standards. There is little evidence to suggest that senior politicians took a strong interest in this work. Prime ministers and senior ministers in both Canada and Britain have had and continue to have their own agenda to pursue and, in both Ottawa and London, ministerial time is the scarcest of commodities. Still, politicians knew that at some point they would be able to issue a media release, hold a press conference, or deliver a major speech on values and ethics in government. In brief, they only saw positive things, politically at least, flowing out of such events, and they were not about to get in the way of a good thing.

Civil servants, however, in their efforts to define or rediscover values and ethical standards looked more to politicians than to their own institution. John Tait began his summary of the report by referring to the traditional bargain that governs the dealings of civil servants and the government of the day: he noted the professionalism of civil servants, their discretion and non-partisan loyalty, in return for which they gain anonymity so that they are not publicly accountable, as well as having security of tenure or lifetime employment.[21] The unstated but underlying message of the Tait report was that relations between ministers and civil servants needed to be clarified, if not updated. The goal was, in the words of an adviser to the Tait task force, to go beyond the 'ad hoc responses to ethical offences by politicians' that had characterized past approaches.[22]

The Tait report concentrated its message on 'four overlapping families of core public service values.' The first centred on 'democratic values.' The Tait report made the case that public service anonymity is designed to protect not only the neutrality of civil servants but also the authority of ministers, thus becoming a key democratic principle. It applauded the doctrine of ministerial responsibility, insisting that it, too, is designed to protect the authority of ministers. It considered the impact of new organizational forms on the doctrine, concluding that they need not involve any fundamental change in ministerial responsibility.[23] That said, it also reported a number of concerns among the civil servants the task force consulted, most notably that the doctrine had become 'unclear, outdated, just unreal or meaningless,' and called for 'clarifying' the responsibility of ministers as essential to promoting values and ethics in government. It was, however, not very forthcoming in pointing the way ahead. It simply pointed out that parliamentary government is inherently evolutionary. Still, the Office of the

Auditor General picked up this recommendation, agreeing with the Tait report's call to clarify 'the responsibility of ministers,' but adding that government should 'extend this clarification to the responsibility of officials who receive delegated authorities.'[24]

The report did have something to say about the civil service, describing it as 'an important national institution in the service of democracy.'[25] It applauded the 'non-partisan' nature of Canada's civil service and the merit principle. It argued that the notion of 'security of tenure' is based on a 'mistaken assumption.' It does not mean a guarantee of permanent or lifetime employment; rather, it means protection from partisan dismissal.[26] It was quite explicit on this point: 'The concept of a professional public service does not include or require a guarantee of lifetime employment,' adding, because it felt a need to do so, that 'a government is quite within its democratic rights to determine the size of the public service or its role.'[27] The report went on to slam 'bureaucratic patronage,' insisting that it is no 'more acceptable than partisan appointments' and that staffing based on merit is designed 'to preclude both the appearance and the reality of favouritism, whether internal or partisan.'[28] It added that the task force had 'heard from experts who observe that over the past two decades there has been a discernible shift in the public service appointment process to favour greater managerial discretion. We do not suggest this is a harmful trend in itself. But we do think that if it goes too far, without appropriate safeguards, it could undermine the institution it seeks to serve by creating the appearance, if not the reality, of bureaucratic patronage.'[29] Canada's civil service, the report insisted, can never enjoy the flexibility of private sector firms. There will always be a requirement for higher 'standards of transparency and due process.'[30] These then are the basic democratic values and accountability that the Canadian government would like to see all civil servants embrace with enthusiasm.

But this hardly constitutes the full story. The Tait report went on to contrast old values associated with traditional public administration with those associated with 'new public management' practices. It reminded civil servants that citizens are not customers but rather the 'bearers of rights and duties in a framework of community.'[31] It spoke about the difference in 'managing up' – the need to respond to the wishes of ministers – and 'managing down' – looking down to employees and the quality of the organization and its performance. It went on to stress the challenge of demonstrating leadership in 'a time of change,' the need to promote decency, humanity, fairness, and ethical values, including integrity, honesty, probity, prudence, equity, and discretion. It concluded with a call for a 'new moral contract between the public service, the government, and the Parliament of Canada.'[32] It outlined a process to develop such a contract but offered little in terms of substance or how the contract should take shape.[33]

The Canadian government liked what it saw in the Tait report. It responded by establishing in 1999 an 'Office of Values and Ethics' in the Treasury Board Secretariat and later decided to re-issue the Tait report and to appoint two deputy ministers as 'co-champions' for promoting values and ethics in government. The next year, the clerk of the privy council and secretary to the cabinet stressed the importance of public service values in his annual report to the prime minister on the state of the Public Service of Canada, and the government's training centre for senior civil servants launched a values and ethics management education initiative.[34]

In 2003 the government released a 'Statement of Public Service Values and Ethics,' designed to 'guide and support public servants in all their professional activities.'[35] It is clear that the statement was based largely on the Tait report. The statement was also built around an 'overlapping' framework of public service values, including 'democratic, professional, ethical and people values.' It declared that the code was now a 'policy of the Government of Canada.' In 2003 the government declared its intention to incorporate it into its new *Values and Ethics Code for the Public Service.* In 2005 the government committed to adopting a new *Charter of Values of Public Service* based, in large part, on the Tait report.[36]

There is no need to list all the values outlined in the statement. The ones most relevant to our purpose are the following: civil servants shall support both individual and collective ministerial accountability; civil servants shall endeavour to ensure the proper, effective, and efficient use of public money; civil servants shall perform their duties and arrange their private affairs so that public confidence and trust in the integrity, objectivity, and impartiality of government are conserved and enhanced; civil servants shall act at all times in a manner that will bear the closest public scrutiny and make decisions in the public interest; civil servants shall ensure that appointments are based on merit; civil servants shall give honest and impartial advice and make all information relevant to a decision available to ministers.[37]

The several 'values' initiatives, however, have not been without their critics both outside and inside government. Some outside government have argued that the government should be very careful in replacing a 'rules approach' with a 'values approach,'[38] making the point that, if the role of the civil service is limited to supporting and serving the government of the day, then a shift away from a rule-based approach could well have important implications. Values, the argument goes, operate on a higher level of abstraction than do rules and regulations.[39] Others pointed out that the 2003 statement contained far too many values, including some that could well contradict each other, notably democratic versus professional values. John Langford, for example, wrote about the 'sheer number of values,' which would enable civil servants to 'value shop,' looking for the ones that suit their most immediate purpose.[40] Peter Aucoin gave the Tait report a positive review but then sought to reduce the number of values to a more manageable and coherent list.[41]

Some senior civil servants, however, fully supported the initiatives. First Jocelyne Bourgon, then Mel Cappe, and later Alex Himelfarb – all three former clerks of the privy council and secretaries of the cabinet – wrote about the importance of the initiatives in their annual reports to the prime minister on the state of the public service. Bourgon, for example, described the Tait report as an 'honest dialogue' that employed an 'inductive approach' that gave it a 'quality of authenticity.'[42] Mel Cappe wrote that 'as public servants, we rely on the four sets of values (as outlined by Tait) to inform and guide us'[43] and added that 'it may be more important to put our values into action than into words.'[44] For his part, Alex Himelfarb wrote that 'values and ethics are the immutable core of the Public Service. Our dedication to values and ethics must be unassailable and unwavering. We must exemplify these values, we must practice them at the highest possible level.'[45] Cappe reminded senior managers that everything they do 'is judged by their employees. If senior managers want to lead effectively, they have to start with promoting values.'[46]

Other civil servants, however, have been less forthcoming. The Treasury Board Secretariat, a strong supporter of the various values initiatives, told deputy ministers in 2000 that most civil servants had not even heard of the Tait report and were not aware of discussions related to it. A wide-ranging consultation process by the auditor general with 'middle managers' in the late 1990s revealed that 'on values and ethics there is a continuing cynicism, embitterment and lack of trust.'[47] A Treasury Board-sponsored survey of civil servants in 1999 revealed a world that did not resonate well with the values outlined in the Tait report. The survey reported, for example, that a significant number of civil servants strongly or mostly agreed that they could not explain to others the values of their department, that they did not have a fair chance of getting promoted, that they could not disagree with their supervisor without reprisal, or that senior management would not try to resolve concerns raised in the survey.[48]

Others spoke about a 'substantial disconnect' between what senior managers in Ottawa say and the way most civil servants 'struggle to make ethical decisions.'[49] Clerks of the privy council, deputy ministers as champions of values, and task force reports can say all they want about the importance of values, but that does not create honesty or probity or ensure that civil servants regard public funds as sacred.

It is more than ironic that, as task force members were meeting to discuss values and ethics in government, as consultants were being hired to assist them in their work, as deputy ministers were being appointed to promote values, as clerks were stressing the importance of values, as the word spread that the 'misconduct of some politicians ... had damaged the image of public servants,' and as his own department launched an ambitious values exercise of its own, Chuck Guité, a career official, was, in the words of the auditor general, 'breaking every rule in the book.' Yet his job description, approved by his deputy minister in 1997, called for a capacity 'for quick action and cutting red tape.'[50]

But that is hardly all. A senior career official at Health Canada was caught setting up a fraudulent scheme with Aboriginal leaders to defraud the government of millions of dollars. Paul Cochrane, an assistant deputy minister, was convicted of fraud and sentenced to one year in jail for accepting $200,000 in 'gifts' between 1994 and 2000 after giving preferential treatment in granting about $70 million to a foundation that had 'a history of highly questionable financial practices.'[51] Another former Health Canada official, Patrick Nottingham, pleaded guilty in November 2005 to fraud for his role in funding an Aboriginal treatment centre.[52] Yet another official, at National Defence, Paul Champagne, was submitting false invoices for information technologies and related services and was later charged with fraud and money laundering. The minister announced that Champagne was implicated in 'a very sophisticated criminal scheme' and that steps had to be taken to recover '$160 million after discovering a massive fraud in computer contracts.' Champagne replied that he simply followed private sector practices in getting the job done and compared himself to 'Wal-Mart,' insisting that his style did not fit the bureaucratic culture.'[53] However, he later 'pleaded guilty to two breach of trust and fraud charges.'[54] Five officials in the Department of Immigration in the Toronto regional office were operating a payback scheme for approving the applications of new Canadians. The officials, including a senior manager, were charged in 2004 with 'conspiracy to commit fraud, breach of trust, fraud upon the government and various charges' after it was learned that they operated a scheme under which bribes, ranging from $4,000 to $25,000, were paid in exchange for helping applicants secure permanent resident status in Canada.[55] A former passport examination officer pleaded guilty in May 2007 to running a scam that allowed non-Canadians to obtain Canadian passports as a result of documents that he falsified between 2003 and 2004.[56]

An audit at the Department of Fisheries and Oceans in 2005 'uncovered rule-breaking by civil servants,' including 'forbidden free travel for spouses.' Civil servants also habitually booked high-priced air fares, each costing on average $5,000 or more per flight. This enabled them to receive more air miles to secure free flights.[57] A federal civil servant was sentenced to five and a half years in prison in 2005 for breach of trust and for dealing in blank Canadian passports. Some 246 blank Canadian passports were stolen and then sold for $1,000.[58] A high-ranking Canadian diplomat was caught recruiting Canadians in Egypt to spy on a Saudi prince and princess. By the time Canadian security officials were informed of this, the diplomat had retired in Saudi Arabia 'and could not be disciplined.'[59]

The government was forced to cancel a contract with a moving and trucking firm after it was discovered that civil servants who oversaw the review process received free golf games and that one who evaluated the bids had accepted a Caribbean cruise with a vice-president from the winning firm.[60] Officials in the Department of Public Works and Government Services (PWGS) were caught claiming too much overtime. A series of 'unusual claims were processed without challenge,' including one that claimed 61.5 overtime hours in one week, which meant that the employee had worked 99 hours that week or more than 14 hours a day for seven days. The government has a policy that strictly limits the number of hours an employee may work each week to 48, unless there are exceptional circumstances, which should be documented. The claims were processed without explanation.[61] Leaving aside the sponsorship scandal, politicians were not involved in any of these cases. There have been more such cases in recent years. Moreover, it is probably safe to assume that there are similar cases that have not been uncovered or have not been made public.

Several years after the values exercise and after two champions were appointed inside government to give meaning to it, the RCMP laid criminal charges against Serge Nadeau, a senior Finance official. The RCMP alleged that Nadeau, general director of tax policy, 'used confidential Government of Canada information for the purchase of securities which gave him a personal benefit.'[62] It will be recalled that the value of income trusts and some dividend paying companies rose sharply in 2005, hours before the then minister of finance, Ralph Goodale, announced that the government would not tax income trusts as some had feared. Some opposition MPs, playing more to the rituals of accountability under Westminster-style parliamentary government than anything else, jumped on the opportunity and called on Goodale to resign. In announcing the charges against Nadeau, the RCMP declared that no charges would be laid against elected politicians or any of the political staffers.[63]

In the case of Guité, at least, had it not been for a journalist working on a hunch, a tip, and an access to information request, Canadians would probably never have known about the sponsorship scandal, and Guité would have been enjoying his retirement in Arizona rather than serving a jail sentence. Senior departmental officials told the court that when the first access to information request on the sponsorship initiative came in, it plunged the department into a state of 'crisis.'[64] Access to information has enabled the media and others to turn their attention to civil servants, not just to politicians. In response to criticisms that civil servants were spending too much on hospitality and travel – including George Radwanski, the privacy commissioner, who spent $500,000 over a two-year period, staying at expensive hotels, travelling first class, and eating extravagant meals – the government in 2004 directed all senior managers to post their travel expenses on their departmental websites. As a result, two of Ottawa's most renowned restaurants – Café Henry Burger and Clair de Lune – closed their doors. The owner of one said that the moment hospitality claims had to be disclosed on the Internet, 'they simply didn't come anymore.' Another reported: 'It wasn't necessarily the politicians, but it was the top civil servants that stopped coming.'[65]

Shortly after Parliament passed Harper's 'Accountability Act,' word began to circulate in Ottawa that a number of senior civil servants were 'out looking for jobs outside of government.' One of the main reasons was the act's 'cooling off period' banning former civil servants from lobbying for five years. Pat Martin, a member of Parliament and a key supporter of the act, argued that 'if there's that many people who had it in mind that they would sell their connections post-tenure with the public service, it just reinforces the need for reform and the changes that were made.' He added that he would be disappointed if more than a few senior civil servants 'would put their own interests ahead of the best interests of the public service.'[66]

The above hardly squares with the claim that flowed from the various values and ethics initiatives that the problem that required attention had everything to do with elected politicians, not with civil servants. Access to information legislation, if nothing else, has revealed that the challenge of promoting values and ethics does not belong exclusively to elected politicians. Some civil servants have acknowledged this to be so, and one had this to say: 'The bottom line here is that senior officials starting with the Clerk do not walk the talk. It is a classic case of do as I say, not as I do.' He went on to point out that the last four clerks were able to secure choice appointments all made by the prime minister. One was appointed to head a crown corporation that was subsequently privatized. The other three secured Canada's best ambassadorial appointments, in London, Paris, and Rome.[67]

Establishing a Code

The British government also set up a number of 'values' initiatives in response to growing concerns that, in the words of the Public Accounts Committee in 1994, government was witnessing 'a departure from the standards of public conduct which have mainly been established during the past 140 years.'[68] It will be recalled that a Ministry of Defence official was sentenced in 1994 to four years in prison for taking at least £1.5 million in bribes from firms with whom he had placed contracts, and in the same year the *Guardian* broke a story that two members of Parliament had agreed to ask questions in Parliament in return for cash payments.[69] Prime Minister John Major asked Lord Nolan to chair a committee to 'examine current concerns about standards of conduct of all holders of public office' and later described the work of the committee as a 'running authority – an ethical workshop called in to do running repairs.'[70]

The Nolan Committee tabled its first report in 1995 and outlined the qualities expected from all holders of public office: selflessness (pursue the public interest, not gain for self, family, or friends), integrity, objectivity, accountability, openness, honesty, and leadership. It also had something to say about the relationship between ministers and civil servants, insisting that political interference 'in the pay and promotion of individuals must be avoided' and that 'more needs to be done' to ensure that civil servants are aware of the standards of conduct required in the public sector.[71]

A year later the British government introduced a Civil Service Code, and three years after that it introduced a Vision and Values Statement. As in Canada, the code speaks to many values but stresses the importance of democratic and ethical ones. (Unlike in Canada, the code does not stress professional values.) As in Canada, the code is mainly concerned with relations between ministers and civil servants. It reads, 'The constitutional and practical role of the Civil Service is, with integrity, honesty, impartiality and objectivity, to assist the duly Constituted Government ... in formulating their policies, carrying out decisions and in administering public services for which they are responsible.'[72] The code was amended in 1999 but only to take devolution into account.

In the summer of 2005, Baroness Usha Prashar, then first civil service commissioner, chaired a working group of permanent secretaries to review the purpose and effectiveness of the Civil Service Code. The group was given a broad mandate to review its principles and values and to determine whether the code itself should be revised. The group decided that, while the code was very important in reinforcing core values, it should be written in more readable or everyday language. The redrafted code appeared on 27 January 2006, together with a consultation process to secure the views of rank-and-file civil servants.

The new code borrows heavily from the old. It calls on the civil service to support 'the Government of the day in formulating and implementing policies and in the delivery of public services' and adds that 'civil servants are appointed on merit.' It lays down the civil service's core values: 'integrity, honesty, objectivity and impartiality.' It calls on civil servants to carry out their responsibilities 'in a way that is fair, just and equitable,' to 'maintain political impartiality,' to 'implement decisions conscientiously,' and not to 'misuse' their 'official position or information' to further their personal interest.[73]

About 2,100 civil servants responded to the revised code through the consultation process. The response, by any standards, was modest. Baroness Prashar observed that she never fails to 'be amazed at the lack of knowledge by civil servants of the Code, not just as a document to which they may turn when things go wrong, but as a document that sets out succinctly and clearly ethical standards they all are expected to apply in going about their daily work.'[74] The great majority of those who responded reported that they were aware of the code's existence and had actually read it (87 per cent of the respondents). When asked if the code had made a difference in how they did their job, 76 per cent said no. When asked if they would be happy to raise concerns about the code with their line manager, 1,637 said yes and 351 said no; with respect to their permanent secretaries, 972 said yes while 940 said no.[75]

Some of the respondents disagreed with the decision to remove from the code the notion that 'civil servants are servants of the Crown.' One argued that 'it is important to me that the line of responsibility runs through to the Crown and nowhere else so that we can continue to be independent and impartial.' Others maintained that the concept of 'servants of the crown' is important because it recognizes their place within the constitution of the civil service and 'its wider relationships, including to Parliament – it has never been simply a creature of the Government of the day.' Yet one respondent made it clear that civil servants are accountable for their actions 'to the elected government, and it is they who are accountable to the public, not us.'[76] The government responded by adding a footnote to the code that reads: 'Constitutionally, all civil servants are servants of the Crown. The Crown's executive powers are exercised by the Government.'[77]

The code makes for interesting reading, but, as in Canada, the challenge is its relevance when the rubber meets the road in the day-to-day work of civil servants. In addition, the code is a one-way street – it does not deal with the obligations ministers have towards civil servants.

The ministerial code in Britain, first made public in 1992, and revised on several occasions since, establishes rules for ministers. The latest revisions deal with access to information requirements. It makes it clear that 'ministers have a duty to Parliament to account and be held to account,' that ministers 'give accurate and truthful information to Parliament,' and be as 'open as possible with Parliament and the public.' The code deals with the relationship with civil servants, and it is worth quoting from it at some length, including what it has to say about the role of the accounting officer, which has not always been properly understood in Canada. It reads: 'Ministers have a duty to give fair consideration and due weight to informed and impartial advice from civil servants, as well as to other considerations and advice, in reaching policy decisions; a duty to uphold the political impartiality of the Civil Service, and not to ask civil servants to act in any way which would conflict with the Civil Service Code; a duty to ensure that influence over appointments is not abused for partisan purposes.' With respect to the accounting officer concept, it explains that 'The essence of the role is a *personal* responsibility for the propriety and regularity of the public finances for which he or she is responsible; for keeping proper accounts; for the avoidance of waste and extravagance; and for the efficient and effective use of resources. Accounting Officers answer personally to the Committee of Public Accounts on these matters, within the framework of Ministerial accountability to Parliament for the policies, actions and conduct of their Departments.'[78]

The ministerial code deals with another issue of strong interest to civil servants – the role of special advisers. It provides for the appointment of two special advisers by ministers who regularly attend cabinet. The purpose is to add a 'political dimension' to the advice already available to ministers, as well as to give ministers access to distinguished experts. The code maintains that this serves to reinforce 'the political impartiality' of the civil service 'by distinguishing the source of political advice and support.'[79] Whatever the purpose, the number of special advisers has increased substantially in recent years. There were thirty-eight special advisers in 1997, and today there are more than eighty.

The Cabinet Office has also published a code of conduct for special advisers. It explains that special advisers operate where government and the government party overlap and where it would be inappropriate for civil servants to be involved. The code lays out in some detail the responsibilities of special advisers, including playing a 'deviling' role for the minister and contributing to policy planning within departments. It calls on special advisers to work closely with career civil servants and reports that they can 'convey to officials ministers' views.'[80]

The notion of writing down how ministers, their political advisers, and civil servants should go about their work and the values they should embrace does not easily square with Westminster-Whitehall traditions. Lord Butler, former cabinet secretary, made clear his views on the ministerial code when he wrote that it was neither 'comprehensive nor absolute. Ministers are accountable to Parliament, not a piece of paper.'[81] Baroness Prashar writes that the government has long favoured a Civil Service Act, but has never got around to it because it has not been able to secure legislative time. Perhaps, she asks, the real reason is that the government sees little need to take up precious legislation time enacting into law such self-evident statements as that civil servants should conduct themselves with integrity.[82] There has been ongoing discussion about the need for a Civil Service Act in Britain for well over ten years, but nothing has come of it. David Cameron's Conservative party, much as Labour did in 1997, has pledged to introduce legislation to Parliament, if elected.

Civil servants may also be hesitant to pursue a complaint under the code, an option described by Richard Wilson, another former secretary to the cabinet, as a most difficult option to pursue.[83] The complaint has to go through the complainant's department, making it awkward for the civil servant who believes that he or she has been asked to break the code. The civil servant may well conclude that pursuing an issue under the code may be too risky a career move and either keep silent or take revenge by leaking damaging information.

Yet another former secretary to the cabinet, Andrew Turnbull, has been less than enthusiastic about a Civil Service Act. He acknowledged that he had been 'accused of not taking values seriously enough, as evidenced by the fact that I have not seen a Civil Service Act as a priority.' He added, 'I have always thought that the proponents of a Civil Service Act had unrealistic expectations of what it would achieve.' He explained that problems between ministers and civil servants arise much more often over behaviour and values than over rules and enforcement.[84]

Dr David Kelly opted to leak information rather than turn to the Civil Service Code when he believed that the government was embellishing the dossier in claiming that Iraq had weapons of mass destruction. We will, of course, never know why Kelly turned to the media rather than to the code to make his accusation that the government was being less than truthful. We do not even know if he was very familiar with the code. What we do know is that he was deeply troubled by developments in the dossier and decided to talk to the media.[85] This led to stories in the media, notably the BBC, that the government had 'sexed up' a report into Iraq's weapons of mass destruction. Kelly may well have considered several options: to remain silent, resign, go public, or leak information. He very clearly had problems with the first option, and history shows that precious few career officials will choose to resign. Going public is also very rarely done, because of the potential impact on one's career and because, traditionally, civil servants have been highly reluctant to engage in a public debate.

Sending Out Mixed Signals

What were rank-and-file civil servants in Canada to make of the clerks' message that 'everything senior managers do is judged by their employees,' while they could see them taking care of their personal interests as they planned for the day when they were no longer clerks? Highly generous pension plans for deputy ministers are especially designed in the Weberian tradition so that they need not pursue personal interests. But that was hardly the only mixed signal.[86] What were rank-and-file civil servants in Britain to make of the proposed Civil Service Act, designed to establish a distinct administrative place for the civil service, while more than one secretary to the cabinet, the top civil servant, disdained any such initiative?

Officials in both countries were told to emulate private sector management techniques and to respond to customers and their needs. Some sought to do this but soon realized that their departmental or program budgets were not determined or even significantly influenced by the actions or views of their customers. Government, leaving aside the establishment of new executive units and special agencies and the measures designed to empower managers and their staff, continued to operate as before when it came to securing resources and accountability. Expenditure budgets were still determined by departmental pull and central agency push back. There were no market forces to determine the size of an expenditure budget, nor was it determined by customer feedback. Yet the talk about transforming the public sector to be more like the private sector has led civil servants to claim that they ought to be treated like their private sector counterparts. They continue to look to the salaries of private sector executives to determine their own salaries, rather than, for instance, the not-for-profit sector or the universities.

The new approach, however, has not been without important consequences for public administration. Public sector managers were told to get on with it, get things done, manage better, and be more responsive to the wishes of both politicians and customers. There was no model to accompany the change, however; more importantly, there were no fundamental changes to accountability requirements. Managers were essentially left to introduce change by 'groping along' while making sure not to get their ministers in trouble.[87]

In the absence of a new model or any fundamental changes in their relations with politicians, senior officials sought to strengthen values as the means to ensure probity in government. In doing so, however, they viewed politicians rather than themselves or their own institutions as the problem or the potential problem. They may well have misdiagnosed the patient. The Office of the Auditor General in Canada carried out a study in 2004 of major management problems and their causes. The office identified six root causes of management problems in government: losing sight of fundamental principles; pressure to get the job done that compromises program integrity; failure to intervene to correct or prevent problems; a lack of consequences for inadequate management; a lack of organizational capacity to deal with risks; and unclear accountability.[88] The study consulted senior government managers, and what they had to say was hardly positive. The interviewees reported that 'There is no institutionalized process: nothing happens at the Cabinet level, nobody asked what happened to business plans'; 'Gross mismanagement is being overlooked; there is an internal crisis'; 'There are no consequences for failure or for disregard of regulations'; 'There is not much of an early warning system and nobody does anything about the problem'; and 'Many contractors per year default, but nothing is done about it.'[89]

Values and ethics exercises do not seem to address these matters. They were perceived in the words of one deputy minister in Ottawa as 'a bit too academic, a bit too far away from real politics and real decisions, to have much relevance.'[90] One observer went further, saying 'all these ethics and values exercises are just pieces of paper.'[91] The challenge, of course, is how to hold someone accountable under an ethics and values package?

Weber's model, with its emphasis on hierarchy, was designed for real politics and for making decisions in an impartial manner. The key element was 'the office,' and the duties and powers of the office were defined by laws. Bureaucracy in Weber's world was strong in ensuring adherence to the law, rules, and regulations. There was little need for the soft side of public administration – statements of values and ethics. Requirements were built into the model; if something went astray, one could simply reach down the hierarchical organization and determine with a degree of certainty what had gone wrong and why. In a simple hierarchical world, it was relatively easy to determine why things had gone wrong and who was responsible.

Real Politics, Real Decisions

The cry to let managers manage, the efforts to emulate private sector management practices, the pressure to make quick decisions in a digital world, and the fallout from bureaucracy bashing have all served to place considerable strain on values and ethics in government. An important element of Chuck Guité's job description, as head of the sponsorship program, was to 'cut red tape' and to make things happen for his political masters. He won promotion after promotion, presumably through the merit principle, and his annual performance evaluation was always very positive. Evidence before the Gomery Commission suggested that Guité had the support of key players in the Prime Minister's Office and his minister's office and of senior civil servants in his department and central agencies.

A former senior federal government official insists that when it comes to values and ethics much depends on the 'tone and the talk of the Prime Minister and Clerk.' He explains that under Chrétien there was too much 'winking and nodding and turning a blind eye.'[92] Elected politicians have significantly fewer opportunities for 'winking and nodding and turning a blind eye' when centralized and tight administrative and financial policies are in place. Ministers can also rely upon government-wide policies and standards of management policed by central agencies to ensure that civil servants comply with well-known administrative requirements. Empowering managers and then relying, at least in part, on a values statement to guide the relationship between politicians and civil servants and to deliver programs is not without potential problems, especially in Westminster-style parliamentary governments.

Senior civil servants in both Canada and Britain continue to make the case that, whether they operate at the highest levels or at the program delivery level, they have no status separate from the government of the day or from the prime minister and ministers. This, combined with the desire of politicians to regain the upper hand in their dealings with bureaucracy in the post-*Yes, Minister* era, has changed the relationship between politicians and civil servants and the way in which civil servants go about their work. Today, the ability to make things happen, to generate administrative energy, and to respond with enthusiasm to the political agenda are all valued skills in the upper echelons of the civil service. A British official put it succinctly when he observed, 'What my job is about is delivering the thing I am told to deliver. It is not my job to write the policy, to believe the policy, to care about the substance of policy ... I am not committed to what I am delivering, I am committed to delivering.'[93] Chuck Guité made a similar point in his defence before the Gomery Commission and in court.

There is also evidence to suggest that civil servants in both Canada and Britain are much more responsive to the political wishes of prime ministers and ministers than they were some forty years ago. For one thing, bureaucracy bashing has had an impact, and the civil service as an institution has lost self-confidence. For another, politicians are today expecting different things from civil servants. As one senior official with the Privy Council Office explains, 'My job here is to fall on hand grenades. Our role here is to manage problems so that they do not become unmanageable political crises.'[94] Given access to information requirements and the power of the media, the need to protect the government and its ministers from what officials describe as 'visible' and 'invisible' errors has come to dominate the work of senior civil servants. Visible errors are those that make it to the front page of newspapers or that surface in Question Period and in access to information requests. Invisible errors are said to be much more common, and they are only invisible because people outside government, most notably the media, have not uncovered them or, if they have, have not made an issue of them. To manage visible and invisible errors is time consuming and takes civil servants more into the territory of good news management and positive press releases than that of good public policies and exemplary administration.

In speaking about the government's growing tendency to focus its efforts on securing favourable media coverage, Robin Butler argued that 'There is too much emphasis on selling, there is too much central control and there is too little of what I would describe as reasoned deliberation which brings in all the arguments.' He went on to say that 'The Cabinet, now, and I don't think there is any secret about this, doesn't make decisions. It isn't wise to listen only to special advisors, and not to listen to fuddy-duddy civil servants, who may produce boringly inconvenient arguments.'[95]

A good number of fuddy-duddy civil servants are also very ambitious, and the road to the top requires networking skills and knowing how to manage political crises. The competence of senior government officials is often in the eye of the beholder, and this explains in part why governments have not been able to make 'pay for performance' schemes work effectively. The problem, simply stated, is how to

determine if a government department has had a particularly successful year. It depends on how one defines 'successful.' To some, a substantial downsizing of both programs and staff is a sign of success,
while to others it may be a sign that the department was unable to
protect itself from spending cuts. The list of pros and cons goes on.
Moreover, even if one is able to state that a department has had a particularly successful year, who is to tell who or what was largely
responsible? Was it the minister, the deputy minister, the permanent
secretary, lack of media attention, political circumstances outside the
control of the department, pressure from interest groups, or what?

Though there is no objective and widely recognized measure to
determine the performance of senior officials, there is one development that can quickly jolt the career of permanent heads of departments and other senior civil servants who aspire to greater things. A
'screw-up' that reaches the media and makes the minister look bad or
not in control, or makes the department look incompetent, can have
grave consequences for those who aspire to reach the top in the civil
service. Civil servants who have learned the art of lying low and not
drawing attention to themselves or to their units from either the media
or politicians will survive and flourish.

Ambitious civil servants know that what matters to their political
masters is an ability to network, to make things happen, and to help in
news management. Christopher Foster writes that the most important
lesson from the Hutton inquiry was that news management on behalf
of government *was* government. It was to a very large extent how 'the
prime minister and those around him and therefore as a consequence
how many others spent their time.'[96] What this suggests is that there is
a convergence of skills between the elected politicians and senior levels
in the civil service. If there is a convergence of skills, there may well
also be a convergence of values.

Boundaries between the political and administrative worlds have
collapsed, particularly when dealing with the media. Given that the
media are increasingly pervasive and capable of going virtually anywhere in government, there is less and less administrative space that
belongs to civil servants. Under Blair, partisan advisers, including his
principal adviser on media and communications, were empowered to
give instructions to permanent civil servants.

Boundaries between the public and private sectors have also become
more porous, and the same can be said about values. The public sectors
in both Canada and Britain have become fragmented. The shift to

make-or-buy policies, to executive units or special agencies, and to policy by networks has forced civil servants to come in contact with outsiders who may well have different values from their own.

The introduction of performance pay schemes is also not without potential implications for public sector values. It promotes economic self-interest. Julian LeGrand points to this in his work on motivation, agency, and public policy. He says that it is 'difficult, if not impossible' to construct a viable measuring and monitoring system to indicate better performance.[97] Performance pay schemes also raise questions about how standards can be maintained and invite 'gaming' to ensure that targets are met so that senior civil servants can secure larger bonuses. It will be recalled that Weber held that fixed salaries were a defining characteristic of modern bureaucracy.

Values Revisited

Peter Aucoin writes that while there may not have been a golden era in the Canadian public service, there was a time when the respect for the civil service was grounded not just on respect for authority but 'first and foremost, on public confidence in the values that were seen to be embedded in the public service and thus guiding its behaviour ... we clearly lost sight of these core values over the past two or three decades.'[98] As confidence waned in the public sector, both elected politicians and senior civil servants rejected traditional civil service values and decided, in the words of the Tait report, to drape 'the public service in the borrowed clothes of the market and of private enterprise.'[99]

Politicians also sought to redefine their relationship with civil servants. Civil servants were to become more responsive on policy issues and partners in dealing with a new, more intrusive media. Policy now needs to be shaped by networks of government departments, agencies, and interested parties rather than by departmental officials working with their ministers. Prime ministers have sought to manage by centralizing into their own offices the issues, both large and small, that matter to them. As for the rest, civil servants are expected to keep the media quiet.

The Canadian and British governments have responded to these developments by launching exercises in values and ethics. Leaving aside the introduction of the accounting officer concept in Canada, they have left virtually intact the accountability relationship between ministers and civil servants. However, the accounting officer concept in Canada has been introduced *à contre coeur* with two sets of rules competing with one another. In addition, the underlying assumption in the exercises in both countries has been that if there is a values and ethics problem that needs fixing, the problem lies for the most part with politicians. Yet there is plenty of evidence to suggest that the problem extends to the civil service. Even when a problem originated at the political level, as with the sponsorship scandal in Canada, civil servants like Chuck Guité acted as accomplices rather than as checks against wrongdoing, and the responsible deputy minister turned a blind eye to the developments.

The desire to strengthen values and ethics in government faces further challenges. It has to accommodate a shift to private sector management instruments and requirements. It has to accommodate a growing number of voices from both within and outside government clamouring for a say or for an oversight role of some kind in how policies are shaped and decisions are struck in government departments and agencies. The next chapter explores this topic.

7 Voices Everywhere

The private sector pursues profit and market share while the public sector deals with voices. The pursuit of profits and market shares is straightforward, easy to understand, and easy to assess. It has stood the test of time. Voices, however, are anything but straightforward. In recent years, they have also both multiplied and become much more demanding. Indeed, we have witnessed a veritable explosion in the number of voices, their purpose, and their approaches to being heard.

Albert Hirschman, in his influential book *Exit, Voice and Loyalty*, outlined ways to register dissatisfaction with an organization – one is to quit (exit), another is to agitate (voice), and yet another is loyalty, which enables voice to play its proper role.[1] Hirschman saw voice as the attempt to change from within, to influence an institution rather than to escape from it. Its relevance traditionally has been to government: a customer can exit a private firm, for example, by simply walking out of a store or selling shares in the firm, if dissatisfied, but a citizen can hardly escape government. Voices can take many forms – voting; joining a political party, an association, or a protest group; engaging in a parliamentary debate; and so on. In brief, then, the private sector has a bottom line that is easily determined. Government has an elusive bottom line. It involves voices that give life to debates, conflicts, contradictions, and tensions.

The purpose of this chapter is to consider recent developments in how citizens, businesses, interest groups, and others voice their views to influence government and to express their concerns. The chapter makes the case that voices today are far more numerous and better informed and considerably less deferential than they were forty years ago. Voices are now everywhere, including within government itself, all trying to be heard, all convinced of their importance, and all having access to resources and new, powerful instruments that enable them to be heard. In addition, governments today function on a much more rapid time scale than at any time in the past: solutions are expected in days and weeks, not months or years, and responses to issues emerging in the media are expected in minutes, not days.

Advice from Everywhere

Andrew Turnbull, the retiring cabinet secretary in the British government, spoke about the tremendous diversity of sources of advice now available to government: 'We no longer claim a monopoly over policy advice. Indeed, we welcome the fact that we are much more open to ideas from think-tanks, consultancies, governments abroad, special advisers and frontline practitioners.'[2] Bureaucracy, over the years, has not been known to welcome outside advice, and it is difficult to imagine that it would do so today.[3] However, it no longer has choice in the matter, since no government today can operate as a closed shop.

Turnbull is right in suggesting that advice, welcomed or not, now comes from many quarters and that bureaucracy has had little choice but to adapt. Indeed, boundaries within government, between governments, between government and the private sector, and between government and citizens are collapsing so that the space politicians and career officials once occupied in relative isolation has been opened up. In many instances, the changes have been subtle and, when taken in isolation, minor, so that on the surface at least, things may still resemble what existed some thirty or forty years ago. However, when one adds all these changes up, they take us into new territory.

Turnbull explains that governments must now 'engage with a variety of partners' and that he was 'actively promoting the philosophy of what matters is what works.'[4] What works requires a much more collaborative approach than in the past, and different skills. What works may well threaten the traditional and fundamental aspects of the machinery of government: boundaries and hierarchy. Turnbull insists that governments must now push things down and out of government and provide a 'greater voice for users.'[5]

The establishment of boundaries to define responsibilities was central to the development of our political and administrative institutions. Hierarchical organization, departmentalization, division of labour, specialization, division of responsibility, the application of the merit principle, specific responsibilities assigned to every position in the civil service, and the doctrine of ministerial responsibility – all these are designed to establish organizational boundaries. Boundaries serve many purposes. They establish who has legitimate access to certain decision-making arenas, as well as departmental mandates and who is responsible for what. They enable those at senior levels to exercise control and to hold subordinates to account for their decisions and activities.

Hierarchy is also an important feature of the machinery of government. Government agencies and departments have historically been organized in a defined hierarchy of offices with clear lines of authority. John Stuart Mill argued more than 125 years ago in his *Considerations on Representative Government* that responsibility is best provided and the work best done if all the functions of a similar subject 'be allocated to single departments.'[6] This notion has guided the development of the machinery of government in both Canada and Britain from the very beginning. For example, a Department of Agriculture was established in 1867 at the time Canada was born. To be sure, the department was small, employing only twenty-seven people. But it had a clear responsibility for the sector. In this sense, the government defined an organizational space, labelled it agriculture, and housed in one department all responsibilities for the sector.

Government departments have been and continue to be organized along such lines. They remain hierarchical, and they have some units responsible for program delivery, others for policy, still others for financial management, and so on. Units and officials in the department in turn are organized hierarchically, with boxes laid out on an organizational chart and with a chain of command running from the minister through the deputy head to the lowest level of official.[7] In this sense, the machinery of government also defines a specific space for every unit and for every civil servant. Departmental units are assigned responsibilities in the organizational charts, as are civil servants through job descriptions.

Much as in the military (which provided the model), hierarchy establishes lines of authority for the transmission of commands and allows a 'calculability of results for those in positions of authority.' It also provides the 'governed' with a clear line for appealing 'the decision of a lower office to the corresponding superior authority' and, as Mill argued, enables a variety of activities to be brought together in one organization.[8] It therefore comes as no surprise that, as in Britain, Canada until recently added new activities and new offices to existing departmental structures or in agencies tied to line departments. This system has served the Anglo-American democracies over the past 100 years with a remarkable degree of stability. Finally, hierarchy enables a minister, who is 'blameable' for both policy and administration under the principle of ministerial responsibility, to reach down into the bureaucracy to secure an explanation for and to find solutions to problems.[9] One can legitimately ask, without hierarchy, what is left of bureaucracy?

The machinery of government was designed around the departmental structure. J.E. Hodgetts argues that the most important legacy of the pre-Confederation bureaucracy was the departmental framework. There was widespread belief in the early 1840s that, without a clear departmental structure, responsible government would be, at best, fraught with danger, at worst, impossible to achieve. As a result, functions were grouped within departments, unity of command was established, and a hierarchy of responsibilities was put in place. This would underpin what Earl Grey described as 'the first principle of our system of government – the control of all branches of administration by Parliament.'[10]

Hodgetts insisted that a 'coherent description of programme allocation' could best be achieved by 'adopting broad functional categories for the basic responsibilities of government.'[11] He listed several and traced the evolution of federal government departments through these lenses. Departments, even as recently as forty years ago, had fairly clear mandates and a distinct turf to protect. In addition, the ability to define clear departmental mandates was approved of in the public administration literature. Luther Gulick had a simple question to guide policy makers: Is there 'little bleeding?'[12] Though departments were hardly ever watertight and self-contained, they could go about their work with limited concern for the work of other departments. Departments could protect their turf because they occupied a fairly well-articulated space. Today, by contrast, departments 'bleed' profusely, and government policies and programs are increasingly linked.

The bleeding has led to two distinct policy processes in both Canada and Britain – one for the prime minister and his court of advisers, usually pitched to the media, and another for everybody else. More is said about this later, but suffice it to note here that when Canadian or British prime ministers and their courts wish to approve a new initiative, they move everything out of the reach of ministers, departments, and career officials and simply get it done. This approach can be described as policy making by announcement. That is, prime ministers simply deliver a major speech to unveil a new policy and then let the government decision-making process pick up the pieces as best it can. Given that the prime minister has a direct say in the career prospects of ministers, aspiring ministers, heads of departments, and aspiring heads of departments, everyone has an interest in seeing the prime minister's initiative come to a successful conclusion.

The process that applies to everyone else is much more complex and less decisive. It involves issues that have not made it to the front pages of newspapers or to the TV screen, issues that are not of sufficient interest to grab the attention of prime ministers and their overloaded agendas. For example, no less than twenty federal departments were directly involved recently in planning new measures to promote development in Canada's north.[13] It took nearly two years for the process to run its course, and it involved extensive consultations with stakeholders and a number of consultants' reports. This is how the bulk of major policy issues are now handled in Ottawa. Indeed, any proposed policy not co-opted by the prime minister, and perhaps the minister of finance, invariably brings together several federal departments or agencies, provincial departments, interest groups, consultants, lobbyists, think-tanks, and pollsters. Things are no different in Britain, where the process has been labelled 'joined-up government.'[14]

John Fraser, former cabinet minister and Speaker of the House of Commons in Canada, often compares government to the military. One way to know in the military if your side is in trouble is simply to ask the question 'Who is in charge?' If the answer is not clear, then, he insists, you know you are in deep trouble. When prime ministers take charge of an issue, the answer is clear to everyone inside government. The problem, of course, is that the prime minister is constantly overloaded and can only focus on a handful of issues. As for the rest, it is less and less clear who is in charge. Ministers may try their hand at 'steering,' but steering a large network of policy specialists from several departments and outside groups is no easy task. They may well feel at times that they are steering a wheel that is not attached to anything.

The concept of ministerial authority changes dramatically when the bulk of the people shaping new policy initiatives are partners and not subordinates. In addition, ministers may prefer to speak their concerns or preferences instead of writing them down, given that words committed to paper may prove embarrassing if they are ever made public. In any event, as Edward Page and Bill Jenkins point out in their aptly named study of 'policy bureaucracy' in Britain, *Public Bureaucracy: Government with a Cast of Thousands,* ministers do not give 'a detailed steer on things at the beginning of the process.'[15] Moreover, it would be difficult to determine precisely when the process begins in shaping policy by networks. Networks and networked organizational forms may well be supplementing hierarchies. They may also have advantages, as some claim, but clarity of purpose and accountability are not among them.[16]

In the case of Britain, Christopher Foster, among others, writes that the Cabinet Office has been transformed into an agency designed to support the prime minister, not the whole cabinet, and that the prime minister now leads a presidential government.[17] A former cabinet secretary in Britain recently wrote about the 'decline of Cabinet government.'[18] There is a new vocabulary that has surfaced in both Canada (horizontality) and Britain (joined-up government). Civil servants in both countries report that this process is 'complex' and 'time consuming.'[19] A senior Canadian official explains, for example, that the 'climate change' initiative has more than 250 programs involving twelve departments. British commentators also report that many joined-up initiatives or cross-cutting actions, ranging from 'crime reduction' and 'the role of the voluntary sector' to 'tackling health inequalities ... involve a large number of programs and several departments.'[20]

In brief, as issues became more complex and interconnected, it became apparent that no single department had all the necessary policy tools and program instruments to deal with them. The result is that each department now comes to the table with only part of the answer in hand, unable on its own to impose a comprehensive solution. The great majority of policy issues no longer respect organizational boundaries; as a result, policy making has now become horizontal, consultative, and porous. To have any chance of making the process work, one must give a voice to all participants so that, in the words of the Treasury Board Secretariat, one can 'ensure consensus and departmental buy in.'[21] To be sure, the senior civil service has had to adjust. Marcel Massé, who could speak from the perspective of both a senior career official and a senior cabinet minister, concluded that 'this means that those who traditionally simply make decisions will have to spend much more of their time explaining situations, setting out the various options and trade-offs, and persuading those involved, before proposed solutions become acceptable. A good part of the present unpopularity of both politicians and civil servants is due to our insufficient adaptation to these new requirements of our jobs.' He saw a new role for career officials. 'In the post-modern government,' he explained, 'the task of understanding, consulting, explaining and persuading must be shared between politicians and bureaucrats.'[22] This compels career officials to engage in a public dialogue with interested parties, take on a public voice, and thus lose some of their anonymity as actors in the policy process. It also calls for similar skills on the part of both elected politicians and civil servants.

Horizontal or joined-up government is not without its critics or its problems. Accountability works much better in a vertical world than in a horizontal structure. Horizontal or joined-up government will often witness bursts of enthusiasm as a proposed policy initiative is first discussed, with many voices both inside and outside government signing on to the proposal, all seeing opportunities for their side. All too often, however, enthusiasm will wane as the proposed initiative bogs down in countless meetings in search of a compromise. Steven Rogelberg writes in the *Journal of Applied Psychology* that private firms that have too many meetings, allow them to go on too long, and have too many people attend risk losing their best workers. He adds that these meetings make the least productive workers happy. He argues that staff members who push to get things done are frustrated with meetings and that those who welcome meeting after meeting are the ones less driven to finish the job.[23] Given the rise of horizontal or joined-up government and the collapse of boundaries between government departments, one can assume that the best workers who want to get on with the job are experiencing similar frustrations, and that this may partly explain some of the low morale in the civil services of both Canada and the Britain.

Horizontal government is a long-term process operating in a world that values initiative and quick decisions. As Christopher Pollitt explains, 'Public servants need to acquire new skills. Different professional practices must be aligned. Mutual trust between different stakeholders must be built. Citizens must have the opportunity to exercise their (diverse) voices and themselves learn the value of participation. None of these things can be accomplished in weeks or even months.'[24] Senior officials speak about 'networking skills' and 'capacity for teamwork,' of 'reaching out and building strategic alliances,' and of a capacity to 'lead or follow the lead of others, depending on the needs of the time at hand.'[25]

Canada and Britain, however, can take comfort in the fact that they are hardly alone in acknowledging the importance of stakeholders and horizontality in the policy-making process. The Organization for Economic Co-operation and Development (OECD) report *Government of the Future*, based on the experience of its member countries, states that 'Policymaking is influenced by a wide variety of players ranging from interest and lobby groups to think tanks and other policy entrepreneurs ... Increased participation by these groups reinforces the democratic process and helps government to better anticipate citizen desires.'[26]

Unless the prime minister has a direct interest in the issue, nothing much of consequence now takes place in government without some type of advisory group attached to it. It seems that politicians and citizens no longer trust government departments to count fish properly (the Department of Fisheries and Oceans in Canada has had since 1993 a Fisheries Resource Conservation Council made up of outside members with a broad mandate to review the work of the department) or to estimate revenues (the minister of finance commissioned a study – the O'Neil report – in June 2005, to review the department's ability to forecast revenue and spending). O'Neil himself argued that the government should seriously consider turning over responsibility for forecasting revenues to the private sector, given that government 'forecasts have been consistently off for decades.'[27] The Harper government, shortly after coming to power, declared its intention to appoint an independent 'Parliamentary Budget Officer' to 'ensure truth in budgeting.'[28] Not only are new voices being created or supported, but there is a belief that voices operating outside the government are more credible and are better suited to speak truth to power. Prime Minister Harper made good on his commitment by making the office part of his accountability reform package.

In addition, hand in hand with the emergence of horizontal or joined-up government has been the growth of a host of new movements giving voice to dissatisfaction with government policies and operations. As already noted, a number of single-issue movements, albeit some with a broad policy agenda, came into their own in the 1970s: women, peace, environment, minority-languages, Aboriginal rights, gay rights, and visible minorities. Canada, in the early 1980s, and more recently Britain have joined the United States in becoming 'rights-oriented' societies.[29] The new movements have been able to attract both financial resources and members, and many of them have carved out a presence in the public policy-making process. They want a straight answer and government action, and this, if nothing else, has narrowed the role of career bureaucrats in the policy process.[30]

When you turn over policy making and decisions to a horizontal process, it becomes not only interdepartmental but also extends to outside players seeking to drive policy development. Gone is the minister working with a line department to bring forward proposals to cabinet. The relationship between the government and citizens is also redefined. Influence is divided and dispersed, and managing the bargaining and accommodation processes becomes the responsibility of civil servants. However, citizens who are not engaged or represented by stakeholders in the processes may well come to view government as slow moving and unresponsive, and individual civil servants as incapable of acting responsibly. They may also come to the conclusion that the policy process is designed only for those with sufficient resources to hire the expertise required to participate in an elaborate, complex, and porous policy-making process. They have a point.

It is now far more difficult for civil servants to provide straight answers to ministers, parliamentary committees, and citizens. To operate in a line department with a clearly defined mandate and a hierarchy is one thing, but to manage a process where influence is widely dispersed, unless the prime minister takes a personal interest in it, is quite another.

Think Tanks, Research Institutes, and Lobbyists also Want In

Think tanks and research institutes have added to the cacophony of voices. They have long enjoyed an important place in the public policy process in Washington. Canada and Britain, however, have made up for lost time since the 1980s.[31] Today, we have think tanks and research institutes covering virtually every area of public policy, and it seems that new ones are continually being created, some through government funding.

It is simply not possible to determine with any degree of certainty the influence research institutes and think tanks have on the public policy process. No major public policy development is the product of a single linear progression of events and ideas. There are many rivulets of thought. What is beyond dispute, however, is that research institutes and think tanks have become a significant part of the public policy architecture. They are paid for their input, and their success is measured by their perceived influence on government and by the attention given to them by the media.

The result is that, leaving aside prime ministers and their courts, power in government has become increasingly diffuse. In the words of Richard Wilson, former cabinet secretary under Tony Blair, power is 'never constant … it moves around from day to day and somebody who was powerful last week is less powerful this … reputations rise and fall like a stock exchange.'[32] There are now specialists who are making a handsome living by keeping tabs on who is up and who is down in government and selling this information to those with the necessary financial resources to influence government.

Lobbyists, in the words of a Canadian journalist, have grown like 'Topsy' in recent years in Ottawa. From a dead start thirty-five years ago in Canada, there are now some fifty lobbying firms listed in the Ottawa directory. This number does not include law firms, which have 'hired guns' to look after lobbying on behalf of customers. By one count, there are now about 2,000 lobbyists in Ottawa. A number of these are highly paid and politically partisan; they could not easily survive a change of political power in Ottawa. However, because they are politically partisan, they have access to ministers and to the prime minister and his or her court. They are always at the ready to offer advice. In brief, they are hired to promote the interests of their corporate customers and paid to sell truth to politicians about government policy, as their customers see it. There are even lobbyists working to promote the interests of the tobacco industry. If nothing else, politicians can now turn to any number of paid lobbyists to get a second opinion on a policy issue. If truth is not absolute, elected politicians now have any number of sources to consult to establish truth as they wish to hear it.

British lobbyists have also made their presence felt in recent years and have become an important part of the political process both in Britain and abroad. British firms top all foreign spending on lobbyists in the United States.[33] There is now a spate of books on how to lobby in Britain, including advice on how to lobby at intergovernmental meetings, how to organize protest campaigns, and how to beat the system.[34] While lobbyists in Canada tend to focus their efforts on ministers and their staff, government departments, and central agencies, lobbyists in Britain are present not only in government but also have a strong presence around Westminster. In recent years lobbyists have been working hand in hand with all party groups, looking into such issues as nuclear power, the pharmaceutical industry, and trade. In some instances, lobbyists actually wrote all-party reports, prompting the parliamentary chair of the committee on standards in public life to express concern, insisting that the matter 'deserves to come into the public domain.'[35]

In both Canada and Britain, senior officials no longer have a monopoly on policy advice to ministers and no longer dominate their policy sectors as they once did. Deputy ministers in Canada and permanent secretaries in Britain were for a long time largely recruited from within their department. They knew their department well – the policies, the programs, the staff, and outside groups with a strong interest in the department. It was an ideal setting to practise 'stovepipe' management and to protect one's turf. Today, senior officials are hired on the basis of their ability to navigate the policy process, to network, to make things happen, and to manage. If senior government officials have a comparative advantage over policy specialists operating on the periphery of government, it is their knowledge of key players in government, an intimate knowledge of how the policy process now works, and an ability to keep their ministers out of trouble or, in the words of a senior Canadian official, the ability 'to fall on hand grenades.'[36]

The Media

The media are all too willing to report on exploding hand grenades. We explored the role of the media in present-day government in chapter 3. We now need to review them as a distinct and powerful voice in their own right. There was a time when journalists respected boundaries and acknowledged that some things were off limits: Churchill's heavy drinking, Mackenzie King's prostitutes, and Franklin D. Roosevelt's polio. But no more. Former prime minister John Major writes about a 'breakdown in trust between the Government and the media.'[37] Robin Sears explains that a whole new generation of journalists began to see themselves as 'Woodward and Bernstein'; the word was that 'politicians are crooks and liars, and it's our job to get them.'[38] He adds that 'gotcha' journalism is 'easy to write and avoids the tedium of having to know anything about the policies or goals of the government you are covering.'[39]

As Richard Wilson, former cabinet secretary, mused in a public lecture, 'I sometimes wonder whether the media understand their own power or the impact they can have on the inner workings of government.' He added that the media in more recent years have not hesitated to put civil servants under the spotlight, explaining that 'being attacked in the press ... is a daunting experience for people who chose a career in which, if they are older, they expected to avoid the limelight.'[40] The question for civil servants, then, is how to reconcile the relentless demands and attacks of the media with sound policy planning and long-term thinking.

The media have of course undergone a sea change in recent years with the advent of twenty-four-hour television news, radio talk shows, TV punditry, the Internet, and political blogs. Forty years ago, political columnists were rare. Today, according to a leading Canadian columnist, they are 'almost a dime a dozen.' Forty years ago, journalists 'worked hard on collecting facts, cross-checking them, reading documents and talking to people. This kind of work is now considered hopelessly old-fashioned.'[41]

The media now have a different voice, one that is less deferential and much more subjective.[42] Journalists will readily agree that the role of the media has changed substantially in recent years. The end of deference, the capacity for self-projection, and a more aggressive approach have had a profound impact on all facets of politics and, by ricochet, public administration. A veteran British journalist, John Lloyd, writes that 'the end of deference, celebrated so uncritically, was also the shared assumption of supreme parliamentary sovereignty ... day to day sovereignty has bit by bit passed to the media.' He adds, 'A half a century ago, the assumption was that political power trumped all others. Now it doesn't: media power comes closer to trumping all others, at least in some things. It is the power of the media which has been one of the largest shifts in society over the past three decades.'[43] Jeffrey Simpson went to the heart of the issue when he wrote about Judy Sgro, a minister in the Martin government, who resigned to clear her name after Harjet Singh made allegations against her that were widely reported in the media. Many journalists decided that she was guilty as charged, and no one in the media came to her defence. An inexperienced minister, new to her post, Ms Sgro decided that she would rather walk away from the daily media onslaught than fight in the Commons to preserve her reputation. It was later established that Singh was anything but a credible witness. He had a criminal record and had lied on numerous occasions to the court, the police, and immigration officials. As Simpson wrote, 'The Sgro affair ought to set off reflections in the Canadian media, and not just for how the file got covered, but because it illustrated how the media have become part of a dysfunctional political culture in which assumptions of wrongdoing are pervasive, cynicism abounds, negativity prevails, and few, if any, breaks are given anyone who serves in public life – except, of course, those paid to be watchdogs on those we elect, such as auditors-general, judges, whistle-blowers, prosecutors, inquiry heads, Democracy Watchers, ethics experts.'[44]

Douglas Fisher, a member of Parliament in the 1950s and 1960s and later a columnist and a television commentator for more than forty years, reflected on his time in Ottawa as he took his leave from journalism in 2006. He noted that, over the years, the 'House of Commons has withered almost to insignificance ... that the influence of cabinet ministers has declined most of all,' and that 'the prime minister and his office now dominate government.'[45] The media, he insists, have also changed. He reports that 'television in almost every sense has altered the behaviour in the House. Part of Question Period every day is kind of an arranged farce, a drama ... The TV people do somewhat a different chore than the print people. The print people are less important and less well known now, but in some ways they remain the basic people in terms of providing the story. You very rarely get, consecutively, from the television coverage of Parliament, much information of worth or weight about, say, an important bill that's coming through. Television tends to report on politics as though it's a game and every day has winners and losers.'[46] Consequently, governments have had to learn the business of news management, to develop an instinct for political survival so as to be perceived as winners before the television cameras.

Christopher Foster, a former senior civil servant, echoes John Lloyd on the matter of media power. He goes so far as to say that, 'if one cannot find a means of detaching ministers – including the Prime Minister – from too much daily absorption in the media preventing them from progressing the real business of government, we cannot have a genuine representative democracy which works.'[47]

It is no longer possible to win elections and to retain power without having a carefully worked out media strategy. This involves shaping tomorrow's news headlines, not simply reacting to them. One must always have at the ready effective sound-bites, instant rebuttal capacity, public opinion surveys, and competent media spin specialists. The Gomery inquiry in Canada and the Hutton and Butler inquiries in Britain revealed the importance governments now attach to twenty-four-hour news management.

It is hardly possible to overstate the importance of the media in shaping voter perception in an era when loyalty to political parties continues to decline. They focus on two things: party leaders and missteps. This and their capacity to cover 'crisis situations,' real or imagined, have led political observers to suggest that governments are now in 'perpetual election campaign' mode.[48]

Party leaders are at the heart of news management mode, a circumstance that has strengthened their hand, especially that of the prime minister, in dealing with their parties and establishing party policies. Indeed, judging by the media focus, party leaders now appear to be the only substantial candidates in an election race. How one does in an election campaign and in the televised leaders' debate can affect the election itself.[49] Increasingly, the objective of all parties at election time is to sell their leaders rather than their ideas, policies, or party. A study by leading students of election campaigns observes that 'Canadian elections, in common with elections in other Westminster-style systems, as well as with presidential elections in the United States, inevitably turn on the question of who – which individual – shall form the government.' If the leader secures a majority it is generally assumed that the party is in his or her debt, not the other way around.

Party leaders – with the help of spin doctors, pollsters, and advisers – run the national campaign, keep a watchful eye on the media, and try as best they can to control campaign developments. Recent history in both Canada and Britain has shown that a sure recipe to win power is to hug the political centre. It is no sin against representative democracy if parties decide to converge on the political centre. But when they do, voters must look to other matters in deciding how to vote. Some may choose to abstain, and there is evidence that this is in fact happening, given the decline in voter turnout in recent years and the weakening of party loyalty. Party leaders and their advisers are well aware that the media will greatly influence how electors will view their credibility and competence; hence the need to score points on air and to avoid political gaffes.

This, in turn, explains the rise of what Christopher Hood and Martin Lodge describe as 'a new politico-bureaucratic class of spin doctors shouldering aside public servants with more traditional analytic skills.'[50] They are a key component of a government's news-management model. They are the hired hands whose job is to manage the media. In the process, they have become important voices in their own right inside government, trying to control a powerful voice on the outside always lurking to spot an exploding hand grenade.

Access to Information: A Voice within a Voice

The media's new, more aggressive voice has been helped greatly by access to information legislation, which, in Canada, broke new ground when it was introduced in 1985. Ottawa circles called it Trudeau's gift to Mulroney. That is, Trudeau would not have to live with the consequences of the legislation produced by his government, but his successor, Brian Mulroney, would.

The central purpose of the act is to provide a 'right of access' for Canadians to information under the control of any government institution. It adds that 'exceptions to the right of access' should be both limited and specific and, further, that decisions on disclosure 'should be reviewed independently of government.'[51]

As senior officials had predicted when the act was proclaimed, the impact of the legislation has been profound. For one thing, it has generated a demand for good political 'firefighters' in Ottawa and has made policy people cautious. As Giles Gherson, former policy adviser in the Department of Human Resources Development and later a journalist, explains, 'To address the access to information issue ... I saw myself that officials are extremely leery of putting things on paper that they wouldn't like to see made public or find its way to the media, several months later, that could be embarrassing to the minister.'[52] Conrad Winn, a pollster, argues that access to information has seriously inhibited the ability of government departments to ask the right questions when commissioning a survey: 'The bottom line for the average public servant is don't embarrass the minister, that is the surest way to have your career stopped or slowed down. If you have polls that ask all kinds of questions that would reveal the truthful complexity of what people think ... then [the polls] will inevitably show the public doesn't like something the government does.'[53] Political journalist Hugh Winsor readily admits that the media often take advantage of access to information to get at a story. But, he argues, they do that 'not so much to find out what the people dislike about the government ... but to try to get an advance look at what the government's agenda might be ... and at the next budget or the next Speech from the Throne by making an access to information request about a public opinion survey which is being commissioned.'[54]

Government officials in both central agencies and line departments readily admit that access to information legislation has made them reluctant to commit their views and recommendations to paper. The concern is for individual civil servants and their ability to speak truth to their ministers under the cover of anonymity. Civil servants fear that their views could well appear in the media and force officials to support or defend them in public. As one senior official at the Treasury Board Secretariat observed recently, 'We are now all sitting ducks. I cringe when I write an email because I never know whether it will appear on the front page of a newspaper six months down the road. It is possible now for someone to ask for all exchanges, including emails, between senior official X and senior official Y. We can no longer blue sky or have a playful mind. We no longer have the luxury of engaging in a frank and honest debate. It is now very difficult to put down on paper – be careful, minister, there are problems with your ideas and what you want to do.'[55] The fear is that anyone outside government could discover what civil servants have said and make it public. One can assume that this leads to less disciplined thinking as strong memoranda give way to PowerPoint presentations. One can also assume that there is less room for critical thinking. Ironically, because advice along the lines of 'Be careful,' if given at all, is no longer committed to paper. In consequence, advice has become less transparent. In addition, officials attempt to attenuate the impact of the access to information legislation to protect their ministers and their policy advisory and administrative roles. In a detailed review of the application of the legislation, one student of public administration reports that 'requests that were identified as sensitive, or that came from the media or political parties, were found to have longer processing time, even after other considerations were accounted for.'[56] More is said about this later.

The concern over media use of access to information has reached the point where the government is actually directing civil servants not to commit anything to paper. For example, the Department of Indian Affairs and Northern Development told consultants in a $132,000 contract not to leave 'a paper trail in government offices' and insisted that they deliver their findings through oral briefings.[57] As well, several months after Harper came to power in January 2006, his government launched a program review exercise designed to cut at least $2 billion from expenditures. Civil servants were instructed to do everything 'orally,' including briefings for their ministers, in identifying potential spending cuts, and to avoid putting anything down on paper.[58] Civil servants did as they were told, and the approach worked, at least from Harper's perspective. His government was able to announce $2 billion in spending cuts on 25 September 2006, including cuts in politically sensitive programs, without media reports on leaks beforehand.[59] The Harper government was not as fortunate on other issues. Access to information enabled the media to obtain briefing books that revealed that the minister of finance and departmental officials were at odds over a cut to the Goods and Services Tax (GST) and that the minister of the environment was not briefed on climate change after nine months in the position.[60]

When access to information legislation was first introduced, it was envisaged that it would be 'first and foremost' for citizens. Today, the media are the 'major users.'[61] It was also envisaged that citizens would turn to the legislation only as a last resort, since government departments would be able to respect the intent of the legislation and share accessible information freely. This, too, has not turned out as expected.

Hugh Winsor, a veteran member of the Parliamentary Press Gallery, claims that he has 'never met a deputy minister who didn't hate the Access to Information Act.' The act, he reports, 'chews up resources,' and senior government officials are 'particularly leery' of 'information fishermen' who file requests for thousands of pages of documents in the hope of discovering something 'hot' that they can shop around to the media. He reported that MPs are now turning to the legislation to get information, a development he described as 'ridiculous and an affront to Parliament.'[62]

Access to information legislation is relatively new to Britain. There are signs, however, that its repercussions may well be similar to the Canadian experience. Nicholas Barrington, a recently retired British civil servant, maintains that 'people are terrified of keeping records which may cast aspersions on people. The Freedom of Information Act is affecting the way the Government works ... in the old days the mandarins wrote things down, that was part of their skill. I think the fact of this fear of the Freedom of Information Act, people's reluctance to put things down frankly on paper is encouraging sofa government, wrong decisions, and is damaging to the government decision-making process.'[63]

Canada's information commissioner wrote some twenty years after access to information legislation came into force that he had witnessed the emergence of 'a deeply entrenched oral culture tolerated if not encouraged at the most senior levels of government.' He added that the government's policy on the management of government information holdings was now 'largely ignored in practice and that accountability for its enforcement and implementation was so diffuse as to be non-existent.' He pointed to the consequences. The quality of decision making in government was being undermined and so was the effectiveness of internal and external audits and the country's historical records.[64] One can be sure that, as Britain learns to live with its freedom of information legislation, there will be increasing demands to extend its coverage. Bit by bit and precedent by precedent, information on what elected politicians and civil servants think and do on policy and management will become public knowledge. In February 2007, for example, MPs in Britain lost their fight to keep travel expenses secret and, as a result, information on which MP turned to the train, cars, taxis, airplanes, and even bicycles to commute to work became an important media concern.[65] The media happily listed the big spenders, including MP Janet Anderson, who claimed more than 60,000 miles in travel to and from her Lancashire constituency by car, suggesting that she made about 270 journeys in one year.[66] The information was released two years after the *Sunday Times* submitted a request under the freedom of information legislation.[67]

Voices from Deep Within

Canada and Britain have both in recent years introduced measures to protect 'whistle-blowers' or 'disclosure of wrongdoing.' There is a growing body of literature on the topic, reflecting a strong interest among governments in strengthening their disclosure processes. One definition of whistle-blowing reads, 'the disclosure by organization members (former or current) of illegal, immoral, or illegitimate practices under the control of their employers, to persons or organizations (internal or external) that may be able to take action to stop the wrongdoing.'[68]

Paul Thomas maintains that whistle-blowing has become more respected within society. To be sure, there are a number of signs suggesting that whistle-blowers are much more admired today than ever. For example, *Time* magazine awarded its Person of the Year award in 2002 to whistle-blowers. It was not always so. As Thomas points out, 'in earlier decades, society looked less favourably on persons who revealed the wrongdoing of other individuals or organizations. Loyalty to employers and respect for authority were more strongly held values within society than is true today. Pejorative labels like "finks," "squealers," "informers" and "rats" were applied to people who blew the whistle. Their motives were assumed to be suspect – they were acting out of bitterness or revenge, for personal gain or simply to pass judgement and claim moral superiority.'[69] But here, too, things have changed. Aggressive media coverage of wrongdoing, campaigns by public service unions in favour of whistle-blowing legislation, and access to information legislation have all contributed to the notion that employees have rights that should be respected, including blowing the whistle on wrongdoing.

The whistle-blowing legislation in Canada went through several twists and turns before it emerged in Harper's accountability package in 2006. The idea first surfaced within government in the Tait report, and it was later pursued by a working group of senior officials. Bills were introduced in Parliament, and subsequently revised. Some felt that the proposed legislation contained 'no framework of ethics and values' and that those responsible for overseeing its legislation should be truly independent of government.[70] Harper met these criticisms head-on in his legislation. He made the Public Sector Integrity Commission an agent of Parliament; gave employers direct access to the commission; created an independent 'Public Servant Disclosure Protection Tribunal,' with the power to decide whether reprisals have occurred and to order action to remedy the situation and ensure that those who took reprisals are disciplined; and introduced specific penalties for offences under the Public Servant Disclosure Protection Act, including tougher penalties for those who wilfully impede investigations of wrongdoing.[71]

In Britain, the Civil Service Code and the Public Interest Disclosure Act (PIDA) deal with the disclosure of wrongdoing. The PIDA covers both public sector (except in such areas as security services) and private sector employees. There are a number of categories of wrongdoing that 'qualify' for protection, including, among others, a criminal offence, a miscarriage of justice, and damage to the environment. The Civil Service Code, meanwhile, calls on employees to report any instances in which they are required to act in a manner that is illegal, improper, or unethical; that are in breach of constitutional convention or a professional code; and that may involve possible maladministration. The Civil Service Code provides that employees who do not believe that their department has given them a reasonable response to their disclosures may appeal to the Civil Service Commissioners, an independent body. If the commissioners' investigation leads them to uphold the appeal, they will 'make recommendations' for remedial action to the discloser's department.[72]

One senior Canadian civil servant had this to say about whistle-blowing: 'It is just another thing for us to worry about. You know that there are problems with the concept, but there is not much that one can do about it. It is like being against motherhood. You just take what's there and do the best you can with it and hope that it doesn't do too much damage to the department.'[73] There is a lack of information on the impact of whistle-blowing legislation on government departments.

Though whistle-blowing has been on the agenda of many Western countries for some years, there is very little information available on its effectiveness.[74] We have virtually no information on the short- and longer-term impact of whistle-blowing on the productivity and the culture and climate of the affected organizations. What harm to other individuals and to organizations did it cause? How often was the wrongdoing corrected as a result of the whistle-blowing, and did the corrective measures prevent its reoccurrence?[75] What we do know is that employees may well have a large amount of knowledge about the goings-on in their department or agency and that the effectiveness of complex organizations depends on a very high level of loyalty and discretion. As Mark Bovens writes, 'if employees expose each assignment, remark, or development which does not please them, this would soon lead to the paralysis of the organisation and confusion in the outside world. In order to work quickly and efficiently, peace and quiet and a certain degree of resolution are indispensable.'[76]

Whistle-blowing, however, squares nicely with the anti-politics and anti-bureaucracy mood in many Western countries, evident particularly since the early 1980s. It is in this environment that whistle-blowers have been transformed from villains to heroes and that measures are being put in place to insulate them from political and bureaucratic pressure. The heroes are given a safe venue to voice their views about what has gone wrong in government. This is a forum dominated by political and media considerations that very often 'amplify, distort and exaggerate' problems inside government.[77] Nevertheless, whistle-blowers now enjoy a special standing and are given a public voice to air their views. The creation of a new position, officer of Parliament, gives the impression that cover-ups are pervasive in government and creates yet another voice completely independent of government whose purpose is to act as a watchdog.

Civil servants have other means of voicing their displeasure. They are now regularly subjected to surveys to determine the state of morale in departments and agencies. The results of these surveys are made public. On 30 September 2006, the *Globe and Mail* reported, for example, from a survey of RCMP officers and civilian employees, that most of them were 'not happy with the way the force is being managed.' It also revealed that 'only 16 percent' said that 'human resources are deployed effectively' and that fewer than one in three (31 per cent) agreed that 'poor performance situations are dealt with effectively.'[78]

Voices from above the Fray

Officers of Parliament are in fashion in both Canada and Britain. Such new positions are being created to ensure that the work is carried out independently of the government. In Canada the most well known officer of Parliament is the auditor general and in Britain, the comptroller and auditor general. These and other officers of Parliament have institutional features to ensure their independence from government. This also explains why they are in fashion. They are perceived to operate away from political and bureaucratic considerations and are thus well positioned to ensure objectivity in audit findings and in looking after access to information and privacy requirements.

Officers of Parliament play by different rules from government departments and agencies. They have their own staffing process and enjoy considerable freedom from central agency requirements. But they are bureaucrats, and they have many of the same characteristics found in government departments and agencies: they will protect their turf and attempt to expand it whenever opportunities arise.

Though they are designed to operate free from political interference, they are also not immune to scandal. It will be recalled, for example, that George Radwanski, Canada's privacy commissioner, resigned in 2003 over allegations of misleading Parliament, extravagant spending, and mismanagement of the office.[79] The Radwanski scandal also revealed that ensuring accountability is even more difficult with officers of Parliament than with government departments and agencies.

Agents of Parliament such as the auditor general have sought to break out of the traditional boundaries to establish new turf for themselves, but not necessarily at the urging of Parliament. Indeed, they now appear to function as free agents accountable to no one. The Office of the Auditor General in Canada once had a distinct mission, with clear boundaries defining its role and responsibility. It was mostly staffed by accountants, and its purpose was to assist the Public Accounts Committee of the House and to report to the committee the results of its investigations of financial probity and compliance with appropriation authority.[80] Today, nearly 60 per cent of its office budget goes to 'qualitative' or 'soft reviews' that 'bear little apparent relationship to efficiency or economy in use of funds, human resources or material.'[81] Neither the office nor the media bother to explain that qualitative or soft reviews can never be as certain or as conclusive as financial audits. But such exercises enable the office to contribute to policy debates and in some ways to participate in the making of public policy. In addition, the office has become particularly adroit at dealing with the media.

The Canadian auditor general became a media star in the sponsorship scandal and gained considerable positive visibility with Canadians. There was talk on a number of open-line shows of 'Sheila Fraser for Prime Minister,' and she was described in the media as a 'folk hero with the electorate.'[82] The office has successfully created its own distinct voice to carry out its work and views Parliament as just another consumer of its reports. But when a new voice is created, existing ones must adjust.

The Canadian privacy commissioner held a press conference in June 2002 to announce a Charter challenge to the RCMP's video-surveillance activities in Kelowna, British Columbia. He was doing so, he explained, after being unable to persuade the solicitor general to 'exercise his responsibility and instruct the RCMP to take down the camera.'[83] His press release made no reference to consulting Parliament in initiating this action. He did report, however, that he had consulted a former justice of the Supreme Court, who, 'prior to his retirement, wrote many of the Supreme Court's most important decisions on privacy rights.'[84]

Agents of Parliament can claim, and many do, to occupy a distinct, relatively self-contained space. John Reid, the information commissioner, admitted as much when he revealed that his annual reports are all but ignored by MPs, 'who are more concerned with exposing political scandals.' As he explained, 'I would expect that they would want to go through my expenditures, my activities with a fine tooth comb.' He added that MPs 'don't take me to task' and that he has never been grilled.[85] The chief human-rights commissioner also called for new measures to 'ensure that there is direct input from MPs and senators on the level of resources and type of work we should do.'[86]

The 'whistle-blower' commissioner will also likely seek to expand his or her mandate, much as other officers of Parliament do. The central purpose of officers of Parliament is to be relevant. Given that, as officers of Parliament, they can only 'bark,' not bite, they have to make sure that their bark is heard.[87]

Britain does not have as many officers of Parliament as Canada, though there, too, the number has increased in recent years. In addition, the tendency to enlarge one's mandate is also evident. The National Audit Office saw its mandate expand in the early 1980s to include value-for-money audits. The 1983 National Audit Act formally made the office an officer of the House of Commons and gave it the power to report to Parliament at its 'own discretion on the economy, efficiency and effectiveness with which government bodies have used public funds.'[88] As with its Canadian counterpart, the mandate of National Audit Office is no longer restricted to investigating financial probity and compliance with appropriation authority. Again, much as in Canada, the office's focus has shifted away from the details of expenditure to broader and more subjective investigations related to value for money and, in the case of Canada, performance reviews. That said, in Britain the relationship between the Committee of Public Accounts and the National Audit Office appears to be much stronger than that between the Public Accounts Committee and the Office of the Auditor General in Canada.

In the 1960s, Britain established the post of parliamentary ombudsman, which was in part modelled on the National Audit Office. In the 1990s, Britain established the Office of Parliamentary Commissioner for Standards, following the first report of the Nolan Committee on Standards in Public Life, and in 2000 the Office of the Information Commission, which holds some characteristics of a parliamentary officer, was established, followed by the Judicial Appointments Commission in 2006.[89] The purpose of this last commission is to 'maintain and strengthen judicial independence from the Executive and the Legislature.' As the secretary of state for constitutional affairs explained, 'In a modern democratic society, it is no longer acceptable for judicial appointments to be entirely in the hands of a Government Minister. For example the judiciary is often involved in adjudicating on the lawfulness of actions of the Executive. And so the appointments system must be, and must be seen to be, independent of Government.'[90]

These new independent voices again square nicely with the current climate of cynicism and mistrust towards politicians and bureaucrats. There is an inherent belief that they will be better because they are above the political fray. Baroness Prashar of the Judicial Appointments Commission explains that the commission is 'required to select solely on merit and to only select people of good character.'[91] That is a requirement the government is apparently not able to meet.

In short, officers of Parliament in both Canada and Britain serve various purposes. They perform audits, they look after judicial appointments and access to information legislation, and they perform various oversight roles. New officers of Parliament have been created in both Canada and Britain in recent years without any effort to define a constitutional niche or to clarify how they fit into the existing constitutional framework.[92] It is not at all clear how they are to be held accountable and by whom. They all have one thing in common – they are independent, and they are free to bark or voice their views even when they may be serving the interest of their own organizations. For the most part, they answer to themselves alone and play to the media.

They join the courts in gaining a voice that operates outside of political influence. Canada's chief justice, it will be recalled, recently made it clear in a public lecture that law and justice rest on rational principles and that 'embedded in the concept of the rule of law is the proposition that there are fundamental and overriding principles of justice binding civilized societies that trump state-made rules where the two come into conflict.'[93] Though they stand above the fray, the courts no longer hesitate to shape the country's social agenda.[94] To be sure, the Charter of Rights and Freedoms that became part of Canada's constitution in 1982 has had a profound impact on the role of Canadian courts, as has the Human Rights Act in Britain.

Revisiting Voices

Voices now take many forms. There are now more voices but fewer issues that speak to a collective purpose. Some voices represent interests on the outside looking in, trying to influence new policy initiatives. But there are also voices on the inside that are being heard publicly for the first time. The cacophony of voices trying to influence prime ministers and their courtiers has become so widespread that in Canada provincial governments have decided to hire lobbyists or set up offices in Ottawa to speak to their interests in court.[95] MPs and ministers representing the provinces, it seems, are no longer up to the task. The various voices can also obtain inside information through whistle-blowing and access to information legislation. They may speak through partnership agreements with the private sector or research institutes. They may take the form of interdepartmental initiatives and involve a multitude of outside actors. The media now have access to inside information in a way that was unthinkable forty years ago. Officers of Parliament are being created for a variety of purposes, all with a voice independent of government. The courts are no longer content to interpret the law.

Parliament, it seems, has turned over much of its accountability responsibilities to officers of Parliament and the media. Officers of

Parliament have somehow projected the image that they are non-political, able to provide objective evidence about almost any public policy and administrative matter. They are new voices independent of both government and Parliament – which is how they are able to project the image that they exist only to provide objective evidence.

Citizens are free to choose which voices they wish to listen to in a cafeteria-style offering. Citizens, civil servants, and elected politicians see little reason to be more loyal to one voice over others, which is the topic of the next chapter. Elected politicians have had to arm themselves with new instruments and media specialists to cope with voices from without and within. Prime ministers in both Canada and Britain have in recent years tended to centralize the policy process to give life to the issues they consider most important and to keep a lid on other matters. The role of the senior civil service on policy matters is now for the most part to act as court advisers to prime ministers on issues of interest to them and their courts, as well as on issues making the headlines. As for the rest, the role is to keep things quiet and out of the media.

8 Searching for Loyalty

To be effective, prime ministers need loyalty from their cabinet ministers, caucus members, the party, and senior civil servants. Senior civil servants, meanwhile, require loyalty from rank-and-file employees. Indeed, loyalty is important right down the hierarchy, to the front-line manager and the workers. The concept of loyalty between politicians and civil servants has long been a central feature of Westminster-style parliamentary systems. It is what Robert Armstrong meant when he wrote in his now famous memo, 'Civil servants are servants of the Crown. The Civil Service serves the Government of the day as a whole ... The duty of individual civil servants is first and foremost to the Minister of the Crown who is in charge of the department in which he or she is serving.'[1] Every government wants the civil service to be loyal to its agenda, if not to be an extension of the government itself. For elected politicians, loyalty gives a degree of certainty in shaping policy and delivering services. It remains a key ingredient for success in both the political and bureaucratic worlds. For senior civil servants, loyalty is important to ensure stability and the smooth operation of their departments and programs.

Loyalty, if anything, should now be more important than in years past. It could act as a check against rampant individualism in society and in government. It could be promoted as a core value as the public sector is increasingly fragmented into different organizational forms and as civil servants work with partners outside of government. It could be crucial to the civil service and its future as government seeks to recruit more managers from outside government. In 2004, British prime minister Tony Blair took great pride, for example, in reporting that 20 per cent of director general posts were now filled by people from outside the civil service and, further, that the proportion was on the rise.[2] He added that 'for all of government, the lessons of the revolution in business management have been highly relevant ... civil servants have become much more in touch with other sectors than they were a decade or so ago.'[3] That may be so, but for someone to make the transition from the private sector to government requires a change in loyalty to a new institution and to a public purpose.

Loyalty, however, was not one of the core values identified in the values and ethics exercises recently undertaken in both Canada and Britain. To be sure, democratic values require civil servants to serve the government of the day. But nothing is said about loyalty to the civil service as an institution or to one's department, or about loyalty to the crown. The purpose of this chapter is to review how loyalty has fared in recent years in the public sector.

Loyalty: Now Just Ambition

We saw earlier that voters are less likely to identify with or remain loyal to a political party than was the case forty years ago. The collapse of political ideology and the need to hug the political centre in order to win power, as well as the rise of image-driven politics in both Canada and Britain, have, if nothing else, made voters considerably less certain whom to vote for or even if they should bother to vote at all. Today, the image and popularity of party leaders are what matters most at election time. For the leaders, the pursuit of political power seems to trump ideology or even holding firm to a policy position.

It appears that party loyalty has also lost its appeal for some elected politicians. Canada has witnessed a number of high-profile political defections in recent years. For instance, Belinda Stronach crossed the floor to the governing Liberal party in 2005, days before a critical non-confidence motion that the opposition appeared likely to win by one or two votes. She was immediately appointed to a senior cabinet post, prompting a columnist to write, 'There are no principles at stake, it is only about power.'[4] Conservative party leader Stephen Harper said that there was 'no grand principle involved in her decision, just ambition.'[5]

Several months later David Emerson, a senior minister in the Martin government, quit the Liberal party to joint the Conservatives, just as Stephen Harper was putting together his cabinet. Harper immediately appointed Emerson to the External Trade portfolio in his cabinet. Only days earlier, Emerson had been campaigning against Harper and his

Conservative party. Harper explained that his invitation to Emerson to join the government was based solely 'on merit.' For his part, Emerson said that had the Liberals been re-elected, he would have 'absolutely stayed on in Paul Martin's cabinet.' His purpose, he explained, was to serve the 'people of my city, my province and my country,' insisting that he had 'always served the people on a non-partisan basis.'[6] Liberal MP Wajid Khan accepted an invitation from Conservative prime minister Stephen Harper to act as his adviser on the Middle East. As Khan explained, 'I think this is non-partisan and the Prime Minister realized that I have experience and depth of knowledge of that region.' His Liberal colleagues asked how he could possibly continue to sit in the Liberal caucus when Middle East issues were being discussed.[7] Several months later Khan decided to quit the Liberal caucus to cross the floor and join the Conservative party.[8]

To be sure, crossing the floor is not a recent phenomenon. Winston Churchill, for example, did it twice, but in both cases he had genuine policy differences with his party. In addition, political defections appear to be on the rise in both Canada and Britain.[9] Nelson Wiseman, a political scientist at the University of Toronto, commenting on the recent rise of political defections in Canada, argues that it could well be a result of 'the fact that elections are now more than ever controlled from the top down in national campaigns.'[10]

If political ideology does not resonate to the same degree as it once did, if party platforms are produced by the leader and a handful of advisers and pollsters, if public opinion surveys have pushed political parties to hug the middle of the political spectrum, and if election outcomes turn on a leader's ability to spin the electronic media, then one can understand why ambitious politicians would find it more advantageous to consider self-interest above loyalty to a political party. Michael Ignatieff declared, during his run for the leadership of the Liberal party, that he was not at all certain that he would run for Parliament in the next general election. 'It depends,' he reported, on 'who's leader.'[11] For Ignatieff, as for many other politicians in recent years, the leader is 'the only game in town.' As for the political party, it now plays a decided second fiddle.

The growing complexity of government, the arrival of governing by network, and the power of the media appear to place a premium on 'merit,' however defined, not just at the bureaucratic level, but also now at the political level. Harper referred to merit in explaining the Emerson appointment to his cabinet. Shortly after Harper came to power, his government asked a number of partisan political advisers to the previous Liberal government if they would be willing to serve as partisan political advisers in his Conservative government. The reason – Harper was 'concerned about a lack of experience within his own ranks.'[12] He was not apparently concerned about any sense of loyalty Liberal political advisers might have to the Liberal party. Nor did he pay heed to the fact that one of the traditional roles of the civil service is to provide a new government with the necessary knowledge and experience for it to take power. For ensuring a smooth transition of power, it appears that the Harper government had more confidence in advisers who only weeks before had been their political opponents than in a non-partisan civil service. Harper also directed his minister of foreign affairs not to hire Graham Fox, a well-known supporter of the Conservative party and a highly regarded policy analyst, as his chief of staff because he had been publicly critical of Harper's leadership in the past. Loyalty to the leader has become more important than loyalty to the party. This, too, speaks to the convergence of skills between the political and bureaucratic levels and makes for bedfellows of convenience.

Loyalty in the Civil Service

In Weber's legal-rational world, the civil service was to operate in a professional structure and remain blissfully impartial and objective. Its loyalty was to the law, to superiors, and to administrative rules and processes rather than to partisan political pressure or personal allegiances, and to the collective organization rather than to self. Hierarchy would serve many purposes, including ensuring that loyalty to the service trumped self-interest. Weber believed that formal rules would shape the motives and attitudes of civil servants and that the resultant loyalty would guarantee the faithful execution of their duties and responsibilities. It is for this reason that civil servants were to be rewarded with a regular (if modest) salary, tenure, prospects of advancement, and a relatively generous pension so that they should not be obliged to find work after retirement that might compromise their career-long loyalty to the civil service.

Loyalty for civil servants usually begins with the policy or program unit to which they belong. They will naturally identify with their co-workers and the work for which they were trained and for which they were presumably hired on merit. Work in policy units is, of course, quite different from work in program units, as are the educational backgrounds and work experience of their staffs. Units in Ottawa and London operate differently from those in Halifax or Liverpool. It is interesting to note that, in Canada at least, staff turnover is much lower in regional offices than it is in Ottawa, which may suggest that loyalty to the unit is stronger in regional offices.[13]

Civil servants will also be loyal to their department. James Q. Wilson has long argued that the behaviour of civil servants is determined by their departments and agencies and by the environment in which they operate.[14] A few years ago, government departments and agencies took up the fashion of producing vision statements that employees could allegedly identify with. It is not at all clear, however, what kind of impact these statements have had on employees. Each department has its own distinct culture and traditions – those of a revenue collection agency, for example, will be vastly different from those of a social services and welfare agency, a central agency, or a policy unit.

Wilson and Henry Mintzberg draw sharp distinctions between government departments and agencies and their organizational culture. Governments no longer consist of clerks producing predictable work and outputs, and one has to observe what kind of outputs or outcomes they produce to classify their departments. Wilson classified government departments and agencies in which both outputs and outcomes can be observed as *production* organizations, agencies in which outputs but not outcomes can be observed as *procedural* organizations, agencies in which outcomes but not outputs can be observed as *craft* organizations, and agencies in which neither outputs nor outcomes can be observed as *coping* organizations.[15]

Wilson used these criteria to classify government organizations in 1989. Though the classifications still apply today, there has been a substantial shift to craft and coping organizations since then. Horizontal or joined-up government has made it much more difficult to measure both outputs and outcomes. One can also assume that loyalty is much easier to promote in production-type agencies than in craft or coping agencies. Identifying with one's department should be easier when outputs, outcomes, and expectations can be established and when the department's purpose is easily understood.

Networks – horizontal and joined-up government – by definition offer a multitude of potential loyalties to civil servants. One's unit and home department no longer constitute the full story. For example, Canada's climate-change strategy in 2004 involved fourteen departments and agencies managing a complex series of 250 programs involving, among others, the international community, public education, transportation, and industrial policies as well as a multitude of activities ranging from incentives to retrofit housing to regulations to ensure energy efficiency. Wilson's organization types encompass all the climate-change activities. The civil servant then has to reconcile his or her loyalty to the home department in this new world while learning to work with officials from diverse organizations.

Climate change is just one example. As already noted, government is being transformed into a world without boundaries. While officials deep down the line may still operate in relative isolation from other government departments and agencies, senior civil servants are expected to have a broader outlook. Former British prime minister Tony Blair spoke to this point in a major address on civil service reform and values. He said that 'The Civil Service needs to encourage and reward lateral thinking. It needs to reward civil servants who look outwards for learning rather than up the hierarchy for approval.'[16] Lateral thinking may be all-inclusive, but it also raises loyalty issues. The Treasury has turned to financial incentives to reshape loyalty, including new funding to encourage departments to engage in 'joined-up' initiatives pushing officials to work outside their departments to shape proposals.[17] The ability to secure new financial resources is widely applauded inside government, but putting money up as a reward for embracing horizontal government is not without consequences for government departments.

Ed Page and Bill Jenkins, in their recent study of Britain's policy bureaucracy, had this to say: 'the department is often assumed to be the prime focus for organizational loyalties among civil servants.' They add that we do not know whether this loyalty 'applies equally to a more mobile top civil servant and a less mobile middle and lower civil service.'[18] There is evidence, however, to suggest that the prime focus for organizational loyalties is under severe strain. As was noted above, loyalty to one's department is under attack on two fronts: from the push to horizontal government and from a fault line dividing senior management from civil servants down the line. Indeed, one can detect differences, even some sharp ones, in the way civil servants regard their department and their role as one goes up the organizational chart. Discussions with present and former line deputy ministers in Ottawa pointed to different preoccupations, values, and loyalties from those expressed by civil servants at the director general and director levels, and farther down the line.

I am not alone in sensing this division. The Task Force on Values and Ethics in the federal civil service also reported that its 'dialogue with public servants revealed to us a certain divide between levels in the public service, perhaps especially where public service values are concerned. Many at the middle and lower levels of the public service to whom we spoke or from whom we heard do not feel connected to the senior levels, and they are not sure whether they necessarily share the same values as those at higher levels.'[19] There are also significant differences in how the two groups view accountability. The more senior managers or, in Ed Page and Bill Jenkins's words, 'the more mobile top civil servant[s],' believe they are accountable to the prime minister, cabinet, their ministers, and the Privy Council Office – or the Cabinet Office in the case of Britain. As one goes down the hierarchy, however, this view is much less apparent. Program managers are likely to look to the public, their 'customers,' and their immediate superiors for a sense of how well they are performing.[20]

Some observers, including the Task Force on Values and Ethics, speak about a fault line in the accountability structure.[21] Deputy ministers, it appears, are much more willing to accept the traditional view of accountability. That is, since the civil service has no constitutional personality, they are there to serve the government of the day and to support its members in performing all the functions for which they are liable to answer to Parliament.[22] The same is not true for program managers, who, as already noted, tend to look more to their 'clients.' When asked to explain why such a fault line exists, a senior government official cited the New Public Management approach: 'You tell program and front line managers that the way ahead is empowerment and to focus on customers, and you repeat that message over and over again, as we have during the past several years. You also explain that the inside of government operations is not very healthy. It is full of red tape, rules, and controls. Now we wonder why our people are looking mostly out to clients and less and less to within government.'[23]

The Treasury Board Secretariat commissioned a study in 1997 to determine why managers were leaving the federal public service at a higher rate than in the past. The study 'clearly showed' that pay was not the main problem. Rather, 140 current and former managers consulted in a focus group explained that their work was being constantly 'distorted' for political reasons. The more senior officials (deputy ministers and assistant deputy ministers) stood accused of turning the public service into a 'ministerial service' and of being overly preoccupied with the political interests of the government, not in a partisan sense, but rather in making every effort to make the government look good.

The study also reported that the concern was more 'acute' among managers in Ottawa, 'especially among those who have already quit.' It added that in the regions, where many of the programs and services are actually delivered, managers were less concerned about the government's political interest.[24] It should be noted that about 65 per cent of all federal civil servants work in regional offices, and about 70 per cent of all executives or senior managers are located in the National Capital Region.

Deputy ministers now constitute a club in Ottawa circles and, to be sure, peer pressure matters. Deputy ministers do not wish to lose face before their peers, and this factor alone promotes close collaboration among club members. How does one lose credibility in the club? Certainly, all deputy ministers prefer walking into their breakfast or luncheon meetings knowing that their minister is in no political controversy or difficulties. All pride themselves on being able to keep their minister out of political trouble. This is now a key measure of success within the club, as indeed it is at the centre of government. To be sure, deputy ministers cannot always deflect a potential crisis; nevertheless, depending on the circumstances, the centre and members of the club may wonder if the deputy minister *could* have done so. On the other hand, when it is apparent that he or she has been able to keep the minister from embarrassment in the media or in Question Period, the club's praise is unstinting.

Deputy ministers and permanent secretaries, as already noted, are not recruited from within the department to the extent that they were in the past or to the extent that they still are in Germany and France, where one in two administrative heads comes from within the department. In addition, deputy ministers and permanent secretaries no longer remain head of the same department for many years and, when their careers end with one department, they no longer retire as before. The necessary skills and knowledge to become deputy ministers and permanent secretaries no longer require an intimate knowledge of a particular department or sector. The necessary skills are now as much political as they are administrative, and loyalty to the department is less strong than it once was. However, loyalty to one's peers or to the 'club' has come to matter a great deal in recent years.[25]

As Ted Hodgetts once observed, deputy ministers occupy a 'curious half-way house.'[26] They are part of the permanent hierarchy of the public service, but they are also in a constitutional sense the alter ego of the minister. They are half in the political world and half in the civil service, sandwiched between the neutral civil service and the partisan political ministers. They must strive to balance a sectoral or departmental perspective with the views of their political masters, which are often political and seldom sectoral. The report of a federal task force summed up the challenge: 'They must represent faithfully and effectively to their employees the wishes, needs and choices of the government of the day so that these may be met or carried out. At the same time, they must represent, and be seen to represent, the values and contribution of public servants to ministers. The second is almost as important as the first, because it undermines morale and corrodes the values of public service if it is not seen to be performed.'[27]

The two realms judge the deputy minister's performance from vastly different perspectives. Policy communities and major customer groups or stakeholders look to see if the deputy minister is able to promote the department's policy agenda and secure more funding for the department and its activities. The political world, meanwhile, has a short-term perspective and gives high marks for responsiveness to the government's political agenda, for flexibility, for making things happen, and for getting them done quickly and quietly.

There is a good deal of evidence in both Canada and Britain that the balance has shifted more to the political perspective.[28] The findings from the focus group noted earlier speak to this point, as many senior officials stood accused of turning the public service into a ministerial service. It is the political world, ultimately the prime minister, who decides who makes it to the very top and, once there, who is promoted to a larger department. Unlike in years past, deputy ministers and permanent secretaries are, like their ministers, increasingly birds of passage in their departments. Again, they are less and less likely to be promoted to that level from within the department. They are also much more likely than in the past to receive an appointment to another department before they retire, and so their loyalty to the department is both relatively recent and temporary. Their focus, or at least part of it, will be on their next appointment, and on the individuals who will have a say in future promotions – the cabinet secretary and the prime minister – not simply on the department they are currently leading.

Deputy ministers and permanent secretaries are ambitious individuals. They make it to the top increasingly because they are visible, because they are responsive to the wishes of the government of the day, and because they are able to establish a reputation that they make things happen and get things done. As one permanent secretary observes, 'There is a certain sort of civil servant, who in the past did well, who over the last 20 years has been edged out from getting to the top. What stopped them getting to that level? It was that they were insufficiently able to move things along and they didn't see that the purpose was to change things.'[29]

Much of the recent change in government in both Canada and Britain has been designed to reassert political control over the civil service and to strengthen management practices. How else can one explain the increased power of the prime minister's office in both countries, the increase in political staff, the establishment of executive units and special operating agencies, the recruiting of senior civil servants from outside or through open competition? In light of these developments, a permanent secretary had this to say about the future of the civil service. Civil servants, he explained, 'will not have a patron to advise on career development. They will not have worked the rites of passage in the private office or at the Treasury and the Cabinet Office. So the public service ethos will be eroded. Loyalty will be conditional, contingent. Informal networks will decline and have to be replaced by formal mechanisms of coordination. The search for the can-do manager will increase the opportunity for, and the temptation to make, political appointments.'[30]

There is precious little empirical evidence to suggest that career planning within government was any more or less successful forty years ago than it is today. Forty years ago, few civil servants wrote about their experience in government, and those who did tended to write about other things, such as the budget process and policy making. Today, former and even current practitioners appear more willing to write or comment on what goes on inside government, but again not much is said about career planning.[31] Consultations with civil servants suggest that attempts to plan a career do not hold much promise for them, at least in Canada. As one director-level official recently observed, 'It is now every man for himself. You try to hitch your wagon to a rising star who looks like he will be an Assistant Deputy Minister or Deputy Minister some day and hope things work out. You try to be visible to key players in town without making mistakes and things may break your way.'[32]

Things appear to be no different in Britain. In their book *The Politics of Public Service Bargains*, Christopher Hood and Martin Lodge compare human resources management in the U.K. government to a 'turkey race.' They explain that the British press once launched a cheap publicity stunt in the Christmas holiday by having turkeys race for their freedom to see which ones would go free and which ones would end up in the festive cooking pot. They report that some civil servants feel that they are now in a turkey race, pitting individual efforts and skills against other civil servants to see who gets the rewards.[33] In their interviews with Whitehall officials, they report that civil servants felt that the 'older conventions' of a system that had 'looked after' its career staff had moved substantially towards a 'turkey race' for promotion or even staying in the service. As one interviewee said, 'The new deal is that you will look after yourself in an environment where the risks and rewards are sharper.' Another, reflecting on thirty years in Whitehall, reported that 'Nowadays ... promotion is a free for all.'[34] In this environment, keeping your eye on the main chance becomes the key ingredient in shaping a career in the civil service.

Looking Out for Number One

Civil servants do not operate in a vacuum. As we saw earlier, society now values individual accomplishments as much as if not more than was the case forty years ago, but collective accomplishments are less valued, and 'belief in the efficacy of state action has been cracked.'[35] The civil service in both Canada and Britain is also now less institutionalized. For this and other reasons, individuals within it matter more.[36] We have also witnessed changes in motivation.[37] This should come as no surprise, given the sustained efforts to make the public sector look like the private sector.

How then do deputy ministers and permanent secretaries manage the border between the political and administrative worlds? Are they more politicized than their predecessors forty years ago? How are they managing their departments? Where do their loyalties lie? Senior civil servants say that no manual exists that describes every possible situation they might encounter with their minister and that they must deal with challenges and conflicts as best they can. The border between the political and administrative worlds is managed by instinct, by a culture handed down through generations of civil servants, by Parliament, and by the need to keep away from the media any hint that a civil servant has become overly political or gone sour.

There is no solid evidence in either Canada or Britain that deputy ministers or permanent secretaries are any more politically partisan today than they were forty years ago. From time to time, an appointment is made that will raise eyebrows because the individual is perceived to be closely connected to key members of the party in power. But things were no different forty years ago.

In their comparative study, R.A.W. Rhodes and Patrick Weller found little evidence that appointments to heads of departments are motivated by partisan political beliefs. They maintain that one needs to move beyond the idea of politicization to 'a different idea, that of personalization.' They report that heads of departments are selected because of their approach and style, not because they are members of the ruling political party. When Margaret Thatcher asked 'Are they one of us?' when considering potential appointments, she was interested in determining not so much whether they were Conservatives but whether they fitted with her definition of a competent civil servant – a can-do manager with a bias for action.[38] When Stephen Harper appointed Kevin Lynch clerk of the privy council and secretary to the cabinet within weeks of coming to power, civil servants in Ottawa understood the message. Lynch, a career civil servant, has never been known to be politically partisan. However, he is well known as a no-nonsense right-of-centre economist. He replaced Alex Himelfarb, a sociologist who came to government only in mid-career and with a limited appreciation of the civil service.[39] Harper also decided to 'shake up' the senior ranks of the civil service, and within several months of coming to office he had announced '41 moves.' However, no one has ever accused Harper of stacking his appointments with partisans of the Conservative party.[40]

Career civil servants, including the more ambitious ones, know intuitively not to cross politically partisan lines. But they have the political skills to recognize what the prime minister, his key advisers, and influential ministers value in the work of senior civil servants. They also know that their role has changed in recent years. Again, gone are the days when they had a monopoly over policy advice. Deputy ministers and permanent secretaries wielded a great deal of influence forty years ago 'because of their control of information and privileged access to the minister.'[41]

Rhodes and Weller explain why things have changed: 'many interests in society are better informed and more demanding: ministers are better educated; pressure groups have the technology and information to offer alternative scenarios, different models of the economy and possible strategies; ministers have an office full of staff who may be political and policy advisers with their own proposals for change; advice is contested; ideas are tested; and solutions are challenged.'[42] The role of departmental heads increasingly consists of 'packaging' for the prime minister and ministers advice they receive from a variety of sources, including consultants, think tanks, academics, and stakeholders or interested parties.[43]

Senior civil servants in traditional departments and agencies are now increasingly loyal to a process designed to promote horizontal or joined-up government. The climate-change initiative, for example, has no home in a formal organization. Rather, it is a process led by the centre with the expectation that line departments will shed their concern over turf and contribute to a government-wide initiative. The centre holds two advantages: it can provide financial resources to those willing to cooperate, not an insignificant advantage, to be sure. In government, the budget steals the stage and lays out in the clearest of terms who wins and who loses. The other advantage is that the centre has a large say in who makes it to the very top of the civil service. Ambitious civil servants know all too well that how they are perceived by the centre will decide whether they make it to deputy minister or permanent secretary.

Loyalty down the Line

If the department is no longer the main locus of loyalty for civil servants, then where does loyalty lie? Civil servants in relatively self-contained units delivering specialized services have specific skills, and they will have a distinct sense of loyalty to their work, their units, and their customers. Executive agencies, in particular, but also special operating agencies in Canada, are growing distinct organizational cultures and a concomitant sense of loyalty. This is deliberate. In his review of executive agencies in Britain, Oliver James maintains that the Cabinet Office and the Treasury promote coordination between agencies but only to 'facilitate sporadic links.' He adds that when the Cabinet Office intervenes, it is to improve 'individual bodies' performance.'[44]

Thus, when it comes to purely program units, loyalty is pushed down to the unit itself, to operating and executive agencies. This squares with their *raison d'être*: the agencies were designed to force managers to focus on management issues, to look outside to clients, and to imitate their private sector counterparts. Loyalty to the civil service as an institution was not part of the grand scheme.

As civil servants are pushed farther away from the centre of government and centrally prescribed rules, their loyalties may shift, as they come to identify with new partners in the shaping and delivering of public services. Some may be more attuned to strong management practices than to their home departments. Others may find themselves embracing a process, one designed to bring different policy actors to the table to shape new initiatives.

Loyalty and Remuneration

The rewards of public service, designed to secure loyalty and a non-partisan perspective, have through the ages contained the following: permanence, career progression, a modest and steady salary, and relatively generous pensions on retirement. The case has been made many times that in the past civil servants have been drawn to government because they are by nature risk averse, that they enjoy the certainty of a steady salary, and that they derive a certain 'psychic income' in other forms, such as having a respected social status or the satisfaction of working for the government.[45] The rewards of a 'psychic income' are much less evident today. Indeed, morale problems plague the bureaucracies of many Western countries, including of course Canada and Britain.

The perception persists that civil servants receive modest pay. It will be recalled that, in his valedictory lecture in 2005, Andrew Turnbull identified 'civil service pay, particularly at senior levels,' in relation to the private sector, to be one of the unresolved issues, as he took his leave from the civil service as cabinet secretary. Ezra Suleiman writes that 'public sector salaries can probably never keep pace with those of the private sector. But they have fallen substantially behind in recent years. This is the case in all democratic societies. But beyond this obvious and glaring disparity, there remains the fact that public service no longer carries with it such advantages as prestige and security of employment.'[46] Suleiman is right about his latter point, but not the first.

Study after study in recent years reveals that, leaving aside the most senior executive levels, workers in the public sector command a 5 to 20 per cent wage premium over private sector workers. The studies make the case that the wage premium, depending on gender and occupation, is higher for the same amount of human capital working in comparable jobs in both sectors. Accordingly, the premium *cannot* be accounted for by increased education, tenure, and the like. Moreover, public sector workers have far more generous fringe benefits, from pension plans to dental care, than their private sector counterparts.

The only private sector workers who earn more than their public sector counterparts are males who are in the top income quartile. However, data here are difficult to secure, given that the number in this category is small and because of confidentiality requirements. The problems with the data employed to account for pay differences between the private and public sectors is that the number of individuals with very high incomes are either so few that it is not possible to make reliable estimates for them from sample surveys or, if census data are employed, Statistics Canada does not allow their numbers to be published for confidentiality reasons. Census data in Canada do not provide data on males who earn more than $200,000 and females who earn more than $120,000. Thus, all entries of $200,000 mean that the individual may earn more than this amount. The same amount will be recorded even if he makes much more. How many individuals would this entail? For females it is 15,535 individuals and for males 39,849. We do not know how many of them work in the private sector. We can safely assume, however, that many occupy senior private sector positions.

Several Canadian scholars have looked at pay differences between government and the private sector. Their conclusion – there is a substantial wage premium in working for government, depending on the level of government. They developed a model controlling unionization rates, and make the case that a large part of the wage differential is a result of higher unionization rates in the Canadian civil service than in the private sector.[47] There have been similar findings in Britain.[48]

Morley Gunderson has broken down differences in remuneration in Canada between pecuniary and non-pecuniary. He writes that public sector workers enjoy better non-pecuniary benefits. He points to job security. Not only are government workers sheltered from market forces, they are more easily shifted to other jobs within government, should the need arise, than private sector workers are within their own firms. He suggests a reason why fringe benefits such as pension plans are better in government than in the private sector – government may have an incentive to save today on current wage costs by granting very generous pension benefits. For example, in lieu of giving a 3 per cent pay increase today, the government can offer a 1 per cent increase today but have a more generous retirement plan as the trade-off.

Table 8.1
Average British hourly income (in £)

	1995		2005	
	Male	Female	Male	Female
Private	7.72	5.3	11.43	8.54
Public	9.47	7.38	13.28	10.96
Average	8.1	5.99	11.78	9.44

Source: Office for National Statistics, Social and Vital Statistics Division and Northern Ireland Statistics and Research Agency. Central Survey Unit, *Quarterly Labour Force Survey, June-August 2005* (computer file). Colchester, Essex: UK Data Archive (distributor), November 2005, SN: 5266. Office of Population Censuses and Surveys. Social Survey Division and Northern Ireland Statistics and Research Agency. Central Survey Unit, *Quarterly Labour Force Survey, June-August 1995* (computer file). *4th Edition,* Colchester, Essex: UK Data Archive (distributor), April 2004, SN: 3490. Please note that the definition employed for public sector employees is pretty broad.

Essentially, this is just a deferred payment that will be borne by future taxpayers. In the private sector this is not possible. Non-pecuniary benefits for government workers, however, are such that the government should be in a position to attract employees without having to pay equivalent private sector wages.

With respect to pecuniary compensation, Gunderson points out that, in government, wages are set under a political rather than a profit constraint, which, he insists, is less binding. He points to important differences between the two sectors: the ability of government to pass the buck to future generations, and the fact that, during a strike, government will continue to see revenues come in while private sector firms may well see a dramatic drop that can threaten jobs, let alone salary increases. It is also assumed that demand for public services is inelastic. Thus the bargaining unit can demand higher wages without having to worry about significant reductions in employment (see table 8.1 for data on Britain). This is largely due to the fact that many of the services government provides have no real substitutes or are considered essential. Coupled with this is the extremely high unionization rate in the public sector and the fact that unions are well positioned to pursue economic advantages for their members, given that market forces are not an issue.[49]

In 2004–5, the Canadian government carried out a comparative review of public and private sector compensation. The government resisted making public the study's findings, employing a number of tactics, including classifying the document as 'a cabinet confidence.' The government finally relented to demands in July 2007 by 'quietly posting' the report on the government website.[50] The study confirmed that workers in 'lower-end' jobs make more than similar workers in the private sector, that those 'in the middle' enjoy better benefits, but that those in 'top jobs' are paid significantly less than their private sector counterparts. The study also reported that compensation for civil servants now accounts for more than one-third of the government's discretionary spending.[51]

To be sure, senior private sector executives enjoy far better financial remuneration than senior government managers, including deputy ministers and permanent secretaries. Compensation for senior bank executives is now in the millions if one includes stock options and performance bonuses. Performance can be tied to a number of objectives and easy-to-understand criteria: market share, profit, share prices, and so on.

Though salaries for deputy heads have not kept pace with those of senior private sector executives, they have increased substantially in recent years. It will be recalled that Thatcher had problems with her own MPs when she decided to give permanent heads of departments a 50 per cent pay increase. In addition, the point of reference for senior civil servants' compensation has become the private sector, not the not-for-profit sector or other criteria.

As was noted in an earlier chapter, many jurisdictions, including Canada and Britain, have instituted performance pay schemes for senior managers. As is the case for other jurisdictions, both Canada and Britain have had problems making the approach work. Governments signed on to performance pay schemes because it was felt that 'uncompetitive' compensation made it difficult to attract the 'highest calibre' of people and that the traditional compensation approach did not encourage and reward outstanding performance. They also argued that 'good leaders' were leaving the public sector.[52] Precious few studies, however, have actually suggested that 'good' leaders were leaving for the private sector because of salary differences or that 'compensation' was the problem in its inability to attract the 'highest calibre' people. We noted earlier that 140 current and former federal government managers reported 'clearly' that pay was not their main reason for leaving or planning to leave the civil service.

In the case of Canada, the pay for performance approach is guided by an Advisory Committee on Senior Level Retention and Compensation composed of 'prominent' Canadians.[53] The approach borrows heavily from the private sector – indeed, one would be hard pressed to differentiate its vocabulary from that of the private sector. It describes the objective of the program as follows: 'to encourage excellent performance by recognizing and rewarding the achievement of results that are linked to business plans.'[54] Neither the advisory committee nor, for that matter, the government, has ever explained how 'business plans' fit into the public sector. They have also never explained how compensation in government can be tied to outstanding performance. At a minimum, the new approach requires a transition from Weber's loyalty to the organization and to formal rules and processes to a new loyalty, one tied to the pursuit of economic self-interest.

Whatever the reason, we know that performance pay schemes have not been a success in government. Senior government officials readily admit to a number of problems. Jean-Guy Fleury, the head of the senior personnel secretariat in the Privy Council Office, reports that 'corporate priorities were too broad for the deputy ministers to easily link them to their own concrete objectives' and that 'more work is required to develop performance indicators that are measurable in the public service environment and within the control of the individual.'[55] Alex Himelfarb, former clerk of the privy council and secretary to the cabinet, pointed to a number of problems with the scheme, including the fact that in government, 'very often, what one discovers is poor performance, or performance that should not be rewarded or acknowledged, several years previous, but it wasn't known during the period of contract and it creates enormous embarrassment. I do believe we have to fix that.' He was referring to the fact that senior civil servants implicated in various high-profile scandals, such as the sponsorship scandal and the Human Resources Development 'boondoggle,' had all received bonuses.[56] He never explained how the problem could be fixed.

Paul Cochrane, for example, the senior Health Canada official at the centre of a fraud case for which he was later found guilty, was awarded a $7,300 performance bonus in August 2000 for 'meeting the expectation' of his job. At the time, however, his branch was subject to a series of audits, and the deputy minister had already moved him out of his position only to appoint him as senior adviser to the department. Four months later, he was suspended from the civil service after his department discovered that he was on a week-long cruise with seventy staffers from the foundation that he was funding.[57] Chuck Guité, the official at the centre of the sponsorship scandal, also consistently received performance bonuses. The head of the Association of Professional Executives of the Public Service of Canada said that performance pay schemes require more 'rigour' and 'discipline' to ensure that there are consequences for those who do not meet job targets. He was responding to the fact that between 93 and 96 per cent of the 4,550 executives in government received performance pay in 2002 and 2003.[58]

The Canada Investment and Savings Agency, one of the government's Special Operating Agencies, saw its four top executives collect about $600,000 in bonuses between 1999 and 2004. The agency's *raison d'être* is to market savings and investment products, notably Canada Savings Bonds. Sales of the bonds dropped substantially over the 1999–2004 period, down to $2.8 billion in 2004 from $7.5 billion in 1995. How senior managers at the agency were able to justify performance bonuses was never made clear. Indeed, an internal note from a senior finance official obtained by the media suggested that the bonuses 'leave us vulnerable to questions.'[59] A survey of senior federal government executives carried out in 2006 found them highly critical of the performance-based salary scheme. They described the scheme as 'arbitrary, subjective, de-motivating and failing to reward team work.'[60]

In Britain, performance pay schemes have not fared any better. They have been adjusted, time and again, ever since their introduction. Initially, performance pay was designed to reward individuals for their performance, but then the emphasis turned to team bonuses. Performance bonuses, however, continued to be available to permanent secretaries. Hood and Lodge report that there is also a 'turkey race' aspect to the pay for performance approach in Britain.[61]

Again, Canada and Britain are hardly alone in their limited success in making pay for performance work. Various OECD countries have also encountered problems. Patricia Ingraham has written extensively on pay for performance programs in the public sector and has identified numerous difficulties in making them work.[62] She has not been able to find many success stories anywhere in the Western world. All governments are facing the intractable problem that it is one thing to say that management in the public sector should adopt private sector practices and quite another to have them do so. No one has been able to establish clear, objective criteria with which to assess the performance of senior civil servants, and no one has been able to design a scheme that avoids 'gaming.' It is also important to note that pay for performance programs, at least in Canada and Britain, have been largely taken out of the hands of politicians. Elected politicians do not decide the level of bonuses on their own. Still, pay for performance programs have an impact on the behaviour of senior civil servants. Individuals and individual interests matter much more than they used to: turkey races and competition for financial rewards have become part of life for senior civil servants.

Introducing the business-management model did change some things in government, albeit not always for the better. Greed may well have accompanied the model into government. Senior government officials are still looked after at the end of their careers with highly generous pension schemes. In Canada, deputy ministers, after ten years in that position, can now enjoy an indexed pension set at 90 per cent of their salaries based on the average of their best five years. Under the special retirement allowance, deputy ministers are credited with two years of service for every year worked, to a maximum of ten years. The special allowance was introduced in 1988 because deputy ministers increasingly work in 'a volatile environment' that does not 'allow most of them to continue to normal retirement age.' This view, however, has been challenged. The head of a civil service union, for example, recently argued that while deputy ministers may get shuffled around, 'I don't know that I have ever heard of a deputy minister getting fired.'[63]

Deputy ministers no longer go quietly into retirement. They now have opportunities to earn money – as consultants or lobbyists and on special government contracts – and a good number of them now pursue these opportunities. Indeed, high-level experience in government has also become a valuable qualification in the private sector, particularly with associations of various kinds and government-relations offices in large national or multinational firms.[64]

The Canadian literature reports that 'a new breed of public servant has emerged with an ethos less oriented to public interest and frugality than towards career advancement and making a mark through bold plans and expenditures.'[65] Civil servants can no longer point their finger at politicians to explain all problems of values and ethics in government. The Public Service Commission noted this development with deep concern. It reported that 'public perceptions of the ethical standards of public servants are currently at their lowest point in seven years ... Many other professions were rated higher. For a public service striving for an exemplary reputation for integrity, these findings are troubling.'[66]

Looking Back

Loyalty in government has taken on new meanings of late. For one thing, loyalty is no longer straightforward. For another, the focus is, by design, increasingly geared towards the individual. For politicians, loyalty to their parties is not as strong as it once was. As parties are less wedded to a core set of principles, beliefs, and values, leaders have come to dominate their parties and the career aspirations of elected party members. In short, parties are fast losing structure and fast becoming more focused on personality. Loyalty to an individual is not the same thing as loyalty to a political party.

Civil servants have traditionally given their loyalty to their institutions and their home departments. But here, too, things are no longer so straightforward. Their institutions have become fragmented, new public/private partnerships have been developed, and horizontal or joined-up governments have reshaped the processes of policy and program formulation. Compensation for government managers has also undergone a substantial makeover. The emphasis is now on the individual and individual performance, however difficult that may be to measure in government. The result is that we have witnessed a shift to 'self first, duty second' and away from 'duty first, self second' among civil servants in both Canada and Britain. All this is to say that self-interest at both the political and bureaucratic levels has been in the ascendant in recent years.

9 The View from the Bottom: A Big Whale That Can't Swim

I asked a middle-level manager working in a Canadian regional line department to describe the state of the civil service. His response: 'It has become a big whale that can't swim.' Despite the recent emphasis on service delivery, empowerment, and emulating private sector management techniques, he believes that things were much better when he entered the civil service in 1973. My next, obvious question was why? His reply: 'It's not fun anymore working in government, too many young university graduates come in just to get a few years experience and then go off to do something else rather than commit to a full career and, believe it or not, there is more red tape now, so that it is a lot more difficult these days to get things done. People just don't come to work happy any more.'[1] By red tape he meant the need to generate performance-related reports and to cope with new administrative requirements in dealing with businesses and community groups in the immediate aftermath of the irregularities at Human Resources Development Canada (HRDC) and the sponsorship scandal. Surveys in Canada confirm that middle managers 'are particularly pessimistic in their view of departmental morale' and that there is a 'significant increase' in the percentage of both 'front line workers and middle managers reporting that they would not choose to become a civil servant if given the same career decision.'[2] Things are not much different in Britain.

The purpose of this chapter is to view government from the bottom of the hierarchy and from the perspective of citizens. To do so, we will focus on the relationship between citizens and government on the one hand, and front-line managers and workers and senior civil servants on the other, by looking at consultations with practitioners, public opinion surveys, and government reports. This chapter makes the case that court government and all its characteristics are being felt down the line and not just in the senior echelons of the civil service.

Citizen Participation

The political leadership in the early 1980s in both Canada and Britain decided that government needed to be reformed in a number of areas. One, as we have already seen, was for government to recast its operations so that in future citizens would be viewed as customers, at least for the purpose of service delivery.

This, however, was not the first attempt to alter the government-citizen relationship. Starting in the 1960s, a number of governments in Anglo-American democracies called for citizen participation in designing and implementing programs. 'Power to the people' and 'participatory democracy,' for example, were at the heart of Trudeau's call for a Just Society and of U.S. president Lyndon Johnson's policies for a Great Society.[3] Governments also said that they wanted public participation in the planning and delivery of regional and community development programs, the thinking being that without community involvement such efforts would have little chance of success.[4]

Without putting too fine a point on it, these efforts soon petered out, and citizen participation became at best spotty and uncertain.[5] For one thing, the bureaucracy had limited interest in including citizens in its work. It was a relatively new concept that held little appeal for civil servants. For another, civil servants were particularly ill-equipped to have citizens participate in their work. The machinery of government, especially accountability requirements, was not designed to include such participation in either policy making or program delivery. As a result, a number of people, particularly those interested in consultation, soon concluded that citizen participation was an empty phrase, as departments continued to pursue their program objectives as before rather than welcoming genuine citizen participation.

Citizen participation came back into fashion in the 1980s and 1990s. This time, however, some citizens became proactive, demanding a place at the policy table, particularly in the areas of the environment, community economic development, and health care. In response, governments set up a multitude of advisory boards, committees, and focus groups and conducted numerous public opinion surveys to secure citizen input in government decision making. Public opinion surveys, as has been well documented elsewhere, have had a profound impact on government. Yet the machinery of government, again particularly in terms of accountability requirements, is still not much different from what it was in the 1960s.

The bureaucracy has been left to adjust to this new scenario as best it can. The environment is now less formal and operates with different sets of rules, depending on the players and the circumstances. Fewer rules means more flexibility, and this should enable civil servants to engage citizens more easily in their work. However, fewer rules also means a riskier environment for civil servants. Rules, when respected, can shelter them from political criticism and from the media when things go wrong. Moreover, if rules are followed to the letter, things very rarely go wrong.

In the absence of rules and clear guidelines and processes, civil servants must now rely on elected politicians and a weakened hierarchy for support and protection. It only takes a moment's reflection to appreciate that, from a civil service perspective, politicians and a weaker hierarchy are less certain allies than rules and processes when things go astray. One only has to look at Canada's so-called HRDC boondoggle to see the evidence of this. The then Human Resources Development minister asked members of Parliament for their input in selecting community economic development projects. MPs enthusiastically responded, promoting projects for their own constituencies. With little patience for due process and red tape, they pushed bureaucrats to get on with things and make decisions. However, when internal audits revealed that projects had been approved without the necessary paperwork and that some files were incomplete, the opposition jumped on the news and put the minister and senior civil servants through 'a year of living hell.'[6] Members of Parliament who had once pushed hard for their projects to be chosen were nowhere to be seen when it came to explaining what had gone wrong. Civil servants had learned an important lesson.

Civil servants in Canada and Britain, perhaps because they have traditionally had no constitutional personality distinct from the government of the day, have never been easy with public consultations and involvement. They regard their work as technical in nature and may wish to consult experts in their fields for policy or administrative input. They understand the rise and requirements of government by policy networks staffed and driven by political or economic elites, but, as Robin Clarke remarks, civil servants still prefer to 'look upwards to please their political masters, rather than outwards.'[7] Clarke disputes the notion that lack of public participation in Britain is due to political apathy. Rather, he maintains that the fundamental problem is 'with the way we do politics.' He insists that citizens do indeed have a strong interest in public policy issues, including strategic national issues and risk issues.[8] Public consultations, however, have very rarely lived up to expectations. In Britain, the Conservative party's Democracy Task Force concluded in 2007 that 'there has never been more consultation in policy making than now, but never has it meant less.'[9]

The Internet

Practitioners have turned to the Internet in recent years to promote citizen participation and to improve the delivery of government services. A number of observers also believe that the Internet is key to effective public participation in shaping public policies and in service delivery. One went so far as to suggest that the Internet will 'change everything, will revolutionize public participation so that citizens can play a more central role in the development of new agencies, policies and rules.'[10] He added, however, that 'rosy predictions' about the impact of e-government may stem in part from the current low level of citizen participation.[11] Political parties in both Canada and Britain have turned to the Internet to promote candidates and party positions, and to track swing voters, target communications, and raise funds. Political blogging is gaining in popularity in both countries, and many maintain that it holds important democratic potential.[12] Though this may well prove to be so in time, it has yet to elbow out the national electronic and print media.

To be sure, considerable progress has already been made through e-government in sharing information with citizens on government policies and programs.[13] It has also armed citizens and associations with important information with which to challenge government departments and agencies and their policies. It is not at all clear, however, to what extent it has enabled citizens to participate in government decision making. All in all, the jury is still out on the extent to which the Internet has promoted public participation. What we do know is that the Internet has proven its worth in its ability to provide information to citizens. It has not, however, been nearly as effective in incorporating the views of citizens in policies and new initiatives.

Former British prime minister Tony Blair got a great deal more than he bargained for when, in the fall of 2006, he agreed to partner with a non-partisan group to invite citizens to set up petitions to be hosted on the Downing Street website, thus enabling anyone to deliver a petition directly to the prime minister. Many citizens happily responded to the invitation. One set up a petition that read, 'We the undersigned petition the Prime Minister to scrap the planned vehicle tracking and road privacy policy.' Blair's government had decided that one way to reduce traffic congestion and cut greenhouse gas emissions was to track cars by satellite and charge motorists on the distance they drive. The taxpayer argued that the proposed charges would be unfair for the poor and decided to establish a petition on the Downing Street website. The petition became highly popular, and within weeks nearly 1.8 million people had signed it.[14] It was also widely reported in the media, prompting Blair to say that he would reply to all those who signed the petition. However, as Stephen Ladyman, Blair's minister of roads, declared, 'I do not take the petition very seriously. Of course, there is a debate to be held. I have said we have a long way to go to convince people.'[15] *The Times* warned the government not to dismiss the petition 'as pure theatre.' Democracy, it argued, is 'different in the digital age and this Government has to address the collective concerns of a generally mild-mannered and very large constituency. If not, there really will be road rage.'[16] In his response to all those who signed the petition, Blair wrote that the petition and his e-mail were 'the beginning, not the end of the debate.'[17] The point is that e-democracy has important challenges to deal with before it can become part of the public policy-making and decision-making process.

Canada and Britain have both been very active on the information technology (IT) front. The international consulting firm Accenture has consistently ranked Canada in the lead in implementing e-government among national governments.[18] That said, the Office of the Auditor General has pointed to a number of flaws in Ottawa's e-government initiative. It warned that, unless some key issues are resolved, the government's on-line initiative could 'become an expensive and underused vehicle' and that it will likely be far more expensive than the government had estimated.[19] Still, IT is now central to the work of virtually all civil servants – in the case of Canada, employees in 94 per cent of its units now have access to computer training. Blackberries are common, and a typical Canadian civil servant spends more than half of his or her time at work on a computer.[20]

Managers report that IT has increased the 'work capacity and effectiveness' of their units. They also say that they have received the necessary support and resources to equip their employees to use technology to its 'fullest advantage.' As is well known, the technology has eliminated a large number of clerical positions in the civil service. Yet government managers in Canada disagree with the suggestion that IT should mean that fewer people ought to be needed in their units. This, however, may well have more to do with bureaucratic unwillingness to part with resources than an objective assessment of the resources required to get the job done.[21]

The British government has also embraced IT with enthusiasm, though it does not appear to be as successful in its implementation as the Canadian government has been. Accenture has consistently placed Britain tenth in its ranking of countries in implementing e-government. Still, going as far back as John Major's government, there has been a minister responsible for IT – more commonly known as 'the e-minister.' It has never, however, fully grabbed any prime minister's attention, necessary in Britain (as in Canada) if a project is to make it onto the government's priority list. This was true even under Blair, though modernization of government was a key part of his agenda. The focus of Blair's government was on performance management and deregulation. This did not, however, prevent the government from several reorganizations to promote e-government. In addition, much as in Canada, the government pledged to have all services on-line at some point in the relatively near future and appointed a chief information officer to promote and coordinate IT activities. Again as in Canada, IT has been used to promote 'joined-up' government (for example, the sharing of information between departments about customers).[22] Studies by market research organizations, however, reveal that citizens in Britain are not using e-government as often as citizens of other countries – ranking sixth out of seven OECD countries.[23]

Canada and Britain share yet another thing in common. Both countries turned to the IT sector to generate substantial cost savings, though no one has ever been able to tally them. Both countries also share a history of public sector IT program failures. E-government spending, broadly defined, is now estimated in the billions in both countries (about £15 billion in Britain). The list of IT initiatives gone bad in both countries is very long.[24] In Canada, one only has to consult the annual reports of the auditor general or follow stories in the media for a growing list of IT failed projects, from Foreign Affairs to the Treasury Board Secretariat. There has been case after case of overspending, gaffes, and outright failures in introducing IT in government departments and agencies.[25] In

Britain, the government, by 2002, was investing more resources in the development of electronic public services than were 'other similar countries.' However, the National Audit Office reported that the investments produced 'mixed outcomes.'[26] IT projects to support the magistrates court, the air traffic control centre, and the passport agency, among others, were both much more costly than anticipated and several years late in becoming operational.[27] Newspaper headlines such as 'The NHS's £20 bn computer isn't working' are not rare in Britain.[28]

Citizens as Customers

A view of citizens as customers is different from a view of citizens as active participants in government. Citizens viewed as voters and taxpayers are part of a community, able to assess what the community, the region, or the nation as a whole receive from government. Such a view speaks to the collectivity in whatever form, be it a country or a community, and to its well-being. A view of citizens as customers, meanwhile, regards them as consumers. It speaks to the individual and his or her well-being. This, in turn, leads us to assess government and government services in terms of what individuals receive rather than what the collectivity receives as a whole. Put differently, a citizen is a member of a community, be it nationally or locally, and possesses certain rights and entitlements and, in turn, has certain duties and obligations. A customer is a recipient of a service, but need not be a citizen.[29] Thus a Canadian citizen in Moncton shares a common purpose and responsibility with a fellow citizen in Vancouver. A shopper in Wal-Mart in Moncton, meanwhile, has no common responsibility with a Wal-Mart shopper in Vancouver other than searching for the best possible bargain.

The notion of citizen as customer has been well debated in the literature, and there is no need to go over the same territory here.[30] Suffice it to note that a number of authors have pointed to important conceptual problems. For example, for a prison worker, who is the customer – the prisoner? For an immigration officer, who is the customer – someone who claims to be a political refugee? For a civil servant working in a tax collection department or agency, who is the customer? Under what circumstances does a citizen become a customer? The list of unanswered questions goes on.

What is of more direct interest to us is what the concept means for the front-line civil servant? The answer is – it depends. Some civil servants have happily embraced the concept of citizen as customer, others have been lukewarm, while still others see little benefit in it. Many front-line civil servants who work in economic or industrial development departments happily and consistently refer to 'customers' in their dealings with citizens. There are several reasons for this. Private sector firms were the first to buy into the idea of citizen as customer. For front-line civil servants dealing with private sector firms to promote industrial development, new technology, research and development, trade, and economic development, it is a relatively straightforward matter – one does not need to ponder for very long the question of who the customer is. In addition, civil servants in the economic development field would readily identify with the private sector and would see advantages in using its vocabulary. As one front-line worker explained, 'I cannot think what else I would call my customers, except customers. We talk the same language, my department is run like a business and we deal with financial and bank statements just like the private sector does.'[31]

The same cannot be said about front-line civil servants working in social policy fields, in security, and in tax collection. Here, they do not employ the term 'customer' with much enthusiasm in their dealings with citizens. This is also true for departments and agencies that deal with cultural and heritage issues and education. They will more often refer to groups and associations than to individuals, and the word *customer* does not sit easily with them.'[32] Still, they use *customer* in some of their planning documents if only 'to feed the beast,' as one front-line civil servant put it.[33]

What is interesting to note is that those who have the resources to deal with government and bureaucracy are more at home with the word *customer* and are the ones who have been quick to embrace it. Studies reveal that businesses are much more adroit at accessing government services through a variety of means (from the telephone and Internet to face-to-face contact) than are individual citizens. Large businesses also have experts, lobbyists, or lawyers to intervene on their behalf before government officials.

Businesses stand to benefit the most from viewing government services in terms of what individuals receive rather than what the collectivity receives. Moreover, if you emulate the private sector and borrow words from its vocabulary, the business community will be pleased. Imitation, after all, is the sincerest form of flattery. It is also interesting to note that governments have not tried to sort out to which departments the notion of citizen as customer applies and to which it does not. In brief, both Canada and Britain have embraced the concept without determining how to apply it or spelling out rules to follow in its implementation.

Feeding the Beast

Front-line government workers share one frustration – the constant demand for information from departmental headquarters and from central agencies. The requests are varied, ranging from financial and administrative data to complete departmental reports on any number of policy and administrative issues. Civil servants report that the demand for these has increased 'exponentially' in recent years and that it eats up a lot of resources. As one front-line manager explains, 'you can't even begin to imagine what it's like now. We spend an incredible amount of time just feeding the beast in Ottawa with all kinds of information.' She added, 'it may have to do with the need for more transparency, the need to provide more information to people, the need to deal with the media, the need to keep our ministers informed of everything, but whatever it is, it consumes an incredible amount of our time and energy. It always seems to be getting worse, never better.'[34]

The centre of government has not only grown, but people who work in central agencies enjoy more senior classifications and higher pay than officials occupying similar positions in line departments (see table 9.1). There are many officials, for example, in the Privy Council Office in Ottawa who enjoy a deputy minister-level classification. In Britain as in Canada, *toute proportion gardée*, there are more officials occupying senior positions in central agencies than in line departments. The number of Cabinet Office officials who now enjoy permanent secretary classification has increased over the past ten years.[35] Nor do these central agency officials have programs to manage and deliver. Thus, they can spend all of their time on policy issues, working on briefing material and micromanaging specific files whenever a crisis flares up, and demanding more and more information from the front line.[36]

Central agencies have a much stronger policy capacity than they had forty years ago. They have strategic planning capacities and, if need be, a direct hand in the day-to-day work of departments. At times, their officials can be heavily involved in transactions or specific departmental files; at other times, not at all. It depends. If it involves the prime minister's interest or if the government's political standing may

Table 9.1
Central agencies, number of employees, 1970–2005

Canada	1970	2005
• PMO-PCO	287	1,032
• Treasury Board	479	1,259
• Finance	417	966

United Kingdom	1970	2005
• PMO-Cabinet Office	716	1,670
• Treasury	989	1,190

Source: Canada, *Budget des dépenses 2005–2006, partie III – Rapport sur les plans et les priorités*, Ottawa, Travaux publics et Services gouvernementaux 2005; Canada, *Budget des dépenses*, Ottawa, ministère des Finances, 13T 31–2, 1970; United Kingdom, Public Sector Employment, National Statistics, 2 October 2006; and United Kingdom, Civil Service Statistics, 1970, London: HMSO 14s Od

be in jeopardy, then central agency officials will be present – even, if necessary, physically in the department directing things.[37] Departments know full well that the centre has them on constant watch to protect the prime minister and the government's political interests, that it also has the human and financial resources to monitor departments – or at least what the media have to say about them – and that, if necessary, it will intervene.

Still, officials in central agencies need to rely on data provided by line departments, and this explains in part the constant stream of requests for information. It should surprise no one that if you add positions in central agencies, as both Canada and Britain have done in more recent years, you will also give rise to more requests for information to line departments and agencies. But that is not all. Ministers need to be briefed on proposed new initiatives and on anticipated questions, both in Parliament and from the media. Just responding to access to information requests and any difficulties they may create for the minister and department can consume a great deal of ministerial time and that of department officials. Andy Scott, the minister of Indian affairs and northern development in Paul Martin's government (2004–6), reports that the department's communications branch employed 118 officials and that 111 of them spent most of their time on work related to access to information requests.[38] A number of new requirements, notably whistle-blowing legislation, will only add to briefing requirements.

It is difficult to determine the amount of time departmental officials spend on 'feeding the beast,' on briefing their ministers, or on dealing with citizens. Consultations with front-line employees suggest that Canadian officials spend more time on providing briefing material for the system than in dealing with citizens. In Canada, there are more central agencies than in Britain, and access to information legislation has been in place for more than twenty years. In addition, federal-provincial relations generate a great many policy papers and a great deal of briefing material. Canada has more oversight bodies than Britain does (for example, the commissioner of official languages), and these also generate paperwork. A government survey of 221,434 positions was carried out in the late 1980s to identify all jobs that had at least some responsibility for dealing with the general public, even if that 'some' amounted to only 10 per cent. The survey found only 92,481 such positions or 41.8 per cent of the total number of positions.[39]

Several years ago, it was pointed out that 'well over half' of senior managerial positions in the government of Canada were staff positions and that 65 per cent of them were located in Ottawa. Today, the number of senior managers occupying staff positions has increased, and well over 70 per cent of them now work in Ottawa.[40] Line managers and a number of observers have long argued that there are far too many people, including managers, performing a staff function. As far back as 1971, J.R. Mallory wrote that 'only a small fraction of the total strength of the public service is directly engaged in carrying out administrative decisions. The rest of the public service is engaged in staff functions.'[41]

Much like ministers, line managers have also come to rely on staff people in the departments to get things done in the system, which explains why there are more staff positions today than in 1971. Indeed, knowing how the system operates and how to navigate in it has become a much-valued competence, even inside the federal civil service. One line manager explains why: 'I simply do not have the time to deal with all the nonsense central agencies keep throwing at us. That is what our staff people in Ottawa are paid to do. When there is a problem with the Treasury Board Secretariat, Finance, or PCO, they take over. I attend some of the meetings when I have to or when I am in Ottawa. Frankly, it is just another world. It is so far removed from what I do, it is unbelievable. Sometimes I think that they speak in tongues.'

But, he adds, 'You need these people around if you want to get things done and to protect your back.'[42] Another reported that he 'tries to avoid involving head office or central agencies' as much as possible. He explains that it is important in a line operation to

> keep your head down, keep things under control here, and don't involve Ottawa people unless you absolutely have to. They will leave you alone if you don't give them a reason to call you. My measure of success is how often that phone rings and someone in Ottawa is on the line. If it rings often, we are doing something wrong. If it doesn't ring, we are doing fine. From time to time, you get head office people introducing a new approach. You know they have to keep busy so that they come around with a new Treasury Board approach in this or that area. We just go along filling their forms while we deliver the programs.[43]

In their study of 'service in the field,' Barbara Carroll and David Siegel confirm this view and quote a government official's claim that officials working in regional offices 'value the ability to work one-on-one with clients. That starts to break down immediately when you get into layers in Ottawa.'[44]

Front-line managers and workers doubt that they dominate their deputy minister's agenda to the extent that they did forty years ago. Though their mandate is not always clear, deputy ministers are very busy people (more is said about that in the next chapter). Suffice it to note here that, according to a detailed study of their workload published in 1997, on average they work eleven hours and twenty-eight minutes a day, or fifty-seven hours a week and spend one hour out of every three on interdepartmental issues. It is interesting to note that a deputy minister typically allocates nearly twice as much time to meetings with his peers as to matters involving his own minister.[45] With respect to issues, deputy ministers on average allocate more of their time to crisis management (16 per cent) than to human resources management (15 per cent). The study also reveals that deputy ministers are at the very centre of departmental activities and that they are always trying as best they can to accommodate 'the urgent,' the 'important,' and the 'unforeseen in [their] daily agenda.'[46]

As noted earlier, deputy ministers are now part of a club. The club meets regularly over breakfast, luncheon, and at special retreats, all chaired by the head of the civil service, the clerk of the privy council. It has its own rules – deputy ministers may have sharp differences with one another, but there is an unwritten understanding that you do not voice those differences outside the club or, in some instances, even inside it. As a former deputy minister explains, 'The department produced a letter for me to sign to the deputy minister of Public Works, which was very testy, if not harsh. I turned it back. I simply could not send that kind of letter to my colleague, although my people had every reason to be upset at Public Works.'[47] As is the case for most other clubs, members are also expected to remain loyal to the club itself.

With all the talk since the Thatcher days about the importance of management, a survey of senior government officials carried out in the 1990s revealed that there has been 'no significant change' in Britain in the proportion of senior civil servants who named managerial skills as a source of job satisfaction.[48] Graham Wilson and Anthony Barker write that 'the truth of the matter is that managerial tasks give satisfaction to relatively few higher civil servants.'[49] Senior civil servants in Britain, like their Canadian counterparts, much prefer being involved in policy making, in particular developing a new policy or creating a new approach or a new project, than in management or government operations. Civil servants down the line know that better than anyone.

Assessing the Relationship

Both Canada and Britain have been ambitious in their attempts to improve service delivery, in the case of Canada, dating back to the early 1990s. Government of Canada officials got a wake-up call when a study they commissioned reported in 1996 that research on 'internal and external perceptions of services vividly reinforces the thesis that there is a crisis characterizing the relationship between citizens and governments.' It surveyed a number of Canadians and reported that on all crucial dimensions of service transaction, customer satisfaction levels were 'depressingly low.' Young Canadians, in particular, had a very negative view of the federal government and its quality of service delivery. The study pointed to 'a wide performance gap' between the government and large banks in client satisfaction, notwithstanding the fact that 'banks are not the most popular institution in Canada.'[50]

The then president of the Treasury Board told Parliament that the government had launched an 'outside-in' citizen approach in order to put a 'new face' on the government within two years. The approach documents Canadians' expectations and priorities for service improvement and outlines measures to support front-line staff and provide training opportunities for managers. It includes the preparation of service improvement plans and the publication of core service standards and establishes a minimum 10 per cent improvement target over a five-year period, based on survey results. All departments and agencies with significant service delivery activities were asked to participate in the service improvement initiative and to measure progress on an annual basis.[51]

The initiative is not limited to the federal government. Governments from all three orders (federal, provincial, and municipal) have joined forces to promote it and to support the Institute for Citizen Centred Service (ICCS). The institute regularly publishes satisfaction surveys and case studies of best practice. The federal government has taken some comfort from the results of these surveys. They report a steady improvement in the quality of service delivery compared with provincial governments (however, the federal government still trails municipal governments) and the private sector. On a quality scale of 0 to 100, the federal government went from 60 per cent in 1998 to 67 per cent in 2005.[52] The surveys also document what drives citizen satisfaction (for example, reaching a live person on the telephone, timely face-to-face meetings, and courteous service).

These surveys, however, do not square with those reporting on low morale within the civil service. A survey made public in July 2006 reports that morale in the federal civil service has not improved and that it remains a serious problem.[53] This seems to contradict the view that there is a direct link between employee satisfaction and customer satisfaction.[54]

How is it, I asked both a middle manager in a line department and a senior Treasury Board official, that service to the public is steadily improving but morale is not? The line department manager maintains that investment in technology and human resources have 'helped a great deal,' adding that 'having someone answer the phone rather than just a recorded voice matters. Our ability to use the Internet to put out information to Canadians has also helped.'[55] The Treasury Board official had a surprisingly different take on the matter, given his central agency perspective, a view that I decided to report at some length and in his own words:

There are two distinct cultures in the federal civil service – one is policy, the other service delivery or management. Policy is the way to the top. Virtually all deputy ministers and the great majority of assistant deputy ministers have come up through the policy route. The heads of central agencies are all a product of the policy route, including the last five secretaries to the Treasury Board, the one place where one would think management would really matter. When deputy ministers meet, what do you think they talk about? Policy issues, ministers and striking deals. People in management and service delivery know this better than anyone. They know that they are second class citizens. They know that their deputy ministers are there for a relatively short time, on their way to another bigger department. They also know that their deputy ministers know very little about service delivery, where the department has been and what their unit is actually doing and what is their main challenge. This is where the morale problem begins.[56]

Many front-line civil servants are puzzled by the sudden emphasis on service to customers on the part of senior officials. After all, a good number of them have spent most of their careers trying to convince senior departmental and central agency officials that service to citizens is important. In their exhaustive study on service in the fields, Carroll and Siegel report on the frustration of Canadian field workers with their head office because they have, over the years, been 'tirelessly inserting as many obstacles as possible to prevent them from providing good customer service. After this history, it is easy to imagine how field staff feel when they see large amounts of scarce funds spent on expensive consultants and glossy publications to convey to them exactly the same message they have been struggling in vain to convey to head office for years.' As they go on to write, 'Despite "empowerment," "decentralization," "TQM," and a myriad of other buzz words, acronyms, and improvements in communication technology, the gulf between head office and the field remains.'[57]

Efforts in Britain to improve service delivery started with John Major's Citizen's Charter. The charter was designed to make bureaucracy more accountable and citizen friendly. Tony Blair, subsequently, consistently claimed that improving service delivery was one of his top priorities. The British government has more reason to make it a priority than the government of Canada, given that it delivers directly many public services that in Canada are delivered by provincial governments.

Blair, among his other service delivery initiatives, announced in November 2005 a 'Transformational Government' strategy. The strategy, much as in Canada, focuses on delivering a citizen- or business-centric service. It also looks to IT, specific targets, and the involvement of citizen and local government in implementing the strategy.[58]

The verdict on Britain's efforts has not been positive. Accenture ranked Canada first and the United States second in leading the way to improving customer service in the public sector. These two countries were labelled 'trendsetters.' Britain was placed among the 'followers' and ranked twelfth among twenty-one countries. The Accenture survey was based on forty-six in-depth interviews with senior officials and 8,600 citizens.[59] However, both Canada and Britain rank poorly when compared with the private sector in terms of innovation in service delivery. Canadian and British citizens also reported that private sector business was doing a better job in developing online services – the perception gap for Canada was established at minus 20 per cent in relation to the private sector (ranking sixteenth among twenty-one countries) and for Britain at minus 24 per cent (ranking twentieth out of twenty-one).

The British government commissioned an independent review of the 'Charter Mark Scheme' and 'Measurement of Customer Satisfaction.' The initiatives are designed to encourage departments and agencies to focus on their customers and to give value for money in the delivery of public services. The review's verdict was that there is a great deal of anecdotal but limited hard evidence of the Charter Mark's effectiveness: 'The Charter Mark scheme continues to prosper, but percentage penetration of the whole public sector – and therefore overall impact – remains quite low. There is now a very low level of public awareness of the Charter Mark, and a general scepticism about quality schemes and awards was displayed by members of the public.'[60]

An official with the Cabinet Office reflected on Britain's efforts to strengthen service delivery and focus on the 'customer.' She found only a mixed success, claiming that the process had become too 'bureaucratic' and had 'little customer feedback.' These shortcomings persisted, she reports, despite efforts to 'devolve more power and responsibility' to those working at the front line. She points out that those working in 'public services sometimes feel little sense of ownership' in their work.[61]

How do citizens view civil servants and their work? We have data for both Canada and Britain over time. Unfortunately, the same questions were not asked in the different surveys. Still, the data provide a picture of how the civil service and its work are viewed in both countries.

Table 9.2 reveals that in 1967 Canadians had a fair degree of respect for civil servants and believed that they were intelligent. They also believed, however, that civil servants were somewhat lazy, overpaid, inefficient, and had little initiative.

Table 9.2
Canadians' assessments of civil servants, 1967

	Lazy	Intelligent	Inefficient	Respected	Overpaid	No initiative
Most	4.26	0.94	3.66	1.43	13.33	7.35
Many	7.90	5.16	7.65	8.46	11.16	9.24
Some/						
don't know	41.22	30.23	43.11	30.25	35.23	39.59
Few	32.38	25.18	35.17	24.15	21.33	32.08
None	14.23	38.49	10.41	35.71	18.96	11.74

Source: David Lanphier Hoffman, C. Michael Morris, Raymond Morris, and Ruth Schindeler, Federal Government Information Study, 1968: A Survey of Canadian Attitudes toward the Federal Government and Its Information Services (machine readable data file). Toronto, ON: York University, 1968

Table 9.3
Canadians' confidence in civil servants, 1993

	Frequency	Per cent	Valid per cent	Cumulative per cent
• A great deal	53	1.1	2.5	2.5
• Quite a lot	660	13.5	30.8	33.2
• Not very much	1,150	23.6	53.6	86.9
• None at all	282	5.8	13.1	100.0
• Total	2,145	44.0	100.0	–
• System	2,726	56.0	–	–
Total	4,871	100.0	–	–

Source: Richard Johnston, André Blais, Henry Brady, Elisabeth Gidengil, and Neil Nevitte, Canadian Election Study, 1993: Incorporating the 1992 Referendum Survey on the Charlottetown Accord (computer file), ICPSR version

In 1993 the national elections survey asked Canadians whether they had confidence in civil servants. Survey results reveal that Canadians had little confidence in civil servants (see table 9.3). Indeed, twice as many Canadians reported that they had 'not very much' confidence or 'none at all' as reported that they had 'a great deal' or 'quite a lot' of confidence in civil servants.

The same question was asked in 2001, several years after sustained efforts to improve service delivery. There was some improvement (see table 9.4), but more Canadians said they had 'not very much confidence' than said they had 'quite a lot.'

Table 9.4
Canadians' confidence in civil servants, 2000

	Frequency	Per cent	Valid per cent	Cumulative per cent
• A great deal	70	1.9	4.7	4.8
• Quite a lot	628	17.2	42.2	46.9
• Not very much	676	18.5	45.4	92.3
• None at all	114	3.1	7.7	100.0
• Total	1,488	40.8	100.0	–
• System	2,163	59.2	–	–
Total	3,651	100.0	–	–

Source: André Blais, Elisabeth Gidengil, Richard Nadeau, and Neil Nevitte, Canadian Election Survey, 2000 (computer file). ICPSR 03969-v1, Toronto, ON: York University, Institute for Social Research (producer), 2000. Ann Arbor, MI: Inter-university Consortium for Political and Social Research (distributor), 2004

Table 9.5
Is the civil service well run?, Britain, 1983

	Frequency	Per cent	Valid per cent	Cumulative per cent
• Well run	684	39.8	42.5	42.5
• Not well run	829	48.2	51.5	94.0
• Don't know	10	0.6	0.6	94.6
• Not answered	87	5.1	5.4	100.0
• Total	1,610	93.6	100.0	–
• No self-completion	109	6.4	–	–
Total	1,719	100.0	–	–

Source: Social and Community Planning Research, *British Social Attitudes Survey, 1983* (computer file), Colchester, Essex: UK Data Archive (distributor), 1984, SN: 1935

In Britain, the general social survey is an important source of information on how citizens view the civil service. Again, the problem is that the same questions were not asked each time, so that it is not possible to see a trend. What we do know is that in 1983 more citizens believed the civil service was not well run than believed it was (see table 9.5).

In 1991, U.K. residents were asked if public services would be better delivered by the private sector. Some 30 per cent of respondents agreed that public services should be provided by the private sector, while 33 per cent disagreed (see table 9.6).

Table 9.6
Should public services be provided by the private sector?, Britain 1991

	Frequency	Per cent	Valid per cent	Cumulative per cent
• Agree strongly	81	2.8	3.0	3.0
• Agree	827	28.3	30.6	33.6
• Neither	629	21.6	23.3	56.9
• Disagree	898	30.8	33.2	90.1
• Disagree strongly	125	4.3	4.6	94.7
• Don't know	100	3.4	3.7	98.4
• Not answered	42	1.4	1.6	100.0
• Total	2,702	92.6	100.0	–
• No self-completion	216	7.4	–	–
Total	2,918	100.0	–	–

Source: Social and Community Planning Research, *British Social Attitudes Survey, 1991* (computer file), 2nd edition, Colchester, Essex: UK Data Archive (distributor), October 1999, SN: 2952

Table 9.7
Will civil service mistakes be corrected?, Britain, 2004

	Frequency	Per cent	Valid per cent	Cumulative per cent
• Very likely	57	1.8	6.7	6.7
• Somewhat likely	314	9.8	36.8	43.5
• Not very likely	339	10.6	39.7	83.2
• Not likely	61	1.9	7.2	90.4
• Can't choose	72	2.3	8.4	98.8
• Not answered	10	0.3	1.2	100.0
• Total	853	26.7	100.0	–
• Skp, B+C version	1,756	54.9	–	–
• No self-completion	590	18.4	–	–
• Total	2,346	73.3	–	–
Total	3,199	100.0	–	–

Source: National Centre for Social Research, *British Social Attitudes Survey, 2004*, (computer file), Colchester, Essex: UK Data Archive (distributor), February 2006, SN: 5329

In 2004, U.K. residents were asked whether mistakes by civil servants would be corrected. More residents believed that they would not than that they would (see table 9.7).

Sense of Ownership

In 2004 I was invited to serve in the Treasury Board Secretariat in Ottawa as the Simon Reisman Visiting Fellow. It was in the immediate aftermath of the auditor general's report on the sponsorship scandal, and my mandate was to give secretariat staff a hand in developing new measures to strengthen accountability requirements. I was in the habit at my university of turning off lights in my own and surrounding offices and in classrooms on my way out of the building at the end of the day – it is my way of saving on the university's electricity bill and, however modestly, helping the environment. The Treasury Board Secretariat is housed in a large sprawling office complex, L'Esplanade Laurier, in downtown Ottawa. I often worked there late into the evening, and the lights were always on. In my early days with the secretariat, I searched for the light switch on my way out the door but with no success. One day I asked a civil servant on my floor to show me where the light switch was located. He had 'no idea' and asked, 'Why would you want to know?' When I explained, he said, 'That really has nothing to do with you – someone else is responsible for turning the lights on and off.'

My experience in this respect is not unlike the work of civil servants. It is exceedingly difficult for front-line workers and their managers or for those working in policy units and central agencies to have a sense of responsibility in their place of work. It is true that their work was once guided by fairly rigid administrative rules and processes. It is also true, however, that a number of these administrative rules have been done away with. In their stead, the work of front-line managers and workers is now subject to many voices, many hands, and many oversight bodies.

Ministerial offices have more staff occupying more senior positions than at any time in the past. Their purpose is to make their ministers look good, an increasingly difficult task given access to information legislation, the role of the media, and the prime minister's dominating presence. Access to information legislation and other developments have served to open up the world of front-line managers and workers to outside scrutiny and, by ricochet, to scrutiny from ministerial offices. This, of course, presents different challenges for front-line workers, who traditionally look to citizens rather than to ministers and their partisan staff in their day-to-day work. Contacts between ministerial staff and front-line workers are now more frequent than in years past. This happens, at least in part, because there are times when a political crisis can start from a transaction between disgruntled citizens and front-line workers. But that is not all. Front-line managers must now also look down to their employees (and the consequences of whistle-blowing legislation) as they go about their work.

Front-line managers and workers have been told to listen to their 'customers,' to work with relevant groups and associations and with private sector partners without changing the rules of accountability. They must also look to other departments in an era of horizontal or joined-up government in delivering services. They must, as well, take into account larger, better staffed, and more demanding central agencies and their insatiable appetite for information about programs and relations with customers. And then there is their minister's office, with its enlarged staff. To be sure, all of the above has made it easier to engage in 'buck passing' or shifting blame to others when things go wrong.[62] It also robs front-line managers of a strong sense of ownership and responsibility for their programs and resources. The establishment of Service Canada takes horizontal government a step farther with its goal of providing one-stop, personalized service to Canadians.[63] The risk is that it will further disconnect citizens from government departments and separate service delivery from service and policy reforms. It could also inhibit the kind of incremental policy change and adaptation that is crucial to any organization that responds, learns, and adjusts to problems.[64]

Managers have also had to learn to deal with collective bargaining, civil service unions, and the courts. The Government of Canada declared its support for collective bargaining in 1963, with the support of all four political parties of the day. British precedent and experience had a great deal of influence in the federal government's decision to proceed with collective bargaining and in its implementation plans.[65]

The public sector in Canada remains largely unionized. From a dead start in the mid-1960s, government workers have embraced collective bargaining and union membership. Table 9.8 compares union membership and collective bargaining between the public and private sectors in 1996 and 2005. It shows two very different worlds, with nearly 75 per cent of public sector workers being members of a union or covered by collective bargaining, compared to less than 20 per cent for the private sector. It is possible for employees to be governed by collective bargaining but not be a member of a union, and such is the case, for example, with the Royal Canadian Mounted Police.

Table 9.8
Union or collective agreement status in Canada

	June 1996		June 2005	
	Public	Private	Public	Private
Union	70.4	19.5	70.1	17.6
Collective bargaining	5.6	2.4	4.1	1.8
Neither	24.0	78.1	25.8	80.6

Source: Statistics Canada, Labour Force Survey (micro-file)

In Canada, at least, the courts have been drawn into management issues. My consultations with civil servants in Canada revealed that many government managers have simply given up trying to terminate employees on the basis of non-performance, fearing that they will have to defend their action in court. Table 9.9 reveals that 451 civil servants were released for 'misconduct' over a six-year period and only 453 for 'incompetence or incapacity' over the same period (about 75 employees on an annual basis). Things are not much different in Britain. In 2001–2, for example, 27,840 civil servants left both the non-industrial and industrial civil service. The number of civil servants 'dismissed or discharged' in that year was 1,160 or 4.2 per cent of the total. This compares with 1,550 (5.6 per cent) who took early retirement, 16,870 (60.6 per cent) who resigned from their positions, and 2,850 (10.2 per cent) who retired at the minimum age.[66]

Recent surveys and studies reveal that the British civil service, like the Canadian civil service, 'is fantastically bad at dealing with poor performance.'[67] As one former cabinet minister explains, 'The most staggering thing about Whitehall is the complete lack of accountability. I would like to write a report evaluating what has gone wrong with the spate of disastrous civil service-led IT procurement programmes. I would include an Appendix listing all those officials who have been sacked as a result of these failures. It would be a blank page.'[68] The former minister is not alone in his view. Civil servants themselves readily admit to the problem. A survey carried out among senior civil servants reveal that only 16 per cent felt that poor performance was adequately dealt with.[69]

The above may well explain why the great majority of front-line managers and workers hardly take annual performance evaluations

Table 9.9
Civil servants, terminated, Canada

Year	Discharge for misconduct	Release for incompetence and incapacity	Total
2000	63	67	130
2001	107	81	188
2002	93	104	197
2003	77	92	169
2004	90	89	179
2005	21	20	41
Total	451	453	904

Source: Data provided by the government of Canada to the Commission of Inquiry into the Sponsorship Program and Advertising Activities, Ottawa, 31 May 2005. See also www.pwgsc.gc.ca/compensation/ppim/ppim-3-5-3-e.html, which provides for a general categorization of the reasons for Public Service of Canada employee departures.

seriously. Carroll and Siegel write that 'virtually everyone' laughed when they asked civil servants in the field about the performance appraisal system. They report that performance appraisal is largely a matter of going through the motions and that neither supervisor nor subordinates take it very seriously. They quote one front-line worker as follows: 'There hasn't been anyone in the last seven years come and tell me I've ever done anything wrong. Nobody ever comes to look ... They don't tell you you've done something right; and they don't tell you you've done something wrong. There's no review of the operation.'[70]

Even senior civil servants have turned to the courts to challenge the government or their own employer. The Supreme Court ruled that the government had to release parts of documents classified as cabinet secrets to its own lawyers, who were suing the Treasury Board for a pay increase. The material in question explained why government lawyers in Vancouver were excluded from salary increases given to their Toronto-based colleagues.[71]

To be sure, it has never been easy to deal with non-performers in government. It is even more difficult today, given collective bargaining and the possibility that employees and their union representatives will go to court if management initiates any action to remove anyone for non-performance. Managers will wish to avoid the hassles and focus on other things over which they have more control. In any event, managers have little incentive to engage in what would likely be a two-year process to terminate an employee for non-performance. Even if they think that they have a solid case, there is no guarantee of success. An arbitrator, for example, instructed a government department to re-hire six civil servants in Ontario who had been fired for exchanging e-mails with pornographic content at work. The content included images of bestiality, nude obese and elderly women, and degrading and violent sexual activity. The arbitrator, however, ruled that the government lacked cause to dismiss the men, and his decision made it to the front pages of Canada's national newspapers. To be sure, the message was not lost on government managers.[72]

It is also revealing that 'no sponsorship-related discipline' measures came to the attention of the 'major government unions.' Union representatives were quick to argue that the problem was at the political level, not with civil servants.[73] Former cabinet ministers who met with Justice Gomery at five roundtables stressed the point that civil servants lacked the ability to impose sanctions or to replace incompetent staff. They also spoke about what they labelled widespread 'institutional inertia' in government departments.[74] Though staff are very rarely penalized for incompetence or mismanagement, civil servants can be dismissed. Three Health Canada officials were 'fired' in June 2004 for speaking out against departmental policies. The three scientists had publicly voiced their concerns over the use of bovine growth hormone to enhance milk production in cows.[75]

How all of this squares with the introduction of private sector management practices to government has never been explained. In any event, the courts represent a new space for government managers – one that they do not know well and cannot control. They also represent one more reason why government managers can never be as free to manage as are their private sector counterparts.

From Management to Measurement

Management can never trump politics, if the two should ever come into conflict. One high-profile scandal can undo the effect of any number of speeches about modernizing government and empowering government managers and their staff. Yet no matter the approach, politicians continue to hammer home the same message – the pursuit of good management.

In speech after speech, Trudeau, Mulroney, Chrétien, Martin, Harper, Thatcher, Major, Blair, and now Brown all talked about 'sound public sector management, accountability and transparency.' Mulroney introduced the Increased Management Authority and Accountability (IMAA) initiative with the purpose of doing away with a number of centrally prescribed rules. Prime Minister Paul Martin and his Treasury Board president, Reg Alcock, in response to the sponsorship scandal, declared that the government of Canada was unable to articulate how well its administrative and financial control mechanisms were working and that important changes were needed. Harper spoke about good management practices when he introduced legislation to strengthen accountability.

Martin and Alcock, it will be recalled, decided to make internal audit committees 'independent' from line management, to introduce new 'key control' requirements across government, and to put in place a number of new reporting requirements. They announced that in future ministers would have yearly 'in camera' meetings with internal audit committees to review any 'concerns about risk, management and control systems in the department.'[76] They also decided to strengthen the role of the Treasury Board Secretariat and to introduce a 'rigorous process to prevent re-employment of or contracting with individuals who were terminated from the public service.'[77] They added an 'oversight committee of independent leaders' to provide advice to the president of the Treasury Board on the necessary 'measures to implement management improvements.'[78] All in all, the Martin government, by its own count, introduced '158 measures' to clean up management in government within ten months of coming to power and pledged to introduce 'another 80.'[79] Martin and Alcock thus served notice to senior civil servants that they could not be fully trusted on management and that the government would be looking outside their ranks for advice.

The Martin-Alcock reforms are in sharp contrast with earlier management reforms. There were sustained efforts between 1983 and the arrival of the Martin government to do away with a number of centrally prescribed rules and to give more freedom to managers. The government did that by having fewer *policies* and by processing fewer transactions from departments, and it succeeded. In 1983, the Treasury Board issued 6,000 decisions.[80] In 1987, the number had dropped to 3,500.[81] By 1997 it had fallen still farther, to 1,100.[82] In 2006 it was fewer than 1,000.[83] Fewer Treasury Board decisions means that decisions are pushed down to departments. The Harper government, however, has pledged to review the Martin-Alcock reforms. What is remarkable is that, throughout these developments, the message remained the same – the purpose is to strengthen management in government operations.

Thus, it does not matter what they do – introduce or remove centrally prescribed rules – the intent remains the same: to improve and strengthen management and accountability.

The Martin-Alcock reforms added still more demands for information from line-department managers. The demand for information to fuel performance measurement and evaluation initiatives by senior departmental and central agency officials in both Canada and Britain has increased substantially in recent years, though few are able or even willing to make the case that these efforts have been very fruitful or led to better management practices.

I heard one complaint after another from departments, from citizens, and from communities about the never-ending demand for reporting documents. I was informed, for example, that Aboriginal communities in Canada need to submit '60,000 reports a year' to the federal government.[84] A federal task force reports that an Aboriginal community in the north, with a population of sixty-three, had fifty-one contribution agreements, each requiring a year-end report.[85] Associations and groups with frequent dealings with the Canadian government also report a sharp increase in demands for 'paper,' 'reports,' 'justification,' and 'evaluations' on the part of civil servants after the 'HRDC and sponsorship scandals.'[86]

In the absence of a rethinking of the accountability framework, evaluations, performance measurement, and independent reviews appear to have replaced centrally prescribed rules and regulations. There are any number of such reports constantly being produced in both Ottawa and London, and civil servants have learned to deal with them.

If one removes centrally prescribed rules and attaches more importance to horizontal government and less to hierarchy, then one has to identify other means to ensure accountability. Establishing management targets and producing evaluation reports appear to be the solutions of choice. The view is that targets and performance evaluations of one kind or another both motivate and promote accountability. The shift has created a performance measurement industry in both Canada and Britain. The industry continues to generate numerous reports in both countries every year. Produced 'in house' by departments and agencies, they will report either that things are improving or that improvements are on the horizon. Precious few reports prepared for public consumption – and most of them now are publicly available because of access to information legislation – will present negative findings.

Things are somewhat different, however, when external reviewers are brought into the picture. In Britain, Whitehall decided in October 2005 to undertake 'capability reviews' to assess the work of departments against three 'core capability areas – leadership, strategy and delivery.' The reviews are prepared in consultation with a number of internal and external experts. The first round of reviews was published in July 2006 and looked at four major public service delivery departments, including the Home Office and the Department for Education and Skills. The second round was published in December 2006 and assessed the Cabinet Office and the Departments of Communities and Local Development and Trade and Industry. The reviews differ from other similar exercises in that they are less hesitant about criticizing government departments. The reviews argued, for example, that 'accountability frameworks ... are not always clearly understood' and that 'there is often a lack of clarity as to precisely how the different models are intended to work together.'[87] What this suggests is that having outside experts brought in to review departmental efforts may well lead to a more objective assessment or to a more 'robust evidence based assessment.'[88] That said, it is important to point out that Sir Michael Bichard, former permanent secretary in the Department of Education, applauded the fact that the reviews included external members but argued that they were still not sufficiently 'independent' from the government.[89]

Civil servants, by tradition, do not wish to draw attention to their work, particularly if the verdict may be critical. Management targets, internal audit reports, and evaluation reports are now accessible to those outside government. Performance in government is now the product of many hands, from the political level down to the most junior front-line worker. There is no incentive for civil servants to draw attention to problems, to explain what has gone wrong, or to suggest why performance targets may not be realistic.

The public administration literature claims that there is 'cheating' on the part of civil servants when producing such reports, and examples abound. We are informed, for instance, that students with a record of lower mathematics and reading scores on previous tests were more likely to be suspended at test time to boost a school's overall test scores.[90] Civil servants assessed on the basis of the number of claims they can process over a time period will focus on the least complicated ones so that they can meet or exceed targets. Complicated cases, meanwhile, do not get the necessary attention. Gwyn Bevan and Christopher Hood report that to deal with the pressure to meet with patients within two working days, many general practitioners simply refuse to book any appointments more than two days in advance, thus meeting performance targets.[91] In brief, governing by targets and measured performance indicators has never lived up to expectations. Many observers question whether it ever will, given major problems of credibility because of, among other things, 'cheating' by both target-setters and managers.[92]

Two former Canadian deputy ministers, one of whom was treasury board secretary, recently wrote an essay on management reform and pointed to significant shortcomings with performance measurement. They argue that 'performance measurement systems are best suited to repetitive industrial activities with simple production functions and direct, unambiguous outcomes.' They add that 'most performance measures are subjective and value laden,' and thus that performance measurement cannot 'be strictly objective.'[93] They reviewed the departmental performance report of the Department of Industry and concluded that one would be hard pressed to call it 'balanced' since they could not find 'a single confession of failure.'[94] In discussing the Department of Indian Affairs and Northern Development, which has been subjected to continuing criticism from the Office of the Auditor General, they remark that in its performance report, its performance 'can be described in most instances in terms of expectations met.'[95]

Evaluation reports that produce these kinds of observations, albeit largely to avoid drawing negative political attention, are not without important implications. At Oxford in the winter of 2006, I participated in a weekly seminar organized by Professor Christopher Hood on 'Ranking Public Service: From Local to Global.' One student put the following question to Professor Rawena Jacobs, who presented a paper on ranking health care services: 'Why is it that people accept, as almost a given, hotel rankings from one to five stars, but have a most difficult time accepting as valid when governments rank hospitals or the quality of their services?' The student did not get an answer from any of the participants.

Isolating Common Services

In the interest of heightened efficiency, governments are centralizing support services for human, administrative, and financial activities. The idea is not to have financial and administrative units in every department but to centralize such functions into one large or several common service agencies serving all departments and agencies. This, however, puts further distance between front-line managers and the critical support services needed to get the job done. It also means that it will be far more difficult for those providing such services to have a first-hand appreciation of the sector, the circumstances, and the challenges confronting front-line managers and their workers.

Notwithstanding these concerns, governments in both Ottawa and London intend to press ahead. Centralization was an important theme in the Gershon review, which sought to identify substantial savings for the British government through better management practices. Sir Peter Gershon, who joined government after a distinguished career in the private sector, was asked to carry out 'an independent' assessment of efficiency in government as part of the government's 2004 spending review. He was requested to look at procurement practices, back office functions, and transactional services (i.e., simplifying access to public services, streamlining policy funding and regulation, and increasing productivity). He came forward with recommendations designed to 'deliver over £20 billion of efficiencies' by 2007–8. He called for new shared processes in procurement and back office functions that alone would eliminate 80,000 jobs and secure £15 billion in savings.[96]

The Gershon recommendations were ambitious, proposing spending reductions amounting to about 2.5 per cent of total annual public sector spending. He looked to IT to organize back office systems between agencies and to overhaul procurement by employing e-auctions and reducing traditional channels of delivery. The chancellor accepted Gershon's recommendations, and departmental and agency targets were adjusted to reflect his decision. There was, however, 'great scepticism' in every sector that the suggested savings would be realized, if only because of 'the long history of public sector IT programs failing.'[97]

Oversight Bodies

Front-line managers have also had to learn to deal with a growing number of oversight bodies. In Canada especially, but increasingly also in Britain, there is no shortage of oversight bodies looking over the shoulders of front-line managers at their work. They sit in judgment on managers and are always ready to point to flaws in their decisions and work. As government managers go about their work in Canada, they must bear in mind what the auditor general, the commissioner of official languages, the access to information commissioner, the Public Service Commission, internal auditors, judicial reviews, the privacy commissioner, whistle-blowing legislation, the Treasury Board Secretariat, and the media have to say about their performance, employing any number of criteria to determine success. In Britain, the Conservative party has pledged to place responsibility for monitoring the ministerial code in 'the hands of a body with powers comparable to those of the National Audit Office, reporting to a Parliamentary Committee.'[98]

Line managers must also deal with employment equity and human rights considerations. A manager who has only white males in his unit will likely be taken to task for not contributing to the government-wide goal of employment equity. The Canadian government has made employment equity a key part of its human resources management for the past thirty years. Women were absent from the more senior ranks of the civil service in Ottawa in 1978. By 16 June 2003, eight of the thirty deputy ministers were women.[99] The British government is pursuing the same goal and recently reported with satisfaction that 24 per cent of those in the very top management posts are women (up from 12.7 per cent in April 1998); that 27.5 per cent of the Senior Civil Service (SCS) are women (up from 17.8 per cent in April 1998); that 3.2 per cent of staff at SCS are from minority ethnic backgrounds (up from 1.6 per cent in April 1998), and that 1.7 per cent of staff at SCS level are disabled (up from 1.5 per cent in April 1998).[100]

Managers have to navigate the work of all oversight bodies, pay attention to government-wide objectives, and constantly keep an eye out for any potentially emerging political crises, while trying as best they can to manage programs and deliver services to citizens. By contrast, forty years ago the Public Service Commission and the Office of the Auditor General in Canada and the National Audit Office in Britain were the only oversight bodies that mattered in the day-to-day work of civil servants, and the work of the audit offices was exclusively focused on financial audits.

Looking Back

It was not supposed to be like this. Thatcher and those who designed the New Public Management approach had a different kind of management in mind than the one that has emerged in recent years. Policy makers were to steer the ship of state, and public services were to be delivered in an efficient, businesslike fashion. Front-line managers and their workers were to be empowered, to have the freedom to manage their operations with a minimum of constraints, much like their private sector counterparts. A number of centrally prescribed rules governing human and financial resources were done away with, and new agencies were established in both Canada and Britain and given a mandate to focus on management. But politics did not change, and once a scandal hit the front page of the newspapers or came to dominate the evening news on television, politicians were always quick to call for new centrally prescribed rules to guide the delivery of public services and the work of civil servants. But that is not all. Both Canada and Britain insisted on involving outside experts or private sector representatives in shaping virtually all their management reform measures.[101]

To be sure, things have changed radically for government front-line managers and workers over the past forty years: reports of one kind or another, performance measurement schemes, management targets, horizontal government, oversight bodies, major developments in IT, political crises (often caused by information obtained through access to information legislation), a much more aggressive media, whistle-blowing legislation, an emphasis on managing publicly not privately, constantly changing priorities, collective bargaining, and unionized workers operating in a world with no bottom line – all speak to the present-day management world in government. Front-line managers and workers firmly believe that getting things done is much more difficult today than it was forty years ago. The new environment may be desirable in the interest of greater transparency. Taken together, however, these factors may well explain the observation of the middle-level manager that the government of Canada has 'become a big whale that can't swim.' Although many things have changed over the past forty years in both Canada and Britain, fundamental accountability requirements and practices have remained essentially the same.

How are things viewed at the top, where the permanent civil service meets the political world? How does it differ from the perspective at the bottom? The next chapter explores these two questions.

10 The View from the Top: 'I'm Like Hank Snow, I Have Been Everywhere, Man'

In the fall of 2006 I interviewed a senior Treasury Board Secretariat official. She was relatively new to the secretariat, had a limited understanding of its history, and was in the process of getting familiar with the work and her unit's *raison d'être*. I asked her where she had worked before coming here. Her reply: 'I'm like Hank Snow, I have been everywhere, man.' She went on to list her last positions with the federal government in the previous ten years or so. She was following the career path of many high fliers and the great majority of those who, today, occupy senior civil service positions in Ottawa.

Mobility in the senior ranks of the civil service is now highly valued and, for many, it is an important measure of success. Mobility has its advantages: it offers a broader perspective than a career in a single department; but it also has disadvantages, since highly mobile officials will not be very familiar with the various departments or sectors they pass through. The idea, which first gained prominence in Canada under Trudeau, is that successful civil servants should be generalists, capable of serving virtually anywhere in government. The thinking was that if one had the necessary policy and administrative skills, then one should be able to apply them anywhere. But there was another reason. Trudeau believed that entrenched bureaucrats in line departments had too much influence, if not power, over policy and administration. He became convinced that they ran departments like personal fiefdoms and all too often left outsiders, including ministers, out of the loop.[1] They could not be easily challenged either by line ministers, central agencies, or cabinet because of their intimate knowledge of the sector, the department, and the department's policy and program history. Rotating civil servants would serve many purposes, one of which was that it would place ministers and senior bureaucrats on a more equal footing, since both would become birds of passage in government departments and agencies.

Though many senior civil servants have now joined their political masters as birds of passage, there are still stark differences in their terms of employment. Indeed, they stand at opposite ends of the employment security spectrum. Politicians must secure the confidence of voters every four years, and perhaps much earlier if they are members of a minority government. Ministers must also secure the confidence of the prime minister, who may terminate their employment at the stroke of a pen. In brief, the risks are very high. Politicians also inhabit a world that is deeply partisan, where the winners get a chance, often for a relatively brief period, to manipulate the levers of power, and the losers are left gazing over the fence. It is a world shaped by images and by ten- or fifteen-second linear bursts of bombast on television or in Question Period. Jean Chrétien, a highly skilled politician, summed up the art of politics: 'learning to walk with your back to the wall, your elbows high, and a smile on your face. It is a survival game played under the glare of light. If you don't learn that, you're quickly finished. The press wants to get you. The opposition wants to get you. Even some of the bureaucrats want to get you. They all may have an interest in making you look bad.'[2]

Senior civil servants, meanwhile, enjoy tenure, and though they may be reassigned to another department, agency, or even to foreign institutions like the World Bank if they fall out of favour with the political leadership, they are very rarely fired. Time is also on their side. They know how to batten down the hatches and wait out any passing political storms. They serve ministers and, in theory at least, they are accountable to them. The great majority are deeply uncomfortable with partisan politics and will do much to avoid it. Yet, there is evidence to suggest that in recent years they have become much more responsive to the wishes of elected politicians. As a former clerk and secretary to the cabinet in Canada recently observed, 'I have lived long enough to remember when public servants knew the difference between governing and partisan politics. I have also lived long enough to see the two merge into one another.' He added, 'resignations have fallen out of fashion. There was a time when deputy ministers went to work with a letter of resignation in their pockets. This no longer appears to be the case.'[3] Hugh Winsor, a former Parliament Hill journalist with Toronto's *Globe and Mail*, observed in 2005 that he had never known a deputy minister to resign on a matter of principle in his thirty years in Ottawa.[4]

Senior civil servants are very skilled at politics and able to sense emerging political crises, and the best of them have an intuitive sense of what is required to get things done. At the top, they value consensus and the ability to sidestep political problems and controversy. They were, and many still remain, comfortable with the expression 'a word of caution here' or 'be careful, Minister.' Farther down, below the fault line described earlier, the world is different again. There the focus is on programs, resources, and dealing with citizens (or customers), and the ability to manage political crises is not nearly so valued. There we have a much better chance of seeing civil servants who have served in the same unit and department for a long time and who are familiar with the relevant sector and their department's program history. There, civil servants are less mobile.

The relationship between senior civil servants and ministers is complex. Indeed, it is anything but clear. One deputy minister made the point that 'I work with my minister, I don't work for him – the distinction is very important.'[5] This may not be how ministers prefer things, but senior civil servants have a multitude of bosses – the prime minister, the secretary to the cabinet, the minister, and central agencies. This situation would simply not be tolerated in the private sector. Ministers, meanwhile, have only one immediate boss – the prime minister. Still, the relationship between ministers and top civil servants remains, for the most part, harmonious.[6]

The purpose of this chapter is to review the relationship at the top and how it has evolved in recent years. Many things have changed over the past forty years or so. Indeed, the world inhabited by ministers and heads of departments today would be barely recognizable to those who were at the top of government forty years or so. Much of this territory has been covered in the previous nine chapters. Thus, this chapter focuses on how individuals at the top of government relate to one another and with others. This is the relationship above the fault line, that grey zone where the world of partisan politics meets bureaucracy.

The Prime Minister and Ministers

Prime ministers, once described as *primus inter pares*, have come to dominate their government to a far greater extent than was the case as recently as forty years ago. This is true in both Canada and Britain. Indeed, observers in the two countries began at about the same time to suggest that the prime minister's domination is a problem for their country's political and administrative institutions.[7] As already noted, it is not too much of an exaggeration to say that the cabinet has been relegated to a kind of 'focus' group in Canada and a briefing group to get ministers on message in Britain.[8] Jean Chrétien, it will be recalled, called Pierre Trudeau 'the boss' when he served in Trudeau's cabinet, and he left no doubt that he was the boss when he became prime minister himself. The prime minister is indeed the boss to many government actors: ministers, aspiring ministers, permanent and aspiring heads of departments and agencies, and many others who seek favours from the government. Christopher Foster, in describing Blair's cabinet and recent developments in the British government, concluded that the monarchy, albeit an elected one, had returned.[9]

The prime minister has come to dominate government at a time when the public policy process has become increasingly complex and cross-cutting and when government is not only larger but also far more open to outside scrutiny than forty years ago. These changes may well explain why prime ministers now feel the need to dominate from the centre. The Glassco Commission calculated in the early 1960s that there were 216,000 employees in the Canadian civil service employed in 80 federal government departments and agencies.[10] During the Trudeau years alone, 117 new departments, agencies, or crown corporations were established.[11] Today, there are 454,000 civil servants employed in 150 federal organizations covered by the Financial Administration Act (FAA), including 43 parent crown corporations; another 140 that fall outside of the FAA; 17 special operating agencies; about 200 semi-autonomous organizations housed within federal departments and agencies; 143 mixed, joined, or shared governance entities; and 26 foundations.[12] In 1967, then prime minister Lester B. Pearson spent a considerable amount of time reading his correspondence and would often reply personally. Today, the Canadian prime minister receives more than 2 million pieces of correspondence every year. These go through an elaborate triage, and only a very small category (e.g., letters from provincial premiers and heads of government) reach the prime minister. The bulk of the correspondence is handled by a special unit in the Prime Minister's Office (PMO) and many of the replies are now signed by an automated signature machine.[13] In Britain, Blair received about '2,100,000 items of post' between May 2005 and November 2006. Though the prime minister does reply to many letters, a large number of replies come from the relevant departmental minister or a Downing Street staff member. Much as in

Canada, the prime minister's correspondence is managed by a special unit within the Prime Minister's Office.[14]

An instinct for political survival, when overseeing large sprawling bureaucracies that have lost their capacity to work both in relative secrecy and in a clear hierarchical structure, also explains why prime ministers have sought to control things from the centre. The view at the very top in both Canada and Britain is that problems are less likely to surface if the centre keeps a tight rein on things when dealing with PMO priorities. The system can manage the rest, or those issues that matter less to the centre, so that departments and agencies keep running on their tracks. After all, it is easy to conclude that you made it to the top because you and your advisers have better political skills than do your ministers and their advisers, including those who also had a run at the party's leadership.

This, however, calls for a different relationship at the top. It explains why prime ministers look for senior civil servants with different skills than were preferred forty years ago. As already noted, having an intimate knowledge of a sector or a government department has become less important. Though senior civil servants in both Canada and Britain still prefer working on policy issues rather than on administration, there is limited capacity in government to evaluate the quality of policy work.[15] It is quite different today than it was forty years ago. Networking in support of horizontal or joined-up government has become an important policy skill. In addition, elected politicians, starting with the prime minister, are demanding that civil servants be much more responsive to their policy agenda, able to assist in managing political crises and in dealing with the media. I asked a senior Canadian official who retired from the federal civil service in November 2006 to reflect on the most important change during his time in government. His response: 'There was a time when the most senior civil servants would not only pursue what the Prime Minister wanted, but also told him what he should want, not just what he wanted to hear, but what he should hear, not just respond to a short term political agenda, but also present a much longer term perspective for him to reflect on. All of this has changed.'[16] This has come at a price. As Christopher Hood argues, demand-led authority and demand-led policy work have led to impoverished policy expertise.[17]

The policy role of civil servants now is less about having an intimate knowledge of a relevant sector and being able to offer policy options and more about finding empirical justification for what the elected politicians have decided to do.[18] In brief, the ability to know when to proceed, when to delay, when to be bold, and when to be prudent; to sense a looming political crisis; to navigate through a multitude of horizontal processes and networks; and then to justify what elected politicians have decided – these have come to matter a great deal.[19]

These skills are much more akin to the political world than those found in Weber's bureaucratic model. Indeed, Weber insisted that political skills need to be vastly different from bureaucratic skills, if not their opposite, for the relationship to work. This is no longer the case. Political skills, albeit not necessarily in a partisan sense, are in high demand, and this may explain in part why deputy ministers and permanent secretaries are rotated more often than in years past. The best stay at the centre of government or are sent to departments that are potential trouble spots or whose ministers need a safe pair of hands by their sides.

Ministers have lost influence in this new environment, and this in turn has had an impact on the relationship between politicians and civil servants. Both the Canadian and the U.K. governments have gradually moved away from formal processes and clear hierarchies to informal relations and flattened hierarchies. This is more akin to court government than cabinet government. Political power no longer resides with prime ministers acting in concert with their 'elected Cabinet colleagues.'[20] Jean Chrétien explained the workings of cabinet government in this fashion: 'within Cabinet a minister is merely part of a collectivity, just another advisor to the prime minister. He can be told what to do and on important matters his only choice is to do or resign.'[21] Resignations on matters of policy or principle are now rare occurrences in Britain and even more so in Canada. Ministers are more likely to resign in order to accept an appointment from the prime minister than to quit over a policy issue.[22]

Both Canada and Britain have moved away from cabinet government more by stealth than by a sudden and high-profile shift in the machinery of government. Walter Bagehot's view of cabinet as the 'efficient' part of the parliamentary system, the part that 'in fact works and rules,' no longer applies.[23] In Britain, the Conservative party's Democracy Task Force, which was assisted by former senior civil servants including a retired cabinet secretary, recently declared that 'Cabinet government has been all but destroyed.'[24] Similar observations have been made in Canada.[25]

Individuals now rule, starting with the prime minister and his most trusted courtiers, carefully selected ministers, and senior civil servants, and they have more power in a court-style government than they do when formal policy and decision-making processes tied to cabinet decision making are respected. It explains why the most powerful individuals in government, starting with the prime minister, have in recent years put aside formal decision-making processes on things that matter to them. They can roam virtually anywhere inside government, focusing on issues that are of direct interest or those that threaten the government's political interest, much as they would in a cafeteria, picking up items at will, without regard to formal processes.

The centre has slowly but surely been made deliberately stronger both in Canada and Britain. Things began to change in Canada under Trudeau in the early 1970s when he put in place measures to strengthen his position, his own office, and the Privy Council Office in relation to his ministers.[26] In Britain, the trend towards centralization can also be traced back to the 1970s under James Callaghan.[27] Both Canadian and U.K. prime ministers now have enough staff in their own offices and in central agencies to develop their own ideas, to pursue policy issues that particularly concern them, and to give life to pet projects.

Paul Martin in his leadership campaign said that under his predecessor, Jean Chrétien, the key to getting things done was the PMO. He made the point that 'Who you know in the PMO' had become what matters in Ottawa. However, according to observers, once in power his government was 'more centralized than anything seen in the Chrétien era.'[28] As one journalist pointed out, 'Need a deal with the provinces over health care? Send in the Clerk [i.e., clerk of the Privy Council and secretary to the cabinet]. Need to negotiate an offshore deal? Dispatch the Clerk to negotiate with Newfoundland's Danny Williams. Need to negotiate with the oil patch over climate change? Get the Clerk a plane ticket. Need a foreign policy review? Make sure the Clerk massages it. Require a Throne Speech? Give the Clerk a pen.'[29] Andrew Turnbull, former cabinet secretary and head of the London civil service under Blair, explained before the Select Committee on Public Administration that recent prime ministers 'clearly wanted a bigger, stronger centre. So it went through a period of very rapid growth, some of it before the election in 2001 and some of it immediately following it, with the creation of new units.'[30] He added that 'a quite conscious change here is that we have moved away from the view that we are simply here to service the Cabinet Office system. We are servicing the Prime Minister in his role as leader, as well as the Cabinet system.'[31] One of Jean Chrétien's former senior policy advisers unwittingly described court government well when he wrote that 'Everything a prime minister says is unfortunately taken by some as coming from the fount of all wisdom. Often the prime minister is just throwing out an idea or suggestion for debate and discussion – it is solemnly transcribed as if it were one of the Ten Commandments.'[32] He was referring to both elected politicians and senior civil servants. Kings Henry II and Henry VIII would have expected nothing less from their courtiers.

Senior government officials understand better than anyone else who holds power and how court government operates. When senior military officials in Canada sought to replace their armoured vehicles, they bypassed cabinet to appeal directly to the prime minister. Lieut.-Gen. Andrew Leslie told the media that he hoped 'Stephen Harper will replace the old tanks,' adding that he expected 'the Prime Minister's decision within about a week.'[33] It is not too much of an exaggeration to suggest that the Privy Council Office in Canada and the Cabinet Office in Britain have become an important part of court government, providing support to prime ministers and their courtiers.[34] Tension surfaced between the Privy Council Office (PCO) and the Department of Indian Affairs and Northern Development (DIAND) after the PCO requested a public opinion survey that Indian Affairs officials regarded as 'politically partisan and inaccurate.' The PCO requested the poll after Prime Minister Harper triggered a political uproar among First Nations people through a letter vowing to oppose 'socially divided' fisheries programs. Shortly after, the PCO commissioned a public opinion survey asking whether people are more likely to agree with 'some' who say the fishery is socially divided or with others who say that First Nations people should have their own fishery. As one Indian Affairs pollster wrote, 'We strongly suggest that the original PCO questions not be used as they appear crafted to support a certain response, contain inaccuracies and, in some cases, do not present balanced choices.'[35]

Court government provides quick and unencumbered access to the levers of power to make things happen and to pick and choose those political, policy, and administrative issues that appeal to prime ministers or that need resolution because the media are demanding immediate answers. Only the prime minister is in a position to provide quick answers to the media on virtually any issue confronting the government. Prime ministers and their courtiers will also look to any number of sources for new policy initiatives: the campaign platform, which they put together; matters that are of strong interest to prime ministers, including their pet projects (see, for example, among many others,

Chrétien's Millennium Scholarship Foundation fund); issues that surface when heads of government meet; issues identified by think tanks, and even by the civil service. Canadian and U.K. prime ministers now report that nothing happens in government unless there is a 'strong central push.'[36] Tony Blair once commented that 'one of the most frustrating things about coming into government is the time it takes to get stuff moving through the system.'[37] Imagine the frustration if one is a line department minister who is not a member of the prime minister's court.

Court government suits prime ministers and their courtiers because it enables them to get things done, to see results, and to manage the news and the media better than they can when formal cabinet processes are respected. Written documents can be kept to a minimum, minutes of meetings do not have to be prepared, records of decisions are not necessary, formal processes can be put aside, and only the most essential interdepartmental consultations have to be undertaken. News management is made easier when only a handful of individuals is involved, rather than full cabinet and many elements of the bureaucracy. To be sure, this streamlined approach holds considerable appeal for prime ministers in their efforts to deal with the government overload problem, to navigate their priorities through the requirements of horizontal government, and to sidestep or involve policy networks of one kind or another, depending on the circumstances. But there is a price to pay. Sir Robin Butler, former cabinet secretary, spoke before a parliamentary committee about the centralizing tendencies of the U.K. government and argued that formal cabinet processes hold distinct advantages. He pointed out that they provide for a collective ownership of policies, and that government works better if everybody feels at one with it and all interests are brought to bear on issues. Also, that it lessens the chance that individual ministers or advisers to the prime minister will become so close to issues that they risk losing perspective.[38]

Butler singled out several important decisions that ought to have been considered by cabinet but were instead brought to the Prime Minister's Office for resolution. One was the decision to ban trade unions in 1984 from the General Communication Headquarters (GCHQ), the spy tracking station. Another was the decision to give independence on monetary policy to the Bank of England, a decision he labelled 'pivotal.' It never went to cabinet for consideration. Butler reports that he pressed on the prime minister the need to go to cabinet. The prime minister dismissed his concerns and assured him that there would be 'a ring around to the Cabinet to make sure nobody dissented.'[39]

New policies, however, hardly take up all or even most of a prime minister's agenda. Prime ministers lead incredibly busy lives. There are many more demands on their time than can possibly be accommodated. They must attend to cabinet, caucus, and House duties; international obligations; in the case of Canada, federal-provincial relations; and in the case of Britain, European Union (EU) issues. They should be available to meet with disgruntled ministers or those with a particular project to promote. They must increasingly pay attention to the media. They are leaders of political parties, a responsibility that requires time and energy. They must deal with the civil service, including appointments to its most senior levels. They must manage their own expanded offices and oversee an elaborate appointments process. They must also manage their ministers and caucus members. A prime minister's focus, even on a handful of priorities, can never be taken for granted. It only takes a crisis to shift his or her attention elsewhere. One can only imagine what it was like in Harper's PMO when national newspapers took his government to task for being asleep at the switch in the summer of 2006 when Canadian citizens were left stranded in Beirut while citizens of other countries were being evacuated, or in Blair's office the day after the weapons inspector David Kelly committed suicide.

Having access to the prime minister is a key sign of who has influence. As the number and status of political advisers have grown in recent years, it has become difficult even for senior civil servants to have time with the prime minister. In consequence, it is also now far more difficult than it was forty years ago for senior civil servants to know the prime minister's policy preferences as well as partisan advisers and assistants do.[40] This also applies to ministers.

Not All Ministers Are Created Equal

The above is not to suggest that ministers have no influence. Though they have less than forty years ago compared to the prime minister, they still have some. Their influence depends on a number of factors, but their relation with the prime minister is usually at the top of the list. There are other factors – their standing in the party and the media and their ability to sell their ideas to the prime minister and his advisers and to navigate the government system are all important. They have, however, all lost some of their influence, for a variety of reasons. Not only have prime ministers become the dominant media stars, they no longer need to rely on their ministers to know where citizens stand on any given issue. Public opinion surveys are more reliable, more objective, more to the point, and easier to cope with than ministers. They can also be used to deal with any public policy issue. Since the 1970s all prime ministers in both Canada and Britain have had their own court pollsters interpreting events and providing advice. Surveys can enable prime ministers and their advisers to challenge the views of ministers. After all, how can even the most senior ministers dispute what the polls say?

Pollsters, better than ministers, can assist a prime minister in deciding what is important and what is not, what is politically sensible and what is not. A pollster in court, always at the ready with data, can be particularly helpful in dealing with the problem of political overload, of 'spinning' the media, now able to ferret out inside information, and can defuse the feeling of being overwhelmed both by events and by the number of matters needing attention. A pollster can also advise prime ministers on 'hot button' issues.

Public opinion surveys, however, can also turn on prime ministers and strengthen the hand of ministers who aspire to replace them. Caucus matters a great deal to all prime ministers. One former Mulroney cabinet minister insists that the prime minister was always more concerned and preoccupied with caucus than with his cabinet, and for good reason.[41] Cabinet ministers have a lot to lose if they get on the wrong side of the prime minister; caucus members less so. This is particularly true when public opinion surveys show that support for the prime minister is slipping and when he or she has been in place long enough for ambitious caucus members to know that they will not make it to cabinet. There is a striking similarity between the Chrétien-Martin and the Blair-Brown struggles for political power. In both instances, when the prime minister's support in public opinion surveys dropped, some caucus members began to call openly for a change in leadership. In both cases, the heir apparent was the second most powerful person in government, the one holding the purse strings. They saw an opportunity to exploit the downturn in the prime minister's popularity and were able to turn to carefully selected caucus members to assist them in their ambition to gain the top prize in politics.[42]

But for the great majority of ministers, making it to cabinet remains the top prize. It is still possible to group cabinet ministers into five broad categories: *status, mission, policy, process,* and *departmental* participants.[43] The main preoccupation of status participants remains visibility. Maurice Lamontagne summed up it well when he observed that, 'If a minister enjoys a good press, he will be envied and respected by his colleagues. If he has no press, he has no future.'[44] Status participants, however, can take public visibility to the extreme by aggressively pursuing every opportunity to look good in the media. At the same time, they are the least troublesome ministers to the prime minister, rarely questioning ongoing policies and programs. If anything, they are likely to encourage their departments to do more, so as to capture media attention. Status participants and their staff are continually on the prowl in search of new initiatives to spin to the media.

Status-participant ministers also try to avoid confrontations with their own staff, their cabinet colleagues, their departments, and especially with the prime minister and his court. They will not want to jeopardize any opportunities to be cast in a favourable public light. A long-running debate with the department over policies and programs (in which they usually have only a limited interest in any event) could well divert attention from initiatives involving the media and public relations.

Mission participants, meanwhile, make quite different cabinet ministers. They will certainly seek a favourable press, like all politicians, but that is not their all-consuming purpose. They have strong views and usually do not avoid confrontation. While their views are ideologically inspired, they also 'seek to serve a cause,' which they happily bring to the cabinet table. Examples of mission participants include Monique Bégin in Canada and Anthony Crosland in Britain. Prime ministers have more difficulty managing mission participants because they are tenacious, because they are confident in their views, and because it is difficult for them to arrive at a compromise.

Policy participants, meanwhile, are rarely numerous in cabinet, at least in Canada. As one former Canadian deputy minister explained in a study on management in government, 'My experience as often as not was that the minister had no view on policy.'[45] The few genuine policy participants in cabinet, however, profess to be in politics precisely to influence and shape public policies. These ministers usually welcome long policy debates with officials. They often have a specific area of expertise and come to office equipped with more than the generalities of their own party election platforms. But their expertise in a specific policy field means that they can usually see all sides of an issue and welcome long debates on the finer points of a particular policy issue.

There is a tendency for prime ministers and their advisers to dismiss policy participants as politically naive and as 'policy wonks,' far too preoccupied with the finer points of public policy. Having an interest and even some expertise in one aspect of public policy is one thing. Knowing how the policy process works and how to bring an issue to a successful conclusion is quite another. Along with the machinery of government, it is now a field of specialization in its own right, one that few outside government, including ministers, can master.

Ministers who become known as departmental participants are those who, after only a few weeks in a department, begin to espouse its policy lines. They suffer from 'departmentalitis' because of their preoccupation with their own department to the exclusion of all other considerations, including the fortunes of their political party, their cabinet colleagues, and government backbenchers. Ministers suffering from departmentalitis are usually convinced that, by following departmental advice, they will seldom get themselves in political difficulty, since most publicized political problems stem from ministers dismissing advice from their officials. It usually does not take long for prime ministers and their advisers to identify ministers who have succumbed to departmentalitis.

The five categories no longer resonate as they once did. Mission participants are not well suited for court government. They need to be heard in a more formal setting, to meet their challengers head-on, and to debate their ideas with cabinet colleagues where the rules are common to all and apply to all. Unlike the prime minister, mission participants cannot walk around government as if it were a cafeteria, picking issues at will. In brief, they need a more formal process and structure for their policy preferences to have any chance of success.

Status participants still aggressively pursue visibility and a positive media profile. But here again the rules have changed. Tony Blair sought to manage media relations from the centre with a firm hand and issued directives to the effect that ministers must coordinate their media relations with his office. Likewise Stephen Harper. The Canadian Press has described Harper's approach as 'PMO seeking total message control.' In brief, status participants no longer enjoy the flexibility and space to pursue a high media profile that they once did.[46] Both Canadian and U.K. prime ministers now reserve the right to announce anything of significance. The relevant ministers are available to provide background information to the media after the announcement. Harper's PMO explains that leaving announcements to the responsible minister will 'not draw television cameras to the show.'[47]

Policy participants can no longer work on policy issues with their departments as they did in the past. Both the British and Canadian prime ministers in recent years have taken policy issues and decisions and the policy processes that matter out of the constraints imposed by formal processes. Jean Chrétien's former senior policy adviser confirmed this when he wrote that final decisions on priorities were 'made solely by the prime minister and the minister of finance rather than by the whole Cabinet.'[48] He explained that, 'in my experience in Ottawa, cabinets don't seem to work in a way to achieve a consensus on what overall government spending priorities should be.' He went on to say that cabinet ministers are not able 'to take into account the whole mix of considerations,' including unanticipated events.[49] This raises the question – What does cabinet do? It seems that only minor policy issues and decisions are submitted to the formal requirements of the cabinet and cabinet committee system. Policy participants are thus often left on the outside looking in, as the more important issues are resolved in the prime minister's court. They, too, would have a much better chance of having an impact if cabinet government operated more as a formal decision-making process, as it once did.

Mitchell Sharp, a former deputy minister in the 1950s and later a minister in the 1960s and early 1970s, has compared policy making before and after Trudeau. As he explained, 'back in the St Laurent and Pearson governments, deputy ministers were clearly responsible for policy and for working with the minister to define policy in your area of responsibility. Your minister would of course challenge your ideas, but then he would agree on a position with you and take the ideas to cabinet and have it out with his colleagues. Things did not work quite like that under Trudeau. It was different.' He added, 'You have to understand that the art of governing was different then. Ministers had a strong base and had strong personalities. They would go to cabinet and take on even the prime minister. Some ministers would threaten to resign over policy, and some actually did. So it was different then for a deputy minister working with a minister. I am not sure that we bothered too much with central agencies like the Prime Minister's Office and the Privy Council Office. They didn't much bother you.'[50] No one would even think of making such a claim today, in either Ottawa or London.

Process participants also have had to adjust to a much different world. A process built on formal requirements focused on ministers and their departments is not only more stable and more accessible but also easier to grasp. The requirements of an informal process are tied to the preference of an individual, the prime minister, to whom chances of success are tied. They are also dependent on the kind of relations the relevant minister has with the centre of government. In addition, the horizontal nature of government has made the process more complicated, thus requiring more time and effort to understand and influence.

Departmental participants have had to adjust, as have all other participants. As boundaries between departments have collapsed and as the centre of government steams ahead on horizontal or joined-up government, it has become increasingly difficult for ministers to influence policy decisions through or with their departments because, when it comes to policy, departments no longer operate in relative isolation from one another.

All in all, no matter what their purpose, ministers must learn to work with the centre of government and with partisan advisers and senior civil servants operating at the centre to have any chance of success or, in many instances, survival. Ministers now have to learn to work with the prime minister's court more than they have to learn to work with cabinet and cabinet colleagues. Harper's PMO went so far as to ask exempt staff working for cabinet ministers to 'secretly provide' an assessment of their bosses' communication skills.[51] Ambitious civil servants, meanwhile, must in turn spend a great deal of time assessing who has influence in court and how to gain access to them so as to move their files forward.

'You Dance with the One Who Brung You'

Former Canadian prime minister Brian Mulroney was very fond of the old saying 'you dance with the one who brung you.' Those who gave of their time and resources to help secure the party leadership for the prime minister and who played an important role in the general election campaign would be rewarded either by being offered a position in government or by having access to its most senior levels. As is well known, loyalty is a much valued asset in partisan politics. Modern election campaigns are today less dependent on foot soldiers than in years past and are now heavily dependent on money, expertise in developing political and policy strategies, and a strong capacity to deal with the media.

A prime minister's immediate political court is partisan and consists of a mixture of outsiders and insiders. The outsiders include media relations specialists, selected lobbyists or government relations specialists, and close political confidants who have contributed money or expertise to the prime minister's political success. They have the skills necessary to staff a political war room, to spin messages to the media, and to craft political and policy positions on short notice.

Paul Martin appointed Cyrus Reporter, a high-profile lobbyist, to lead his political 'war room' in the 2006 general election campaign. Reporter, lobbyist for a number of global firms, including BP Energy and Bayer, did not see any potential conflict of interest because, he explained, he was taking a leave of absence from his firm and would temporarily de-register as a lobbyist. He maintained that there is now a frequent 'crossover' between those who work in politics and government relations. He added that 'People who engage in lobbying as part of their professional activities are very much involved with all political parties and will be playing a significant role with all the political parties.'[52] Still, access to senior government officials now or in the future is very lucrative for lobbyists, communication firms, and large firms. It will be recalled, for example, that a lobbyist sought $9 million in 2005 simply to organize a meeting with U.S. president Bush.[53]

Large businesses always have interests to promote. They know what they want or do not want from government, even when the product is to emerge from an elaborate horizontal policy process. What they do not know is how the process works, the key actors in the process, and how one goes about getting access to them. But now they can hire help to deal with these matters. Close associates of senior elected politicians know the key actors and can also hire former senior civil servants or long-serving political advisers who know how the process works. Large businesses will make a point of knowing who has access to the court. This explains why there is a turnover in staff and even ownership in lobbying firms when there is a change of government. It also explains why Derek Burney, the head of Stephen Harper's transition team, reacted strongly against a call to stop transition team members from lobbying government for a five-year period. He explained that 'I put a premium on loyalty and most people in politics do, and this is affecting one of my team members in a manner I find unfair.'[54] Lobbying and access to key government actors now constitute the modern version of political patronage. To the victors and their political advisers now go the economic spoils. Harvie André, a former cabinet minister in Brian Mulroney's cabinet, referring to lobbyists in Ottawa, once observed that 'it pays more to know Harvie André than to be Harvie André.'[55]

Those who opt to serve in the Prime Minister's Office or in ministerial offices are no less politically partisan. There are now more of them in both Canada and Britain than in years past, and again they enjoy higher pay and status. They also enjoy greater influence, especially in their dealings with senior civil servants. It is much more difficult for partisan advisers to have influence in a formal setting with clearly defined rules and processes than when the prime minister brings key decisions to his court. Civil servants must learn to respond to the court and its members rather than to cabinet and its formal processes. This and the growing importance of news management have strengthened the hand of politically partisan advisers as, for example, when two members of Tony Blair's political staff were delegated authority to direct the work of civil servants.

Governments, in response to a more aggressive media, appear to be fighting a permanent election campaign; hence the need to manage the news on a daily basis.[56] News management is also often regarded by many civil servants as a partisan activity, and some have simply decided to turn the steering wheel over to the politicians and say, 'OK, now you drive.' But spinning tomorrow's headlines is not without implications for how power and influence are distributed in government or for relations between elected politicians, their partisan advisers, and civil servants.

Relations with Civil Servants

The public sector reforms of the 1980s were designed to strengthen the hand of elected politicians in their dealings with civil servants. Relations between elected officials and career officials have not always been easy, as earlier chapters report. Joel Aberbach, Robert Putnam, and Bert Rockman, in their seminal work, point to a number of tension points: bureaucrats tend to look to yesterday, not tomorrow, while politicians tend to look to tomorrow, not yesterday; bureaucrats are likely to be biased against change until it occurs, while politicians are far more willing to embrace change; bureaucrats will ask 'Will it work?' while politicians will ask 'Will it fly politically?'; and the list goes on.[57]

What politicians have wanted, from Thatcher to Mulroney, to Chrétien, to Martin, to Harper, to Major, and to Blair and Brown, is a more responsive bureaucracy, and the literature suggests that they have been successful.[58] Yet bureaucracy in Canada and in Britain has traditionally been regarded as a secondary institution, an institution without a constitutional personality, in contrast to the all-powerful bureaucracies in continental Europe.[59] The point here is that politicians under our Westminster-style parliamentary system should have had all the political authority they could ever need. So what changed? The centre has changed. Making the centre stronger has significant implications for relations between elected politicians and civil servants. Ambitious politicians and senior civil servants will want to be members of the court or, if not, at least be able to influence it. Prime ministers, like monarchs of past years, will always value and reward loyalty. Prime ministers, like monarchs of past years, do not appreciate inconvenient counsel, particularly when it comes to their pet projects or policy preferences.

There is evidence to suggest that senior civil servants have become more responsive to the prime minister's court in both Canada and Britain. Political journalist Lawrence Martin writes that in Ottawa bureaucrats now either 'fall in line or fall out of favour.' He quotes a deputy minister as saying, 'When you live in a world where options aren't necessary, I suppose you don't need much of a bureaucracy' and makes the point that the 'government does not want high level bureaucrats to exercise the challenge function.'[60] Jim Travers writes that the view among senior bureaucrats in Ottawa is that 'instead of sous-chefs helping the government prepare the national menu, bureaucrats complain that they are being used as short-order cooks.'[61]

Testimonies from both politicians and senior civil servants and documents tabled before the Gomery Commission have revealed the extent to which a former cabinet secretary was right when he observed that he had lived long enough to see partisan politics and governing merge. Testimonies before commissions of inquiry or before parliamentary committees can provide fresh insights into the changing relationships between elected politicians and civil servants, and we have had a good supply of them in recent years in both Canada and Britain.

The central message, at least from recently retired civil servants and independent observers, is that senior civil servants have been highly responsive to the wishes of elected politicians, perhaps overly so. Even some ministers who appeared before Gomery felt that things have gone too far. Former Treasury Board president Lucienne Robillard expressed her astonishment before the commission that a government document had been submitted to ministers stating that 'ministers should recommend strengthening the Liberal party organization in Quebec. This means hiring organizers, finding candidates, identifying ridings where the party can win.'[62] She said it was 'unusual' for such a document to be submitted by civil servants to Jean Chrétien, as prime minister, rather than by party organizers to the leader of the Liberal party. The fact that the majority of cabinet documents in Canada are now produced by consultants rather than by career civil servants may explain the content of this and other government documents.

The testimonies of other ministers and senior political staff before Justice Gomery also reveal that they now exert considerable influence even over the administrative responsibilities of civil servants. Prime Minister Jean Chrétien acknowledged that he interviewed one career official, Roger Collet, before he was appointed to a civil service position, though he insisted that he was not a 'micro-manager.'[63] He claimed that he simply wanted to make sure that Collet understood the challenge at hand and that he was up to the job. This suggests that Chrétien felt that he was in a better position to apply the merit principle than were senior civil servants.

Chrétien's chief of staff, Jean Pelletier, told Gomery that civil servants were not happy with his involvement in the sponsorship program. But, he explained, 'This is part of a system that civil servants jealously guard as their prerogative and when they do not decide everything, they are not happy. There was one Deputy Minister or one Assistant Deputy Minister that wanted to control the program by himself. I think that the Clerk did not agree with this and even more obviously the Prime Minister did not agree.'[64] He added, 'I recall very well that officials in the Privy Council Office wanted to decide everything on the "use" of the fund under the sponsorship program and they were not happy that they were not taking the final decision, but rather the Prime Minister. That I remember very well.'[65] This did not deter Pelletier from having a hand in the management of the sponsorship program. Pelletier also acknowledged that he had sent a letter to all ministers to say that he had designated a partisan official from the Prime Minister's Office to oversee the application of a new policy on advertising.[66]

One Chrétien minister, Stéphane Dion, claimed with pride before Gomery that he had been a member of Chrétien's court. He stated that he had an extremely strong working relationship with the prime minister, saying that 'few ministers had that kind of direct relationship with him.'[67] Denis Coderre, another former Chrétien minister, acknowledged that he had advised 'against the hiring of additional civil servants to deliver the Sponsorship Program.'[68] He explained that to deliver the initiative through an external agency would not be more costly.[69] It will be recalled that the bulk of the sponsorship program was delivered by outside consultants. Coderre's message was not lost on civil servants – if they were not sufficiently responsive, they could be replaced in both policy and administrative matters by outside consultants. Court government gives elected politicians, among other things, the ability to pick and choose the delivery mechanism that best suits their partisan political interest.

Warren Kinsella, the chief of staff for the minister at Public Works and Government Services (DPWGS), the department that housed the sponsorship program, wrote to the deputy minister stating that 'in my view, Mr. J.C. Guité, current Director General of Advertising and Public Opinion Research, should be assigned to carry out a review of advertising and sponsorship activities on a full-time basis. It is requested that he be assigned to a position that will allow him to carry out these tasks and that he be provided with the appropriate resources consistent with such an initiative.'[70] The minister, David Dingwall, said that he 'certainly instructed Mr. Kinsella to write the note.'[71] He explained that 'others in the Department and elsewhere within the government at the senior official level had universally acclaimed that Guité had done a first-class job' and that 'the matter had never been raised with me as the minister of the day by the deputy or anyone else in the department, suggesting that the action was not appropriate.'[72] The deputy minister told Justice Gomery that he found the note unacceptable, but acknowledged that he did not raise the matter with the minister.

Alfonso Gagliano, who replaced Dingwall at DPWGS, bluntly told Gomery, 'Public servants run the government.'[73] He said that a minister often hears about a problem in the department only when it hits the front page of a national newspaper, and then everybody in the department runs around getting information to the minister because it is he or she who 'must face the music in Question Period' or in the media. He added, 'I don't blame individuals,' but rather '[I] blame the system,' for this state of affairs.[74]

Gagliano reported that immediately after being appointed minister of public works and government services, he received a full briefing over several days from his deputy minister, Ranald Quail. During the briefing sessions, the deputy minister asked Gagliano to sign the delegation-of-authority form. The form, tied to a long-standing practice in the government of Canada, serves to delegate administrative authority to manage the department and its programs. As he told Quail in reply, 'Why do you need ministers? If I sign this, I delegate everything and I can stay home. I will have nothing to do.'[75] Gagliano added that, after discussions lasting about one year with senior department officials, he finally agreed to delegate some authority. He also agreed to meet with his deputy minister twice a week, early Monday and early Thursday, and to be available at all times if Quail needed to see him.

There was disagreement on Gagliano's and Pelletier's roles in approving the sponsorship program. While both insisted that they played only an advisory role, providing input to the process, Guité had a different version. In response to the question, 'And let us be specific here. What did input mean in the case of Mr. Gagliano? Did it mean comment and discussion or did it mean decision?' Guité replied, 'decision.'[76] Notes and memos were also tabled suggesting that Pelletier and Gagliano approved or turned down sponsorship requests. Among many such memos, one showed that Gagliano overturned a decision 'in response to a request from a Cabinet minister, Denis Coderre, to do so.'[77] The deputy minister also testified that Gagliano 'certainly chose the events. I agree with that.' Gagliano insisted, however, that he provided only input and that decisions were always made by the bureaucrats.[78] He never explained the difference between ministerial input and a ministerial directive.

Gagliano also involved himself in personnel issues. Guité raised with him the possible reclassification of his position to a higher level. Gagliano told the commission that he decided to discuss Guité's request with the deputy minister, asking him 'to look into it.'[79] Gagliano testified, too, that his executive assistant, Pierre Tremblay, consulted him before applying to replace Guité as head of the sponsorship initiative. As Gagliano told the commission, at the time he expressed some concern over the possibility that his executive assistant would take a civil service position as head of the sponsorship program while he himself was the minister responsible and suggested that Tremblay might wish to look at other positions in the bureaucracy.[80] In any event, Tremblay did replace Guité, and Gagliano informed the commission that he had a strong working relationship with both Guité and Tremblay.[81] Gagliano's problem, it appears, was not with individual civil servants, notably those he supported for a promotion or higher classification, but rather a system run by bureaucrats that, he felt, took too much power away from elected politicians.

Gagliano, like Pelletier, told the commission that he was always pressed for time and that he had to manage his agenda very carefully. He explained that a typical day started at 6:30 a.m. and ended at 8:00 p.m., five days a week. He looked after his riding on weekends, had to spend time elsewhere in the province because he was political minister for Quebec, and also had to visit other regions of the country because of his departmental and crown corporation responsibilities.[82] Pelletier, likewise, told the commission that his workload and urgent matters requiring his attention were extremely demanding. He reported, for example, receiving a foot-high stack of written material and hundreds of telephone calls every day. His working day typically began at 8:00 a.m. and ended around 8:00 p.m.[83] Given these circumstances, he testified, he had to select issues on which to focus his attention. To deal with the flow of paper and the constant demands on his time, Pelletier had his correspondence and government documents vetted so that the more important items would be identified.[84] Notwithstanding their heavy agendas, Gagliano and Pelletier made time to meet with Guité, who operated one or two levels below the deputy minister, in order to review files, to provide 'input,' and to assist him in securing a promotion. In light of the other demands on their time, one is led to conclude that they were providing something more than simple 'input.' If their views had not prevailed, they would quickly have turned their attention to other matters.

Civil Servants: It's a Changing World

But what about deputy ministers? Where do they come from? In the case of Canada, they all come from inside government, except for one, from the private sector. Efforts by the Mulroney, Chrétien, Martin, and Harper governments to recruit deputy ministers from outside government have all met with little success.

Almost all deputy ministers appointed since 1997 held senior management positions in the Privy Council Office (PCO) prior to their appointments. This speaks to the 'rising star' approach by which someone is identified early in his or her career as having the qualities to assume senior positions.[85] It also speaks to court government, since the more senior officials in the PCO are members of the prime minister's court and have a very strong say on who makes it as deputy minister. They will look to the court itself or to their own in the PCO to identify future members of the court.

At the risk of sounding repetitive, deputy ministers are no longer appointed from within the ranks of the department. They come to a department with a mandate from the centre to accomplish certain tasks. Their loyalty, as Jacques Bourgault argues, is to the centre 'rather than departmental.'[86] A former agriculture minister, Eugene Whelan, told a Senate committee meeting in 2006 that deputy ministers of agriculture no longer know 'a sow from a cow' and that he longed for 'the glory days of the public service when the deputy minister of Agriculture lived and breathed farming and stayed in the job for 20 years. They would rather quit than be shuffled somewhere else. Some think that all you need now is a good education and you can run anything.'[87]

Deputy ministers, unlike in years past, when they usually stayed with the same department throughout their career, now range through a 'multiplicity' of departments before retirement. Indeed, some can have up to five assignments as a deputy minister before leaving government. Gordon Osbaldeston, in his study of accountability in government, was highly critical of the short stay of deputy ministers in line departments, claiming, among other things, that it made accountability more difficult.[88] The length of time a deputy minister stayed in one department between 1867 and 1967 was on average 12 years, but fell to only 3 years between 1977 and 1987.[89] C.E.S. Franks concluded that the stay between 1996 and 2005 dropped still further, to 2.3 years. He reports that on 17 July 2006 (after thirteen years of uninterrupted Liberal rule), nine of the twenty-two serving deputy ministers had served six months or less in their current office.[90] In addition, eleven of the twenty current deputy ministers had previously served as a deputy minister in another department. Jodi White, the head of Canada's Public Policy Forum, asked how proper management leadership could be exercised or how a deputy minister could represent a department properly in one such as Industry Canada, which had had 'thirteen deputy ministers in twenty years.'[91] She could have added that between 1984 and 2002 the Canadian government had six clerks of the privy council, seven secretaries to the treasury board, and seven deputy ministers of finance.[92]

Deputy ministers no longer retire at the end of their civil service career. As already noted, the private sector now offers them lucrative business opportunities as consultants or as lobbyists for large corporations where they can apply their knowledge of the 'system' on behalf of corporate customers. The result is that 'immediate retirement' for deputy ministers has 'become almost non existent.'[93]

What about politicization of the senior ranks of the civil service? As we also noted earlier, there is little evidence that Chrétien or Martin under the Liberals or Mulroney or Harper under the Conservatives sought to appoint high-profile Liberals or Conservatives as deputy ministers. That said, those recently appointed had the background to be very sensitive to political considerations. Among the thirty deputy ministers in office in June 2003, seven had served as chiefs of staff to ministers.[94]

Ministerial staff in the government of Canada have traditionally enjoyed priority rights in that, subject to certain conditions, they have access to a civil service appointment without competition. The Public Service Employment Act, including revisions that came into force on 31 December 2005, permits priority appointments, provided, among other things, that a ministerial assistant under consideration has served for a period of time – usually three years. Prime Minister Harper, however, decided to do away with this provision as part of his 'Federal Accountability Action Plan.'

The Public Service Commission of Canada carried out a study in May 2006 to determine the extent to which ministers' staff were appointed as a result of their priority right. Between 1993–4 and 2003–4, 243 persons from ministers' offices became civil servants as a result of a ministerial priority, about one-third of those who were eligible for a priority appointment. The great majority of them had at least three years of continuous service as a minister's staff member (88 per cent). About one-third were appointed to senior positions (i.e., senior management or EX levels), and almost half were appointed to positions involving program administration.[95] The point here is that ministerial staff can overnight move from a partisan position to a senior management position without competition. The prime minister and ministers quite naturally regard each of these newly minted senior managers as one of their own.

It will be recalled that, when Margaret Thatcher asked 'Is he one of us?' before appointing a permanent secretary, she was not asking whether or not he was a card-carrying member of her Conservative party, but rather whether he or she shared her policy orientation. Her view also resonates in Canada. Addressing a group of senior federal officials, Peter Aucoin spoke about senior civil servants' practice of 'demonstrating enthusiasm for the government's agenda either as a tactic to advance their own personal career or in the mistaken notion that neutral public servants should all be, as one British scholar put it, "promiscuously partisan," that is, partisan to the government-of-the-day, but willing to change when a different party takes over.'[96] Aucoin went on to argue that the pressures that have produced the politicization of government and public administration are 'not likely to abate, let alone be reversed.'[97] Colin Campbell also writes about the recent tendency of senior civil servants to 'resolutely associate' themselves with political leaders and their agenda to advance their careers.[98] They are more likely to support a government's agenda if they have served in various central agencies and departments than if they have only served in a single department.

The desire to have senior civil servants wholeheartedly embrace a political agenda may well explain why the Harper government included a clause in its accountability bill to appoint 'special advisors' to deputy ministers or place authority in the hands of the government of the day through an Order in Council rather than through the Public Service Commission. Maria Barrados, president of the Public Service Commission, estimates that there are about 200 such advisers in government, something she finds unacceptable. She maintains that it gives the government 'access to the bureaucracy that is inappropriate to me and violates the spirit and core of what the Public Service Commission is all about and supposed to do.' She fears the further politicization of the civil service, not in a politically partisan sense but 'in the sense of civil servants being too accommodating to their political masters.'[99]

Regardless of who ultimately will have the authority to appoint special advisers, it is clear that the rapid rotation phenomenon is no longer limited to deputy ministers. The Hank Snow syndrome has permeated farther down the line to include assistant deputy ministers and directors general, who now frequently move from job to job and from department to department. As Brian Marson, a senior Treasury Board Secretariat official, writes, 'The systematic rotation of executives extends to ADMs and directors general in the federal system ... This means that some public organizations have three layers of executives at the top who have very limited knowledge and experience about the department, its history, its policies and business lines. As long as there were expert middle managers and professionals, rotational senior executives could draw on this knowledge and experience below to guide them.' Now, he insists, 'senior civil servants are leading organizations that have lost their memory.'[100] This loss of institutional memory makes it more difficult for senior civil servants with limited experience in the line department in which they are currently serving to say, 'No, Minister, we tried this before and it did not work,' or 'Be careful, Minister, because people served by the department will have a very strong negative reaction to your proposal.'

Looking to the United Kingdom

Shortly after coming to power, Tony Blair told Canadian prime minister Jean Chrétien that 'I want to know all about what my ministers are
doing.'[101] History tells us that he gave it a good try. He insisted, for
example, that all ministerial 'major interviews and media appearances,
both print and broadcast, should be agreed with the No. 10 Press Office
before any commitments are entered into.'[102] Indeed, the similarities in
how Canadian and British prime ministers have in recent years sought
to strengthen the centre are remarkable. A journalist coined the phrase
'sofa government' after listening to former cabinet secretary Robin
Butler describe the current approach to policy and decision making in
the U.K. government.[103] As in Canada, formal cabinet processes no
longer apply as they once did, and the prime minister has also adopted
a less formal approach to governing. The expression 'sofa government'
captures the situation well.

The similarities do not end there. Britain has also had public inquiries that, like the Gomery Commission and committees of Parliament,
have explored the relationships at the top, notably the Hutton, Butler,
and Budd inquiries and the work of the Select Committee on Public
Administration. In May 2003 a journalist reported that a senior civil
servant had been told by the Prime Minister's Office to make the file
on Iraq's weapons of mass destruction (WMD) more exciting. The government decided to table a report on Iraq's supposed possession of
these weapons to provide a 'serious and sober' account of the intelligence material that had convinced the government that action against
Iraq was necessary. A few weeks later, the Ministry of Defence identified the journalist's source as David Kelly, a departmental scientist.
Kelly was asked to appear before a parliamentary committee, where he
faced hostile questions. A few days later, he committed suicide. Blair
then asked Brian Hutton, former chief justice of Northern Ireland, to
conduct an investigation into the circumstances surrounding the death
of David Kelly.[104]

The Hutton inquiry was able to shed some light on the inner workings of government and the importance of media spin to the perceived
success of a government initiative and efforts to gain favourable media
coverage. The inquiry had access to all background material, including
exchanges of e-mails within 10 Downing Street. These e-mails spoke to
the importance of the media and how the file should be managed to
gain maximum positive media coverage.[105]

Hutton concluded that the government did not include information against the wishes of the defence experts working on the file. The inquiry, however, did 'raise a number of issues, including the possibility that senior civil servants may be unconsciously influenced by contacts with Downing Street – a desire to be helpful and to please.'[106] The inquiry also revealed that the file had been the 'subject of comments and drafting suggestions' from Downing Street, a process that 'had in part the explicit aim of strengthening the presentation.'[107]

Blair asked Robin Butler, who had served as cabinet secretary, to review the 'accuracy of intelligence on Iraqi WMD up to March 2003 and to examine any discrepancies between the intelligence gathered, evaluated and used by the Government before the conflict, and between that intelligence and what has been discovered by the Iraq Survey Group since the end of the conflict.'[108] Blair did not ask Butler to review the role of politicians in the file, arguing that Hutton had already looked into this issue. The five-person review was critical of the government's Secret Intelligence Service, making the case that it had not checked its sources well enough. The review also concluded that making public that the Joint Intelligence Committee (JIC) had authorship of the file was 'a mistake.' The JIC consists of senior civil servants heading the British intelligence agencies and representatives of the ministers at Defence, the Foreign Office, and the Commonwealth Office. Butler insisted that it served to put the 'JIC and its Chairman into an area of public controversy.'[109] This is a role for elected politicians, he argued, not for civil servants.

The issue gripped the entire country. The media, starting with Andrew Gilligan, the BBC journalist who first broke the story, gave the matter sustained coverage. One senior civil servant argued that the case was evidence of 'policy led intelligence, or evidence manipulated by the political leadership to fit the government's case.'[110] The point was also made that the publication of an intelligence report invariably called for political input, a development that would set a precedent 'bequeathing its own problems.'[111] A senior career diplomat argued that the intelligence agencies 'had bowed to government pressure to use secret intelligence to justify a war when other arguments were cutting too little ice with the public.' He saw a line separating things political from things administrative that was not respected.[112] A memorandum from Alastair Campbell, a senior media adviser to Blair, made available through the Hutton inquiry, suggests that Blair and his senior partisan advisers did see that the political world could easily merge with that of the civil service. Campbell's notes report in considerable detail Blair's views of the 'draft' report on WMD. Campbell, meanwhile, wrote the preface and told John Scarlett, the senior civil servant, that he found the draft 'convincing,' but called for a 're-ordering of chapter 3.' He also worried about how the draft 'expressed the nuclear issue,' asked for more 'pictures,' and then went on to offer his own 'detailed comments on the draft.'[113] Obviously, the purpose of the observations by Blair and Campbell was to make more convincing the case in support of the government's decision to join the United States in the Iraq war.

Testimony by current and former senior civil servants before the Select Committee on Public Administration was remarkably similar to what senior Canadian civil servants said to Justice Gomery and the Public Accounts Committee. Three themes dominated the testimony on both sides of the Atlantic: the role of the centre is different and considerably more powerful than in years past; the role of the media and the business of news management is now much more persuasive or 'stronger'; and elected politicians and their partisan advisers are much more present in the day-to-day activities of civil servants.[114] Richard Wilson, cabinet secretary under Blair, summed it all up before the Select Committee on Public Administration when he observed, 'I think that Sir Humphrey would be completely lost today if he were here.'[115] To be sure, Sir Humphrey would not approve.

On the role of the centre, Richard Wilson told the same committee that 'the role of Number 10, the size of Number 10 and the concentration of special advisors in Number 10 are different from what they have been before.'[116] Richard Mottram, permanent secretary at Transport, told the same committee that the government now 'has a very strong centre and the networks around the centre have a much bigger input from non-civil servants.'[117] On the role of the media, senior civil servants maintain that the presence of the media is constantly felt inside government, and that the media are mostly interested in the drama of individuals and are in a constant search for winners and losers to make good headlines. Richard Wilson spoke about the power of the media and their ability to report something that might be 'inaccurate, but with the media the story has a way of becoming the reality.'[118] As Robert Armstrong, a former cabinet secretary, noted, 'There has never, in my experience, been a time when considerations of political spin did not enter into the business of news management, but it seems to me that the balance has now swung too far in that direction.'[119] On the pervasive presence of partisan political advisers, Armstrong told the *Spectator* that the lines separating partisan political advisers and civil servants 'have been blurred.'[120] Richard Wilson told the committee that the number of special political advisers has increased (the number, as already noted, is around eighty) and that two in the Prime Minister's Office now have the authority to direct civil servants.

Richard Mottram also spoke to the committee about the growing influence of partisan political staff.[121] Mottram had every reason to be concerned. It will be recalled that Jo Moore, special adviser to transport secretary Stephen Byers, had served the Labour party during the 1997 general election campaign and that, after Blair's victory, she went to work with a leading lobbying firm. Byers subsequently appointed Moore as special adviser in February 1999. She was embroiled in a controversy when an e-mail she wrote was leaked to the media. She wrote, on 11 September 2001, 'it's now a very good day to get anything out we want to bury.'[122] Indeed, the following day the department did announce some controversial measures. A year later, Jo Moore was once again embroiled in a controversy when Martin Sixsmith, a civil servant in the department, alleged that she had written yet another e-mail suggesting that bad news from the department be released on the day of Princess Margaret's funeral. Within days, both Moore and Sixsmith resigned after Prime Minister Blair intervened to resolve the matter.[123]

Sixsmith, a civil servant, resigned after pressure from the minister and Number 10, and after it became evident that Moore had not written the second e-mail. The Transport select committee, however, took Blair to task on the issue, accusing him of 'meddling.' It also made the point that 'never in peacetime has a prime minister gathered about himself such an assemblage of *apparatchiks* unaccountable to parliament.' It added. 'A small number of people ... with few relevant qualifications, with the ear of the prime minister, second-guess the work of experienced civil servants.' Consequently, civil servants' work is 'inhibited by the attentions of the "prime minister's department," and their time is wasted sorting out ill-considered interventions.'[124] The department's permanent secretary told the House Select Committee on Public Administration that he had been 'forced to work hard over several months to manage an unusually active special advisor and a communication sector in which some failed to uphold profes-

sional standards.' He explained that, while he could deal with Martin
Sixsmith, a civil servant, Jo Moore was a different matter since, he
added, 'a special advisor is a political animal' personally associated
with the government.[125] Still, it was a civil servant who fed the media
inaccurate allegations about Jo Moore's activities concerning Princess
Margaret's funeral.

The U.K. civil service also suffers from the Hank Snow syndrome,
although to a lesser degree than in Canada. For one thing, loyalty to
prime ministers and their courts appears to be less important to aspiring permanent secretaries in Britain than it is to deputy ministers
in Canada. Though more and more younger civil servants are being
appointed to top administrative posts, permanent secretaries are for
the most part still appointed later in their careers than their Canadian
counterparts. There is also a somewhat greater tendency in Britain to
appoint heads of department from within the department. However,
much as in Canada, permanent secretaries no longer serve in the same
department as long as they once did.[126] U.K. officials whom I consulted
in February 2007 told me that, increasingly, permanent secretaries are
younger and drawn from outside the departments they are being
asked to direct.[127]

In Britain, as in Canada, the prime minister is advised by the cabinet
secretary, as head of the Home Civil Service, in appointing permanent
secretaries. The head of the civil service, meanwhile, is assisted by a
Senior Appointment Selection Committee, consisting of senior permanent secretaries. The U.K. model differs from the Canadian in that the
committee includes two external members.[128]

The above has led some observers to argue that permanent secretaries are less 'agents' of the prime minister than their Canadian counterparts.[129] But, again, things are changing. 'Personalization' on the part
of prime ministers, a desire for greater political control, and efforts to
promote an open civil service with no tenure for its senior ranks continues to have an impact on the upper echelons of the civil service.[130]
One student of government argues that the U.K. model is moving
closer to Canada's. Peter Aucoin maintains that in Britain partisan
political staffers are exercising more and more pressure on civil servants, and that a cadre of senior civil servants is increasingly 'staffed
and managed by a prime minister who expects them to be fully
responsive to political directions and to actively promote the implementation of the government's agenda.'[131]

In terms of length of stay in a position, however, Britain exhibits the same Hank Snow syndrome as Canada. Whitehall, for the past twenty years, has actively promoted a high level of movement for senior civil servants to further develop their skills. Guy Lodge and Ben Rogers argue that the efforts have gone too far, that they undermine both performance and the civil service's institutional memory. They report that the average time spent in a position at senior levels is now down to four years. They add that 'anecdotal evidence' suggests that the problem is even more pronounced at junior levels with 'younger civil servants often spending no more than a year in the post before moving on.' They add that one cabinet minister they consulted joked that he was his 'department's institutional memory, as he has been in the post longer than any of his senior officials.'[132] This, among several other reasons, also explains why there has been a convergence of skills between elected politicians and senior civil servants.

Looking Back

The following questions are being asked on both sides of the Atlantic. Has there been a loss of institutional memory? Are civil servants too cowed to speak truth to power to protect the general interest? Have civil servants been overly preoccupied with protecting a government's political interest? Have the media fundamentally changed the work of civil servants?

A central message that former senior civil servants had for Justice Gomery at the five roundtables held across Canada in the summer and fall of 2005 was that the Canadian civil service had lost much of its institutional memory. Many spoke about the extremely high turnover in senior civil service positions. How could ministers, how could departments, how could departmental employees, and how could the collective interest be properly supported and served under such circumstances, they asked?[133] In Britain, one keen observer of government wrote that 'people joining central government departments are often struck by how limited the institutional memory is.'[134]

Senior civil servants no longer stay in the same position, let alone the same department, long enough 'to see through the delivery of long term objectives.'[135] But that is not all. As Christopher Foster argues, there was a time when, no matter what the meeting or however small the group, what was said was always recorded.[136] The importance of having minutes recorded was widely accepted everywhere in government. The shift to court government and to less formal requirements in striking decisions and the uses to which access to information legislation are being put have meant that as little as possible is committed to paper. Recall, for example, in Harper's first program review exercise, that deputy ministers were instructed not to put anything down on paper as they sought to identify potential spending cuts.

This suggests that senior civil servants may no longer have the experience, the knowledge, or the institutional memory to speak truth to power. It is one thing to be too cowed to speak truth to power; but even those who are not cowed need the capacity to do so. In their study of the relations of 'bureaucrats and politicians' over time in Britain, Graham Wilson and Anthony Parker write that 'what may well have changed is the self-confidence of Whitehall, its willingness to argue against government policies it thinks unwise and ill-considered.'[137]

Senior civil servants on both sides of the Atlantic now attach a great deal of importance to protecting the prime minister, ministers, and their government. It was always thus, but the balance has tilted further towards protection. The prime minister and ministers are more exposed today than ever before to a constant barrage of criticism and to potential political crises of one kind or another, and senior civil servants now see the protection of ministers to be a much more important part of their responsibilities than previously. Senior civil servants have strengthened their ability to manage up or to manage political crises for prime ministers and their courtiers, but have left unattended the need to strengthen their capacity for identifying and rectifying weaknesses in their organizations. This is yet another example of the convergence of knowledge and skills required of elected politicians and senior civil servants.[138]

Guy Lodge and Ben Rogers, in their review of accountability and Whitehall, concluded that there 'is trouble at the top' and that there are 'new tensions and challenges' in the relationships between senior civil servants and ministers.[139] Senior civil servants have to deal with the realization that it is considerably easier to speak truth when buttressed by formal processes and structures than it is to confront one individual and his or her court, particularly when that one individual is in the position to decide who makes it to the top in both the political and bureaucratic worlds.

Media relations have become supremely important in both Canada and Britain. The prime minister and ministers today spend far more time with their partisan advisers and lobbyists than their predecessors ever did. These, in turn, have built up a barrier between heads of departments and their ministers and contributed to a more pronounced political atmosphere in which senior civil servants must operate. Senior civil servants who offer inconvenient counsel are increasingly left outside the loop. This raises the question whether these developments have blurred the lines of accountability. The next chapter explores this topic.

11 Accountability: 'I Take the Blame, but I Am Not to Blame'

In her testimony before Justice Gomery, during the inquiry into the sponsorship scandal, Jocelyne Bourgon, former clerk and cabinet secretary, explained that 'where authority resides, so resides accountability, and if one has authority to strike a decision, then one has an obligation to provide an account.'[1] The Privy Council Office (PCO) has long argued that responsibility shared is responsibility shirked.[2] The U.K. Cabinet Office speaks a similar language and also insists that the doctrine of ministerial responsibility continues to apply much as it has done through the ages. Canada's PCO, meanwhile, maintains that 'the operation of ministerial responsibility does not differ widely from that of 200 years ago when it first became clearly distinguishable in the constitution.'[3] However, the Privy Council Office did not take into account a number of major developments that have shaped the 'operation of ministerial responsibility.' For one thing, the principle of collective ministerial responsibility existed in only a rudimentary form some 200 years ago. For another, the departmental structure, as we know it today, did not exist 200 years ago; the crown still managed defence and foreign affairs, and many of those activities were not discussed by Parliament.[4]

Senior civil servants in Canada and Britain, perhaps more than elected politicians, regard the doctrine of ministerial responsibility as a fundamental principle of the constitution and the cornerstone of democratic government in that it provides the basis for the control of power.[5] Yet the doctrine remains an unwritten convention, and there have been many exceptions to it. The doctrine 'vests' ministers with the constitutional responsibility to Parliament and thus places them in a unique position in relation to others who hold office under the crown.[6] For whatever reason, senior civil servants in both countries have resisted the attempts of elected politicians to move away from the doctrine. As noted earlier, Margaret Thatcher, not known for turning, did change her mind about revising the doctrine of ministerial responsibility in her decision to establish executive agencies. Stephen Harper also attenuated his plans to strengthen accountability shortly after coming to power on the advice of senior civil servants in the Privy Council Office, while Jean Chrétien simply gave up on his efforts to introduce the accounting officer concept in Canada.[7] In brief, for senior civil servants there is nothing more important than the doctrine of ministerial responsibility to underpin their work and to guide their relations with ministers, Parliament, and citizens.

The doctrine, rooted in military history and in Weber's hierarchy, requires that the individual in charge of the organization should answer publicly for the actions of both the organization and its employees or, to put it another way, whoever is at the top should take responsibility. In the Westminster-Whitehall model, civil servants have traditionally been expected to respect hierarchical accountability, to refrain from any public profile, and to remain anonymous; if they should have to speak out, they must do so under the minister's authority. Ministers are in charge of departments, answer in Parliament and in public, and speak to the media on behalf of their departments. Consequently, they expect loyalty from civil servants, starting from the deputy minister all the way down to the front-line workers.

Critics of the doctrine maintain that it is no longer appropriate to hold ministers responsible for their department while civil servants, who may have committed the errors, are allowed to go unpunished, at least publicly.[8] They believe that the doctrine of ministerial responsibility acts as a cloak for a lot of murkiness in departments and agencies.[9] Some observers, including practitioners, argue that attempts to draw a distinction between accountability and responsibility have been unconvincing.[10] They have a point. While Jocelyne Bourgon insists that 'where authority resides, so resides accountability,' Alex Himelfarb, another former clerk and cabinet secretary, insists that 'authority can be delegated, but accountability can't.'[11] If two former cabinet secretaries cannot agree on what the doctrine actually entails, then what are MPs to make of it? The PCO has also introduced the notion of 'answerability' into the mix, and this has served to complicate matters further. One can easily appreciate that the distinction between answerability, responsibility, and accountability was lost on senior civil servants who came under attack before parliamentary committees for their role in the sponsorship scandal or the Al-Mashat affair.

Other observers argue that accountability in government under the doctrine breaks down because, on the one hand, civil servants are constrained from being critical of their ministers while, on the other, they are shielded from direct public scrutiny. The doctrine makes ministers accountable, responsible, or answerable for administrative matters. Yet everything else points the other way. There are many subtle and not-so-subtle signals to ministers suggesting a hands-off attitude when it comes to administration: the non-partisan nature of the civil service and its accompanying requirements; repeated calls in both Canada and Britain to empower managers; and statutes, in the case of Canada, delegating management authority directly to departmental heads.

The result is that both elected politicians and civil servants can serve up a menu of plausible deniability to Parliament and to the public whenever errors are committed. In the sponsorship scandal, Chrétien and Gagliano, the minister, blamed the bureaucrats for not assuming their responsibilities, while Guité, the senior civil servant in charge of the program, blamed Chrétien's political staff and the minister for getting involved in administrative issues such as the selection and location of projects and the advertising firm.[12] Guité, it will be recalled, had to testify under oath before a commission of inquiry and in a court of law. It will also be recalled that Justice Gomery asked 'how can we have responsible government, but no one is prepared to take responsibility when things go wrong?' What was remarkable from the testimony before Justice Gomery was that neither elected politicians nor civil servants evinced any sense of guilt or acceptance of responsibility. Instead, they pointed the finger at one another, from Jean Chrétien and his office, to the minister responsible, right down to Chuck Guité.

Ministers are happy to claim credit when things go right. When things go wrong, they are expected to own up to the problem and, if they were not directly involved, to admit that an error has been made, that they will look into it, and that they will take steps to prevent its recurrence. Civil servants, meanwhile, are to remain anonymous under the protective cover of the doctrine. It thus makes it very difficult to get to the bottom of things and to identify accurately who should be held responsible at either the political or the bureaucratic level.

The doctrine, the argument goes, was designed for a bygone era, when government was very small (the U.K. home secretary oversaw the work of one chief clerk and ten civil servants in 1782). The doctrine has become increasingly irrelevant recently because of legislation prescribing detailed program criteria. It is much more difficult for governments today to be specific in legislation, and they now produce vague statutes to enable civil servants to make government programs work and to provide the required flexibility to respond to rapidly changing political and economic circumstances.[13] In addition, managers have also been empowered to handle human and financial resources in line with private sector practices. Through all of these changes, however, basic accountability requirements have not evolved. All of this has prompted some to make the point that the doctrine of ministerial responsibility is today better at serving political and administrative institutions that are structured to protect their own than at holding elected politicians and civil servants to account.

Critics point to still other issues. How can the doctrine, which tends to focus on a single individual – the minister – when things go wrong, remain effective in an era of horizontal or joined-up government? How can it continue to apply when borders between countries and boundaries between and within governments are collapsing? How can the doctrine adjust to constant demands for increased accountability and transparency, combined with the unwillingness to accept previously acceptable standards of secrecy?[14] How can the doctrine continue to apply when so many voices have a say or want to have a say in shaping new policies and in delivering public services? This chapter reviews how the doctrine squares with recent developments in government and in the changing relationship between elected politicians and civil servants.

Managing Publicly

Gérard Veilleux, former secretary to the treasury board and subsequently a senior private sector executive with Power Corporation, explained the difference between the public and private sectors in this fashion: 'in the public sector, you manage publicly, in the private sector, you manage privately.' He went on to point out that an important error in the private sector, unless it involves criminal charges, will more often than not make it only to page two in the business section of a national newspaper for one day, and be all but ignored by the electronic media. A similar gaffe in the public sector, however, often involving less money, can erupt into a full-blown political crisis, with the inevitable calls for the concerned minister to resign, and can then go on to dominate the front pages of national newspapers and the evening news for days and weeks, if not months.[15] Accountability in the private sector is straightforward, and concerns are handled quietly.

In government, every effort is made to handle things quietly and away from the limelight when things go wrong, but the efforts are not always successful. Nor is accountability a straightforward matter. Indeed, it is anything but, and depends on a number of factors, starting with partisan political considerations.

There are, however, some similarities between the two sectors when it comes to assuming blame. People at the very top in both sectors are willing to assume responsibility, but only up to a point. Jean Chrétien, in his testimony before Justice Gomery, accepted full responsibility for the sponsorship program, but insisted that he knew 'nothing about specific sponsorship contracts, their values or the amount of commissions paid to Liberal-friendly firms.'[16] Enron founder Kenneth Lay took the very same line when he appeared in court on criminal charges related to the firm's collapse. He took full 'responsibility for what happened at Enron,' but not for any of the illegal activities.[17] The message from both Chrétien and Lay was the same – 'I take the blame, but I am not to blame.' It is also a position that ministers in both Canada and Britain will assume when things go wrong in their departments. Civil servants, meanwhile, will insist that accountability should not be about assigning blame but that, if blame is to be assigned, it should be in the political arena, an arena reserved for elected politicians.

The differences between the two sectors are sharp. The 'I take the blame, but I am not to blame' stance permeates down through many levels in government, but much less so in the private sector. As already noted, the private sector is concerned with stock prices, quarterly earnings reports, market share, and profits. The top and the bottom lines are there for everyone to see. If the firm meets expectations, all is well. If it does not, particularly over a few quarters, then some changes are likely to be made to senior management or even, if things are bad enough, to the business model. Shareholders, financial analysts, and management will wish to pinpoint the problem, whether it is with the product, marketing, sales, or top management. But this is done without fanfare because few of the key actors have any interest in making the difficulties public. Moreover, a private firm doesn't have to deal with Question Period, organized groups, a caucus, or an auditor general or National Audit Office bringing management flaws, misguided activities, and wasteful spending to light. Politicians new to Parliament and to government are often surprised at the extent to which government operates in a fishbowl, compared to the private sector. As Belinda Stronach – former CEO of Magna International, a large global firm in the auto parts sector, and a minister in the Martin government – observed a few years after being elected to Parliament, 'When I decided to enter public life, I didn't realize how public it would be.'[18]

In government, any issue, however trivial, can take on a life of its own and inflict substantial political damage. Managing publicly means that civil servants must constantly bear in mind that any decision can become the subject of a public debate, a question in Parliament, or a fifteen-second clip on the television news. For example, several years ago a middle-level manager decided that all the windows in the Department of Foreign Affairs and International Trade in Ottawa needed to be replaced one by one, given that a number of them were defective. It was determined that, over time, it would be more expensive to replace them as their defects became obvious. The manager never expected the decision to receive intense media coverage, give rise to questions in Parliament, and move the minister of government services to declare that the decision was 'stupid' and that he 'wanted a full explanation,' since he had never been made aware of the file.[19] The minister was prepared to answer in the House of Commons on this matter, but certainly not to take the blame. The manager may well have given a full explanation to the minister, but he or she said nothing publicly and was left to wear the 'stupid decision' in silence outside of government. Private sector managers, meanwhile, are free to replace windows without fear that their decision to do so will raise any eyebrows, let alone unleash a frenzy of criticism.

Lucie McClung, the commissioner at Correctional Service of Canada, knew she was in difficulty when she saw an *Ottawa Sun* story on 9 March 2004 that reported on her 'extravagant travel expenses.' The newspaper had obtained her travel expenses through an access to information request and revealed that she had made 'pricy jaunts' to Hong Kong, New Zealand, Brazil, Barbados, and Europe over a two-year period. Predictably, the opposition called on the minister to investigate the expenses, insisting that there was 'no tangible evidence as to what benefit came for the people of the country.'[20] Opposition MPs did not explain on what basis they could make such a claim. The minister, meanwhile, chose not to respond, leaving it to departmental officials to deal with the matter as best they could.

Two contract officials in the Department of Public Works and Government Services also realized that they would have problems when the Toronto *Globe and Mail* reported that they had not shown up for some meetings while on a fact-finding mission to London, England. It was also revealed that their trip report contained a large portion of documents taken from British websites but without attribution. The two officials had been hired on contract for a three-year period to help the department find savings in purchasing and real-estate management. When the story broke, the minister claimed no knowledge of the case and called for an investigation. He simply put it back on the department. A few weeks later the contracts for both officials were terminated.[21] The matter would have been much more complicated had the two been career civil servants. I asked a senior deputy minister what would have happened if this had been the case. His reply: 'perhaps they would have likely been cast aside in an obscure office somewhere and left there to wait for their first retirement cheque to come in.'[22]

There are other examples. But there are also many gaffes that are never uncovered by the media or the opposition. Then there are some that do become public but neither pique public interest nor are exploited by the opposition. In 2002, for example, Ottawa had inadvertently transferred an extra $3.3 billion to several provinces between 1993 and 1999. The error came to light only during a computer system upgrade.[23] There was mild interest in the story for a few days and then it dropped below the radar. Contrast this with the sponsorship scandal, which involved only about $250 million in public funds but came to dominate the media for several years. It led to a public inquiry, cost the governing Liberal party a number of seats in the 2004 general election, and led to the first minority government in twenty-five years. The first Gomery report came out in November 2005, and its conclusions led all opposition parties to say that they would topple the government at the first opportunity. This they did, and Martin subsequently went on to lose the January 2006 general election.[24]

The fact that managers are now expected to manage in a more public and transparent fashion has prompted the Privy Council Office to do what it never did before – publish a 'how to' manual for managers and make it publicly available. *Crisis Management* declares that 'a crisis is a crisis when the media, Parliament and/or credible or powerful interest groups identify it as a crisis.' Someone *outside* the civil service decides that a crisis exists – speaking truth to power turned on its head. Although each crisis is different, the media and interest groups react with 'predictable sameness.' They all want to blame someone and ask, 'When will the party at fault be fired and when did the organization discover the problem?' The publication tells career officials that the usual argument, for 'being silent must be resisted, such as the need to assemble more facts.' Civil servants should 'take the initiative and make news.' It adds, 'Do not hesitate to admit that you do not have all the answers,' because 'a crisis is *not* the time to defend policies on the basis of a superior record or outstanding performance in the past.'[25] Thus, the emphasis on crisis management has forced career officials to shed some of their anonymity and to become part of the political process, explaining to the public what transpired. The manual is an admission that civil servants can no longer hide behind the minister's screen as easily as they could in the past.

The Privy Council Office simply admitted the obvious. In the private sector, it does not much matter if you get it wrong 60 per cent of the time, so long as you turn a profit. Robert Behn argues that in the public sector it does not much matter if you get it right 99 per cent of the time, because the focus will be on the 1 per cent you got wrong. This is why, he writes, the 'Ten Commandments of Government are – Thou shall not make a mistake. Thou shall not make a mistake and Thou shall not make a mistake ...'[26] Mistakes invariably happen, and the media, if not the opposition, are bound to uncover some of them. While opposition parties will exploit mistakes to score political points, elected politicians and senior civil servants will do whatever they can to deflect criticism and, if at all possible, lay the blame at someone else's door.

It is not too much of an exaggeration to suggest that accountability in government is now about avoiding mistakes, even the most trivial ones, so as not to embarrass the minister and the department.[27] Failing that, the objective is to manage the mistakes, to play them down, and to ensure minimum damage to the minister and department. This at a time when there has been a movement away from rules and administrative prescriptions to an increased emphasis on results, a circumstance that increases the probability of mistakes. The assumption is that, with fewer rules and under a new set of incentives, all parties will remain honest, continue to look to the public interest rather than self-interest, and be forthcoming in providing information on their activities.[28]

We saw in an earlier chapter that it was believed that a renewed emphasis on values and ethics would place the public interest above self-interest. Rules and centrally prescribed processes may have made for more bureaucratic government, but they kept people with power and influence in check so that they would not use them for their own ends.[29] They also made it more difficult for the media to uncover gaffes. Senior civil servants told Justice Gomery that every political scandal and major bureaucratic error is rooted in the need for urgent action and the setting aside of rules for the sake of political expediency.

The report on government-media relations of Britain's Select Committee on Public Administration concluded that it would be 'naïve to imagine that the clock can be turned back.' It added that 'both career civil servants and special advisers are today seen on public platforms to an extent that would surprise the officials of 30 or 40 years ago' and that they 'have become fair game, exposed as never before to media scrutiny.'[30] Civil servants know full well that their future promotions may well be in jeopardy if they become the story in the media, something that neither the PCO manual nor the U.K. select committee addressed.

Accountability is now played out in full public view to a far greater extent than ever before because it is considerably more difficult today to keep politically embarrassing developments away from public knowledge. The decision to pursue an issue in the House is linked to the ability of opposition MPs to be theatrical – to engage in 'gotcha' accountability – and to the wish to score partisan political points. MPs are still debating whether it was a good idea to let television cameras into the House, with some insisting that it has only served to play into the hands of those on the lookout for the fifteen-second television clip.[31] Former prime minister Brian Mulroney maintains that television cameras in the House of Commons transformed Canadian politics and that there is 'no going back.' He adds, however, that it has made for 'easy headlines' and 'cheap shots' and that a 'young man or woman with a serious interest in policy is not getting much in terms of publicity.'[32]

The media's reaction to political scandals has come to matter more than the principles involved. Indeed, cycles of scandal and corruption, not principles, are what galvanizes voters and, by ricochet, politicians to call for stronger accountability.[33]

Chrétien's sponsorship scandal dominated Question Period and the media for four years. The Conservative party saw it as a gift, the key to their achieving political power, and consequently focused their efforts in Parliament on it. Hugh Segal, a long-serving Conservative party strategist, maintains that his party's determination to attack Liberal corruption may have been a major factor in the party's success, but that it also gave both the Chrétien and Martin Liberal governments 'a remarkable respite from any real, competitive public policy debate.'[34]

To the public and the media, individuals matter, processes and policy substance are considerably less interesting, and everybody in government is vulnerable to attack if it means scoring political points. The media, especially the electronic media, prefer to focus first on individuals, next on a process, and later on a complex policy issue. Political and personal rivalries, wasteful public spending, or political or bureaucratic scandals make for far better stories than does the substance of a policy. In response to the threat of negative publicity, governments in both Canada and Britain and of all political stripes developed defensive means to protect their political interest – hence the rise of spin doctors and aggressive news management. Once spun, however, the media came to distrust government even more, and this, in turn, increased the distrust on both sides.[35] For journalists, spin is simply another word for not coming clean and telling the truth. Government reacted with attempts to conceal even more and to manage news precisely at a time when access to information legislation was making its mark on government administration. .

Added to the above is the fact that this environment no longer separates the political world from the bureaucratic world. As Sheila Copps, Canada's former deputy prime minister, argues, there was a time when 'people were more hands-off, but now everything is fair game.'[36] She could have added that everyone in government is also fair game.

The Search for Sleaze Pays

Elected politicians who have served for any length of time have sought to adjust to this new environment, and the more successful ones have learned the art of deflecting difficult questions and criticisms. A former senior adviser to Jean Chrétien writes that ministers and the prime minister often competed 'to see who could obfuscate the best in responding to Opposition questions in the House of Commons.'[37] Chrétien praised one of his senior ministers, Ralph Goodale, for his ability to be quoted at some length on a sensitive issue 'without uttering a word of substance.'[38]

Political accountability on the government side is measured by the ability to keep mistakes under wraps and, failing that, to minimize political damage to the prime minister, to the government, and to individual ministers. Hence the strong pressure to manage the news, to cover up errors, and to put a 'spin' on damaging information.[39] Bureaucratic accountability, meanwhile, involves protecting one's minister, but also protecting the department, its budget, and its employees. Accountability in government is seriously lacking in several areas. Opposition parties, the lead actors in making accountability work, find a direct political advantage in embarrassing the party in power and the government, including its administrative side. The governing party will react defensively, spin whatever it can in a positive light, be as economical as possible with information that may reflect badly on the government, and resist admitting that something is wrong. Civil servants will intuitively try to avoid the noise and heat produced by partisan clashes. That said, there is a convergence of interests between elected politicians and senior civil servants because the latter know that if their ministers look competent, they too will look competent.

Canada's former auditor general, Denis Desautels, wrote in his final report to Parliament that managerial and political accountability should be different, but that they 'merge at the top of the system.' As he explained, 'public servants are not inclined to produce information that could embarrass their ministers.'[40] Senior civil servants, as they have been told to be time and again, are loyal to the government of the day, and objective program evaluation and performance assessments tend to be sacrificed or their findings attenuated or minimized for Parliament and public consumption so as to cause the least political damage. A former senior civil servant told Canada's Public Accounts Committee that the 'typical attitude of bureaucracies to bad news is that we shoot the messenger: if it happened in my ministry or division, then it's a negative reflection on me, and no news is good news.'[41]

It appears that much more than program evaluation and performance assessments have been sacrificed in the process. A review of the government's internal audit function in Canada revealed that internal auditors have not in recent years always stood their ground in their dealings with elected politicians. The review reports that political interference can and, in the case of the sponsorship program at least, did influence how internal auditors go about their work. The review also looked at the impact of the access to information legislation on internal audits. It concluded that, when the legislation opened the door to public disclosure of internal reports, 'everything changed.' It is worth quoting at length the review's findings:

> The Government failed to anticipate the inability of the public to understand and distinguish between the various types of internal and external audits or how the media and opposition might exploit this misunderstanding for their own professional or partisan purposes. It should come as a revelation to no one, given human and bureaucratic nature, that the consequence of compelling departments to hang out their dirty laundry in public is more often than not a whitewash of the linens. Indeed, as evidence from the sponsorship audit indicates, this has had a self-censoring effect on

the auditors themselves. The raw objective of internal audit as a candid tool of oversight has been placed at cross-purposes with the larger obligation of departments to protect themselves and their Minister from public criticism. In that contest, the management function is inevitably sacrificed. The result is now a tendency towards increased obfuscation in internal audit reports, if not the outright removal of any damning information.[42]

Blameless Accountability

Left to their own devices, civil servants would opt for blameless accountability. They insist that blaming someone may make for good political theatre but serves no other purpose. Accountability, they argue, in an organization as large as a national government, should not be about assigning blame but about putting lessons learned to good use, to revising policies or processes to ensure that the problem does not resurface. In the immediate aftermath of the sponsorship scandal, the Treasury Board Secretariat produced a paper on the doctrine and practice of ministerial responsibility and argued that 'Accountability should not be directly equated with blame ... The challenge is to develop a capacity for capturing lessons learned and putting in place corrective measures rather than pointing the finger at individual public servants for things that have gone wrong ... that is in the interest of better government.'[43] Robin Butler, in his review of intelligence on Iraq and weapons of mass destruction, argued that the decision to make public the Joint Intelligence Committee report was an error in judgment, but he insisted that 'no single individual was to blame.'[44] Sir Alan Budd, also a former senior civil servant, found a 'chain of events' in his inquiry over Home Secretary David Blunkett's involvement in fast-tracking a visa application by his former lover's nanny: it was processed in 52 days rather than the usual 172 days. He reported that meetings took place but that no records were kept and minutes were not prepared. Budd did not, however, point the finger of blame at anyone.[45]

Most politicians and citizens do not see things in the same light as senior civil servants. They want to assign blame and see sanctions imposed. Justice Gomery's website received thousands of e-mails from Canadians, many of whom asked how it is that no civil servant involved in the sponsorship program was ever fired? How could it be, they asked, that the civil servants in charge were still able to secure bonuses and promotions? Why were there no sanctions imposed? Justice Gomery himself asked on many occasions how it was that the system itself did not uncover the problems and why no one was ever fired or punished. Why is it, he asked, that a journalist working on a tip and through access to information could uncover the problem but that thousands of civil servants employed in the relevant departments and central agencies could not?[46] His question remains unanswered.

Elected politicians see the finger of blame constantly being pointed at them and ask why it cannot be pointed at civil servants when it is they who are at fault. Some ministers have begun to scapegoat senior civil servants so as to make it clear that they themselves were not responsible for the mistake.[47] There is no set pattern to this trend. It depends on the minister, the circumstances, and the case. It seems that the more attention the media and the opposition give to a case (see, for example, the Al-Mashat case in Canada), and the more a minister is on the defensive, the more he or she will be tempted to deflect the blame to civil servants.

Ministers see that sanctions can be imposed by voters or by the prime minister. Voters can turf ministers out at election time. Ministers can be dropped from cabinet – and a number of them are dropped in every government. Gagliano, Andy Scott, and Judy Sgro in Canada, and Blunkett, Stephen Byers, and Estelle Morris in Britain, among many others, were forced out of cabinet for committing a variety of gaffes or errors in judgment. When it comes to ministers, there is little tolerance for errors, either in the media or among opposition parties. In her review of ministerial resignations in Britain, Diana Woodhouse points out that 'most cases of resignation in the last 50 years owe something to the media.'[48] She maintains that there has been a shift in the location of accountability to the media and away from politicians, particularly Parliament. The opinion of the press now matters more and sends a more powerful message to ambitious ministers than the opinions of cabinet colleagues (leaving aside the prime minister), MPs, party members, and the House of Commons.[49]

All in all, there are precious few voices anywhere suggesting that, when it comes to ministers, prime ministers should limit their interventions only to putting corrective measures in place so that the ministers under attack will know better what to do the next time. In brief, *deux poids, deux mesures* may make sense for civil servants but not for many elected politicians. Ministers have every right to ask why blame can point to them, resulting in a good number of them having to resign, while senior civil servants claim that, when it comes to them, accountability is about lessons learned and preventing similar mistakes in future. Blame, it seems, should only be assigned to ministers.

That said, ministers in both Canada and Britain have on occasion been successful in establishing some distance between themselves and departmental errors and in making a distinction between policy and operations. When it comes to departmental mistakes that a minister had no knowledge of or involvement in, it is now widely accepted by most observers, including many in the media, that the minister's duty is simply to provide an account to Parliament of what transpired and to stay on message that similar errors will be prevented in future. Few observers expect ministers to resign when someone down the line in the department makes a mistake or even commits a felony, such as fraud or the misappropriation of public funds, provided that the minister had no involvement in or knowledge of the incident. A minister's resignation may be required only 'for serious departmental errors in which the minister was involved or of which he knew, or should have known.'[50]

Citizens also want to assign blame and see sanctions imposed, and few concern themselves with the finer points of the doctrine of ministerial responsibility. The tax and spending bond has traditionally been one of the strongest connections between citizens and government. Patrick Boyer, a former Canadian MP, writes that it is through this bond that 'citizen and government will make its strongest claims on the other – the government for money, the citizen for accountability in its use.'[51] Boyer points to the views of Gordon Robertson, former cabinet secretary and clerk of the privy council under prime ministers Diefenbaker, Pearson, and Trudeau, who maintains that, when government started growing 'exponentially' in the 1960s and 1970s, it lost its sense of frugality.[52] To be sure, the tax and spending bond between citizens and government was stronger when government had, as one of its key values, a sense of frugality and when government was smaller and its programs and operations less complex.

Citizens need not dig very deep to find waste in government. The annual catalogue of examples of government waste from the auditor general, always widely reported in the media, is one source. In Canada, they range from a serious cost overrun in establishing the gun registry (from an estimate of $117 million to more than $1 billion) to $300,000 in advertisements to promote the government's budget, and the list goes on.[53] The media will happily report that one senior civil servant (Canada's ambassador to France) spent $311,800 mostly on 'hospitality' over a two-year period and that Sandra Lavigne, a mid-level manager, spent $7,727 on airfare alone to attend a conference in New Zealand; here, too, the list goes on.[54] Civil servants will answer these charges by explaining that travel and hospitality spending represent 'a mere fraction of government spending' and that the press 'tends to overplay rare instances of misconduct' (it should be pointed out that Ottawa spends $1.2 billion a year on travel).[55]

It is likely very difficult for taxpayers to accept the logic that they ought to be complaisant about wasteful spending because it represents 'a mere fraction of government spending.' The comment speaks directly to the loss of the parsimonious culture that was once a defining characteristic of the civil service. There have been any number of costly administrative mistakes by civil servants that were completely free of political involvement. For example, Canadian civil servants set out to overhaul the job classification system that had 840 pay rates. For twelve years, from 1990 to 2002, tens of thousands of employees from some sixty departments and agencies spent countless hours, and the government committed millions of dollars to consulting contracts, but the efforts had precious little impact and produced few changes.[56] There is no evidence to suggest that those responsible for the initiatives suffered any negative consequences.

A debate raged in Ottawa throughout the period Paul Martin was prime minister over who was responsible for dividing the Department of Foreign Affairs and International Trade. The decision was widely condemned, with officials in both departments spending considerable time fighting over turf and who would get what in the divorce. The change required the approval of Parliament, but Parliament said no. The government decided to proceed with the divorce just the same, all the while saying nothing about cost. The media and retired diplomats became highly critical of the decision and the waste it entailed. Suddenly, no one in government would accept responsibility for proposing the change. As Andrew Cohen explains, 'Some say it came from the Clerk of the Privy Council, Alex Himelfarb. Some say it was Rob Fonberg, the deputy trade minister, who wanted a promotion ... Whoever its father may be, the reorganization is now an orphan. No wonder. Rarely has an idea been denounced so widely. Active and former diplomats see it as another blow to the ebbing power of Foreign Affairs, once the aristocracy of the bureaucracy. As Raymond Chrétien, Canada's former ambassador to Washington and Paris, says, 'If the Prime Minister can find the culprit who recommended dismembering our foreign service, he should fire him!'[57] Neither the prime minister nor anyone else has been able to find the culprit, and no one has been fired.

Things are no different in Britain, where citizens are fed a constant stream of examples of government waste by the media. Citizens have been informed, for example, that, among other things, twenty out of twenty-four government departments overspent their budgets by a total of £7.1 billion in 2005, that the Art Council spent £77,000 sending a team of artists to the North Pole to make a snowman, and that the Department of Health spent £225,000 teaching grannies how to wear slippers.[58] Citizens were also told that public sector absenteeism cost £1.1 billion more than absenteeism in the private sector and that the cost of central government administration grew by 40 per cent from 1998 to 2004. Had the cost gone up in line with inflation, the savings to taxpayers would have been £2.1 billion. Taxpayers saw no evidence that the responsible civil servants were taken to task or that any kind of sanctions were imposed.[59] MPs appear to share the same frustration. We are informed that 'a question MPs often ask' in the Public Accounts Committee in the U.K. Parliament when reviewing administrative fiascos is 'how many civil servants have been sacked over this? The answer is always the same – none.'[60]

MPs are always on the lookout for cases of government waste and, when successful, they are sure to score political points with ease. There is no need to pore over volumes of material to get at the right question. All that is required is to keep an ear open for the latest gossip and to follow up in Question Period. If one is not sure of the answer before asking the question, then one can always submit an access to information request. Opposition MPs, for example, were able to gain both visibility and political mileage when they were able to report that Pierre Pettigrew, Martin's foreign affairs minister, brought his chauffeur on one of his international trips at a cost of $10,000 to taxpayers.[61] The story dominated the print and electronic media for several days.

The opposition parties' focus on waste and sleaze has led them to make accountability an important part of their election campaign commitments. Again, this is true in both Canada and Britain. It will be recalled that Chrétien made doing away with sleaze and strengthening accountability in the post-Mulroney era a key part of his red book of campaign promises in 1993 and that Harper said the very same thing in his successful 2006 campaign against Martin. It will also be recalled that John Major stressed the importance of values and integrity in government in his widely reported 'back to basics' speech.[62] Tony Blair, in speaking to his party's 1997 election manifesto, said that a 'lack of accountability was a problem of both the left and right,' and that his party was strongly committed to 'democratic renewal.'[63] David Cameron, meanwhile, has highlighted political sleaze under Blair and pledged a series 'of changes to strengthen accountability,' if elected.[64]

Grabbing Smoke

Sleaze and political missteps are relatively easy topics to master and use to secure media attention. Members of Parliament, however, have a more difficult time grasping the government's proposed spending plans and securing media interest in their efforts. Spending estimates are submitted in some detail in both the Canadian and British parliaments. The difficulty is finding time to develop a capacity to understand what is being put forward. Indeed, one Canadian MP describes his attempt at working with the government estimates as 'an exercise in grabbing smoke.'[65] A multi-party task force of MPs established to consider parliamentary reform in Canada concluded that 'Parliament has lost its ability to scrutinize government activity' and that 'most Parliamentarians admit that they are simply overwhelmed.'[66] The problem may well be more pronounced in Canada where the turnover of MPs is higher in general elections than is the case in Britain.[67] But even if one had the time and expertise to review spending estimates, no MP could possibly secure the necessary information on more than a handful of programs to appreciate how and on what the government proposes to spend.

Horizontal and joined-up government have complicated still further the government spending estimates tabled annually in both the Canadian and British parliaments. As one senior Privy Council Office official explained, 'I think it's the result of the increased horizontality. Everything we do in government has horizontal impact. You can no longer identify easily one single department or one single agency that is responsible for making sure that a complex set of answers is presented to a particular problem. The impact is that it does reduce the overall accountability for the individual departments and agencies.'[68]

Budgets are by design and purpose geared to programs, hierarchy, and departmental structure, not horizontal or joined-up government. But that is not all. In Canada, the federal and provincial governments are tangled up in each other's jurisdictions, and this makes it very difficult to establish who is responsible for what. Britain is going down that same road with Europe and with the devolution of responsibilities to Scotland and Wales. MPs, with a multitude of responsibilities, often operating with limited knowledge of the spending estimate process, with limited access to expert staff, and with little hope of having an impact on government spending plans, are expected to find the time to make sense of it all and hold government to account on this basis.

In theory, voting supply remains an invaluable instrument to enable the House to scrutinize government plans under the Westminster parliamentary system. Parliament every year approves the government's request to spend. In the case of the Canadian government, the request for 2006–7 was for nearly $200 billion, of which more than $70 billion was for programs that require Parliament's annual approval of their spending limits, and more than $128 billion was for statutory spending.[69] The estimates are submitted to Parliament in a sea of information that is divided into part 1 (overviews), part 2 (the main estimates and the spending authorities or votes to enable the government to spend), and part 3 (broken down into two components: reports on plans and priorities, which provide detailed expenditure plans; and performance reports, which report on results achieved). Every year, literally cartloads of documents are sent up to Parliament for MPs to review and ponder, but MPs complain more than ever that they have lost the ability to hold the government to account through its spending estimates. They have a point. Canadians were informed, for example, that even some central agency officials were unclear about the location of the government spending plans for the sponsorship initiatives.[70] Until quite recently, civil servants were also free to move funds earmarked for capital spending to operating expenditures.[71]

In Britain, the spending request for 2006–7 was for £552 billion.[72] The national government plays a much larger role in British society than in Canada, where jurisdiction over key sectors, such as health care and education, belongs to the provinces. Big government does complicate accountability. However, Britain has moved much farther than Canada in separating service delivery from the policy function and in breaking down proposed spending. Britain has a 'vote on Account,' which provides resources and cash to allow existing services to continue during the early months of the financial year. Parliament normally passes the Appropriation Act towards the end of July. The amounts in the Vote on Account are normally a standard 45 per cent of the amounts already voted for the corresponding services in the current year.[73] Canada does not have a system of sub-votes and virement like that of the U.K. Parliament. Sub-votes can allow Parliament to review spending in greater detail, and virement is a process by which funds are moved between subheads so that additional spending on one is met by savings on one or more others. Still, MPs on the Liaison Committee are exploring new ways to strengthen further the parliamentary ability to review the government's spending plans.[74] The Canadian government does control departmental spending through 'allotments,' but these are internal to the government and are not reported to Parliament.

It is widely believed in Canada that parliamentary committees in Britain are better at what they do than their Canadian counterparts. Britain has more than twice as many MPs as Canada, and the turnover of Canadian MPs is higher than in Britain. In Canada, if you take out MPs who serve as ministers and parliamentary secretaries and the government MPs who are, for obvious reasons, reluctant to raise issues that may embarrass the government, there is only a very small number of MPs who are willing to attempt to hold the government accountable. There is also a much stronger tradition among MPs on the government side in Britain to take 'seriously the work of holding the government' accountable. Peter Aucoin writes that one ought not to exaggerate this difference between MPs in Canada and Britain, in part because U.K. MPs willing to take their responsibility seriously are 'a diminishing number.' Still, he argues that U.K. parliamentary committees remain reasonably effective, at least when compared to their Canadian counterparts.[75] However, consultations with MPs, government officials, and staff of parliamentary committees suggest that things in Britain are fast moving towards Canadian standards.

There are other differences. In Britain, the authority of permanent secretaries has emerged through custom and practice, while in Canada the authority of deputy ministers is statutory. In Britain, the prime minister is expected in the Commons once a week (on Wednesdays) to answer questions for half an hour. The Prime Minister's Questions (PMQs) period is certain to be widely reported in the media. The leader of the opposition may make up to six interventions during PMQs, and the leader of the Liberal Democrats will normally ask two questions. Prime Minister's Questions follows a different format to that of questions to other ministers. MPs do not normally give the prime minister prior notice of the subject they are going to raise. This element of surprise allows opposition MPs, in particular, to try to catch the prime minister out with a difficult question. Government backbenchers can normally be relied upon to ask a 'helpful' question that will allow the prime minister to tell the House about successful government policies. The chance to ask the prime minister a question is highly prized. The names of the MPs who will get the chance to ask the prime minister a question are drawn in a weekly lottery managed by the Speaker. Several years ago, the prime minister also agreed to appear before the Liaison Committee (the chairs of all the select committees) twice or more yearly. Sessions last over two hours and are open to the public. Committee members are free to ask the prime minister any question, and the sessions allow for more extensive discussions of policy than do PMQs.

Canadian prime ministers attend Question Period most days when in Ottawa, and the element of surprise is always present for them and their ministers. It is rare that an opposition MP will give notice of the subject he or she will raise in question period. The prime minister does not, however, appear before a parliamentary committee on a regular basis. Voted appropriations in Canada are very broadly worded. Government departments typically have a 'vote one,' which includes the bulk of the department's spending plans. The U.K. government also concentrates spending plans in one or a few votes for each department.

It is important to note that a 'vote' is a fixed sum voted by Parliament for an identified agency, department, or program for a purpose or purposes identified normally by legislation. Ideally, the vote structure should correspond with the government program structure – one vote should equal one program. But governments in both Canada and Britain have shifted to large votes that cover many programs. The shift provides added flexibility and discretion to senior government managers, but it also serves to conceal how much is actually spent on each program.[76]

Spending under voted appropriations in Canada has gone down over the years in relation to statutory spending. In 1963, Parliament saw 58 per cent of government spending approved under voted appropriations and 42 per cent under statutory spending. However, by 2004, voted expenditures amounted to only 35 per cent of total spending. Thus the role of Parliament in reviewing the government's annual spending plans has been attenuated further over the past forty years since the bulk of the expenditure budget is authorized on a continuing basis through enabling legislation.[77] This may well be one factor, among others, that explains the lack of interest MPs have in reviewing the government's spending estimates.

There was a time when the Commons did make better use of the estimates process to review government plans in detail and to establish guidelines to hold the government accountable, if only because votes were better aligned to programs. It is today much more difficult in both Canada and Britain to ask specific questions about the rationale for increasing individual salaries, enlarging departmental organizations, raising operating costs, or increasing program spending. Information accompanying the estimates is now complex, voluminous, and – in the eyes of many – convoluted. In short, it is not easily accessible to MPs.

Departmental officials do appear before standing committees. One senior deputy minister explains candidly that the estimates process reminds him 'of Brezhnev and the old Soviet Union. Workers pretended to work and the Government pretended to pay them. We pretend to provide full information to Parliament and MPs pretend to hold us accountable.'[78] Even if the information provided is clear and concise, scrutinizing proposed departmental plans and holding departments to account is no easy task. It requires patience, skill, and knowledge. Inexperienced MPs, at least in Canada, with limited access to expert staff, face long-serving officials who are well versed in the ways of government and who have ready access to expertise and the elaborate interdepartmental consultative process.

In both Canada and Britain, civil servants appearing before parliamentary committees follow, as best they can, the Osmotherly rules. This calls on them to give evidence on behalf of their ministers and under their direction. More specifically, civil servants may describe existing policies and explain ministers' reasons for adopting them but should not give information that undermines collective responsibility or get into a discussion about alternative policies; officials may not divulge advice given to ministers by officials; and officials may not divulge information about interdepartmental exchanges on policy issues, the level at which decisions were taken, or the manner in which ministers consulted their colleagues.[79] Accordingly, civil servants must deal with significant constraints when appearing before parliamentary committees, constraints that seriously inhibit a free flow of information between them and elected politicians. Where they do have some flexibility and are expected to be more forthcoming, particularly in Britain – because of the accounting officer concept, but also in Canada when civil servants appear before the Public Accounts Committee – is in dealing with administrative and financial issues.

However, senior civil servants in both Canada and Britain argue that MPs and Parliament should ignore the details of administration.

Andrew Turnbull, cabinet secretary under Blair, wrote in his valedictory lecture that 'Parliament should be holding us to account on the outcomes we achieve, not details of our internal management.'[80] Former and current senior civil servants who appeared before Justice Gomery also argued that elected politicians and Parliament would serve Canada better if they would focus on the broad policy picture and on how well policies and programs are performing rather than on the details of the day and administrative issues.

However, if MPs have difficulty grasping detailed information on proposed spending plans, one can only imagine how difficult it is for them to understand program evaluation reports, performance targets, performance indicators, outcomes, and achievements. In any event, such efforts at evaluating performance on both sides of the ocean remain, at best, works in progress. Governments in every Western country have poured a substantial amount of money and human resources into making program evaluation and performance indicators work. The record everywhere has been disappointing. We are told that 'no national jurisdiction that has been independently audited appears to have received a high score for its achievements in results-based reporting.'[81] This, as we saw in earlier chapters, is no less true for Canada and Britain.

Central agencies, as noted in an earlier chapter, have sought for the past forty years or so to link performance measurements to expenditure planning and management but with very little success. When spending cuts have to be introduced, governments still look to across-the-board cuts or ways of squeezing departmental spending not the findings of program performance reviews or evaluation exercises. Canada's much-touted program review (circa 1995–7), for example, was built around across-the-board spending cuts not program evaluation or assessments of program outcomes.[82]

Britain has, arguably, made more advances than Canada in promoting performance targets, or at least in generating noise about their importance. Blair has often talked at length about the need to focus on outcomes and on achieving policy targets. His government's 'Modernising Government' efforts aim to strengthen departmental accountability by producing several documents: public service agreements, service delivery agreements, the expenditure plan, and annual reports. The agreements are designed to link government and departmental priorities and to clarify accountability, expectations, and results.[83] The government reported in 2005 that it had about 130 public service agreements in place. The Prime Minister's Delivery Unit, established by Blair in 2001, focuses on the agreements to ensure that the prime minister's priorities are pursued.[84] Notwithstanding these developments, the Treasury still imposes broad spending limits in managing the expenditure budget.[85] The government also turned to an independent review of government spending, prepared by Peter Gershon, to identify spending cuts.[86]

Those who have looked at Britain's efforts to emphasize outcome measurement and performance reports have not been positive. This is even true for executive agencies, which, by design, are more managerial and self-contained in their work. A government report on outcome reporting in executive agencies concluded that 'at present annual reporting is generally seen as an expensive and resource-hungry exercise that is of little value except as confirmation of a high level audit.' It maintains that both departments and agencies consider that there are too many targets, and 'rewards incentives or penalties' bear no relation to performance. It quotes one chief executive officer as saying 'target setting is a game.'[87]

If ministers with extensive briefings from senior civil servants have difficulty with program performance and evaluation reports, then one can appreciate why MPs would prefer to be on the lookout to score political points by pointing to things that anyone can understand and relate to. One does not need an evaluation report to make the case that spending $10,000 of public money to have your chauffeur accompany you on a trip to Europe will not be well received by taxpayers. Cartload after cartload of information on program evaluation and performance targets are beside the point. For MPs, accountability is about politics – about assigning blame and scoring political points in the media. Performance measurement, meanwhile, seeks to de-emphasize politics in a highly political environment. There is precious little appetite among opposition MPs for this or the material being produced.

There are two issues we need to underline here. First, holding government to account must compete with various demands on MPs, such as the time they make available for their constituencies, their party and party caucus, House duties, and parliamentary committees. Most MPs, but particularly those in Canada, must travel long distances to and from their constituencies. MPs will naturally focus their time and efforts where there is a greater return. We need not go over the same material we reviewed in an earlier chapter. Suffice it to note here that being seen in one's constituency and in contact with party supporters and the local media will quite naturally matter a great deal to MPs.

The second issue is the complex nature of the documents submitted to Parliament. In response to demands for better information, the government has increased the number of documents detailing longer-term plans and providing still more information on performance and results. The government and its central agencies, not Parliament and its committees, have specified the information that Parliament should receive. As governments have increased the number of documents they send to Parliament, they have also, over the years, reduced the number of votes in their spending estimates. They have thus provided more flexibility to managers by giving them the ability to transfer funds from one activity to another without having to go back to Parliament. This, however, has weakened parliamentary oversight. It may explain, for example, why the Canadian gun registry cost overrun and the sponsorship scandal were not picked up by MPs for years. The Gomery Commission revealed, for example, that the Chrétien government deliberately concealed the sponsorship initiatives in the estimates sent to Parliament by including them in the department's general vote one, without identifying them or their purpose.[88]

The same can be said about Canada's gun registry fiasco. The government of Canada, in introducing its gun registry initiative, argued that it would cost no more than $85 million over five years. Several years later, it became clear that the registry would cost well over $1 billion. The auditor general insisted that Parliament had been kept in the dark, and opposition MPs lined up to ask for the minister's resignation, calls that were ignored.[89] Later, the auditor general concluded that bureaucrats in the firearms centre 'misinformed' Parliament with respect to '$39 million in 2002–3 and $22 million in 2003–4 not recorded in the books as the rules required.'[90] It was civil servants, not the minister, who made the decision to use 'an accounting treatment' of the expenditure to avoid political controversy.[91] In considering the auditor general's findings, MPs made the case that it 'is not the role of public servants to make political decisions for their ministers.' John Williams, a Conservative MP, has this to say: 'We like to think we have an apolitical public service, but when things get dicey they circle the wagons around the government of the day and that does not bode well for the public service.'[92]

To be sure, MPs would have benefited if the vote in some programs, such as gun control or sponsorship, had been isolated. Two long-time students of Canada's Parliament now report that 'Members of all parties were troubled when information on the cost of carrying out the gun control program surfaced. There was a widespread feeling among MPs that, had they seriously reviewed Estimates, they could have identified the problem earlier and pressed for cost controls. Many Members also feel that Parliament would have been able to identify and publicly expose much more quickly the financial mismanagement related to the Sponsorship Program.'[93]

Governments submit estimates, and Parliament and committees have until an established date to review them and to vote supply (in the case of Canada, by the end of May, in the case of Britain, by the end of July). In a number of cases, estimates are approved by relevant parliamentary committees with precious few questions asked. In the case of Canada, most committees will devote very few meetings to reviewing the estimates, and some committees do not even 'move to approve them, since under the Standing Orders, even if they have not been adopted by the committee, they are deemed to have been approved.'[94]

The Parliamentary Centre in Canada surveyed MPs and concluded that the documents in support of the estimates the government sends to Parliament are unnecessarily complex, that MPs 'often admitted – sometimes with regret – that they did not pay much attention to the estimates,' and that 'because they achieve little, most MPs find time spent on the Estimates unrewarding.'[95] The result is that the estimates tend to emerge from Parliament 'unchallenged' and 'unchanged.'[96] In another report, the Parliamentary Centre reported that in 2001 only ten committees tabled reports as part of the estimates and supply process, and of these only one dealt with a performance report. They concluded that parliamentary committees added 'very little' to the supply process and that the actual voting on supply provided 'little, if anything, more.' The centre concluded that the problem was that 'the information and the process were too complex to understand.' MPs, the centre added, regard both the process and documentation to be 'virtually impenetrable.'[97]

Opposition MPs must also bear in mind that in their dealings with civil servants in attempts to gain a better understanding of the government expenditure budget, the primary loyalty of civil servants is to the government of the day. This is much more obvious in Canada and Britain than it is, for example, in the United States. Career officials regard MPs as real or potential adversaries to be helped as little as possible. They see every reason to keep quiet about any real or potentially politically sensitive issue.[98] As this study explains, this can mean anything and everything. Thus, senior civil servants will wish to avoid providing targets to the opposition. Failures in administration and inability to reach performance targets could offer inviting opportunities to score political points and embarrass the government. If objectives are vaguely stated to avoid potential problems down the road, then performance indicators are not likely to reveal much.

Walking without Order

Matthew Flinders writes that the British state is 'walking without order,' as major structural changes are taking place and the boundary between the private and public sectors is becoming increasingly opaque. He expressed concern that a large number of public bodies were being created without legislation and that Parliament's capacity to hold to account a number of organizations was limited.[99] In Canada, the auditor general stunned the nation as far back as 1976 when he wrote that 'Parliament – and indeed the government – had lost or was close to losing effective control of the public purse.'[100] The government, in response, established a Royal Commission on Financial Management and Accountability and an Office of the Comptroller General. By the time the commission tabled its report, the political storm created by the auditor general's observations had passed, and the government, on the advice of senior civil servants, dismissed the bulk of the commission's recommendations. A key recommendation, which was rejected, was to import the accounting officer concept from Britain. A few years later, the government did away with the Office of the Comptroller General, again on the advice of senior civil servants, notably the secretary of the treasury board.[101] The government, however, subsequently decided to re-establish the office in the aftermath of the sponsorship scandal.

That, it seems, is the story of accountability in both Canada and Britain. A high-profile scandal, a major political or bureaucratic gaffe, or a warning from a credible voice that accountability in government has broken down will lead the government to announce a flurry of measures, ranging from the establishment of a royal commission or a commission of inquiry to new centrally prescribed rules. Political circumstances more than anything will determine the approaches taken. Management rules are tightened or loosened depending on the country's political circumstances. Once the storm has passed, things are expected slowly to get back to the way they were. The government will decide on tighter or more relaxed management rules without regard to formal processes and with little regard for what is best for the civil service as an institution and its management and administrative requirements. The two options are always there on the shelf for the government to pick at will to suit the political circumstances of the day. The objective is always to protect, as best one can, the government's political interest, the minister, and the department. The focus is on the minister, the one who must carry accountability and defend past actions before Parliament and the media. The doctrine of ministerial responsibility, as one student of government so aptly described it, is 'an accountability shield rather than a sword.'[102]

The accountability shield, the hunt for sleaze, and the notion that elected politicians should focus on outcomes rather than administrative details have left a number of issues unattended. It seems that the size and cost of bureaucracy are, for the most part, matters best left to senior civil servants to sort out. Whenever a new program or activity is launched, the immediate response from departments is to ask for more personnel rather than look at how existing resources could be reallocated. Billions of dollars and pounds are spent every year on consultants in Canada and Britain, but MPs are left scratching their heads in trying to understand why. The prime minister and ministers have neither the time nor the interest to pursue the matter in depth. MPs, meanwhile, do not have the knowledge or the resources to explore the issue to any level of detail. Indeed, they do not know if they should be asking questions about this spending, let alone what questions to ask. To be sure, elected politicians may well meddle in administrative matters to keep a local office open or to nudge government jobs to certain constituencies, but they will see little merit in concerning themselves with management issues.[103] Reg Alcock, former treasury board president, claimed that his cabinet colleagues thought that he 'was nuts for taking a strong interest in management issues.'[104] The result is that the civil services in Canada and Britain have largely become self-governing institutions that see accountability in terms not of assigning blame when things go wrong but of applying lessons learned at some vague point in the future.

Voters believe intuitively that there is waste in government bureaucracies, as public opinion surveys reveal. Canadians, for example, believe that of each dollar Ottawa spends, it wastes forty-seven cents.[105] But we have learned that to achieve cuts in government overhead requires one of two things – a politician like Margaret Thatcher, who simply lays down a number and directs her officials to make it happen, or a fiscal crisis of the kind that Canada witnessed in 1995 that led to a program review and cuts in the civil service. As we saw in an earlier chapter, senior civil servants will never volunteer cuts in their departments. Indeed, when things go wrong, they are likely to point to previous spending cuts imposed by politicians as the likely explanation. Alex Himelfarb, clerk and cabinet secretary under Chrétien and Martin, claims that the 1995 program review cuts in the civil service were one of the reasons for the sponsorship scandal. He argued that there ought to have been more civil servants occupying oversight functions.[106] How can anyone in cabinet or Parliament possibly be in a position or have the necessary knowledge to challenge this view?

Revisiting the Doctrine

A number of elected politicians in both Canada and Britain are asking if the doctrine of ministerial responsibility should continue to apply as it has down through the ages. Canada and Britain, among parliamentary systems based on the Westminster model, have been the most protective of the authority of ministers and the anonymity of civil servants.[107] Senior civil servants, more than anyone, have resisted change, turning to such concepts as accountability and answerability to make the doctrine work. In Canada, Parliament has explicitly assigned authority to deputy ministers to manage human and financial resources and the application of the Official Languages Act. Yet the Privy Council Office insists that ministers should still be held accountable for authorities assigned to deputy ministers by statutes. The office has never squared this view with Jocelyne Bourgon's opinion that 'where authority resides, so resides accountability.' It is interesting to note that in Britain, senior civil servants who defend the doctrine make the point that a civil servant has 'no power conferred to him by Parliament, has no direct responsibility to Parliament and cannot be called to account by Parliament. His acts, indeed, are not his own.'[108] This is not the case in Canada, where Parliament has conferred statutory powers directly on civil servants; yet the Canadian government clings to the doctrine of ministerial responsibility – if anything, more firmly than the British government. The point here is that civil servants start from the premise that the doctrine needs to be protected at all cost and *quitte à trouver* the argument to support it.

One Canadian member of Parliament explained the problem of plausible deniability under the doctrine before the Public Accounts

Committee. He told the president of the treasury board that deputy ministers have 'actual statutory responsibilities.' But, he added, 'when tough questions are put to them – why was that done, who made those decisions? – the deputy minister says: "I can't answer that; that's up to the minister. I can't speak to that. That's ministerial responsibility."' He added that 'The minister rolls in, we ask the minister exactly the same question and the minister says: "I don't run the department. The deputy minister runs the department. I don't make those decisions."'[109] The president of the treasury board responded, 'I think that's a very important question and I appreciate it' but did not say how things could be improved.[110] This supports David Judge's argument that the doctrine of ministerial responsibility now serves as an accountability shield rather than a sword.[111]

The public sector has changed substantially over the past forty years in terms of size and approaches to policy making (e.g., horizontality), service delivery (e.g., public/private partnership), and the creation of somewhat autonomous agencies, particularly in Britain but also in Canada. Yet the doctrine continues to provide for a single point of accountability at a time when government policies and activities are the product of many hands. Imagine how the doctrine of ministerial responsibility applied in Britain in 1782 when the home secretary oversaw the work of one chief clerk and ten civil servants. Now consider the responsibilities of Canada's minister of transport. The Department of Transport is a 'relatively' large department by Canadian standards, but not by any means the largest. It has a budget of $1.6 billion and 4,900 employees or 'full time equivalents.'[112] The minister oversees the work of the department, has responsibility for Canada's Infrastructure Program, and is the designated minister responsible for the province of Quebec. In addition, he is responsible for twelve Transport crown corporations, eight non-Transport crown corporations, and forty-nine Shared Governance Organizations, which include twenty-one airports and nineteen port authorities.[113] Little wonder that senior civil servants have sought to update the doctrine by adding new concepts such as 'answerability.'

But the doctrine, both Canadian and British officials maintain, as we noted in the introductory paragraphs to this chapter, should continue to operate much as it did 100 or even 200 years ago. There is evidence of this everywhere. One only needs to look at what senior civil servants told the U.K. Parliament after the government introduced sweeping management reforms, including the Next Steps program, to appreciate their position. Senior civil servants insisted that the 'traditional doctrine of ministerial accountability was unaffected.'[114] Robin Butler could not have been clearer: 'I think there is a misunderstanding, particularly about Next Steps Agencies. People often refer to them as quasi-autonomous. They are not. They are part of the Civil Service. The Chief Executive of a Next Steps Agency is a Civil Servant like anybody else, responsible to the Minister, and the Minister is accountable for him. I say there is no accountability gap because a Minister is accountable, in the sense that he can be called to account for everything.'[115]

Access to Information: How to Minimize Its Impact

Alasdair Roberts, a leading authority on access to information, published a paper on the topic titled 'Lessons for the U.K. from Canada.' Canada had more than twenty years of experience with the legislation by the time Britain's legislation came into effect in 2005. He wrote that, much as in Canada, there is 'evidence' to suggest that the legislation would be employed extensively by the media, legislators, and advocacy groups seeking information for the purpose of embarrassing the government.[116]

Roberts documents how the government and in particular civil servants have devised ways to minimize political damage to their ministers. These include the failure to place some organizations under the ambit of the legislation and the putting in place of an elaborate 'special' process to handle 'politically sensitive' requests. For instance, civil servants in Canada alert the Prime Minister's Office to new requests that may be politically embarrassing. These requests, Roberts reports, usually come from the media and Parliament and deal with high-profile policy debates or with travel and hospitality expenses. Strategies to deal with requests that may be embarrassing include ways to delay responding or even ways to thwart the request. Roberts points out that delay in processing information requests 'can be very important, particularly for journalists, members of Parliament or other party representatives. The news cycle has its own rhythm – an issue will not remain in the foreground indefinitely and will soon be displaced by other topics.'[117]

There has also been a running battle in Ottawa between the government and the access to information commissioner. The battle has led to court cases and charges by the commissioner that the government is deliberately keeping a tight hand on the office's expenditure budget to reduce its effectiveness. The hostility between senior civil servants and the commissioner has been evident for years, and there is no sign that things are improving.[118] An aspect of his proposed accountability program that Harper watered down shortly after coming to power was his plan to strengthen access to information legislation – a decision attributed to recommendations from senior civil servants during the transition period.

The most popular strategy to minimize political or bureaucratic damage flowing from access to information legislation is simply to avoid putting anything that matters on paper. My consultations with government officials at both the political and bureaucratic levels reveal that this practice is now widespread in both Canada and Britain. Important decisions are made by elected politicians and civil servants with nothing or precious little being written down. I was informed that Blair led the discussion in cabinet on going to war in Iraq through a PowerPoint presentation. It will also be recalled that Harper led a $2 billion expenditure reduction by instructing civil servants to do everything orally, and civil servants in one department directed consultants to deliver their findings through oral briefings.

Government officials also pointed out that the fear of litigation is a factor in the growing unwillingness to commit to paper. Some added that there was a time when nothing could move in government unless it was on paper but that today the opposite is true. Accountability pays a heavy price. A long-serving Westminster MP and former cabinet minister under Thatcher maintains that the shift away from committing things to paper not only leads to bad government, because policy makers do not have access to the necessary information on an equal basis, but also 'erodes accountability because it is not possible to hold someone accountable in government if there is no paper trail.'[119]

Looking Back

Mark Bovens, in his comparative study of accountability, concluded that 'Life is often more complicated than doctrine.'[120] The doctrine of ministerial responsibility, if it were to apply as it was originally conceived, implies that ministers are fully empowered to determine what happens inside their departments.[121] This is no longer practical. For this reason, we have narrowed the definition of the doctrine so that, unless they were directly involved, ministers no longer resign when civil servants commit a serious mistake. Lord Carrington is the only minister in either Canada or Britain who has resigned over the past forty years within the traditional view of ministerial responsibility for the civil service. It will be recalled that Lord Carrington resigned his position as foreign and commonwealth secretary in the Thatcher cabinet over his department's failure to foresee the Argentine invasion of the Falkland Islands. Thus, he resigned for the failings of his civil servants and not because of any personal responsibility for the failure to foresee the invasion. But this is the exception that proves that there is something quite wrong with the doctrine. If nothing else, it leaves a 'hole' in the doctrine. Colin Turpin, writing about this hole, argued that 'the system does not appear to provide adequately for the accountability of civil servants, who nowadays themselves formulate policies and take numberless decisions of importance without reference to ministers.'[122] Though not always – as the study shows – sleaze is generally the product of elected politicians, and, again not always, waste is the product of bureaucracy.

To be sure, the public sector has changed substantially over the past forty years. But so have society and its values. An earlier chapter noted that citizens are better educated, better informed, and less deferential than in the past. The emphasis has in recent years increasingly turned to individual achievements. In the market, if an actor does something wrong or commits a blunder, then the actor is punished. However, if the actor does something good, then the actor is rewarded – think of a salesperson, an information technology worker successfully developing a new product or building a new firm, or a lawyer winning an important case. The market, because it is built on competition, is rigorous when it comes to accountability – in the end, failing firms do go bankrupt.[123]

Voters would like to see the same discipline imposed on governments. The Organization for Economic Co-operation and Development, in its review of accountability in public organizations, concluded that 'both legislators and investigative journalists seek to go beyond the system and to allocate credit or blame to individuals.'[124] Weber thought that he had the answer – accept hierarchy and ensure that elected politicians and civil servants stick to their jobs. To be sure, hierarchical bureaucracy has the advantage of clarifying individual accountability and roles. The politician's role was to take a stand, to be passionate, and to be a political and community leader. The civil servant's was to execute conscientiously the orders of the superior authorities, to have moral discipline, and to practise self-denial.[125] However, society, its expectations, and government have changed substantially over the past forty years, and the old machinery is now in need of repair. Parliament has lost the ability to hold government to account. The establishment of inquiries in both Canada (MacDonald, O'Connor, and Gomery) and in Britain. (Butler, Budd, Scott, and Franks) speaks to the 'perceived limits of the parliamentary process' to hold ministers and civil servants to account.[126] All in all, it is not too much of an exaggeration to say that MPs in both Canada and Britain have contracted out their accountability responsibilities to commissions of inquiries, to officers of Parliament, and to the media.

The doctrine of ministerial responsibility, in the words of the first civil service commissioner in Britain, 'needs to be reviewed ... we no longer understand what it means.'[127] The Home Office recently sought to clarify the doctrine by establishing a 'compact between Ministers and the Home Office Board.'[128] The compact states that ministers are responsible for 'accounting to Parliament and the public for the policy and delivery of the Home Office' while civil servants are responsible for 'increasingly answering externally for operational matters for which they are responsible.'[129] The compact falls short on a number of fronts. The House Select Committee on Public Administration correctly points out that 'it is still far from clear who is accountable when operational matters affect delivery as a whole.'[130] The compact calls on ministers to account to Parliament and the public while it makes civil servants 'increasingly' answerable.

Time will tell what 'increasingly answerable' will mean. Still, U.K. ministers and civil servants appear much more open to reviewing the doctrine than their Canadian counterparts. Both Prime Minister Harper and the clerk of the privy council and secretary to the cabinet have made it clear in published letters and speeches that the introduction of the accounting officer concept did not alter 'in any way' the doctrine of ministerial responsibility since the 'framework of responsibility and accountability to Parliament ... remains unchanged.'[131]

How, then, should accountability fit in our new political environment? What happens when hierarchy becomes less important and organizations and programs are pushed farther away from ministers either by design or by force of circumstances? The challenge now is how to structure the machinery of government to recognize the policy advisory and management responsibilities of civil servants while preserving the requirements of democratic accountability.[132] The next chapter explores these issues.

12 Power: Locating It and Holding It to Account

Our machinery of government was designed for another era, for small government serving a small population in relatively self-contained jurisdictions at a time when educational opportunities were limited and deference to authority and a rigid hierarchy within the civil service were widely accepted. Democratic legitimacy was based on a limited number of people who had the right to vote. The relationship between elected officials and civil servants was relatively straightforward at the time. Parliament was able to hold government to account, and it could and did review proposed spending plans down to the most minute of details.

Power drifted first from monarch to an executive Parliament selected from and accountable to it, then to cabinet, and more recently to prime ministers and their courtiers. The machinery adjusted. Students of government wrote about a golden age for Parliament (before disciplined political parties took control), for cabinet (before the prime minister and courtiers turned it into a focus group), and for the civil service (in the aftermath of the Second World War until the 1970s, when talented and committed people joined the service to build the welfare state and to guide activist governments). Throughout these developments, it was relatively easy to determine where power was located and how to hold it to account.

Things are different today. For one thing, the market has been in the ascendancy for some thirty years or so, and the most talented continue to flow to the private sector. For another, we have witnessed in recent years a significant drop in public interest in national politics and in civic engagement, together with a sharp decline in public confidence towards the entire set of government institutions. We have also witnessed an important shift in society that favours the attributes of individuals over those of the community.

It is now less clear where power is located. To be sure, political power has never been static. However, one could in the past know its location, the key actors involved, and how it was being employed. This is much less true today, when power moves around in the form of relations between individuals and networks of interests. We know that prime ministers and their courts have concentrated power in their own hands in recent years at the expense of cabinet as a collective policy-making and decision-making body. The following is one of many such examples increasingly evident in both Canada and Britain. It will be recalled that Stephen Harper tabled a motion in Parliament in 2006 that read 'This House recognizes that the Québécois form a nation within a united Canada' after consulting only a handful of his closest advisers. Cabinet was left outside the loop.[1] Even the minister responsible for intergovernmental affairs was not informed, let alone consulted, before the decision was made and before full caucus was told. The minister subsequently resigned, not because he felt slighted but because he is opposed to special status for any particular ethnic group, even when that group is one of the country's two founding peoples.[2]

Prime ministers and their courts, however, can deal with only a limited number of issues. The rest is turned over to the government system, broadly defined, and involves networking with other levels of government and an array of departments and concerned parties outside of government. Power also flows up to regional or international institutions and down to interest groups, to lobbyists who constantly roam the corridors of political power and bureaucracy to influence policy and decision making, and to communication specialists working inside and outside government to protect and polish the image of prime ministers and their governments. It explains why only bold decisions are essentially taken by prime ministers and their courts (e.g., the decision to participate or not in the war in Iraq). Other decisions are increasingly the product of hidden hands – of networks and interdepartmental and intergovernmental consensus. The media, meanwhile, inspired by the requirements of 'gotcha' journalism, will focus on personalities rather than processes, on events rather than substance, and on the prime minister rather than ministers. The new media also have had a profound impact on a government's political and policy agenda.

Many bureaucrats have been turned into 'networkers' in search of partners to shape new policy initiatives and to deliver public services. They know full well that the days when they had a monopoly of policy advice are gone and that they have to share their influence with a wide array of partnership arrangements. If they have a comparative advantage over other policy actors, it is their ability to keep their ministers and departments out of political trouble – or, failing that, to manage political crises – and their capacity to initiate partnership arrangements. But that alone has changed the relationship between elected politicians and civil servants.

This is a world that has blurred the lines between the public and private sectors and between the political and the bureaucratic arenas. It plays to the advantage of the political, intellectual, and economic elites. The instruments of governance and their accompanying power and influence are now distributed across certain segments of society and the economy. Relationships are now more horizontal than hierarchical, so that one can no longer expect to locate power within the hierarchy and to hold it to account. It takes a deep knowledge not only of the relevant policy issue but also of the ways of the machinery of government if one sets out to influence public policies and government decisions. However, with sufficient financial resources, one can hire both the knowledge and the contacts inside government to get things done. This is what many private firms now do. 'Have knowledge and political connections, will travel' provides lucrative business opportunities in a world where the private sector is king.

Those who are familiar with a sector or a particular policy field will also have opportunities to voice their opinions and to be heard. In both Canada and Britain, consultants are billing governments billions every year to work on virtually every conceivable project or issue. As noted earlier, former elected politicians and retired senior civil servants no longer go off into the sunset to retire. They offer their experience and their inside knowledge to firms and associations wishing to influence public policy and government decisions. Knowledgable academics will more often be seen in the corridors of government buildings than in the classroom. One can hardly overstate the point that, without knowledge of the issue or the ways of the machinery, it is simply not possible to know how public policy is being shaped, let alone how to influence it. At the same time, recent governments in both Canada and Britain have, on certain issues and with the prime minister's court on side, moved away from formal policy and decision making, away from carefully prepared written submissions and towards oral briefings and

Powerpoint presentations. As has already been noted, discussions in the Blair cabinet on whether Britain should join the United States in Iraq centred on a PowerPoint presentation. There were no written documents carefully considering all the issues available to ministers, no expert advice. Nor did the Cabinet Committee on Defence even meet to take stock of the matter. We are informed that Blair, with the help of a handful of senior ministers (i.e., members of his court) drove the decision.[3] Chrétien, meanwhile, consulted only a handful of individuals before deciding not to go to war in Iraq. He did not even bother to secure cabinet's approval.[4] In Britain, the Conservative party's Democracy Task Force concluded that 'Cabinet government has been all but destroyed' and pledged that, if elected, the party would 'establish that no major decision of government should be taken before full papers have been submitted in good time to Cabinet, and the opportunity has been given for a full decision in Cabinet ...'[5]

Court government has enabled those with political power and bureaucratic influence to roam around, strike deals, pick things up at will, and make important decisions without formal processes to guide them or to act as a check. We are discovering in both Canada and Britain that when the cabinet system is dislocated from its traditional parliamentary moorings, as it has been in recent years, the impact is felt in virtually every corner of our political-administrative institutions.[6]

The purpose of this chapter is to take stock of recent developments in our political and administrative institutions from a comparative perspective. Our concern is to assess the state of the relationship between elected politicians and civil servants at the top and between civil servants and citizens at the bottom. We seek to shine light into the increasingly shadowy corridors of power and influence. We draw on the findings of earlier chapters to position how Parliament relates to the government, how elected politicians deal with civil servants and how citizens deal with government. It is now important to define and locate which powers and responsibilities should fall to elected politicians and which to civil servants, and how they should be held to account, in order to give citizens a chance of knowing where power and influence are located and to have a sense that someone in government can be held accountable.

Parliament: On the Outside Watching the Court

Max Weber's ideal-type bureaucracy requires a strong parliament. As he wrote, 'Only a working, not merely a speech making parliament, can provide the ground for the growth and selective ascent of genuine leaders, not merely demagogic talents. A working parliament supervises the administration by continuously showing its work.'[7] For Weber, a strong working parliament has three distinct roles: controlling the power of the bureaucracy, generating political leadership to direct bureaucratic activities, and holding that leadership accountable. Weber not only believed that a strong parliament would counterbalance bureaucracy, but also that the key to accountability was to hold the political leadership to account. Parliament would force the hand of the executive to show where power was located, show its work, and explain its actions.

Parliament once played this central role in the political life of Britain and Canada. Doing well in Parliament still matters to prime ministers and ministers, but doing well means keeping the government out of political trouble, appearing to be in control of government, and having, on occasion at least, the capacity to circle an issue without landing.[8] We saw in chapter 3 that there was a time when Parliament met with some success in making government behave, in holding it to account, in expressing the 'mind of the people,' and in informing both government and citizens of the nation's grievances and problems. One would have to search far and wide to find anyone, particularly in Canada but also in Britain, willing to make the case that Parliament still plays these roles.

A bipartisan committee of Canadian MPs concluded in late 2003 that 'Parliament has lost its forum quality so that it is no longer the place in which meaningful debate occurs, lost its ability to scrutinize government activity and no longer contributes meaningfully to policy debates.'[9] Ed Broadbent, a widely respected parliamentarian who served as leader of the New Democratic Party and as an MP for twenty-three years, had this to say as he left politics: 'After many cumulative years in politics, I have become much less enamoured with the British parliamentary model of confrontation. It is almost intellectually bankrupt in terms of serious debate.'[10] Former British prime minister John Major echoed the views of Canadian MPs in a paper suggesting that 'A malaise is undermining parliamentary democracy. I do not pretend that we have reached the point at which this is irreversible. But I do believe that if we do not act now, then it may become too late.' He added, 'The House of Commons is losing control over decision making and, as it does so, many in the electorate look on in disinterest, not least because of the peripheral factors that have brought politics into disrepute.'[11] If Parliament no longer constitutes the leading political body and is no longer capable of making the government behave, then relations between elected politicians and civil servants at the top and between civil servants and citizens at the bottom will have to adjust.

There appears to be a disconnect between what citizens consider to be the most important role of a member of Parliament and how MPs themselves view their role. For one thing, there is no consensus on what constitutes a proper role for a member of Parliament. It depends on a number of factors – on the MP, on the constituency, on the political party, on the number of MPs the party has in Parliament, and on the state of relations between government and Parliament. MPs, for example, tell me that the role of an MP from a Toronto constituency is vastly different from that of one representing rural New Brunswick.

MPs in Canada ranked helping individuals with their problems and protecting the interests of their constituency at the top in terms of importance. Ensuring that bureaucracy is administering government policy they ranked at the bottom of their priorities, and keeping in touch with constituents about what government is doing at number four out of five possible roles they were asked to consider and rank. Citizens, meanwhile, had quite a different ranking. They ranked keeping in touch with constituents about what government is doing at the top, ensuring that bureaucracy is administering government policy third, and helping people who have personal problems with government at the very bottom.[12] Without putting too fine a point on it, Canadian MPs attach a great deal of importance to playing an 'ombudsman' or 'social worker' role but much less to holding the government and the bureaucracy to account. Citizens, meanwhile, particularly those from urban areas, do not attach much importance to the ombudsman role of MPs but highly value being kept informed of what the government is doing and holding it to account.

Jean Chrétien sought to explain the role of an MP during the 'Shawinigate' scandal. It will be recalled that Chrétien personally lobbied the head of the Business Development Bank, a crown corporation, to approve a $615,000 loan to a hotel adjacent to a golf course. The bank approved the loan, despite having misgivings about the hotel's long-term viability.[13] It was alleged that Chrétien owned shares in the golf course. However, throughout the affair, which dominated the Canadian media for several months, Chrétien denied that he owned shares and insisted that he was only assuming his role as a member of Parliament. His constituency, he stressed, depends on tourism for economic development. He said: 'I will not apologize to anybody for doing my job as a member for Saint Maurice.'[14]

He repeated this claim time and again and pointed to the findings of his own government's ethics counsellor, who reported that it was entirely appropriate for the prime minister to call the bank on behalf of a constituent. Prime ministers and ministers, he argued, have responsibility as members of Parliament and have every right to intervene in government on behalf of their constituencies.[15] The ethics commissioner explained that 'in our constitutional system, one of the most important responsibilities that Members of Parliament have is to represent the interests of their constituents. They do not lose their responsibility ... merely because they are now Ministers.'[16] It should be noted that, at the time, the ethics commissioner reported to the prime minister, not to Parliament.

It doesn't take much to appreciate the difference between how the president of a crown corporation would respond to a request from a prime minister on behalf of a constituent and a similar request from a backbench opposition MP. The president owes his current appointment and possible future promotion to larger crown corporations directly to the prime minister. Prime ministers have tremendous power to reward and punish. Backbench MPs do not. The president of a crown corporation will be certain to take a call from the prime minister but may well refer a call from an opposition MP to someone else down the line. There is nothing in our constitution that would inhibit either Canadian or British prime ministers from using the full force of their office and their power of appointment to pressure a senior government official to take a decision favourable to their political or personal interest.

Chrétien is hardly the first politician to claim that the role of an elected politician is to look after the interest of his constituency. Representatives of all political parties appear to sing from the same hymn book on this matter. A senior political adviser in the Conservative party, for example, insists that 'political influence is the very reason politicians are elected in the first place. To stop them from exercising this influence would be apolitical.'[17] How MPs can go about influencing decisions has never been defined. They are free to push and pull levers and exploit connections they may have with ministers or, better yet, to gain the prime minister's ear to get what they want. One thing is certain: some MPs will have more influence than others. Consequently, some constituents will receive more benefits than others. Civil servants, for whom impartiality and objectivity are core values in their work, will presumably have to accommodate these side deals as best they can. Some former senior civil servants have argued that this factor alone will make the accounting officer concept difficult to implement in Canada. Political considerations and the regional factor, they insist, are invariably present in many government decisions. Establishing a solid working relationship between the deputy minister and minister would be very difficult given the constant need for the minister to override on paper a deputy minister's objections to pursuing a given project.[18]

It may be that one of the reasons Canadian MPs attach a great deal of importance to constituency issues is that, unlike in Britain, there are precious few safe seats. In the 1993 general election, for example, the Progressive Conservative government was soundly defeated, going from a majority mandate to winning only two seats. In most elections, something like 30 per cent of constituencies will change party affiliations. The average tenure of an MP in the Commons in Canada over the past sixty years has been about five years, in contrast to the longer terms achieved by prime ministers.[19]

Although there is no job description against which one can assess an MP's performance in Canada, the U.K. House of Commons has published a short paper on the role of an MP. It singles out three responsibilities: to their constituents, to Parliament, and to their political party, in that order. The publication concentrates almost exclusively on an MP's responsibility to constituents. It states that 'There is no job description for an MP and it is up to an individual MP which cases they take on.' However, it adds, 'MPs are generous with their help and advice, and they will generally try to assist their constituents with a wide range of problems.'[20] The publication makes it clear that an MP cannot interfere with decisions made by the courts but can help with a wide range of problems for which Parliament or the central government is responsible. It mentions, among others, tax problems, problems with the National Health Service, and problems with the Home Office over such matters as immigration and school closures.[21] It adds that an MP has a number of ways to help constituents and, as a last resort, can turn to the parliamentary ombudsman – the Parliamentary Commission for Administration. The ombudsman can deal with issues where there has been administrative incompetence, but only an MP can submit cases to the parliamentary ombudsman.[22] A cursory look at MPs' websites and speeches in Britain also reveals that they see acting as ombudsman to their constituents to be a high priority. One MP, for example, writes that though he is not able to support every cause, he pledges to 'do everything I can to help my constituents.'[23]

Canadian MPs have, over the years, focused more of their efforts on their constituencies than have their U.K. counterparts. But again, that is changing. Students of British politics suggest a number of reasons. Most MPs did not live in their constituencies in the 1950s, but this is no longer the case. There are fewer safe seats in Britain than there were forty years ago, so that promoting the interests of one's constituency is a way to gain attention and achieve electoral success. It is now recognized that lobbying ministers on behalf of local firms or industries and leading delegations to see ministers now constitute an important part of an MP's work and that such activities have increased over the past decades.[24] Moreover, the constituency role appears to be gaining greater importance among recently elected MPs. Questioned for a survey for the U.K. Parliament, 86 per cent of the new intake of MPs regarded 'the most important role of the MP is being a good constituency member,' while less than half identified checking the executive and developing an expertise.[25] However, many in Britain are arguing that MPs are spending too much time on constituency work, a responsibility that they are also ill-equipped to carry out. Betty Boothroyd, former Speaker of the House of Commons, expressed her concern that constituency work had become so dominant that it detracts from an MP's ability to perform his or her other responsibilities.[26] The Fabian Society made the same case in a study carried out in 1998.[27] In both Canada and Britain, MPs can deal with only a very small percentage of their constituents' problems, and surveys reveal that most voters do not reward their MPs on the basis of their constituency work.[28] Indeed, recent surveys in Britain suggest that the great majority of people have had no face-to-face contact with their MP within the past year. Eighty per cent report that they have not written to their MP, 84 per cent have not visited their MP's website, only 18 per cent trust politicians, and only 16 per cent now trust political parties.[29]

In December 2006, I wrote to a number of MPs in Britain, asking them to rank their duties in terms of importance along the same lines as their Canadian counterparts in the survey reported above. I outlined the same five duties (protecting interests of constituency, helping people who have personal problems with government, ensuring that bureaucracy is administering government policy and holding it to account, keeping in touch with constituents about what government is doing, debating and voting in Parliament). Seventeen responded, and their responses unexpectedly mirrored the views of their Canadian counterparts. Thirteen MPs gave 'protecting the interests of their constituencies' and 'helping individuals' at the top (ranking them first and second, out of five) and ranked 'ensuring bureaucracy is administering government policy and holding it to account' at or near the bottom, with eight ranking it fourth or fifth in terms of that importance and only three ranking it first. In contrast, twelve out of seventeen MPs gave 'helping people who have personal problems with government' a ranking of one or two.[30] I write 'unexpectedly' because, as noted, we have always believed – a belief supported by the literature – that Westminster MPs are much less preoccupied with their constituencies than are their Canadian counterparts.[31]

Robert Key, an MP since 1983, recalls seeing MPs increasingly focusing their attention on their constituencies and helping their constituents with problems during his twenty-four years in Parliament. He explained that, in his own early years as an MP, he would likely have told a constituent to contact a certain government department or a civil servant to deal with his or her problem. Today, he remarks, he and his staff are far more likely to handle constituents' problems directly. Twenty-four years ago, he explains, his staff consisted of one person, whom he shared with another MP. Today, he has three staff members, two of them full time in his constituency office. Key also reports that more than half of MPs have also decided to locate the majority of their staff in their constituencies.

He explains that MPs are much less likely to take their constituencies for granted than was the case forty years ago. Constituency associations have grown much more independent from their national party offices and increasingly guard their prerogative to select party candidates to run in national elections. He adds, 'you must understand that for an MP, his entire political life depends on how he is perceived by his constituency.'[32]

The machinery of government in both Canada and Britain has been adjusted somewhat to deal with the increasing tendency of MPs to focus on assisting their constituents. Some government departments in Ottawa and London have added units to deal with requests from MPs to intervene on behalf of their constituents. The Home Office, for example, now has a well-staffed unit dedicated to dealing with 'queries from MPs on immigration matters.' I asked a Home Office official – does this mean that an MP has a better chance of success than someone acting on his or her own behalf? The answer: 'not necessarily, but the MP will very likely get a much quicker response.' The official added that 'this gives MPs a sense of accomplishment.'[33]

Though there is hardly a consensus on this point, focusing on their ombudsman role may well help MPs in their re-election bids. Greg Power, for example, writes that, even in Britain, MPs and academics agree that constituency work now has 'a positive electoral benefit.'[34] That said, it may well have more to do with an MP's perception of what he or she can hope to accomplish while in Parliament. Indeed, it is one area where an MP can exert some influence and thus bolster his or her self-esteem.[35] It provides a purpose – unlike the House of Commons, where MPs 'lose their sense of power and purpose in the boredom of toeing the party line.'[36]

Parliament continues to move away from one of its central roles as described by Gladstone when he told his MPs that 'You are not here to govern, but rather to hold to account those who do.' The House of Commons in both Canada and Britain has been programmed to the convenience of the government, and its ability to hold those who govern to account has waned.[37] Estimates are now approved by a certain date with very little debate, and the accompanying documents are considered inaccessible by many MPs. Accountability has come to signify little more than Question Period and the search for political sleaze.

MPs have largely been relegated to a kind of social worker or service role, and Parliament is seen mainly as a forum for political party gamesmanship. The Canadian and U.K. parliaments have in common the fact that they are not seen as effective in performing their roles in legislative and financial oversight.[38] One veteran observer of Canadian politics exemplified the extent to which Parliament has been brought low by noting that MPs are increasingly turning to the Access to Information Act in order to get information from the government. This he describes as 'ridiculous and an affront to Parliament.'[39]

Spending estimates show how the government plans to implement its program and legislation. The estimate documents are the most important ones to be tabled in the Commons and represent the key source for holding the government accountable to Parliament and citizens. Studies of Parliament's performance in carrying out its budgetary oversight role have highlighted the complexity of both the process and the material brought before Parliament. As a result, as already observed, estimates are now approved without the active involvement of parliamentarians.[40] But that is not all. The traditional purpose of supplementary estimates is to finance unanticipated spending. The auditor general of Canada maintains that in more recent years they have become a vehicle for launching new programs and spending outside of the budget cycle. She writes, 'During the fiscal years from 1997–98 to 2004–05, supplementary appropriations averaged 10.5 per-cent of the total appropriations, up from an average 4.5 percent in the previous eight years.'[41]

MPs readily acknowledge that Parliament's scrutiny and account-ability functions have been reduced to a few partisan skirmishes and that there are limited opportunities to consider important issues and major expenditures. They also readily acknowledge that Parliament now has little impact on public policy. Parliament is regarded by prime ministers and their closest advisers as an obstacle to be overcome or, if possible, avoided. By the time issues are brought to Parliament, posi-tions have been set, partisan lines drawn, and outcomes established.[42] The prime minister, the one dominating force in the government, does not participate in many aspects of the work of the Commons. Prime ministers attend Question Period, but they do not attend committee meetings or, as a rule, testify before committees, apart from the prime minister's appearance before the Liaison Committee in Britain. But Question Period is not without its many critics. John Major insists that 'Prime Minister's Questions has degenerated to pointless farce. Its pur-pose was never so much to impart or extract information as to embar-rass the Prime Minister – or, in the Prime Minister's eyes – to expose the inexperience of the Opposition.'[43]

MPs do not invest much of their time and energy in the work of par-liamentary committees. Their work on a committee in Canada accounts for only about four hours weekly when Parliament sits. That estimate assumes that they attend all committee meetings, which they do not. They also do not have access to much expertise in crafting their participation. More importantly, they see limited political advantage in their work with parliamentary committees. As one Canadian official remarked, 'An MP would trade all his or her work on a Parliamentary Committee for the chance of being seen for fifteen seconds on the evening news on television asking a tough question during Question Period.' She added, 'visibility matters a great deal to MPs and much more often than not there are no journalists covering Parliamentary Committees, let alone television cameras.'[44] In Canada, parliamentari-ans now receive, among other documents, more than ninety reports on plans and priorities, a similar number of departmental performance reports, and various reports from some forty crown corporations – but spend precious little time going over them.[45]

In Britain, parliamentary committees have produced more than 150 reports in twenty years, but MPs have made very little use of them in holding the government to account.[46] Members of select committees in Britain have concluded that, with the limited resources at their disposal and the sheer volume of paper generated by 'modern government, it is simply not possible to monitor in depth the full range of responsibilities' of departments.[47] There was much hope for stronger accountability in 1979 when the newly elected Conservative government moved to set up a full range of standing departmental select committees. The new structure appears to have given parliamentary committees a higher 'public profile' and generated 'lots of papers' but little else.[48] Indeed, a number of observers argue that some thirty years of expectations have not been met. Nevil Johnson, for one, maintains that the 'preservation of party government in the chamber of the [British] House of Commons sets strict limits on the ability of select committees to challenge head-on the policies and performance of a government.'[49] The result is that MPs serve on parliamentary committees because it offers the 'best prospect of being kept reasonably busy until something better comes along.'[50] This is no less true for Canada.

But there is yet another reason to explain the failure of parliamentary committees to make their mark. They do not have the resources and expertise to assist MPs to mount an effective challenge to government departments and agencies. Parliamentary committees in Britain typically have access to about six staff members – two clerks, one committee assistant, and three committee specialists. There is also a small scrutiny unit (about twenty officials) from which they can draw information and possible questions to ask of ministers. Contrast this with the Home Office, with tens of thousands of employees.[51] Things are not much different in Canada, though its Parliament does not have access to a scrutiny unit. Both Canadian and British MPs also have some support from their respective Libraries of Parliament.[52]

The Public Accounts Committee is different from other committees in that the chair in both Canada and Britain can draw on the vast resources of the Office of the Auditor General or the National Audit Office for help. Committee members are able to put questions to civil servants rather than to ministers. The work of the committee, however, is to examine past programs and how they were managed. Both hearsay and the literature in Canada suggest that Britain's Public Accounts Committee is more effective than its Canadian counterpart.[53] British MPs and parliamentary staff confirm that appointments to the committee are sought after and that it ranks in the top three or four committees.[54] One student of the U.K. government describes the Public Accounts Committee as 'highly traditionalist and self-consciously authoritative.'[55] The same cannot be said about Canada. The fact that the accounting officer concept has a long history in Britain and none in Canada may explain the difference. In addition, the work of the Public Accounts Committee in Britain is considerably less partisan than the work of other parliamentary committees, again perhaps because it has learned to work with accounting officers. One committee staff member reports that he has heard MPs tell one another that they may disagree in the strongest of terms on policy but that when it comes to the Public Accounts Committee they all share the same interest – better administration and more effective public spending. He mentioned that he had worked with another parliamentary committee prior to the Public Accounts Committee and that the Public Accounts Committee is a great deal less partisan.[56]

U.K. MPs and committee staff members, however, argue that the Public Accounts Committee could be more effective. They report that senior civil servants tend to 'fuddle' answers and can sidestep difficult questions because MPs have only 'ten minutes' to grill a permanent secretary. They add that, all too often, senior civil servants are there to defend the political interests of their ministers rather than to come clean on management matters and on public spending.[57] Things are not much different in Canada on this front. This should come as a surprise to no one, including MPs, since the government tells civil servants that they have a duty to the crown but that, for all practical purposes, the crown means the government of the day.

Government MPs, particularly if they see that the prime minister's hold on the government is weakening, may well challenge the government. Chrétien experienced some difficulty in getting his legislative agenda through Parliament in his last two years in office. In Britain, Blair saw his Labour MPs vote against his government on the Education and Inspection Bill in 2006. Revolts of government MPs are not without consequences. Revolts suggest weakness in the party, which will likely hurt government MPs in their re-election prospects.[58] For this reason alone, government MPs will revolt only when it becomes clear that the prime minister may not stay in office for long or that he or she would be of little or no help in securing re-election. At other times and in other circumstances, the roles of government MPs are to act as cheerleaders for their party and lobbyists for their constituencies.

Political Parties: Empty Vessels

Previously we noted that few observers either in Canada or Britain would disagree with the following: political parties are not effective vehicles for policy formulation; they offer precious few meaningful opportunities for citizens to participate in the policy-making process; and their main purpose now is to be election-day machines.[59] Wherever political power now resides, it is not in political parties. When we move away from political parties to pursue more narrow interests, the connection between citizens and their government is further fragmented. It also speaks to the rise of more 'personalized realities.'[60]

Membership in political parties, as we have already seen, has fallen sharply in both Canada and Britain, and national party meetings are not much more than pep rallies. Party leaders and their courtiers dominate their parties to the point where the more substantive issues centre on the leader not the party. The hollowing out of political parties has left the leaders and their advisers rather than the wider membership to define policy preferences. Michael Foley's observation that political parties in Britain are 'permanently enthralled with the projected utility and leverage of their actual or potential leaders' also resonates very well in Canada.[61] The one constant message from think tanks, political scientists, political parties, and politicians themselves in recent years is that political parties have lost their place to the 'celebritization' of party leaders. The competition in contemporary politics is now between choices in personalities rather than between political parties and policies.[62]

Citizens may wish to see strong political parties capable of competing with public opinion surveys and focus groups in shaping new initiatives and policy positions for party leaders, but they are not prepared to make the effort to help this process. Fewer and fewer of them want to be involved with political parties, and volunteer political activity is no longer regarded as a civic virtue or something to be valued by society. In fact, it is quite the opposite. The media are constantly on the lookout for appointments to boards or commissions to see if there is any link to the party in power. The media applauded, for example, the fact that the last two governors general, Adrienne Clarkson and Michaëlle Jean, had no political affiliation. They argued that Clarkson had 'removed the tarnish of political patronage that had marred previous appointments.'[63] In other words, citizens should avoid joining political parties if they wish to avoid tarnishing their image.

We have also made life much more difficult than in the past for elected politicians, who are now subjected to demanding conflict-of-interest legislation and who must be constantly on the lookout against a misstep in their professional or even their personal lives. Their very political survival may well depend on it. Again, things were very different forty years ago. In Canada, a former ethics counsellor writes that C.D. Howe, Canada's minister of industry after the Second World War, would review his extensive stock portfolio on the basis of the government's decisions and the information he had learned inside government during the week. No one thought anything of the fact that Howe was an active investor and a minister at the same time: 'there was no chorus of claims that he was corrupt or that his decisions were tainted by his own personal interests. It was felt that he would never take a decision as minister that was not in the public interest. Howe saw no contradiction between doing good for his country and doing well for himself. There was a high level of trust in public officials. Those days are long gone.'[64]

One leading Canadian journalist wonders if we have gone too far in our suspicion of those who run for office: 'Egged on by a voracious press, we have lost all trust in politicians and public servants. We have placed so many restrictions on them, stripped them of so much privacy, that many citizens decide to remain in private life rather than face such scrutiny.'[65] It may well be that, in our inability to influence horizontal or joined-up government – tied as it is to policy networks, consultants, lobbyists, and the international community – we are taking it out on politicians and civil servants and forcing them to face a level of public scrutiny that we would not tolerate anywhere except in government.

Observers in both Canada and Britain, supported by a host of public opinion surveys, agree that political parties no longer have the appeal for citizens that they once did. Practitioners maintain that the high point for political parties in their ability to attract members and to engage in meaningful policy debate was from the Second World War until the 1970s.[66] Tom Axworthy, one-time chief of staff to Pierre Trudeau, writes that in Canada in the 1960s if one were interested in policy, the place to be was on the floor of a party convention. That, he insists, is simply not a recognizable model today.[67]

While in power, cabinet ministers and even MPs and rank-and-file members will, for the most part, remain silent about the location of political power and about the apparent inability of their party to play much of a role in shaping government policy. Not long after being turfed out by voters, however, they feel free to speak out. Senior Liberal party members, including former ministers, won 'sustained applause' at a Liberal party convention when they spoke about 'party oligarchy' replacing 'party democracy' and about Paul Martin's top-down approach to governing, after pledging to be different from Jean Chrétien on this front. One former minister said that she and her colleagues are simply 'fed up with platforms that have not even been run by the party membership. We're fed up with the fact that campaign ads can be approved by focus groups on Bay Street instead of by Liberal party members.'[68]

Many recent studies in both Canada and Britain have telling titles: 'Parties without Members,' 'Empty Vessels?' and 'Parties without Partisans.'[69] William Cross, one of Canada's leading students of political parties, recently observed that Canada's 'political parties are not effective vehicles for policy study and development. They neither offer voters meaningful opportunity for involvement in the policy-making process nor do they regularly generate policy alternatives for consideration and examination by those in elected office or in the senior bureaucracy. It is fair to say that Canadian parties have long seen their primary role as being electoral machines.'[70]

Political parties in both Canada and Britain are concerned with winning power and have little interest in analysing political or policy issues that are not connected to winning the next election. In a comparative study, Pippa Norris maintains that the loss of support for political parties is particularly evident in affluent, established democracies. She explains that there are various aspects of modern society that lead to a weakening of the bond between citizens and political parties. Some individuals now are much more able to become self-reliant. Well-educated people will pick and choose what they want from government and ignore the rest. This suits the political, intellectual, and economic elite just fine. One can easily appreciate why a small group of political advisers would wish to produce election campaign platforms in a vacuum, working with the leader.[71]

The problem is that interests not represented by this inner circle of political elites may be frozen out of the political process. The alternative is for individuals with genuine policy concerns to join interest groups to promote their point of view. But, as Robert Young points out, this serves to degenerate parties 'further into domination by leaders and their personal entourages, who play the politics of image and strategic vagueness, who take office with little sense of direction, and who end up as brokers among interest groups.'[72] The lack of formal policy-making processes tied to a political party permits party leaders and their inner circles to pick and choose which interest groups they will respond to and which issues they will address. There is a much better chance that the concerns of average citizens will be heard when political parties and their members prepare broad policy preferences, rather than when this responsibility is concentrated in the hands of party leaders and their advisers. Similarly, the concerns of the average citizen in shaping policies are less likely to be taken into account when political power is concentrated in the hands of party leaders and their courtiers. In other words, the hollowing out of political parties is not without important consequences for representative democracy. If nothing else, it places even more pressure on other political institutions and makes it more difficult for citizens to establish where political power and influence are located.

Politicians and Political Power

It is still possible, as we saw earlier, to recognize status, mission, and policy participants among politicians. The difference is that the rules have changed and what matters to all of them in their search for success is their link to the party leaders and their courts. Conventional party politics and cabinet processes have come to matter a great deal less in this pursuit.

As in the past, the challenge is to manage voices as best one can. The difference now is that some voices are louder, more pervasive, and less deferential, while others have simply gone mute. We have seen that the number of people who are bothering to vote in both Canada and Britain has fallen sharply in recent years. This may well be the result of voters feeling dismayed by what they got, or what they were able to influence in return for their votes.[73]

The lack of formal processes favours private money, the economic and political elites, and special interests with the necessary resources to be heard. Ordinary citizens require formal processes if they are to be heard and if they are to have public services on an equal basis. Court government is better suited to the elites, who can roam around picking issues to influence or can hire expert help to do so on their behalf. Ordinary citizens have neither the resources nor the knowledge to thrive in a world of court government.

Elected politicians will react to influential interest groups, the economic elites, the media, and public opinion surveys. Those in government will, in addition, look to policy networks and to people who can advance their agenda and their political or bureaucratic interests. But here, too, the world has changed. As we noted in earlier chapters, gone are the days when the ministers would work with their departments to define proposals and then go to cabinet and have it out with cabinet colleagues. Today, influence, responsibility, and even authority on issues that do not hold the interest of prime ministers and their courtiers are parcelled out across policy networks and public-private partnerships designed to deliver public services.

We are no longer sure what role a politician should play in society.[74] There was a time when MPs went to Ottawa and London to (among other things) represent the views of citizens. Public opinion surveys are now much better and more accurate at doing that. In years past, MPs were also sent to Ottawa and London to bring home the bacon, to push and pull as many levers as they could to gain things for their constituencies. Citizens may still expect as much from their MPs if benefits flow to their communities, but when this does not happen, they will cry 'Inappropriate political intervention!' There was a time when an MP could claim to have the influence to locate a local post office outlet. Today, the media will take him or her to task for attempting to influence what should be a fair, transparent process.[75] There was a time when aspiring and elected politicians were expected to help shape party positions and plan election campaign strategies, but that role has now been taken over by paid professionals and consultants or lobbyists on loan to a political party hoping for future benefits. Lastly, in the nineteenth century, private bills were more important and members, particularly in Britain, could more easily work on behalf of their constituents, notably wealthy individuals, and get charters for railways and canals.

Once elected, MPs are expected to promote the party line and to voice criticism of the government only in private or in caucus. But even here the bargain has broken down, both in Canada and Britain. MPs are saying less of significance in a leaky caucus and more to ministers, and preferably to the prime minister, in private.[76] MPs in their one-on-one meetings will pursue issues of personal interest, and this reinforces the tendency to focus on single issues rather than on the community as a whole and on the 'me' versus the 'we' perspective.

This is not to suggest that the 'me' perspective works. A quick and private tête-à-tête with a minister may not actually get things done.

But it does sidestep dealing with the inherent frustration of trying to navigate the government's horizontal policy and decision-making process with limited knowledge of how the process works. It also reduces the scope for informed collective political assessments and judgments.

Bureaucrats: A Shadow on Their Shoulders

I asked a government official who had held a number of senior level positions in the private sector before joining the federal government to compare the two sectors. His response: 'I always feel that there is a shadow on everybody's shoulder working in government.'[77] To be sure, civil servants *should* go to work feeling that there is a shadow on their shoulders: this is a good way to differentiate the public sector from the private. The more important question is – what is the source of that shadow? Responsibility for administering public funds is vastly different from that for managing private money. Civil servants should, at all times, be guided by a sense of equality, impartiality, integrity, objectivity in staffing, and promotions based on merit. The public interest and a parsimonious culture in their handling of public funds should be paramount. If this is what constitutes the shadow, then all to the good.

This study, however, makes the case that these forces no longer constitute the shadow, or are no longer alone in shaping it. The shadow today speaks to political realities – do not get the minister in trouble, do not get the department in trouble, protect your department. And the measure of your success will be how well you were able to keep everyone out of the media. This may not be much different from the way public administration was practised forty years ago. But other things have changed. Society has changed. It is, on the one hand, more demanding of government and, on the other, less trusting of public institutions. The parsimonious culture is no longer evident, and elected politicians are looking for senior civil servants who are particularly responsive to their political agenda. One can also question to what extent self-interest among senior civil servants remains in check – for example, the three most recent clerks and secretaries to the cabinet in Canada were all able, through their own efforts, to secure three of the most sought-after diplomatic appointments, although none of them had any expertise or had even worked in foreign affairs before their appointment.

What do civil servants think about in the morning when they leave their home to go to their office? To whom do they feel responsible?

What role is expected of them? Again, on the face of it, not much has changed. The civil service exists to provide policy analysis, to formulate policy under political direction, to implement policy, to deliver services to the public, and to manage resources. It should perform all these tasks with professionalism, neutrality, fairness, and integrity. Some civil servants, much like their predecessors forty years ago, will go to their offices to deal directly with citizens and deliver public services. They will process passport applications or income-tax returns, or deal with prisoners. Others will go to work to serve ministers, attempt to put political objectives into practice, and develop policy. The gulf between the two groups is what has changed. It has widened considerably in recent years.

Civil servants who work on policy, evaluating programs and assisting ministers to govern, now have to manage three fairly distinct processes. The first and the most important for ambitious civil servants is the prime minister's priorities and policy agenda. Starting in earnest with Trudeau in Canada and Callaghan in Britain, prime ministers have brought key decisions to their own offices. The Privy Council Office and the Cabinet Office now serve prime ministers more than they serve cabinet. The role of senior civil servants in these offices is to pursue the prime minister's agenda, to make things happen, and to ensure that departments and agencies know what the prime minister expects of them. In addition, prime ministers have established special units in those agencies to drive their agenda. Tony Blair, for example, established the Prime Minister's Delivery Unit in the Cabinet Office and the Treasury, but decided essentially to have the unit report directly to him. The unit's purpose is to drive a cultural change to improve delivery performance and speaks to Blair's 'personalism' in pursuing his duties as prime minister.[78]

The growth of central agencies over the past thirty-five years speaks to the above. We saw in a previous chapter that central agencies in both Canada and Britain have increased substantially during this period, with some agencies now well over three times larger than they were in 1970. It is important to stress once again that central agencies do not deliver public services and have precious few contacts with citizens.

The second process, closely tied to the first, involves the media and the issues of the day. As many studies have pointed out in recent years, the media can have a significant impact on the government's agenda, a point that was made time and again in my consultations with current and recently retired elected politicians and senior civil servants in both

Canada and Britain. Richard Rose puts it very well when he writes that 'the box that counts is the television set rather than the dispatch box.' He adds that what is said on television has come to matter a great deal more than what is said in Westminster, with the result that the more the prime minister counts on the media to promote his message the less he will communicate or 'feel the need to communicate with MPs at Westminster.'[79] Given that only prime ministers can provide a response without consulting cabinet or navigating through the traditional policy-making process, they and their courts will drive the process, involving only senior officials from the relevant departments and agencies. They will want to move quickly and to be seen to be in control of issues dominating the media – an example in Canada is the summer of 2006 when measures had to be taken to remove citizens from Lebanon.

The third process is the one tied to horizontal government, where many departments and practitioners are involved. As we saw earlier, the process is elaborate and the consultations are slow. Here, the process has many hands from both inside and outside government. The role of civil servants is to network, to find common ground, and to strike partnership arrangements. The process requires patience and negotiating skills. It holds little appeal for those who would like to embrace bold tries and who have a strong sense of ownership of their work. It is a form of government by paralysis. It also requires civil servants to become policy actors in their own right, able to present and defend policy positions outside of government circles, although they are constantly reminded that they serve in an institution that does not have a personality distinct from the government of the day.

The above explains why there has been a convergence of skills between elected politicians and senior civil servants. It may also explain why, according to Graham Wilson and Anthony Barker, senior civil servants have lost some of their self-confidence and their willingness to argue against policies they think unwise.[80] In many ways, civil servants have lost some of their ability or willingness to speak truth to power. The balance has shifted so that elected politicians now feel less inhibited about speaking political power to those who might wish to speak truth to them.

One has only to read the testimony of recently retired civil servants before parliamentary committees and public inquiries to appreciate the extent to which the balance has shifted. Paul Tellier, former clerk of the privy council and secretary to the cabinet, accepted in November 2006 an invitation by Prime Minister Harper to co-chair an advisory committee on the renewal and future development of the public service.[81] He told the media that senior civil servants need to rediscover the capacity to 'say no to ministers when required ... A deputy minister has to be able to put his foot down and say – I don't think the government should do this.' He added, 'It's a question of leadership – and the first challenge is to protect integrity and promote ethics, which is leadership. The sponsorship scandal should never have happened and I think that public servants have to carry some blame for this.'[82]

Tellier's desire to strengthen the capacity of senior civil servants to speak truth to power may well have to do with the location of political power and its use. It is one thing to say no to a minister when required, but it is quite another matter to say no to the prime minister. Ministers do not appoint deputy ministers and permanent secretaries, the prime minister does. Deputy ministers and permanent secretaries have an accountability relationship with the prime minister that is stronger than the one they have with their ministers. They will pay particular attention to the wishes of the one who has the power to appoint, dismiss, or promote them. Speaking truth to the prime minister is not without risks for those who would wish a more senior appointment or a plum foreign posting. They know full well that if they have a major disagreement with their ministers, they can appeal to the secretary to the cabinet in Britain, or to the Privy Council Office in Canada. The PCO directive reads, 'Ultimately, a matter which results in an apparently irreconcilable difference becomes a matter for resolution by the Prime Minister, with advice from the Clerk. Deputy Ministers should also consult the Clerk in cases where problems have occurred in the management of the department or the Minister's portfolio, and which may have an impact on the Ministry's ability as a collectivity to maintain the confidence of the House of Commons and move forward its legislative and policy agenda.'[83] Recall, as well, the observation of a deputy minister, which we noted in the last chapter, that she works 'with' her minister, not 'for' the minister.

When it truly matters, deputy ministers and permanent secretaries work for the prime minister. Ministers know full well that deputy ministers or permanent secretaries have a direct reporting relationship to the secretary to the cabinet and the prime minister and that they need to be on solid ground if they are to challenge them. There is a story that has made the rounds for years in Ottawa: a minister went to Trudeau with a request to have his deputy minister sacked or transferred elsewhere. Trudeau replied that he knew the deputy minister well and that he had more confidence in the deputy minister than in the minister. The minister swallowed his pride, went back to the department, and carried on.

Deputy ministers can hardly speak truth to a horizontal policy process. For one thing, they would not know to whom they should speak truth. The growing pluralism of policy advice means that senior civil servants must now share truth with multiple actors – from inside government, from other governments, and from an elaborate network of interested parties, consultants, and lobbyists. Truth in such a situation is now held in many hands, no longer simply in those of a permanent head of a government department.

Some elected politicians have always sought to have a say in program implementation. New Public Management was to change that by empowering front-line managers and their employees. As we have seen, program managers in both Canada and Britain have been delegated greater authority to manage financial and human resources, and a number of centralized prescribed rules and regulations have been done away with. Particularly since the introduction of New Public Management measures, politicians and bureaucrats in Western democracies regard program implementation as the one area where they consider that they have principal responsibility.[84] But here again, it depends. Some ministers, albeit a very small minority, with the prime minister's blessing or direction, may take a strong interest in management. Nick D'Ombrain, who served as head of the Machinery of Government Secretariat in the PCO for several years, explained that a minister may or may not be involved in management, depending on the minister and the circumstances.[85] It is the prime minister who usually decides when the circumstances are appropriate, not the minister.

Prime ministers, of course, are free to roam wherever they want and deal with whatever management issue they wish, provided that they have enough time to do so and that it does not violate any statutes. It seems that nothing is off limits any more for prime ministers. They and their courtiers are free to have files 'sexed up' to enable them to sell or spin a new initiative to the media. Chrétien, it will be recalled, was accused of turning the RCMP into an extension of his own office. Lawrence Martin wrote that the RCMP was all too willing to help Chrétien in both the Shawinigate and the sponsorship scandals. He pointed out that the court condemned the RCMP raids on a house and cottage owned by the president of the bank, the head of the crown corporation, after the bank president had raised questions publicly about the prime minister's personal intervention to secure a loan on behalf of a hotel. The court called the raid 'an unspeakable injustice.'[86] The machinery of government, it seems, had been asked to assist the prime minister and his court, and there is now little in the way of formal processes or defined authority to check their interventions.

Whether or not ministers have an interest in management issues, nothing prevents elected politicians from intervening to try to influence program decisions or the pace of program delivery. We have seen from senior civil servants' testimonies before the Gomery Commission that a number of them were unhappy with the extent to which politicians and their political advisers were involved in program administration but that there was little they could do about it other than raise questions. One senior Privy Council Office official told Justice Gomery that his role was to prepare briefing notes to go up the line, recommending what PMO officials wanted. He said, 'I was responsible but I had no role other than to validate decisions made by PMO officials. I did not feel good about this but that was that.'[87]

Though he was never asked to appear before Gomery, a former deputy minister went public with his concerns about political interference in day-to-day administration. He recalled that, after the PCO had supported the preparation of a paper on public service values and ethics, he spent a great deal of his time 'dodging political entities to use my agency as a slush fund, even as officials in the Privy Council Office were helping the Prime Minister's Office pressure my staff to approve dubious projects.'[88] To be sure, if prime ministers and their courts decide on a course of action, whether it involves a policy or a management issue, then departments have little choice but to pursue the matter. As Norman Spector, a former official of deputy minister rank under both Mulroney and Chrétien, writes, 'I know a former public servant who is raising dogs and walking the beach in Nova Scotia because she refused to knuckle under to the Privy Council Office and PMO.'[89]

The point is that officials in the Prime Minister's Office in both Canada and Britain think that they can help themselves to a department or an agency's programs to serve their own partisan political interests. We do not differentiate how elected politicians and their political advisers should deal with departments and agencies with respect to their purpose, their legislated mandate, and the degree to which program requirements are outlined in statutes, and this enables them to walk through government departments, picking up items at

will. The fact that governments have moved away from formal processes and requirements has also made it easier for elected politicians
to do this, particularly prime ministers and their courtiers. Still, prime
ministers and their advisers are held in check by the possibility that
using their power improperly could well generate bad publicity.

Tony Blair's office in Britain has even sought to strengthen its hand in
program delivery. His purpose was not to direct activities to certain
areas but rather to monitor the progress departments and agencies were
making in strengthening program delivery and in meeting performance
targets. As noted earlier, Blair established in 2001 a Prime Minister's
Delivery Unit (PMDU) to develop a formal direct control over implementation, which, in the past, had been a 'relatively autonomous area of
departmental activity.' This added an institutional mechanism to the
'personalism' factor in strengthening the hand of the prime minister. As
David Richards and Martin Smith suggest, 'Blair explicitly wanted to
augment Prime Ministerial influence over departments and in a way
that does not rely on the personal interests or intervention of the Prime
Minister.'[90] PMDU is headed by an official of permanent secretary rank
and is designed to work in close partnership with the Treasury, the
Prime Minister's Office, and the Cabinet Office.[91]

This, in turn, has implications for civil servants. It suggests that the
centre of government not only sets the policy agenda but also has a
hand in program delivery. It involves the centre in the details of administration, it gives the centre a capacity to generate data about departments and agencies rather than being dependent on them, and it speaks
to the old adage that 'the man in Whitehall knows best.'[92] It also means
that prime ministers and their courtiers can intervene in whatever policy issue – and now in whatever area of administration – they wish.

All of the above has serious implications for accountability and for
relations between elected politicians and civil servants and between
civil servants and citizens. It suggests that a new map is being drawn
in charting the democratic policy process from voters to politicians to
civil servants. It also suggests that new relations are being forged.

Citizens Looking for Who Has Power

Citizens want more opportunities to influence government decisions,
but a majority do not want to participate in political activities other
than voting.[93] It may well be that the policy process has become
extremely complicated and inaccessible to the average citizen. Either

because they have given up on policies or because political issues have become too complex, citizens demonstrate 'deep pockets of political ignorance and political illiteracy.' As part of the Canadian election survey, efforts were made to assess how well Canadian voters were informed. The study revealed that about one-third of Canadian voters could not correctly attribute a single election promise to the party that had made it, even when the questions listed the most basic elements of a party's platform. Many Canadians were also confounded by the most basic of political terms.[94] Whatever the reasons, it is clear that if citizens are not prepared to commit the time and effort to participate in the political process, they will need to strengthen conventional representative democracy and recapture a meaningful role for elected officials beyond that of the prime minister.

An unprecedented volume of information, ideas, and policy positions is now circulating and making it difficult even for government officials to cope. One can hardly imagine what it must be like for citizens. It is extremely difficult for citizens to inform themselves about policy issues, let alone know how the policy process now works. There was a time when both were more straightforward. There was also a time when there was a stronger element of trust between citizens and elected politicians and between citizens and civil servants than exists today. As we have seen, the trust factor has eroded at both levels. Scandals, many of which, like the sponsorship scandal, go beyond the political class, have also weakened the trust between civil servants and citizens.

Citizens are left to vote and to be the source of public opinion as captured from time to time by public opinion surveys. Still, some citizens feel impotent and believe that their lack of participation in government, broadly defined, has been thrust upon them.[95] A number believe that voting has limited impact and that it is the media that controls public opinion. Many citizens now believe that self-interest is paramount with civil servants. Milton Friedman would agree: California, he argued, is a state run by bureaucrats for bureaucrats.[96] William Niskanen, too, has pointed to weak legislative oversight and bureaucratic inefficiencies as the main challenges confronting Western democracies.[97]

Citizens who do focus on the operations of national political institutions are, as earlier chapters argue, finding accountability lacking, and with good reason. Ministers, as we saw, have started to blame civil servants, with some civil servants responding by blaming politicians.

Even prime ministers are now disregarding civil service anonymity, once an important component of the doctrine of ministerial responsibility. Prime Minister Harper, for example, publicly expressed his 'anger' at his Foreign Affairs officials for not 'even trying to be at a trial' to support a Canadian citizen charged with promoting terrorist activities in China. Mr Cahil, a Canadian citizen, born and raised in China, was sent to prison for promoting what Chinese officials described as terrorist activities following his efforts to secure more autonomy from Beijing for the Uyghur minority. Harper and some of his senior ministers had raised the Cahil case with senior Chinese officials as a 'serious human rights case.' The day after Harper's public outburst, Canadian diplomats were 'dispatched' to the court in a remote part of China to support Cahil.[98]

Some ministers are no longer willing to answer for the activities of civil servants, let alone be held accountable for their activities. Ministers, including some highly respected former ministers, are also pointing the finger at civil servants for what they label 'bureaucratic patronage.' Marc Lalonde, a former finance minister in the Trudeau cabinet, spoke of bureaucratic patronage before Justice Gomery, suggesting that it was worse than political patronage because elected politicians are 'accountable to Parliament and can be put on the spot in the House of Commons.'[99] John Crosbie, a senior minister in the Mulroney cabinet, made the same point as Lalonde, insisting that 'patronage is now controlled by deputy ministers, not ministers.'[100] Citizens see ministers hiding behind civil servants and civil servants hiding behind ministers or, in the words of a permanent secretary, 'in reality the current arrangements let everyone off the hook.'[101] Nor do citizens have access to the invisible public sector, the one populated by consultants, lobbyists, and think tanks. The invisible public sector is largely Ottawa- and London-based and is populated by political, economic, and knowledge elites. Citizens, meanwhile, will often acquire what knowledge they have of public policy and government decisions through fifteen-second sound bites on the evening news.[102]

The central issue in public administration is to decide where one ought to focus efforts to strengthen the relationship between elected politicians and civil servants and between the government and citizens. Some believe that we ought to look to individuals and see what motivates them. Others maintain that the key lies in institutions, in how they shape the behaviour of elected politicians and civil servants. Thus, the debate is between those who believe that institutions, notably their norms and values, shape what elected politicians and civil servants believe to be possible and desirable in their work and those who look to individuals and incentives. The next chapter explores this debate.

13 From Formal Processes, Rules, and a Doctrine to the Individual

The history of public administration is a record of a struggle between senior civil servants who would extend their authority and managerial space to take decisions versus those who would wish to hold that power in check, to impose constraints on its application. The latter would like to introduce measures to ensure transparency about how and why decisions were made and to intervene in administrative decisions. The struggle has been evident at all levels in government, but it now encompasses actors outside government. It pits individual against individual and individuals against processes. We have seen, over the past forty years, a deliberate shift away from formal processes to an emphasis on the individual. The implications for the relationship between elected politicians and civil servants and between civil servants and citizens are far reaching.

The return of court government, the introduction of private sector management to government operations, and access to information legislation, among other developments, all focus on the individual rather than on formal processes. Governing by networks involves consultative processes, but it, too, focuses on the relative influence of individuals and their access to key decision makers in government. Governments have of late even begun the practice of singling out individuals inside government to become 'champions,' their remit being to promote a variety of causes, from affirmative action for visible minorities to ethics and values. Citizens have recently been turned into customers, one more indication that it is individuals who matter. Scholars have also turned their interest during the past forty years or so to the individual, as work on public-choice and principal-agent theories attests. Everyone, it seems, is focused on the individual, but no one has

sought, in light of this trend, to adjust basic accountability requirements. As a result, individuals in government are free to embrace traditional processes whenever it is to their advantage and to ignore them
when it is not.

The shift has concentrated political power further into the hands of
prime ministers and their courts and has made individual civil servants more visible, even to those outside government. Richard Wilson,
a former cabinet secretary, explains that civil servants now 'need to
have good presentation skills to be prepared to appear in public on
television, before select committees and to be prepared to give interviews to the media and to understand the needs of modern management.'[1] Wilson did not attempt to reconcile this with the view still
espoused by the U.K. Cabinet Office and the Canadian Privy Council
Office that the civil service does not have a constitutional personality
distinct from that of the government of the day.

Peter Hennessy writes about the personalization of public administration in Britain and the importance of loyalty to the prime minister
rather than to the cabinet, the civil service, or the government.[2] The
very same has been written about Canada.[3] I asked a senior deputy
minister, for example, how he and his colleagues were adjusting to the
arrival of the Harper government to power, the first Conservative
government elected in thirteen years. His reply is very telling: 'It seems
that the Prime Minister likes us as individuals but he, some of his
Ministers and his advisers do not much like us as a group or as a profession.' He added, 'they may like individual civil servants, but they
do not much like the civil service.'[4]

The point is that it is not cabinet, but prime ministers and their
courts of advisers, which will include only a few key ministers, who
hold effective political power. Similarly, individual civil servants now
have influence, but the civil service does not. Individual lobbyists, partisan political advisers, and key participants in policy networks with
access to prime ministers and their courts can also wield considerable
influence. More to the point, as has already been noted on numerous
occasions, when things matter to prime ministers and their courts,
power is concentrated in the hands of selected individuals and decisions are made. We cannot predict what issues prime ministers will
decide to focus on, but we can predict that they will invariably concentrate on a selected number of files and that their views will easily pre-
vail, particularly when they lead a majority government. We can also
predict that the prime minister's policy preferences, partisan political

expediency and considerations, and the watchful eye of the media will contribute to his or her interest on selected issues. It is no longer clear, in either Canada or Britain, what is meant when we refer to cabinet's collective decision-making role. We simply no longer know what decisions, if any, require some kind of collective deliberation. To be sure, cabinet may come in handy, but, in both countries, it no longer directs the work of the government.[5]

At least some authority on management matters has also shifted to individual civil servants or to front-line program managers and away from formal processes. This is a direct result of the decision by the centre of government that individual managers must have greater flexibility over financial and human resources. A number of centrally prescribed rules and regulations have been done away with in both Canada and Britain in the hope that government operations and programs will be better managed.[6] It should be noted, however, that new rules were subsequently introduced in Canada in the aftermath of Chrétien's sponsorship scandal.

Whether or not their increased authority over operations leads to better management practices, senior civil servants and front-line managers will continue to press for more of it. It would be rare indeed for a manager to object to increased authority and ask for some to be taken away. Managers invariably have an answer when it comes to accountability – give us the freedom to manage, do away with constraints and red tape, assess our performance, and let us deal with non-performers. Their answers are not as easily forthcoming, however, when one asks just how the performance of civil servants can be properly evaluated or how one ought to hold them to account. There is also precious little evidence to show that non-performers, however identified, suffer many, if any, consequences.

The personalization of public administration extends to both the formulation of policy proposals and the delivery of programs and services. The prime minister's inner court will concentrate on policy issues that matter to the prime minister, and here the key individual will be well known both inside and outside government, including in the media. Program managers, meanwhile, have also become visible, and this by design. In the total scheme of things, individuals have come to matter more than hierarchy, and individual civil servants now matter more than does the civil service itself. The civil service may not have a personality distinct from the government of the day, but it has become quite another matter for individual civil servants.

There is plenty of evidence to suggest that citizens would like to hold the reins more tightly on government spending and that they believe in holding individuals to account when things go wrong, whether they be in politics or the civil service.[7] Indeed, we have witnessed in recent years what Nevil Johnson describes as the 'ever-stronger urge on the part of the public to see culprits identified, to be able to blame them and, if possible, to see them penalised or at least made uncomfortable.'[8] The focus here again is on the individual, not on processes. The changes in society and values outlined in chapter 5 explain in part the urge to see culprits identified. However, the widely held view that government wastes taxpayers' money has also pushed citizens to search for those playing fast and loose with their money. There is also plenty of evidence to suggest that Parliament and government no longer control spending to the extent that they once did.[9]

Elected politicians and senior civil servants have, for the past forty years, been busy searching for things that work or, in the words of a former cabinet secretary, Andrew Turnbull, 'actively promoting the philosophy of what matters is what works.'[10] However, by focusing on what works, we have left unattended the most important issue confronting public administration today: accountability. More to the point, we have misdiagnosed the patient. The focus on the individual covers everything except accountability.

The Court and Accountability

Before the sponsorship scandal erupted in the Canadian media, Chuck Guité had been the poster boy for government efforts to introduce private sector management to government operations. Here was an individual who could get things done. He was told to cut red tape and to make things happen. This he did, and it will be recalled that he was awarded several promotions over a relatively short period of time. Indeed, he was described as 'a man of action, a man of decisions, it did not take him 50 years to reach a decision. In terms of client services, there were few who could beat him.'[11] Here was a modern-day bureaucrat, praised by senior elected politicians for his ability to respond to their wishes and to get things done. The Prime Minister's Office and the minister responsible for the sponsorship initiatives all supported Guité's rapid promotions through the senior ranks of the civil service. Guité did what he believed was expected of him.

When Canada's sponsorship scandal began to hit the front pages of the country's daily newspapers, however, both politicians and senior civil servants ran for cover, and the doctrine of ministerial responsibility and resorting to the traditional politics-administration dichotomy came in handy for all of them. Although we suspected all along who the key actors in the sponsorship initiatives were – Prime Minister Chrétien; Jean Pelletier, his chief of staff; Alfonso Gagliano, the minister responsible; and Chuck Guité – one by one, they pointed the finger of blame elsewhere. Chrétien said that he was responsible but not to blame. Pelletier, falling back on the politics-administration dichotomy, said that civil servants, not he, were responsible for managing programs. Gagliano, taking the same stance, maintained that civil servants had been delegated full authority to manage programs and that he, like Pelletier, had merely provided input and advice to Guité. Ranald Quail, the deputy minister, said that he had been kept out of the loop, but that he had assumed that his minister and senior departmental officials were reaching the right decisions. Guité, meanwhile, insisted that he was simply responding to the wishes and direction of elected politicians.

The minister, working hand in hand with the Prime Minister's Office, had, he felt, every right to make decisions because elected politicians would eventually have to carry the accountability responsibility in Parliament. In brief, the sponsorship scandal happened because (1) the prime minister and his court, not cabinet, decided that they wanted to launch a special initiative; (2) senior officials in the Privy Council Office did not defend basic civil service values; (3) deputy ministers decided that the wishes of the prime minister and his court were more important than the law; (4) and a minister and his political staff ignored due process and basic public administration and public finance requirements. Civil servants, if they are to be believed, simply turned the steering wheel over to elected politicians and their advisers, saying, 'Here, you drive,' since the prime minister and the minister had full political authority to make decisions and to be held accountable before Parliament. Senior civil servants believed that if something were to go wrong, then the prime minister and his ministers would stand up in the Commons and take full responsibility and that, in the end, no civil servant would be held accountable for the politicians' actions. They were wrong. In any event, deputy ministers have statutory responsibilities in their own right.

Elected politicians, from Thatcher to Blair and from Trudeau to Harper, have sought out individual civil servants who would be responsive to their wishes. They have got what they wanted. This and other developments have muddied further the chain of accountability. As is well known, the Westminster model differs from the U.S. presidential system in many important ways. There is no need to review here the differences in any detail.[12] Suffice it to note that they start at the very top. The President of the United States is chosen by voters and by a separate election from that of the two houses of the legislature, while in a parliamentary system, the prime minister leads the majority party in Parliament. Thus, the legislative and executive branches are joined, which tends to lead to more discipline among political parties and, in itself, makes accountability more difficult. Members of the party in power will go to great lengths inside and outside Parliament to deflect criticism and protect the government's political interest. Political parties are expected to play a very important role in parliamentary democracy because, again, executive power is linked with the legislature so that no government can survive unless it enjoys the confidence of Parliament. Political parties are or should also be important because they provide another link between citizens and politicians.

This study, however, makes the case that the link between citizens and political parties has weakened in recent years in both Canada and Britain (again, one only has to look at the substantial drop in party memberships in both countries for evidence). The 2006 national Liberal party leadership convention in Canada spoke to the personification of party politics. The party held a number of policy workshops that were very poorly attended, with television cameras showing nearly empty rooms. The focus of the delegates was largely on who would be the next leader. They recognized that the party leader and his court of advisers would in the end shape party policies to their own liking and that it was best to concentrate their efforts in this area.

The principal-agent relationship does not get much better going up or down the accountability chain.[13] *Principal-agent* refers to the contractual relationship between buyers and sellers. The theory centres on delegation – that is, when the principal turns to an agent or agents to accomplish tasks that the principal cannot perform. Two issues – adverse selection and moral hazard – are central to the theory. The first focuses on whether the right agent is hired, the second on whether the agent does the job appropriately. Moral hazards become a problem because the principal and agent can have conflicting objectives and because the principal cannot always assume that the agent will pursue the principal's best interest. One can monitor the agent's performance, but this can become costly, difficult, and uncertain.[14]

One also needs to establish the level of discretion that one is prepared to delegate to the agent. One can attempt to design fairly specific contracts or bargains to establish the relationship between principal and agent, but there are at least two issues that will inhibit this: both principal and agent will try as best they can to maximize their benefits under the arrangement, and it is extremely difficult in modern government to articulate with any degree of precision what will be expected under any contractual arrangements. Individuals in government can look to any number of measures to protect their interests, to hide their errors or inactivities, and to explain their inability to perform. They can always point to the work of central agencies, the lack of adequate funding (always a popular one and very difficult to counter), and the role of their political masters (even more difficult to counter). A principal can always decide not to delegate responsibilities, but this too is difficult. When you overlay all of this with an emphasis on the individual and a shift away from formal processes, you pose still new challenges for accountability requirements.

Governing through networks has also made accountability much more complex. There is no longer a single, standard, formal process for establishing policy or striking decisions, so that it has become extremely difficult to hold processes to account. There are different processes for different decisions and for different individuals. Prime ministers and their courts can and do announce bold policy or program decisions after consulting only a handful of individuals. They have little patience with formal, drawn-out processes; hence their tendency to deliver policy by announcement. But things are vastly different for other decisions. Those taken by ministers and senior officials are developed not only by lower departmental units but also by organizations and individuals formally outside the department, sometimes even outside government. Civil servants know that their contribution can be costly to future promotions if proposed initiatives go sour or if a program is mismanaged and reported in the media. Individual civil servants also know that their work will be a trivial contribution to the overall success of the group's work – hence the temptation to 'free ride' and the tendency to give the appearance of change while standing still.

There are decisions informed by legislation that direct civil servants to administer programs following clear criteria. There was a time when the great majority of programs were designed along these lines, and it made sense to look to hierarchy and formal processes and structures to make sure they were respected, and thus ensure accountability. But the world and socio-economic circumstances have become much too volatile, not only for hierarchies but also for rigid program criteria. To be sure, program flexibility has its advantages, particularly for civil servants delivering programs or services. But it also makes the principal-agent relationship much more complex and enables the agent to produce broader and ill-defined objectives and to easily work around benchmarking or program evaluation exercises. It can even allow the agent, rather than the principal, to establish the goals to be pursued. It also makes it more difficult for principals to ensure that agents are pursuing principals' or the public interest, as defined by the government. To ensure that agents respect accountability requirements and do not pursue their own interests requires specialized knowledge, resources, time, and commitment from an already overextended agenda on the part of the prime minister and ministers. Time is always tight in the senior echelons of government. In short, it is the desire to get things done as quickly as possible that has led prime ministers to break out of formal processes, to embrace court government, and to look to key individuals to get things done.

All of the above leads to unstructured political institutions, unstructured government organizations, and unstructured policy and decision-making processes. Some individuals can establish their own rules, starting with the prime minister. Institutions, administrative organizations, norms, rules, and expected behaviour are today more amorphous and transient than at any time in the past. Individuals, meanwhile, are far more visible because of access to information and whistle-blowing legislation, the new media, and the fact that boundaries are collapsing between the political world and bureaucracy, particularly between elected politicians and senior civil servants. However, accountability mechanisms in Westminster-style parliamentary systems have essentially been left intact through all these developments. The doctrine of ministerial responsibility has continued to survive on 'a wing and a prayer,' enabling ministers to shelter behind civil servants and vice versa.[15] This has provided an ideal setting for the free riders and for those who would wish to sidestep accountability. It is no exaggeration to write that accountability in both the Canadian and the U.K. parliaments has been ritualized so that there are no real consequences for decisions made or for modifications in policy and management action.[16]

Practitioners, for the most part, prefer to focus on institutions and the machinery of government to explain the behaviour of political and bureaucratic actors and in their search for accountability solutions. They insist that institutions hold the key to a better understanding of how government works and what shapes the behaviour of both elected and career officials. Practitioners will also point to the obvious by insisting that delegation is necessary and that the key is to design accountability mechanisms that work. Many maintain that political and administrative institutions all have an inherent logic of appropriateness that guides the behaviour of both elected politicians and career civil servants.[17] They will point out that businesses must, most of the time, make business decisions (they simply could not compete if they were to make other than business decisions), that elected politicians must, most of the time, make political decisions, and that bureaucrats, notwithstanding the introduction of New Public Management measures, must, most of the time, follow some kind of due process. All three cases share one objective in common – survival.

All three also have their own internal logic of appropriateness to guide decision making. Here, however, they differ in important ways. Norms, formal rules, and expectations of how things are done, or should be done, are very different. Accountability in the private sector, as we have noted on several occasions, is straightforward, at least when compared to the public sector. Provided one does not break the law, one is free to pursue profits and market share and have a sense of ownership of one's work. It is also, in most cases, relatively easy to assess performance of the firm (look at the top and bottom lines) and individuals within the firm (look at year-over-year sales growth and productivity). Incentives are self-centred and straightforward, as individuals and firms have a direct interest in creating products that are valued in the market.[18] In brief, you compete to survive, and the market will decide which firms – and often which individual – will survive, prosper, or fall. We know, for example, that about 35 per cent of departing chief executive officers of large North American companies left involuntarily in 2005.[19]

Elected politicians and senior civil servants, meanwhile, operate under vastly different circumstances and constraints, and the basis on which their performance is evaluated is different. Politicians often say that, in politics, perception is reality. This is a far cry from the unbending verdict of the market. Perception aside, politicians and civil servants also have to keep a watchful eye on public finances, on fairness in their dealings with citizens, and on their own performances, however defined and however determined. To be sure, it is difficult for accountability requirements to deal with perceptions.

How citizens assess the performance of elected politicians and government has changed dramatically over the past forty years. Citizens are today better educated and better informed. But the challenge of gaining comprehensive information about government has never been greater for citizens. They have to rely on others: political parties to screen potential candidates; the media and oversight bodies to ensure probity in public spending and to promote their interests. Anyone who sets out to do this on his own will be lost in a sea of collaborative arrangements, complex policy and program processes, and delegation and accountability mechanisms that are no longer readily accessible to elected politicians, let alone citizens.

Both Canada and Britain have made attempts to strengthen the bond between government and citizens. Access to information legislation is just one of several efforts to make government operations more transparent. In addition, governments in both countries have launched sustained efforts to improve services to individual citizens, from the introduction of the Citizen's Charter in Britain to a series of one-stop shopping measures in Canada.

Notwithstanding the above, and as reported in the introductory chapter, a multitude of public opinion surveys reveal that citizens no longer trust their governments.[20] This study also documents the tendency of citizens in Canada and Britain to be less involved in political parties and less inclined to vote. Something has gone wrong in the chain of accountability from citizens or voters to their members of Parliament, to the top policy makers, and to the front-line civil servants. This is all the more perplexing since, as this study has shown, MPs now attach considerable importance to helping constituents in their dealings with government and since governments continue to introduce measure after measure to strengthen management practices in government, improve the delivery and quality of services, and encourage the participation of citizens, associations, and policy networks in shaping policies and delivering programs.

Part of the problem may well be farther up in the chain of accountability. Public opinion surveys reveal that citizens would like to be better informed about government operations; they want to be assured that the government spends taxpayers' money wisely and that it is properly accountable for its spending. Citizens can easily predict the views of their MPs on the government's performance. If the MP sits on the government side, the assessment will be positive; if the MP sits on the opposition benches, negative. Citizens could dig deeper for information, though not many do. They could consult any number of government documents that report on the performance of departments and their programs. Those who do will quickly discover that departments and programs are invariably cast in a positive light. Government departments, as we observed above, are not in the business of being critical of their own efforts, activities, or officials.

Precious few citizens have the knowledge, expertise, or time needed to comb through government documents to determine if they provide *l'heure juste* and to accurately assess the performance of government departments and agencies let alone the efficiency and probity of government spending. Citizens can always turn to oversight bodies, but these have their own inherent limitations. For the most part, they can only provide a retrospective scrutiny, since they only report on what has gone on after the fact or after the misdeeds have been committed.[21] Oversight bodies also have to cope as best they can with incomplete information, and they will view the world from the prism of their own bias and mandate.[22] As well, they are staffed by bureaucrats, who will be reluctant to address the overhead cost of government departments and agencies, perhaps out of fear that someone may turn their arguments and findings on their own operations. In any event, citizens would much rather be aware of individuals who have committed misdeeds and who may have wasted taxpayers' money through errors of commission or omission than wade through performance appraisals and reports from oversight bodies.

Elected politicians, meanwhile, sit at the top of a vastly expanded government. The expansion since 1960 has transformed how public policies are struck, how expenditure budgets are prepared and reviewed, and how decisions are made. Most accountability issues relate to the government's expenditure budget and how public funds are spent. We have seen in this study that governments have moved away from line-item budgeting, which once held considerable appeal for both MPs and citizens – it was relatively simple to grasp and it enabled them to compare the input costs of one program over another. Rather than specifying spending on every item, including detailing civil service positions, spending plans have now been consolidated into broad categories. In Canada, many departmental expenditures (except capital spending) are consolidated into a single amount or a single departmental vote. This has given public sector managers considerable flexibility in reallocating financial resources. They can, for example, add new positions and increase travel budgets while reducing program spending or level of services. Accountability requirements, meanwhile, have not been revised to accommodate this development.

We have lost the parsimonious culture in government. This became evident as government grew and as its budgeting shifted from a line-item to a program approach. This suggests that the behaviour of public sector managers is shaped by institutions, processes, and procedures – or the lack of them – and that accountability is all about how the three work in a 'world of hard, practical realities' and how they relate to individuals.[23] It should also be noted that the budget has also become an important instrument to guide and stabilize the economy, a development that serves to focus the attention of policy makers away from spending plans and programs to broader economic issues.[24]

Politicians have seen their role transformed. They are now expected to be more managerial and to understand the finer points of performance reports. Contrary to Weber's credo, their views on budget matters are now to be based less on political judgment and more on technocratic considerations. MPs have been given additional staff, but for the most part the new staff assist in helping constituents.[25] The government tables its expenditure budget, and government MPs are left to sing its praises and opposition MPs to condemn it. The result is that, in both Canada and Britain, the expenditure budget is approved every year with no changes or just a few minor adjustments.[26] Party discipline inhibits MPs from performing their oversight and accountability role to the full, with the result that the House of Commons is 'not able to participate effectively in the determination of the budget.'[27] In addition, spending estimates can be increased only with a royal recommendation – in other words, through the executive. MPs have given up a good part of their accountability responsibilities to officers of Parliament and to the media, neither of which is reluctant to single out individuals in assigning responsibility and blame.

The cabinet has, in more recent years, suffered the same fate as the House of Commons. Today, cabinets in both Canada and Britain scarcely participate in determining the expenditure budget. Prime ministers and the minister of finance or the chancellor of the exchequer, together with key advisers, will determine the broad outline of the expenditure budget and decide which new major initiatives the government will support. Cabinet ministers wishing to promote a particular initiative must now convince the prime minister and the minister of finance or the chancellor of the exchequer of its worth, rather than putting it to their cabinet colleagues. In short, the way to secure funding is to focus on key individuals in the prime minister's court, certainly not on formal processes and procedures or on cabinet.

As for other budget matters, effective power has shifted from elected ministers to non-elected civil servants. Allen Schick explains that it is no longer 'an easy task for legislators to control a state that has grown so large and active.'[28] The chain of accountability breaks down because MPs do not have the necessary information, let alone the expertise, to hold government units to account. Asking MPs to acquire the skills and knowledge to assess expenditure budgets on the basis of economic models and performance reports requires a set of skills that, in the past, belonged to civil servants. It is also asking too much.

Senior civil servants, meanwhile, will argue that they suffer from accountability overload. In both Canada and Britain, they are expected to accommodate incessant demands to produce accountability reports in one form or another. But that is not all. The idea of audit has been transformed from its original financial context to deal with non-financial processes and systems. They must also contend with a growing number of oversight bodies established to pass judgment on their work and make public any misstep. But performance reports reveal as little as possible, at least in terms of negative findings. They also map strategies to assist ministers in sidestepping 'gotcha' journalism. Still, some insist that accountability overkill has discouraged innovative and entrepreneurial behaviour in senior civil servants precisely at a time when political and business leaders are asking bureaucrats to become less bureaucratic and more entrepreneurial.[29] In no other field of endeavour have signals been so mixed, if not contradictory.

Senior civil servants have also had to learn to share their policy advisory space. There are any number of new policy actors on the stage: partisan political advisers, lobbyists, research institutes, think tanks, academics, and community or sectoral groups. Senior civil servants have had to come to terms with the fact that their ministers no longer have the clout that they once had. Key policy decisions are taken by prime ministers and their courts, and so, to have influence, they must be members of the court, or at least have access to one. Not all ministers hold such an advantage.

A fault line has developed between the world of senior civil servants on the one hand, preoccupied with things political and with broad policy issues involving policy networks, and the world of program managers on the other, concerned about citizens or customers. The differences between the two groups are great. The top group is transient, focused on the government's political interests and on managing real or potential political crises and relations with the media. The bottom group has a more intimate knowledge of the sector, the department's program history, and its customers. The two groups are connected less by a shared sense of purpose than by numerous performance reports that front-line managers and their employees must produce or contribute to. But, when it comes to accountability, both groups are lumped together as one.

All civil servants share a common challenge, and that is the barrage of criticism coming from different quarters, including their political masters. They have come to regard virtually any kind of criticism as just another round of bureaucracy bashing, best ignored. This has become a convenient defence mechanism for civil servants; no matter what they do, they will be criticized because, as they point out, they can never emulate the private sector when it comes to managing human and financial resources. They will use this kind of argument to make the case that there is no point in reducing spending or cutting back positions in their units. In addition, many civil servants maintain that accountability should be not about assigning blame but about putting to use lessons learned. Again, elected politicians and voters do not always see it that way.

Many civil servants will readily admit that management could be substantially improved. However, they insist that all too often their management hands are tied by political demands, by contradictory objectives, by civil service unions, and by different and at times contradictory requests from many quarters. They report that elected politicians will often agree that difficult decisions need to be made, but when the time comes to make them, will invariably say 'this is not a good time.' In short, officials will assert that it is forces beyond their control – the prime minister, ministers, and others – who are behind shortfalls in administration; rarely do they fault themselves. This is convenient because it enables them to avoid making tough decisions or accepting accountability for their work. The solution, then, is to encourage civil servants to explain publicly how and why their management hands are tied by political demands.

It is simplistic and misleading, if convenient, to blame elected politicians and political realities for weak management in government. As reported earlier, Arthur Kroeger, a former senior deputy minister who served in several large federal departments in Canada, has observed that 'general management with a capital M and management theory never interested me very much.'[30] This raises the question – who *did* have an interest in the management of these departments? Kroeger's statement does not square with the traditional understanding of public administration, whereby the minister deals with policy issues and the deputy minister with administration. The Financial Administration Act certainly suggests that the deputy minister should have more than a casual interest in management. A House of Commons committee in Britain recently made it clear that it is 'civil servants, not ministers, who are responsible for the dismissal of underperforming civil servants' and that it had 'no wish to change this.'[31]

As noted earlier, front-line civil servants dismiss their performance appraisal system as laughable. To repeat the comment of one front-line worker quoted by Barbara Carroll and David Siegel, 'there hasn't been anyone in the last seven years come and tell me I've done anything wrong. Nobody ever comes to look. They don't tell you you've done something right and they don't tell you you've done something wrong. There's no review of the operations.'[32] One can hardly blame elected politicians for this state of affairs. As was also reported earlier, a 2004 study, based on interviews with senior government officials, identified a number of 'root' causes of management problems in government. They included, among others, a lack of consequences for inadequate management, failure to correct or prevent problems, and unclear accountability.[33] Surely, one cannot possibly pin all or even most of the blame for this on elected politicians.

It is extremely difficult for ministers, with their overloaded agendas, and for MPs, subject to party discipline and increasingly looking to their constituencies as their main preoccupation, to find the time to challenge departmental 'A' base or expenditure budgets in support of continuing programs and activities. Performance and evaluation reports and management and performance targets have been of little help. Those within a department have a sense of who makes a contribution, who the free riders are, and where waste lies. However, there is no incentive for them to identify the free riders or point to waste. If anything, they have an incentive to leave well enough alone, so as to avoid losing resources and making tough decisions.

Why make tough decisions when there is no good reason to do so and when there are no consequences for not doing so? In fact, the incentives point the other way. The result is that, whenever feasible, departmental officials will ask for new resources. If the prime minister's court or ministers want to launch a new project or an increased level of services, civil servants will tell them that they will have to find new financial resources in order to do so. When program spending or service levels are reduced, government managers will claim that there is no room to reduce staff. To be sure, one can point to budget maximizers as the cause. The more likely causes, however, are the tendency to follow the path of least resistance, bureaucratic lethargy, the inability of MPs to get at the information to challenge departmental officials, and misaligned incentives. In short, political and administrative institutions simply no longer correspond to present-day requirements. This, in turn, is the result of the failure in both Canada and Britain to clarify the roles and responsibilities between the prime minister, ministers, and civil servants.

What's Next?

Kate Jenkins sums up the situation well when she writes that our institutions have their 'feet firmly planted in the pre-democratic past.' As she explains, 'Parliament appears stuck somewhere between Magna Carta and Dr. Arnold's Rugby, the civil service still reflects Victorian social structures, the government, harried by the need for action, takes any opportunity to extend its powers without recognizing constitutional constraints.'[34] The result is that the constitutions of both Canada and Britain have effectively been dismantled. There has been a centralization of political authority, and the departmental structure has been torn apart by the requirements of horizontal government. In addition, the two civil services have lost their way, while their responsibilities have been redefined by stealth, and Parliament has seen part of its role shift to officers of Parliament and the media.

There are many forces that have led to these developments, among them a significant change in values in society, the rise of new and influential voices both inside and outside government, including a less deferential media, and a shift in loyalty away from our political and administrative institutions. These developments have favoured – if not been promoted by – political, bureaucratic, and economic elites that have little interest in constitutional matters and the finer points of accountability.[35] What matters to them is what works.

It is not possible to turn back the clock to the way things were 100 or even 40 years ago. To be sure, one can always ask prime ministers to attenuate or share some of their political power. However, it is unlikely that they will take to this suggestion. Indeed, in Canada two recent prime ministers (Martin and Harper) who pledged to reform the machinery of government so as to strengthen the hand of ministers and others, notably government MPs and Parliament, changed their minds soon after taking the prime minister's chair. One could also ask the media to exercise some self-control and to be accountable for their work. But here, too, the call is very likely to go unheard.[36]

A basic constitutional principle in representative democracies is that we should be able to identify political power, the source of that power, and the users and use of that power. When people know their place in political administrative institutions and know that formal policy-making and decision-making processes are present, there is a much greater chance that they will 'walk with order' and that accountability will be more transparent and effective.[37] Earlier chapters in this study argue that attempts to replace formal rules and processes by values and ethics exercises have not been very successful.

Citizens have assumed that political authority lies with elected politicians. We know that Canadian and U.K. prime ministers have in recent years concentrated political power in their own hands and in their offices. To be sure, the need to respond quickly to rapidly changing circumstances and the tactics of the new media have pushed things up to the prime minister. But that explains only part of the problem. The power of the prime minister has never been defined, and prime ministers essentially do what they want to do when they want to do it.[38] Jean Chrétien simply redefined the role of the prime minister's relationship with ministers by stating that 'within Cabinet a minister is merely part of a collectivity, just another advisor to the prime minister. He can be told what to do and on important matters his only choice is to do or resign.'[39] When prime ministers can establish their own rules so as to get things done, as has happened in both Canada and Britain in recent years, then rules and formal processes are no longer in equilibrium, and institutions that are designed to oversee them are in peril. When institutions and formal processes are no longer in equilibrium, it is a great deal easier for some individuals to have their way. The strong are favoured over the weak, both inside and outside government. This, in turn, suggests that accountability requirements should be geared to the individual rather than to processes or a doctrine that speaks to collective responsibility and to ministerial responsibility for the activities of civil servants.

Other than prime ministers and their courtiers, it is not at all clear who else believes that substantial political power should be concentrated at the centre of government. There are no effective checks and balances from cabinet, the civil service, or Parliament to prevent prime ministers from grabbing power and abusing it. Chrétien's role and that of his office in the sponsorship scandal is a case in point. The fact that our constitution relies on Parliament to hold prime ministers and ministers and, through ministers, the work of civil servants to account is cold comfort. We now need to go farther and define in law the role and responsibilities of the prime minister, ministers, and the civil service.

The flexible constitutions in Canada and Britain have enabled elected politicians to change their relationship with civil servants in pursuit of what works, with little regard for accountability requirements. Any promoter of representative democracy will and should support the supremacy of the elected representatives over the civil servant. Still, our constitutions should provide for a degree of independence for our civil service so that prime ministers and their courtiers cannot consider civil servants simply to be appendages to their courts. The 'what works' requirement of modern government has buffeted the senior civil service in both countries.

The notion that the civil service has no personality distinct from the government of the day has served both the political and the bureaucratic elites well. They are not about to part with this advantage, despite what the political elites may say when they sit in opposition. Stephen Harper, within days of his accountability bill being approved by Parliament, wrote that 'the fundamental accountability between a Minister and Parliament and between a Minister and his or her Deputy Minister have not been altered in any way.'[40] Harper sang quite a different song while in opposition and in his 2006 election platform, when he made it clear that the deputy minister should be designated the department's accounting officer and that he or she 'will be responsible to Parliament for the departmental spending and administrative practices' of the department and that in the event of a 'disagreement between a minister and a deputy minister on a matter of administration, the minister must provide written instruction to the deputy minister and notify the Auditor General [an officer of Parliament] ... of the disagreement.'[41]

It is no secret that senior civil servants operate in a more challenging environment today than they did forty years ago and that elected politicians have been able to secure a much more responsive civil service. The political shadow hovering over the shoulders of civil servants, particularly those at the more senior levels, has never been so evident and so large as it is today.

This study argues that what has become the main task for senior civil servants is to accommodate the wishes of the prime minister and to keep ministers out of political trouble. It is far less important than in times past for them to give independent advice to political power. It points out that the prime minister's decision to make a statement on television rather than in the Commons, or to leak information, counts more than the requirements of the House of Commons; that managing access to information legislation to protect political and bureaucratic interests counts more than respecting an Act of Parliament; that political parties, once an important instrument of representative democracy, have been turned into election-day organizations; that the job of a member of Parliament has been, to a much larger extent than in the past, relegated to playing an ombudsman role for constituents or, for the most fortunate MPs, a first step to a cabinet post; and that the virtually unlimited resources of the government, when compared to what is available for Parliament, can easily be marshalled to defend the administration of any government program that has come under attack by a parliamentary committee. Further, if cabinet has been turned into little more than a focus group, if the self-restraint of judges now belongs to the history books, if there is a need to come up with three distinct processes to define policies, if hierarchy has lost its relevance in government organizations and in ensuring accountability between subordinates and superiors, if Parliament can no longer establish clear lines of accountability for spending public funds, and if government by networks has become so complex that it is no longer possible for citizens to hold it accountable through their MPs – then one can only conclude that our constitution is now under tremendous strain.[42]

The challenge this presents extends beyond the rebalancing of power away from the executive towards Parliament. The goal now should be to alter substantially the internal logic of appropriateness both at the elected level in government and in the bureaucracy. If individuals – rather than a collective body like cabinet or a cabinet committee – have come to be the driving force in government, then individuals should also become accountable. For this to happen, we need to express in binding and enforceable legal norms the basis for organizing and controlling political and administrative power.[43]

Court government, by which political leaders shape and reshape instruments of political power at will, should no longer be tolerated. Britain's constitution and Canada's British-inspired constitution are based on the premise that elites should rule. In more recent times, deference 'has largely collapsed' and the very idea of 'elite rule is widely rejected.'[44] Political and bureaucratic elites have an interest in the status quo, and on this point I can do no better than quote Kate Jenkins: 'It is a dangerous time for an unwritten constitution when it no longer works effectively and there is no serious pressure from those involved to reform it.'[45]

The reform agenda will need to be brave. It will have to reconcile increasing demands for transparency and concerns with the decline of governability.[46] It will need to

1 define in statutes the role of the prime minister;
2 establish in statutes a distinct personality for the civil service so that civil servants have a legal basis for resisting instructions from elected politicians to perform essentially political acts;
3 resolve the confusion between accountability, responsibility, and answerability;
4 establish a distinction between civil servants operating at the centre and in the most senior echelons in the bureaucracy and those who deliver government programs and services to the public; and
5 look to the spending estimates to track accountability in governing by networks and establish a publicly accessible process to hold civil servants accountable for administrative overhead costs and the management of financial and human resources.

We will need external examiners to review the overhead costs of government units and to drive up performance. In turn, civil servants will have to get better at being candid and learn to deal more effectively with criticism. It has become too easy and convenient to dismiss criticism as just another round of bureaucracy bashing.

We have been all too willing to buy into the notion that we cannot separate what is political from what is administrative in running a hospital, a prison, or an income-tax processing unit. The result is that no one, including Parliament, can distinguish between authorities and responsibilities of ministers and senior civil servants. All we know is that, at times, the political sphere will have a deep influence on the administration of a government program, but that at other times a virtually impenetrable wall may protect the civil service from political intervention. It always depends. It depends on the individuals, on the circumstances, and on the issue. Most of all, it depends on the prime minister. Accountability is then lost in a world of 'it depends' and plausible, if not mutual, deniability. Elected politicians and civil servants will happily employ the politics-administration dichotomy when it suits their purpose but will point to all its flaws when it does not. Senior civil servants in Britain, it will be recalled, explained that special advisers were being established at the political level to 'distinguish the source of political advice and support.' They will not hesitate to argue, however, that the doctrine of ministerial responsibility should continue to apply because one cannot separate politics, policy, and administration into compartments.[47] In short, it is an argument for all seasons to be applied to any purpose whenever convenient.

The critical question is whether we should continue to accept the 'it depends' and 'what matters is what works' approach to governing. To be sure, court government has its advantages for some. In concentrating political power in the hands of prime ministers and their courts, things that matter to them get done. But the price, as this study shows, is high. The chain of accountability – from voter to MP, from MP to PM and cabinet ministers, from cabinet to line ministers, from line ministers to the heads of government departments and agencies, and from senior civil servants to front-line managers and their employees – has broken down at every level. The solution lies in acknowledging legally that the political and administrative worlds can, with some imagination and tolerance, occupy different spaces. Above all, it lies in recognizing that the problems of accountability in both Canada and Britain are greater than commonly accepted and that the direction of our efforts should be towards the individual.

The performance of prime ministers and ministers will continue to be assessed in a political environment, and that is the way it should be. The performance of senior civil servants should now be externally examined. Internal scrutiny simply no longer works in either Canada or Britain. The process has been described by a senior U.K. official as one in which 'permanent secretaries write letters to themselves.'[48] A rigorous external assessment of a group of senior officials selected randomly on an annual basis would enable tough management questions to be asked and answers elicited. It is quite common to have the performance of university faculty members reviewed by someone outside of their home university to ensure an objective assessment before promotions are awarded. University departments are also reviewed by outsiders to provide a thorough and detached assessment of their performance. There is no reason why the performance of aspiring deputy ministers and permanent secretaries and departmental units could not be reviewed in the same fashion. In brief, senior civil servants should no longer be allowed to mark their own exams.[49]

Parting with the Doctrine

Rebuilding the chain of accountability requires loosening the doctrine of ministerial responsibility. The doctrine is partly to blame for turning purely administrative matters into political issues. For one thing, it invites opposition MPs to point the finger at ministers for administrative gaffes. For another, it invites ministers to meddle in administrative matters when it suits their political interests to do so, because they can rightly claim that the doctrine makes them responsible for both policy and administration.

The need to avoid confusion about where responsibility lies is now greater than ever, as is the need to assert that, when it matters, elected politicians are in charge. It is they who should decide 'when it matters' and deal with the consequences of their decisions. It is no less important, however, that there be a public forum in which the accountability of civil servants is clearly spelled out for all aspects of their work. The purpose is not only to strengthen accountability but also to give all civil servants, including those delivering programs and public services, a greater sense of ownership of their work.

Prime ministers and their ministers should retain full authority to make policy, to allocate financial resources, to establish how policy should be delivered, to decide on the size and shape of the civil service, and to make appointments at the most senior levels in government departments, agencies, and corporations. They should have the authority to overrule civil servants in all matters not covered by statutes, provided that such decisions are made public. Senior civil servants should also remain accountable 'to' the government in the sense that only the prime minister and ministers should be able to impose sanctions and make appointments at the most senior levels.

But other things have to change. The anonymity of civil servants should now be a thing of the past. The cloak of anonymity has, in recent years, been a major contributor to the rise of plausible deniability. The anonymity aspect of the doctrine of ministerial responsibility has also promoted prime-ministerial and ministerial overload by suggesting that elected politicians have a role in operational matters, though few profess to have a genuine interest in them. It pushes senior civil servants to think of the prime minister and ministers at the expense of everyone else, including Parliament and citizens. It enables prime ministers and their courtiers to exercise a growing and informal authority over civil servants that, in turn, has enabled court government to take shape in both Canada and Britain.[50] It places the full onus of accountability on the prime minister and ministers. Given the developments outlined in this study, this is no longer realistic.

Civil servants, meanwhile, need an administrative space that they can occupy relatively free from political interference, a capacity to resist improper demands from elected politicians, and a sense of ownership, however tenuous, in their work. We reported earlier that Paul Tellier, former cabinet secretary to the Mulroney government, recently told the media that senior civil servants need to rediscover the capacity to 'say no to ministers when required.'[51] This will not happen because we wish it to happen or because a former cabinet secretary suggests that it should happen. We need to give civil servants a statutory capacity and duty to do so. If this is not possible, then citizens need to accept that their civil service will never measure up to expectations. It will remain riddled with inefficiencies and will be far more costly to taxpayers than it need be. It will become increasingly difficult to attract the best and the brightest to the civil service, despite generous salaries and highly attractive employment benefits. It will also mean that ministers will continue to claim that 'bureaucratic patronage' exists in the civil service.

Giving civil servants their own administrative space means that they will be subject to external accountability. The doctrine of ministerial responsibility has seriously inhibited external accountability because ministers are always implicated in any criticism of their departments and their civil servants. Yet, as a former permanent secretary points out, the doctrine does not provide ministers with the necessary power to hold bureaucrats to account 'without breaching the conventions which surround the impartiality of the Service.' The doctrine also protects the civil service 'from any real form of external accountability.'[52]

Giving an administrative space to civil servants may well prompt civil servants to challenge their ministers publicly over administrative issues, and vice versa. Students of public administration have recognized for well over sixty years that Woodrow Wilson's politics-administration dichotomy does not fully reflect reality. Paul H. Appleby, as far back as 1949, wrote that 'public administration is policy making, and administrators are continually laying down rules for the future, and administrators are continually determining what the law is and what it means in terms of action.'[53] Precious few have been willing to challenge Appleby's thesis. Yet, the politics-administration dichotomy goes to the heart of public administration and accountability in government. It underpins British constitutional theory, suggesting that elected politicians decide on policy, while civil servants give advice and implement policy.

To this day, the dichotomy haunts students of public administration and practitioners operating at all levels of the public sector, from international organizations down to the smallest municipality. It provides an enduring image of how policy and management decisions should be struck in government. The challenge now is to give new life and definition to the dichotomy by focusing on individuals operating in the political world and in the civil service.

The dichotomy has come to mean everything or very little, and the doctrine of ministerial responsibility has certainly not helped matters. If anything, the dichotomy has contributed to the doctrine in the sense of 'everything and very little.' Some call for adjustments to the dichotomy, claiming that policy is made at all levels of administration and that there is thus a need to bring democracy into administration. David Levitan, for one, argues that 'democratic government means democracy in administration, as well as in the original legislation. It is of supreme importance that the administrative machinery established for the execution of legislation be permeated with democratic spirit and ideology.'[54] Civil servants use this line of argument to support the doctrine of ministerial responsibility, suggesting that politics permeates virtually every aspect of their work.

This argument plays to the advantage of both elected politicians and civil servants. Some former senior civil servants in Canada insist that applying Britain's accounting officer concept and other attempts 'to draw a clear line of division between the political world and the administrative one' are undemocratic. Arthur Kroeger provides an example that he would consider undemocratic, if it were allowed. In an article titled 'The Elected Should Have the Last Word,' he writes, 'A regional director could close local offices and lay off staff at will in areas of unemployment. Any intervention by the responsible minister and local MPs would constitute political interference.'[55] That said, civil servants will also make the case, very often with success, that elected politicians have no business in administrative matters. The merit principle, the Financial Administration Act, and other statutes in Canada and the accounting officer concept in Britain, as well as the turning over of the management of performance pay schemes to civil servants assisted by a body of outside advisers, all provide ammunition to civil servants to push elected politicians away from their offices and responsibilities.

Frederik Mosher wrote in the 1960s that 'on the theoretical plane the finding of a viable substitute to the [politics-administration] dichotomy may well be the number one problem of public administration.'[56] No substitute has been found, and there are none on the horizon. The dichotomy is still employed to explain or justify many things, including the introduction of the New Public Management initiative. The dichotomy's application has been sufficiently flexible to accommodate this initiative and many other developments. It has been employed to empower front-line managers and their employees without, at the same time, introducing new accountability requirements. It has enabled senior civil servants to compare their work and their salaries to their private sector counterparts. The problem, then, with the politics-administration dichotomy is that it has become a theory for all seasons, for all purposes, and for all to turn to whenever political or administrative issues need to be accommodated. But it still remains the most vivid and well-understood image of how things should work in government, and we should make every effort to make it appeal to elected politicians, civil servants, and citizens as the basis for strengthening accountability.

If conflicts over a management decision between politicians on the government side and civil servants should become public, so be it. Surely it is not a sin against representative democracy for citizens to be informed that a minister has forced civil servants to keep an office open in a high unemployment region. It is far more democratic to have this done in the open for all to see than to have it hidden behind the doctrine of ministerial responsibility. The prime minister and ministers should have the final say on such issues, but when they meddle in administrative issues, then it should be a matter for Parliament to debate – or at least be informed of – and for citizens to be told.

Britain has already learned to manage such cases well, including ministerial involvement in the Advanced Jet Trainer-Hawk 128 and the Pergau Dam project.[57] Both cases illustrate the fact that the civil service does indeed have a personality and that democracy is better served when citizens have access not only to the information that led to decisions but also to the political and administrative forces behind them. The same can be said about the Howard-Lewis affair and the management of U.K. prisons discussed earlier. The case has reverberated in Westminster and Whitehall for years. It brought home the point that executive agencies did little to clarify the line between politics and administration where it truly matters – in accountability.[58] The tension between Howard, then home secretary, and Lewis, a civil servant, became untenable after Howard turned an administrative matter into a political issue. Howard's permanent secretary had warned Lewis that the case was 'getting white hot and I don't want it to become nuclear.'[59] History reports that, by intervening in an administrative matter, Howard caused the issue to become nuclear.[60] But there is an important lesson to be learned from this type of case: namely, that it is best to air such issues in public rather than to handle them quietly, as has traditionally been done in both Canada and Britain in attempts to accommodate the political interests of ministers.[61] Cases such as Howard-Lewis, when played out in public view, can shed light on the relationship between politicians and civil servants and assist in giving life to the politics-administration dichotomy. But, all too often, such cases have been deliberately hidden, from both Parliament and the public.

Civil servants in Britain have been reluctant, however, to look to the accounting officer concept to stake out a position in public in support of strong management decisions. They have described exercising their prerogative under the concept as 'the nuclear option.'[62] Their Canadian counterparts, meanwhile, were able to resist attempts to introduce the concept until Harper did so with his accountability package, although he considerably watered down his election campaign promise – on the advice of senior civil servants. To be sure, challenging one's minister in public is not always a good career move. Nor does a public debate with an elected politician give much immediate advantage to civil servants. However, other developments are removing the veil of anonymity. Unless a distinct administrative space is carved out for civil servants so that probing management questions can be put to government managers in a public forum, they will neither have a proper sense of ownership of their work nor be able to recapture the credibility needed to enjoy the kind of public support they once had.

Civil servants should have the right to defend themselves and to explain their management decisions and actions. The solution is to define in law rules that will govern the participation of civil servants in public debate. These rules should protect them from inappropriate questions from elected politicians and strive to retain the professional characteristics of the civil service. If it is not possible to turn back the clock to a possible 'golden era,' when government was small, when the doctrine of ministerial responsibility made sense, and when ministers and civil servants operated in relative secrecy, then our political and administrative institutions need to adjust. Having one foot in the past, operating under rules and processes that belong to a different era, and the other in a political environment that focuses on the individual, that is much more transparent, and that believes that the public sector should emulate private sector management practices no longer serves representative democracy, bureaucracy, Parliament, or citizens well – let alone accountability.

Focusing on the individual, whether at the political or bureaucratic level, would not only strengthen accountability by promoting transparency, it would also serve as an antidote to the overbearing presence of court government, governing by networks, horizontal or joined-up government, complex intergovernmental and interdepartmental processes, and a multitude of voices all clamouring to be heard. It would also inhibit the ability of elected politicians and civil servants to serve up a menu of plausible deniability. It would provide individuals with a greater sense of achievement and success, would push them to accept responsibility for failure, and – perhaps most important – would shed light on an expenditure budget that few outside government departments and central agencies even pretend to understand.

Notes

1. Introduction

1 Joseph S. Nye, Philip D. Zelikow, and David C. King, eds, *Why People Don't Trust Government* (Cambridge, MA: Harvard University Press, 1997), 2.

2 Peter Hennessy, *Whitehall* (London: Fontana, 1989), 82.

3 D. Marquand, *Decline of the Public: The Hollowing-out of Citizenship* (Cambridge: Polity Press, 2004), 140.

4 For a history of government, see S.E. Finer, *The History of Government from the Earliest Times*, 3 vols (Oxford: Oxford University Press, 1997).

5 Ibid., 1: 63.

6 Ibid., 64.

7 Carl K.Y. Shaw, 'Hegel's Theory of Modern Bureaucracy,' *American Political Science Review* 86, 2 (June 1992): 381–9.

8 Max Weber, 'Bureaucracy,' in Hans Heinrich Gerth and C. Wright Mills, eds, *Max Weber: Essays in Sociology* (New York: Oxford University Press, 1946), 215–16.

9 Ibid., 233.

10 Weber, quoted in Erik Olin Wright, 'To Control or to Smash Bureaucracy,' *Berkeley Journal of Sociology* 19 (1974–5): 25–6.

11 Patrick Overeem and Mark R. Rutgers, 'Three Roads to Politics and Administration: Ideational Foundations of the Politics/Administration Dichotomy,' in Mark R. Rutgers, ed., *Retracing Public Administration* (London: JAI, Elsevier Science, 2003), 173.

12 Ibid.

13 David Osborne and Peter Plastrick, *Banishing Bureaucracy: The Five Strategies for Reinventing Government* (New York: Addison-Wesley, 1972), 17.

14 Weber, 'Bureaucracy,' 2: 841.

15 Ibid., 3: 1163.
16 Andrew Knapp and Vincent Wright, *Government and Politics*, 2nd ed. (London: Unwin and Hyman, 1996).
17 See, among others, Donald J. Savoie, *Thatcher, Reagan, Mulroney: In Search of a New Bureaucracy* (Pittsburgh: University of Pittsburgh Press, 1994).
18 Christopher Foster, *British Government in Crisis* (Oxford: Hart Publishing, 2005), 218.
19 *News – Canadians Distrust Government, Embrace Volunteerism* (Montreal: Trudeau Foundation, 11 November 2005).
20 'Stop Talking about Fixing Government, Just Do It, Public Says,' *Citizen* (Ottawa), 21 April 2006, A1.
21 'Living in Cyn,' *BBC News*, 2 April 2001.
22 *Power to the People* (London: The Power Inquiry and York Publishing Distribution, 2006), 16.
23 Foster, *British Government in Crisis*, chapter 15.
24 Ezra Suleiman, *Dismantling Democratic States* (Princeton: Princeton University Press, 2003), 2.
25 Julian LeGrand, *Motivation, Agency and Public Policy: Of Knights and Knaves, Pawns and Queens* (Oxford: Oxford University Press, 2003), 143.
26 See, among others, A.W. Johnson, *Social Policy in Canada: The Past as It Conditions the Present* (Halifax: Institute for Research on Public Policy, 1987), 1.
27 Peter Hennessy, *Never Again: Britain 1945–51* (London: Jonathan Cape, 1992), 44.
28 See, among others, *Public Citizen*, at www.citizen.org/pressroom/release/ CFem, 14 January 2004.
29 B. Guy Peters and Jon Pierre, *Bureaucracy and Democracy*, at www.sog.org/ paper/ipsaprop.doc. A conference sponsored by the International Political Science Association.
30 See among others, C. Offe, 'Political Authority and Class Structures: An Analysis of Late Capitalist Societies,' *International Journal of Sociology* 73, 2 (1982): 108.
31 See, among others, Peter Hall, *Governing the Economy* (New York: Oxford University Press, 1986).
32 Bertrand Russell, *The Impact of Science on Society* (London: Allen and Unwin, 1967), 37.
33 Patrick Weller and R.A.W. Rhodes, 'Introduction: Enter Centre Stage,' in R.A.W. Rhodes and P. Weller, *The Changing World of Top Officials: Mandarins or Valets* (Philadelphia: Open University Press, 2001), 1.
34 Woodrow Wilson, 'The Study of Administration,' *Political Science Quarterly* 2, 1 (1887): 198, and Herbert Kaufman, 'Emerging Conflicts

in the Doctrines of Public Administration,' *American Political Science Review* 50, 4 (December 1956): 1057–73.

35 For a brief but excellent discussion on this, see John D. Huber and Charles R. Shipan, *Deliberate Discretion? The Institutional Foundations of Bureaucratic Autonomy* (Cambridge: Cambridge University Press, 2002), 18–26.

36 William A. Niskanen, Jr, *Bureaucracy and Representative Government* (Chicago: Aldine-Atherton, 1971).

37 This is particularly true in the case of the United States. See, among many others, Nolan McCarty and Rose Razaghian, 'Advice and Consent: Senate Responses to Executive Branch Nominations, 1885–1996,' *American Journal of Political Science* 43, 4 (1999): 1122–93.

38 See, among others, Suleiman, *Dismantling Democratic States*, 4.

39 '1991: Tories Launch Citizen Charter,' www.bbc.co.uk, 23 March 1991.

40 See, among others, Donald J. Savoie, *Breaking the Bargain: Public Servants, Ministers, and Parliament* (Toronto: University of Toronto Press, 2003); Foster, *British Government in Crisis*; and Suleiman, *Dismantling Democratic States*.

41 Suleiman, *Dismantling Democratic States*, 5.

42 Giovanni Sartori, quoted in Neil Nevitte, *The Decline of Deference* (Toronto: Broadview, 1996), xvii.

43 Larry Diamond and Marc Plattner, 'Introduction,' in Larry Diamond and Marc Plattner, eds, *The Global Divergence of Democracies* (Baltimore: Johns Hopkins University Press, 2001), x.

44 See, among others, Robert Young and Christian Leuprecht, eds, *Municipal-Federal-Provincial Relations* (Kingston: Queen's University, School of Public Studies, 2006). See also 'Too Much Government Everywhere,' *Globe and Mail*, 12 July 2006, B2.

45 See, among others, Savoie, *Breaking the Bargain*.

46 Dani Kodrik, *Has Globalization Gone Too Far?* (Washington, DC: Institute for International Economics, 1997).

47 Ronald Wintrobe, *The Canadian Dictatorship*, working paper 2003–1, Royal Bank of Canada (RBC) Financial Group, Economic Policy Research Institute (EPRI) Working Paper Series, University of Western Ontario (June 2003), 30–1. See also Thomas Friedman, *The Lexus and the Olive Tree* (New York: Anchor Books, 2000).

48 The Honourable Pierre S. Pettigrew, 'Seattle: The Lessons for Future Governance,' The 2000 John L. Manion Lecture, Ottawa, Canadian Centre for Management Development, 4 May 2000, 8–9.

49 Ibid., 12.

50 See, for example, J.G. March and J.P. Olsen, 'The New Institutionalism: Organizational Factors in Political Life,' *American Political Science Review* 78, 4 (1984): 738–49.
51 'Stop Talking about Fixing Government, Just Do It, Public Says,' *Citizen* (Ottawa), 14 August 2006, A6.
52 Henry Mintzberg, 'Managing Government, Governing Management,' *Harvard Business Review*, 1 May 1996, 75–83.
53 Ralph Heintzman, 'The Effects of Globalization on Management Practices: Should the Public Sector Operate on Different Parameters?' paper presented to the Institute of Public Administration of Canada (IPAC) National Conference, Fredericton, New Brunswick, 31 August 1999, 7–9.
54 Vernon Bogdanor, 'Oxford and the Mandarin Culture: The Past That Is Gone,' *Oxford Review of Education* 32, 1 (February 2006): 162.
55 B. Guy Peters, *Institutional Theory in Political Science: The New Institutionalism*, 2nd ed. (New York: Continuum, 2005), 17.
56 I owe a special thank you to C.E.S. Franks for pushing me to identify the major changes at play in the relationship between politicians and civil servants.

2. How Did We Get Here?

1 P. Pierson and T. Skocpol, 'Historial Institutionalism in Contemporary Political Science,' in I. Katznelson and H.V. Milner, eds, *Political Science: State of Discipline* (New York: Norton, 2002).
2 The most ambitious and thorough is S.E. Finer, *The History of Government*, 3 vols (Oxford: Oxford University Press, 1997).
3 Ibid., 1: 133.
4 Richard Mulgan, *Holding Power to Account: Accountability in Modern Democracies* (New York: Palgrave Macmillan, 2003), 12.
5 Ibid., 346.
6 S. Andrews, *Enlightened Despotism: Readings, Problems and Perspectives in History* (London: Longman, 1967), 135.
7 See, among others, M.I. Finlay, *The Ancient Greeks* (Harmondsworth: Penguin, 1977), 91–3.
8 James Madison, *The Federalist Papers, No. 10: The Utility of the Union as a Safeguard against Domestic Faction and Insurrection* (New York: Daily Advertiser, 22 November 1787).
9 Cheryl Simrell King and Camilla Stivers, 'Citizens and Administrators: Roles and Responsibilities,' in Richard C. Box, ed., *Public Administration and Society: Critical Issues in American Government* (London: M.E. Sharpe, 2004), 272.

10 Christopher Hitchens, 'The Export of Democracy,' *Wall Street Journal*, 12 July 2005, A16.

11 See, among many others, Encyclopedia Britannica Online.

12 Finer, *The History of Government*, 1: 542.

13 Ibid., 543.

14 Ibid., 548.

15 See, for example, W.T. Chan, *A Source Book in Chinese Philosophy* (Princeton: Princeton University Press, 1963).

16 Finer, *The History of Government*, 1: 583–5.

17 L. Bernier, *Les institutions de l'empire byzantin* (Paris: Albin Michel, 1949), 80.

18 Charles Benn, *Daily Life in Traditional China: The T'ang Dynasty* (Westport, CT: Greenwood Press, 2001).

19 Finer, *The History of Government*, 1: 764.

20 H. Maspero and E. Balazs, *Histoire et institutions de la Chine ancienne* (Paris: Presses universitaires de Paris, 1967), 173.

21 Adam Tomkins, *Public Law* (Oxford: Oxford University Press, 2003), 42.

22 The Acts of Settlement 1701 established that Parliament could control the identity of the monarch by altering the line of succession.

23 See, among others, Jeffrey Goldsworthy, *The Sovereignty of Parliament: History and Philosophy* (Oxford: Oxford University Press, 2001), 16–18.

24 Quoted in Joyce Lee Malcolm, 'Doing No Wrong: Law, Liberty, and the Constraint of Kings,' *Journal of British Studies* 38 (April 1999): 161.

25 'Magna Carta,' Wikipedia, the free encyclopedia, undated.

26 Goldsworthy, *The Sovereignty of Parliament*, 140–1.

27 Finer, *The History of Government*, 1: 1340.

28 L.G. Schwoerer, 'The Contributions of the Declaration of Rights to Anglo-American Radicalism,' in M.C. Jacob and J.R. Jacob, eds, *The Origins of Anglo-American Radicalism* (London: George Allen and Unwin, 1984), 112.

29 Tomkins, *Public Law*, 44.

30 W. Bagehot, *The English Constitution* (London: C.A. Watts and Co., 1964), 220.

31 Quoted in Sir Norman Chester, *The English Administrative System, 1780–1870* (Oxford: Clarendon Press, 1981), 81.

32 Goldsworthy, *The Sovereignty of Parliament*, 230.

33 Ibid., 232.

34 Sir Ivor Jennings, *Cabinet Government* (Cambridge: Cambridge University Press, 1959), 14.

35 Harold Wilson quotes Walter Bagehot to make the point on the role of the prime minister in Harold Wilson, *A Prime Minister on Prime Ministers* (London: Weidenfeld and Nicolson, and Michael Joseph, 1977), 10.

36 Henry Parris, *Constitutional Bureaucracy* (London: George Allen and Unwin, 1969), 28.
37 Jennings, *Cabinet Government*, 20.
38 Ibid., 15–16.
39 Quoted in Chester, *The English Administrative System*, 81.
40 Jennings, *Cabinet Government*, 14.
41 Quoted in Parris, *Constitutional Bureaucracy*, 80.
42 Ibid.
43 Ibid., 81.
44 A.V. Dicey quoted in ibid., 81.
45 Geoffrey Marshall and Graeme C. Moodie, *Some Problems of the Constitution*, 5th ed. (London: Hutchinson University Library, 1971), 55.
46 For an excellent paper on this issue, see Donald Desserud, 'The Confidence Convention under the Canadian Parliamentary System' (Ottawa: Canadian Study of Parliament Group-Parliamentary Perspectives, October 2006).
47 Sir Ivor Jennings, *The Law and the Constitution* (London: University of London Press, 1959), 208.
48 Marshall and Moodie, *Some Problems of the Constitution*, 65.
49 Goldsworthy, *The Sovereignty of Parliament*, 230.
50 R.H. Lord, quoted in P. Spufford, *The Origins of the English Parliament: Readings* (London: Longman, 1967), 21.
51 David Held, *Models of Democracy* (Stanford: Stanford University Press, 1996), 119.
52 Joseph A. Schumpeter, *Capitalism, Socialism, and Democracy* (New York: Harper and Row, 1950), 122.
53 John Stuart Mill, 'Considerations on Representative Government,' in H.B. Acton, ed., *Utilitarianism, Liberty and Representative Government* (London: Dent, 1951), 230.
54 Jennifer Smith, 'Democracy and the Canadian House of Commons at the Millennium,' *Canadian Public Administration* 42, 4 (1999): 414.
55 R. MacGregor Dawson, *The Government of Canada*, 4th ed. (Toronto: University of Toronto Press, 1963), 340.
56 See, among others, David C. Docherty, *Legislatures* (Vancouver: University of British Columbia Press, 2005), chapter 3.
57 See, among others, Nevil Johnson, *Reshaping the British Constitution: Essays in Political Interpretation* (Basingstoke: Palgrave Macmillan, 2004), 12.
58 Kenneth McNaught, 'History and the Perception of Politics,' in John H. Redekop, ed., *Approaches to Canadian Politics* (Scarborough, ON: Prentice-Hall of Canada, 1978), 108.
59 Roger Gibbins, *Regionalism: Territorial Politics in Canada and the United States* (Toronto: Butterworth, 1982), 29.

60 J.M. Roberts, *The Hutchinson History of the World* (London: Hutchinson, 1976).

61 Sidney Low, Sir Ivor Jennings, and Lord Morrison of Lambeth, quoted in Geoffrey Marshall, *Constitutional Conventions* (Oxford: Oxford University Press, 1984), 61–6. These statements, however, do not square with the accounting officer concept that has been in place in Britain for about 140 years and much more recently in Canada.

62 Parris, *Constitutional Bureaucracy*, 106.

63 Ibid., 127.

64 Ibid.

65 J.E. Hodgetts, *Pioneer Public Service: An Administrative History of the Upper Canadas, 1841–1867* (Toronto: University of Toronto Press, 1955), 49.

66 This information was provided by C.E.S. Franks in correspondence with the author, dated 9 April 2007.

67 See Robert C. Brown, *Robert Laird Borden: A Biography*, vol. 1, *1854–1914* (Toronto: Macmillan, 1975), 215.

68 Chester, *The English Administrative System*, 27.

69 Ibid., 370.

70 Quoted in Kevin Theakston, *The Civil Service since 1945* (Oxford: Blackwell, 1995), 176.

71 See, among others, Edward Greenspon and Anthony Wilson-Smith, *Double Vision: The Inside Story of the Liberals in Power* (Toronto: Doubleday Canada, 1996).

72 Gordon Robertson, *Memoirs of a Very Civil Servant: Mackenzie King to Pierre Trudeau* (Toronto: University of Toronto Press, 2000), 316.

73 See, for example, Chester, *The English Administrative System*, 120–49.

74 Report of the Committee on Public Expenditure, tabled in 1808; quoted in ibid., 149.

75 See, for example, Donald J. Savoie, *The Politics of Public Spending in Canada* (Toronto: University of Toronto Press, 1990), chapter 2.

76 Quoted in Chester, *The English Administrative System*, 26.

77 Quoted in Peter Hennessy, *Whitehall* (London: Fontana, 1989), 38.

78 Tomkins, *Public Law*, 85.

79 Geoffrey Marshall, *Constitutional Conventions: The Rules and Forms of Political Accountability* (Oxford: Clarendon Press, 2001), 54.

80 Ibid.

3. Was There Ever a Golden Era?

1 See, among others, Vernon Bogdanor's review of Sir Christopher Foster's *British Government in Crisis*, in *Review No. 29* (London: the Public Management

and Policy Association [PMPA], 2005), and C.E.S. Franks, 'A Clarion Call for Clarified Boundaries between Politicians and Public Servants,' *Policy Options* (December 2003–January 2004): 110.

2 Lord Wilson of Dinton, 'The Mandarin Myth,' fourth lecture in a series on Tomorrow's Government, London, Royal Society for the Encouragement of Arts Manufacturers and Commerce, 1 March 2006, 4.

3 Tom Ginsburg, *Judicial Review in New Democracies: Constitutional Courts in Asian Cases* (Cambridge: Cambridge University Press, 2005), 43.

4 Tom Bentley, *Everyday Democracy: Why We Get the Politicians We Deserve* (London: Demos, 2005), 9.

5 Quoted in Sue Cameron, 'Mandarin Dynasty,' *FT Magazine* (London), 8/9 (April 2006): 16.

6 Lowell Murray, 'MPs, Political Parties and Parliamentary Democracy,' *Isuma* 1, 2 (Autumn 2000): 103.

7 Christopher Foster, *British Government in Crisis* (Oxford: Hart Publishing, 2005).

8 Donald J. Savoie, *Governing from the Centre: The Concentration of Power in Canadian Politics* (Toronto: University of Toronto Press, 1999).

9 See, among many others, the work of the Institute for Research on Public Policy on Democratic Reform at www.irpp.org in the case of Canada and *Power to the People* the centenary project of the Joseph Rowntree Charitable Trust and the Joseph Rowntree Reform Trust (London: The Power Inquiry and York Publishing Distribution, 2006).

10 Ralph Heintzman, 'Public Service Values and Ethics: Dead End or Strong Foundation?' (Discussion Paper, University of Ottawa, 2006), 3.

11 Jeffrey Goldsworthy, *The Sovereignty of Parliament: History and Philosophy* (Oxford: Oxford University Press, 2001), 233.

12 Walter Bagehot, *The English Constitution* (London: C.A. Watts and Co., 1964), 215.

13 Ibid., 220.

14 C.D. Yonge, *The Life and Administration of the Second Earl of Liverpool* (London, 1868), 3: 340.

15 Quoted in Goldsworthy, *Sovereignty of Parliament*, 227.

16 Ibid., 277.

17 S.E. Finer, *The History of Government* (Oxford: Oxford University Press, 1997), 3: 1593–4.

18 Adam Tomkins, *Public Law* (Oxford: Oxford University Press, 2003), 165.

19 Ibid.

20 C.E.S. Franks, *The Parliament of Canada* (Toronto: University of Toronto Press, 1987), 5.

21 John D. Huber and Charles R. Shipan make this very point in their *Deliberate Discretion? The Institutional Foundations of Bureaucratic Autonomy* (Cambridge: Cambridge University Press, 2002), 28.

22 Tomkins, *Public Law*, 164.

23 Jennifer Smith, 'Democracy and the Canadian House of Commons at the Millennium,' *Canadian Public Administration* 42, 4 (1999): 407.

24 See, among others, Foster, *British Government in Crisis*, 8.

25 Lord Hailsham, *Dilemma of Democracy* (London: Collins, 1978).

26 Jeffrey Simpson, *The Friendly Dictatorship* (McClelland and Stewart, 2001).

27 Peter Hennessy, *Whitehall* (London: Fontana, 1989), 327.

28 Frank Cooper, 'Changing the Establishment,' *The Political Quarterly* 57 (July 1986): 269.

29 Foster, *British Government in Crisis*, 131.

30 *Power to the People*, 136.

31 Both quoted in ibid., 129–30.

32 C.E.S. Franks, 'The Decline of the Canadian Parliament,' *Hill Times* (Ottawa), 25 May 1998, 15.

33 Franks, *The Parliament of Canada*, 175.

34 'Senior Students Get Tory Dollars,' CBC online news, www.cbc.ca, 27 March 2003.

35 Geoffrey Marshall, 'Re-making the British Constitution,' a special lecture delivered before the Faculty of Law, McGill University, Montreal, 5 October 2000, 4.

36 Europe, *Human Rights Act of 1998*, www.opsi.gov.uk/Acts/acts1998/1980042.htm.

37 'Canadians Challenging Authority, Report Says,' *National Post*, 21 January 2002, A2.

38 My conversations with a senior official at the Department of Fisheries and Oceans, Ottawa, May 2002.

39 My conversation with a senior official at the Department of Justice, Ottawa, July 2002.

40 My conversation with a senior government official, Ottawa, 24 February 2002.

41 Ibid.

42 Ibid.

43 Chief Justice Beverley McLachlin, 'Unwritten Constitutional Principles: What Is Going On?' Remarks given at the 2005 Lord Cooke Lecture, Wellington, New Zealand, 1 December 2005, 11–12.

44 Peter McCormick, 'New Questions about an Old Concept: The Supreme Court of Canada's Judicial Independence Decisions,' *Canadian Journal of Political Science* 37, 4 (December 2004): 858.

45 Franks, *The Parliament of Canada.*
46 Peter Hennessy, *Never Again: Britain 1945–51* (London: Jonathan Cape, 1992), 44.
47 Julian LeGrand, *Motivation, Agency and Public Policy: Of Knights and Knaves, Pawns and Queens* (Oxford: Oxford University Press, 2003), 4.
48 Vernon Bogdanor, 'Oxford and the Mandarin Culture: The Past That Is Gone,' *Oxford Review of Education* 32, 1 (February 2006): 160.
49 Ibid., 147, and Beatrice Webb, *My Apprenticeship* (Cambridge: Cambridge University Press, 1979), 143.
50 Consultation with the Assemblée des évêques catholiques du Québec, 10 May 2006.
51 Hennessy, *Whitehall*, 194.
52 Consultation with a former senior civil servant, Oxford University, 12 February 2006.
53 Canada, Canadian Centre for Management Development, *A Strong Foundation: Report of the Task Force on Public Service Values and Ethics* (Ottawa: Author, 1996), 27–43.
54 Heintzman, 'Public Service Values and Ethics,' 29.
55 R. Armstrong, *The Duties and Responsibilities of Civil Servants in Relation to Ministers: Note by the Head of the Civil Service* (London: Cabinet Office, 1985), 2.
56 Christopher Hood in an interview with the author. See also Christopher Hood and Martin Lodge, *The Politics of Public Service Bargains: Reward, Competency, Loyalty and Blame* (Oxford: Oxford University Press, 2006).
57 London, House of Lords, *Parliamentary Debates–Hansard* 679, 113 (3 March 2006): 470.
58 Britain, Cabinet Office, *The Civil Service*, Guide to Government (London, undated), 1.
59 Canada, Privy Council Office, *Constitutional Responsibility and Accountability*, section VII, Accountability in Parliamentary Government – the Minister (Ottawa, 1993).
60 Canada, Office of the Prime Minister, *Federal Accountability Action Plan: Turning a New Leaf* (Ottawa, 11 April 2006), 30.
61 U.K., Treasury, *Responsibilities of an Accounting Officer*, Memorandum (London, undated), 6.
62 Canada, Office of the Prime Minister, *Accountable Government: A Guide for Ministers* (Ottawa: Author, 2006).
63 Canada, Privy Council Office, *Guidance for Deputy Ministers, section 4, Accountability for Addressing Errors in Administration* (Ottawa: Author, 2003), 4.

64 Canada, Privy Council Office, *Guidance for Accounting Officers* (Ottawa: Author, March 2007).

65 Privy Council Office, Accounting Officers: Guidance on Roles, Responsibilities, and Appearances before Parliamentary Committees, 2007, www. pco-bcp.gc.ca.

66 Based on material provided by Professor C.E.S. Franks in correspondence with the author, 16 August 2007. Professor Franks acted as consultant-adviser to the Public Accounts Committee in drafting the protocol spelling out the roles and responsibilities of MPs in relation to the accounting officer.

67 U.K., Treasury, *Corporate Governance in Central Government Departments: Code of Good Practice* (2005), 5.

68 Canada, Privy Council Office, *Notes on the Responsibility of Public Servants in Relation to Parliamentary Committees*, Section Swearing of Public Servants (Ottawa: Author, December 1990).

69 See, among others, C.E.S. Franks, 'The Respective Responsibilities and Accountabilities of Ministers and Public Servants: A Study of the British Accounting Officer System and Its Relevance for Canada,' in Canada, Commission of Inquiry into the Sponsorship Program and Advertising Activities, *Restoring Accountability*, vol. 3 (Ottawa, 2006).

70 J. Jowell and D. Oliver, eds, *The Changing Constitution* (Oxford: Oxford University Press, 2000), viii.

71 Hood and Lodge, *The Politics of Public Service Bargains*, 49.

72 U.K., House of Commons, Treasury and Civil Service Select Committee, 1993–4, *The Role of the Civil Service*, HC27, paragraph 132.

73 U.K., *The Civil Service: Taking Forward Continuity and Change*, Cm. 2748 (London: Her Majesty's Stationery Office, January 1995), 25–30.

74 U.K., Review of Prison Service Security in England and Wales and the Escape from Parkhurst Prison, Cm. 3020 (London: Her Majesty's Stationery Office, October 1995), and Diana Woodhouse, 'The Reconstruction of Constitutional Accountability,' Newcastle Law School Working Paper 2000, number 10.

75 See, among others, Peter Barberis, 'The New Public Management and a New Accountability,' *Public Administration* 76, 4 (Autumn 1998): 451–70.

76 Britain, House of Commons, Public Service Committee, *Ministerial Accountability and Responsibility*, 1995–6, 313, paragraph 20.

77 Ibid., paragraph 19.

78 Britain, House of Commons, *Debates*, vol. 292, cols 1046–7 (19 March 1997).

79 For a full account of the debates that led to the parliamentary resolution, see Tomkins, *Public Law*, 152–9.

80 Lorne Sossin, 'Defining Boundaries: The Constitutional Argument for
    Bureaucratic Independence and Its Implications for the Accountability of
    the Public Service,' in Canada, Commission of Inquiry into the Sponsorship
    Program and Advertising Activities, *Restoring Accountability: Research Stud-
    ies*, vol. 2, *The Public Service and Transparency* (Ottawa, 2006), 27 and 65.
81 Ibid., 43.
82 Peter Aucoin and Mark D. Jarvis, *Modernizing Government Accountability: A
    Framework for Reform* (Ottawa: Canada School of the Public Service, 2005), 75.
83 Ibid., 79.
84 Franks, 'The Respective Responsibilities and Accountabilities of Ministers
    and Public Servants,' 210.
85 Canada, Office of the Prime Minister, 'Prime Minister Announces New
    Ethics Guidelines for the Ministry and the New Appointment Procedure
    for Ethics Counsellor,' News Release, 11 June 2002.
86 Canada, House of Commons, Public Accounts Committee, *Governance in
    the Public Service of Canada: Ministerial and Deputy Ministerial Responsibility*,
    10th report (May 2005), 16.
87 Conservative Party of Canada, *Stand Up for Canada*, Platform for the 2006
    general election. See section on 'Strengths, Auditing and Accountability
    within Departments' (Ottawa 2006), 9.
88 Ibid., 13.
89 Canada, Office of the Prime Minister, *Federal Accountability Action Plan*, 31.
90 Geoffrey Marshall, *Constitutional Conventions* (Oxford: Clarendon Press,
    1984), 75.
91 Gordon Osbaldeston, *Organizing to Govern* (Toronto: McGraw-Hill Ryerson,
    1992), 1: 115.
92 A.D.P. Heeney, 'Mackenzie King and the Cabinet Secretariat,' *Canadian Pub-
    lic Administration* 10 (September 1967): 373.
93 Canada, Treasury Board Secretariat, *Government Response to the Tenth Report
    of the Standing Committee on Public Accounts* (Ottawa, 17 August 2005), 7.
94 Gordon Robertson, 'The Deputies' Anonymous Duty,' *Policy Options* (July
    1983): 13.
95 Canada, Canadian Intergovernmental Conference Secretariat, *First Minis-
    ters Meeting: Documents*, 800–042/004, Verbatim Transcript (Ottawa,
    16 September 2004).
96 'Politicians, Not PS to Blame for Scandal,' *Citizen* (Ottawa), 24 March 2006.
97 See U.K., Information Commissioner's Office, 'Freedom of Information –
    One Year On' (1 January 2006).
98 See, among others, Donald J. Savoie, *Breaking the Bargain: Public Servants,
    Ministers, and Parliament* (Toronto: University of Toronto Press, 2003).

99 See, for example, Hugh Heclo and Aaron Wildavsky, *The Private Government of Public Money* (London: Macmillan, 1981).

100 Quoted in Franks, 'The Decline of the Canadian Parliament,' 15.

101 Quoted in 'Simpson Takes a Swipe at the Year's Political Books,' *Globe and Mail*, 31 December 1994, C12.

102 Jeffrey Simpson, 'Finding Harmony on the Linguistic Front,' *Globe and Mail*, 9 October 2002, A17.

103 Michael Colsden, 'Read All about Him,' *Globe and Mail*, 20 July 2002, D15.

104 See, among many others, Jim Travers, 'Harper's Closed Shop,' *Toronto Star*, 23 March 2006.

105 See, among others, 'PMO Wanted Crisis Kept under Wraps, Sources Say,' *Globe and Mail*, 20 July 2006, A1.

106 Murray, 'MPs, Political Parties and Parliamentary Democracy,' 137.

107 Savoie, *Governing from the Centre*, chapter 8.

108 See, among many others, Margaret Thatcher, *The Downing Street Years* (New York: HarperCollins, 1995).

109 Sir Christopher Foster, *Why Are We so Badly Governed?* (London: Public Management and Policy Association, 2005), 11.

110 George Pitcher, *The Death of Spin?* (London: Demos, 2002), 12.

111 'Cameron and the Sex Clinic Mystery,' *The Times*, 6 February 2006, 1.

112 John Crosbie, *No Holds Barred: My Life in Politics* (Toronto: McClelland and Stewart, 1997), 300.

113 'Cuts Won't Disconnect Government Cell Phones,' *Globe and Mail*, 29 June 1994, A5.

114 U.K., Information Commissioner's Office, 'Freedom of Information – One Year On' (2006), 1.

115 Nevil Johnson, *Reshaping the British Constitution: Essays in Political Interpretation* (Basingstoke: Palgrave Macmillan, 2004), 234.

116 Kevin Theakston, *Leadership in Whitehall* (New York: St Martin's Press, 1999), 257.

117 See, among others, Savoie, *Breaking the Bargain*.

4. Disenchantment Sets In

1 Ralph Heintzman, 'Public Service Values and Ethics: Dead End or Strong Foundation?' (Discussion Paper, University of Ottawa, 2006), 2.

2 Donald J. Savoie, *Thatcher, Reagan, Mulroney: In Search of a New Bureaucracy* (Pittsburgh: University of Pittsburgh Press, 1994).

3 See, among others, S.H. Barnes, Max Kaase, et al., *Political Action: Mass Participation in Five Western Democracies* (London: Sage, 1979).

4 An excellent example here is John K. Galbraith. See *Dimension* (Moncton) (Winter 1986): 13.
5 Quoted in Peter Hennessy, *Whitehall* (London: Fontana, 1989), 590.
6 Quoted in Sheldon Ehrenworth, 'A Better Public Service Needs Freedom to Manage Its People,' *Globe and Mail*, 15 April 1989, B21.
7 Canada, Royal Commission on the Economic Union and Development Prospects for Canada, *Report* (Ottawa: Minister of Supply and Services, 1985), 3: 148.
8 Alan Cairns, 'The Nature of the Administrative State,' *University of Toronto Law Journal* 40 (1990): 345.
9 J.K. Galbraith, quoted in *Dimension*, 13.
10 Tony Benn, 'Manifestos and Mandates,' in Tony Benn and Shirley Williams, et al., *Policy and Practice: The Experience of Government* (London: Royal Institute of Public Administration, 1980), 62.
11 Shirley Williams, 'The Decision Makers,' in Benn and Williams, *Policy and Practice: The Experience of Government* (London: Royal Institute of Public Administration, 1980), 81.
12 Donald J. Savoie, *Governing from the Centre: The Concentration of Power in Canadian Politics* (Toronto: University of Toronto Press, 1999).
13 Richard Crossman, *The Diaries of a Cabinet Minister* (London: Hamish Hamilton and Jonathan Cape, 1975), 1: 90.
14 David Lipsey, ed., *Making Government Work* (London: Fabian Society, 1982), 37.
15 Lord Wilson of Dinton, 'The Mandarin Myth,' fourth lecture in a series on Tomorrow's Government, London, Royal Society for the Encouragement of Arts Manufacturers and Commerce, 1 March 2006, 3.
16 Sandford F. Borins, 'Public Choice: "Yes, Minister" Made It Popular, but Does Winning a Nobel Prize Make It True?' *Canadian Public Administration* 31, 1 (Spring 1988): 22.
17 Carol H. Weiss, 'Efforts at Bureaucratic Reform,' in Carol H. Weiss and Allan H. Barton, eds., *Making Bureaucracies Work* (Beverley Hills, CA: Sage Publications, 1980), 10; Stephen Michelson, 'The Working Bureaucrat and the Working Bureaucracy,' in Weiss and Barton, *Making Bureaucracies Work*, 175; Herbert Kaufman, 'Fear of Bureaucracy: A Raging Pandemic,' *Public Administration Review* 59, 3 (1981): 1.
18 Charles T. Goodsell, *The Case for Bureaucracy: A Public Administration Polemic* (Chatham, NJ: Chatham House, 1983).
19 Prime Minister Margaret Thatcher in an interview with *Women's Own* magazine, London, 31 October 1987.
20 See, among others, Savoie, *Thatcher, Reagan, Mulroney*, chapter 3.

21 See, among many others, Christopher Pollitt and G. Bouckaert, *Public Management Reform: The Case of the European Community* (Oxford: Oxford University Press, 2000), and Savoie, *Thatcher, Reagan, Mulroney.*
22 Peter Aucoin, 'New Public Management and New Public Governance: Finding the Balance,' in David Siegel and Ken Rasmussen, eds, *Power, Professionalism, and Public Service: Essays in Honour of Kenneth Kernaghan* (Toronto: University of Toronto Press, Institute of Public Administration of Canada [IPAC] Series in Public Management and Governance, 2006), chapter 2.
23 See, among others, Walter Williams, *Washington, Westminster, and Whitehall* (Cambridge: Cambridge University Press, 1988), 11.
24 Henry Mintzberg, *The Structuring of Organizations* (Englewood Cliffs, NJ: Prentice Hall, 1979); Thomas J. Peters and Robert H. Waterman, Jr, *In Search of Excellence: Lessons from America's Best-Run Companies* (New York: Harper and Row, 1982), chapters 5, 6, 7, 11; Peter Block, *The Empowered Manager: Positive Political Skills at Work* (New York: Jossey-Bass, 1988), 75.
25 See, among others, Les Metcalfe and Sue Richards, *Improving Public Management* (Sage: London, 1987), chapters 1, 2, 4, 10 (quotation is from 218).
26 Consultations with a government official, Oxford, England, 10 February 2006.
27 See, among others, Patrick Dunleavy, H. Margetts, S. Bastow, et al., 'New Public Management Is Dead – Long Live Digital-Era Government,' *Journal of Public Administration Research and Theory* 16, 3 (2006): 467–94. Also consultations with Professor Dunleavy, London, 8 February 2007.
28 See, for example, Peter Curwen, *Public Enterprise: A Modern Approach* (Brighton: Wheatsheaf Books, 1986), 42.
29 Ibid., 266.
30 Peter Aucoin, 'New Public Management and New Public Governance,' 40.
31 Jean Robert Gauthier made this statement in opening the Public Accounts Committee, Ottawa, 14 May 1992.
32 www.news.bbc.co.uk/on this day/22 July 1991.
33 C. Campbell and G.K. Wilson, *The End of Whitehall* (Oxford: Blackwell, 1995), 50–3.
34 Christopher Foster, *British Government in Crisis* (Oxford: Hart Publishing, 2005), 217.
35 John Major, *The Erosion of Parliamentary Government* (London: Centre for Policy Studies, 2003), 1.
36 Ibid., 9–10.
37 See Donald J. Savoie, *Breaking the Bargain: Public Servants, Ministers, and Parliament* (Toronto: University of Toronto Press, 2003).

38 U.K., 'Speech by the Prime Minister: Reform of Public Services' (10 Downing Street, 16 July 2001), 6.
39 See, among others, Foster, *British Government in Crisis*, 221.
40 Sir Andrew Turnbull, 'Continuity and Change,' in Baroness Usha Prashar, ed., *Changing Times: Leading Perspectives on the Civil Service in the 21st Century and Its Enduring Values* (London: The Office of the Civil Service Commissioners, 2005), 70.
41 See, among others, 'Public Servants Cannot Escape All the Blame,' *Globe and Mail*, 3 May 2004, A13.
42 Savoie, *Breaking the Bargain*.
43 Canada, Parliament, *Building a Higher Quality of Life for All Canadians*, Speech from the Throne to Open the Second Session of the Thirty-Sixth Parliament of Canada, Ottawa, 12 October 1999, 14.
44 Quoted in Peter Aucoin and Donald J. Savoie, 'Launching and Organizing a Program Review Exercise,' paper prepared for the Canadian Centre for Management Development, Ottawa, 1998, 2.
45 Ibid.
46 See, among others, 'Shawinigate Bank Exec Wins Dismissal Suit,' www.cbc.ca/story/news/national, 3 March 2004.
47 Canada, Commission of Inquiry into the Sponsorship Program and Advertising Activities, *Who Is Responsible? Fact Finding Report*, 1 November 2005.
48 Consultations with the president of the Treasury Board, Ottawa, June 2004.
49 Canada, Department of Finance, *Focussing on Priorities*, The Budget Plan 2006, 2 May 2006, 51–2.
50 U.K., *The Citizen's Charter*, presented to Parliament by the prime minister (London: Her Majesty's Stationery Office, July 1991).
51 See, among others, 'The Two Tonys,' *New Yorker*, 6 October 1997.
52 U.K., *Modernising Government*, a document presented to Parliament by the prime minister and the minister for the Cabinet Office, 1999, 11.
53 Canada, Office of the Prime Minister, Address by Prime Minister Paul Martin, in reply to the Speech from the Throne, Ottawa, 6 October 2004, 3.
54 Christopher Hood, 'De-Sir Humphreyfying the Westminster Model of Bureaucracy: A New Style of Governance,' *Governance* 3, 2 (April 1990): 206.
55 Edie N. Goldenberg, 'The Permanent Government in an Era of Retrenchment and Redirection,' in Lester M. Salamon and Michael S. Lund, eds, *The Reagan Presidency and the Governing of America* (Washington, DC: Urban Institute Press, 1984), 384.
56 See Michael Keating and Malcolm Holmes, 'Reply to Aucoin and Hood,' *Governance* 3, 2 (April 1990), 217–18.

57 George Post, *Conversations with Canadian Public Service Leaders* (Ottawa: Canadian Centre for Management Development, March 1996), 13.

58 Gordon Robertson, *Memoirs of a Very Civil Servant* (Toronto: University of Toronto Press, 2001), 38.

59 A.W. Johnson, 'The Role of the Deputy Minister,' *Canadian Public Administration* 4, 4 (1961): 363.

60 John Hilliker, *Canada's Department of External Affairs*, vol. 1, *The Early Years, 1909–1946* (Montreal and Kingston: McGill-Queen's University Press, 1990), 243.

61 J.L. Granatstein, *The Ottawa Men: The Civil Service Mandarins, 1935–1957* (Toronto: University of Toronto Press, 1982), 9–10.

62 Ibid., 10.

63 U.K., *The Civil Service*, vol. 1, *Report of the Committee 1960–68* (London: Her Majesty's Stationery Office, June 1968), 105.

64 U.K., House of Commons, *Debates* (London), 8 February 1966, vol. 210, 13.

65 See Royal Commission on Government Organizations, *Final Report* (Ottawa: Queen's Printer, 1962), 91.

66 Ibid.

67 Ibid., 156.

68 See, among many others, Pollitt and Bouckaert, *Public Management Reform*.

69 U.K., 'Prime Minister Announces Change in Way Whitehall Delivers Services,' Press Notice (10 Downing Street, 18 February 1987). See also the section 'Notes to Editors.'

70 U.K., *Hansard* (London), 18 February 1988, col. 1159.

71 See Geoffrey Fry, Andrew Flynn, William Jenkins, et al., 'Symposium on Improving Management in Government,' *Public Administration* 66, 4 (Winter 1988): 443.

72 Butler, cited in U.K., House of Commons, London, *Official Report*, 18 February 1988. See also Hennessy, *Whitehall*, 621.

73 See, among many others, Savoie, *Thatcher, Reagan, Mulroney*, chapter 7.

74 Douglas G. Hartle, 'The Role of the Auditor General of Canada,' *Canadian Tax Journal* 23, 3 (1975): 197.

75 See, among others, Gwyn Bevan and Christopher Hood, 'Have Targets Improved Performance in the English NHS?,' *British Medical Journal*, 332 (18 February 2006): 419–22.

76 'Senior Civil Servants Use Up Entire Budget for Bonuses,' *National Post*, 29 August 2002, A1 and A9.

77 See, among others, Savoie, *Breaking the Bargain*, 224.

78 Savoie, *Thatcher, Reagan, Mulroney*, 205.

79 'Sir Andrew Turnbull's Valedictory Lecture,' London, 26 July 2005, mimeo, 21.
80 Lord Wilson of Dinton, 'The Mandarin Myth,' 7.
81 Consultations with former senior officials in the British government. See also Geoffrey K. Fry, 'The Thatcher Government, the Financial Management Initiative and the New Civil Service,' *Public Administration* 66, 2 (Spring 1988): 7.
82 Consultations with former senior British government officials, London and Oxford, various dates.
83 'Treasury Hopes Senior Cuts Will Boost Employee Morale,' *Citizen* (Ottawa), 18 April 1980, A3.
84 See Peter F. Drucker, 'The Deadly Sins of Public Administration,' *Public Administration Review* 26, 2 (March-April 1980): 103–6.

5. Society Then and Now: From an Obligation to Others to an Obligation to Self

1 Ezra Suleiman, *Dismantling Democratic States* (Princeton: Princeton University Press, 2003), 9.
2 Francis Fukuyama, *Social Capital and Civil Society* (Fairfax, VA: The Institute of Public Policy, George Mason University, 1999), 1.
3 Robert D. Putnam, *Bowling Alone: The Collapse and Revival of American Community* (New York: Simon and Schuster, 2000).
4 Robert D. Putnam, 'Turning In, Turning Out: The Strange Disappearance of Civic America,' the Inaugural Ithiel de Sola Pool Lecture, December 1995, American Political Science Association, 4.
5 Peter Hall, 'Great Britain: The Role of Government and the Distribution of Social Capital,' in Robert D. Putnam, ed., *Democracies in Flux: The Evolution of Social Capital in Contemporary Society* (Oxford: Oxford University Press, 2002), 47.
6 U.K., Office for National Statistics, *Social Capital: A Review of the Literature* (London: Author, 2001), 3; and M. Johnson and R. Jowell, 'Social Capital and the Social Fabric,' chapter 9 in R. Jowell, J. Curtice, A. Park, and K. Thomson, eds, *British Social Attitudes: The 16th Report, Who Shares New Labour's Values?* (Aldershot: Ashgate, National Centre for Social Research, 1999).
7 Jane Jenson, *Mapping Social Cohesion: The State of Canadian Research* (Ottawa: Canadian Policy Research Network, 1998), v.
8 Caroline Beauvais and Jane Jenson, *Social Cohesion: Updating the State of the Research* (Ottawa: Canadian Policy Research Network, 2000), 28.

9 F. Baum, 'Social Capital, Economic Capital and Power: Further Issues for a Public Health Agenda,' *Journal of Epidemiology and Community Health* 54 (2000): 409.

10 Statistics Canada, 'Overview: Canada Still Predominantly Roman Catholic and Protestant' (Ottawa: Author, 2001).

11 Ibid., 5.

12 Ibid.

13 U.K., Office for National Statistics, *Social Capital*, 13.

14 Statistics Canada, 'Overview,' 5.

15 Putnam, 'Turning In, Turning Out,' 4.

16 Barbara Dafoe Whitehead, *The Divorce Culture* (New York: Alfred Knopf, 1997), chapter 1.

17 Putnam, 'Turning In, Turning Out,' 10.

18 'All Work and No Play Leads to Divorce,' *Sunday Times*, 12 March 2006, 6.

19 David Owen, *English Philanthropy 1660–1960* (Oxford: Oxford University Press, 1965), 597.

20 See, among others, Social Development Canada, *The Voluntary Sector Initiative* (Ottawa: Author, undated).

21 Quoted in Hall, 'Great Britain,' 42.

22 Canada, 'Notes for an Address by Prime Minister Jean Chrétien to the 15th Biennial World Volunteer Conference at the International Association for Volunteer Effort,' Edmonton, Alberta, 24 August 1998, 2.

23 See, among many others, Steven Cohen and William E. Micke, *The New Effective Public Manager* (San Francisco: Jossey-Bass, 1995).

24 Putnam, 'Turning In, Turning Out,' 16.

25 Ibid., 18.

26 See World Values Survey on television watching and newspaper readership in the case of Britain (2002) and Canada (2003).

27 Blake Andrew and Stuart Soroka, 'From Ink-Stained Wretches to Telling Heads: A Short History of the Press Gallery,' *Policy Options* 27, 6 (July-August 2006): 12.

28 Arend Lijphart, 'Unequal Participation: Democracy's Unresolved Dilemma,' *American Political Science Review* 91, 1 (March 1997): 2.

29 Mark Franklin and Thomas T. Mackie, *Electoral Change: Responses to Evolving Social and Attitudinal Structures in Western Democracies* (Cambridge: Cambridge University Press, 1992), and Mark Franklin, *Voter Turnout and the Dynamics of Electoral Competition in Established Democracies since 1945* (Cambridge: Cambridge University Press, 2004).

30 Martin P. Wattenberg, 'Turnout Decline in the U.S. and Other Advanced Industrial Democracies,' Centre for the Study of Democracy Research

Paper Series in Empirical Democracy Theory (Irvine, CA: University of California, Irvine, Center for the Study of Democracy, 1998), 14.

31 Putnam, 'Turning In, Turning Out,' 40.

32 Canada, Consejo Regional Indigena del Cauca, (CRIC) Survey on Trade, Globalization and Canadian Values, in *Opinion Canada* 3, 73 (21 June 2001).

33 See Neil Nevitte, *The Decline of Deference: Canadian Value Change in Cross- National Perspective* (Peterborough, ON: Broadview Press, 1996); Neil Nevitte and Mebs Kanju, 'Canadian Political Culture and Value Change,' in Joanna Everitt and Brenda O'Neill, eds, *Citizen Politics: Research and Theory in Canadian Political Behaviour* (Toronto: Oxford University Press, 2001), esp. 71.

34 Ibid., 37.

35 Michael Adams, 'Death of Politics,' *Globe and Mail*, 30 November 2000, A6.

36 See, among others, Scott Proudfoot, 'Political Parties Lose Ground Steadily,' www.hillwatch.com, 1 June 2006.

37 Trudeau Foundation, *News – Canadians Distrust Government, Embrace Volun- teerism* (Montreal: Author, 11 November 2005).

38 George Perlin, *Canadian Politics: Canadian Democracy in Critical Perspective* (Toronto: CBC Newsworld, 2001).

39 Graham Fox, 'Rethinking Political Parties,' discussion paper, Ottawa, Pub- lic Policy Forum, November 2005, 3 and 4.

40 'Main Political Parties Facing Oblivion,' www.demos.co.uk, London, 28 September 2004.

41 Allan Gregg, 'Party Loyalty Is Dead,' www.allangrefgg.com, 7 April 2006.

42 World Economic Forum, 'Trust in Governments, Corporations and Global Institutions Continues to Decline,' Geneva, Switzerland, 15 December 2005, 1.

43 Ibid., 2.

44 Nevitte, *The Decline of Deference*, 55.

45 'Public Trust and APEX Perspectives on Trust and Ethics,' Ottawa, APEX Symposium, 7 October 2004.

46 Putnam, 'Turning In, Turning Out,' 10.

47 Hall, 'Great Britain,' 35.

48 See various OECD publications, including *The Well-Being of Nations: The Role of Human and Social Capital* (Paris: OECD, 2001), and S. Knack, 'Trust, Associational Life and Economic Performance,' in J.F. Helliwell, ed., *The Contribution of Human and Social Capital to Sustained Economic Growth and Well Being* (Paris: OECD, 2001).

49 Elisabeth Gidengil, Elizabeth Goodyear-Grant, and Neil Nevitte, 'Gender, Knowledge and Social Capital,' in Brenda O'Neill and Elisabeth Gidengil, eds, *Gender and Social Capital* (New York: Routledge, 2004).

50 Hall, 'Great Britain,' 37.
51 Ibid., 57.
52 Ibid., 56.
53 Nevitte, *The Decline of Deference*, 9.
54 Ibid., 70.
55 Ralph Heintzman and Brian Marson, 'People, Service and Trust: Is There a Public Sector Value Chain?' *International Review of Administrative Sciences* 71, 4 (2005): 551.
56 Lord Wilson of Dinton , 'The Mandarin Myth,' fourth lecture in a series on Tomorrow's Government, 1 March 2006, 7.
57 'Rural Residents More Ready to Help,' *Globe and Mail*, 17 July 2006, A1. The article was based on a study produced by Statistics Canada.
58 See www.bowlingalone.com.
59 Putnam, *Bowling Alone*, 104.
60 See, among others, Tom Bentley, *Everyday Democracy: Why We Get the Politicians We Deserve* (London: Demos, 2005), 7.
61 'Generation Y Speaks: It's All Me, Me, Me,' *Sunday Times*, 4 February 2007, 25.

6. Searching for Values

1 'Guité Found Guilty,' *Globe and Mail*, 7 June 2006, A3.
2 Ibid.
3 'Guité Sentenced to 3½ Years in Prison,' *Globe and Mail*, 19 June 2006, A1.
4 See, among many others, Frederick Mosher, *Democracy and the Public Service* (New York: Oxford University Press, 1968).
5 See, for example, Leonard White, *Introduction to the Study of Public Administration* (New York: Macmillan, 1955), 460–1.
6 Canada, Office of the Auditor General, *Values and Ethics in the Federal Public Sector* (Ottawa: Report of the Auditor General of Canada, October 2000), chapter 12, 12–7.
7 Ibid., 12–18.
8 U.K., Cabinet Office and Office of the Civil Service Commissioner, 'Summary of Responses to 2006 Consultations on New Civil Service Code,' 6 June 2006, 1.
9 Donald J. Savoie, *Breaking the Bargain: Public Servants, Ministers, and Parliament* (Toronto: University of Toronto Press, 2003).
10 Kenneth Kernaghan, 'Towards a Public Service Code of Conduct – and Beyond,' *Canadian Public Administration* 40, 1 (Spring 1997): 40.
11 Ibid.

12 Canada, Privy Council Office, *Public Service 2000* (Ottawa: Author, 1990).
13 John Tait, 'A Strong Foundation: Report of the Task Force on Public Service Values and Ethics (the summary),' in *Canadian Public Administration* 40, 1 (Spring 1997): 1.
14 U.K., Committee on Standards in Public Life, *First Report* (London: Her Majesty's Stationery Office, 1994), cmd 2850–1, 1: 16.
15 See, among others, Stephen K. Bailey, 'Ethics and the Public Service,' in Roscoe Martin, ed., *Public Administration and Democracy* (Syracuse, NY: Syracuse University Press, 1965), 282–3.
16 See, among others, Christopher Foster, *British Government in Crisis* (Oxford: Hart Publishing, 2005).
17 'Cash for Peerages Affairs,' www.news.bbc.co.uk, 14 July 2006.
18 'Blair Battles for Survival,' *Daily Telegraph*, 2 February 2007, 2, and 'Blair's Fixer Arrested over the Honours Cover-up,' *Daily Telegraph*, 31 January 2007, 1.
19 Stevie Cameron, *On the Take: Crime, Corruption and Greed in the Mulroney Years* (Toronto: Random House, 1995).
20 Liberal Party of Canada, *Creating Opportunity: The Liberal Plan for Canada* (Ottawa: Author, 1993), chapter 6.
21 Tait, 'A Strong Foundation,' 1.
22 Kernaghan, 'Towards a Public Service Code of Conduct – and Beyond,' 40.
23 Tait, 'A Strong Foundation,' 3–5.
24 Canada, Office of the Auditor General, *Values and Ethics in the Federal Public Sector*, 12–17.
25 Tait, 'A Strong Foundation.'
26 Ibid., 8.
27 Canada, Canadian Centre for Management Development, *A Strong Foundation* (Ottawa: Author, 2006), 23.
28 Tait, 'A Strong Foundation,' 9.
29 Canada, Canadian Centre for Management Development, *A Strong Foundation*, 27.
30 Tait, 'A Strong Foundation,' 10.
31 Ibid., 11.
32 Ibid., 15–17.
33 Ibid., 19–20.
34 John W. Langford, 'Acting on Values: An Ethical Dead End for Public Servants,' *Canadian Public Administration* 47, 4 (Winter 2004): 432.
35 Canada, Treasury Board Secretariat, *Statement of Public Service Values and Ethics* (Ottawa: Author, 2003).

36 Canada, Office of Public Service Values and Ethics, *Values and Ethics Code for the Public Service* (Ottawa: Her Majesty the Queen in Right of Canada, 2003).
37 Ibid.
38 Langford, 'Acting on Values,' 432.
39 Ibid., 433.
40 Ibid., 437.
41 Peter Aucoin, 'A Profession of Public Administration? A Commentary on A Strong Foundation,' *Canadian Public Administration* 40, 1 (Spring 1997): 23–39.
42 Jocelyne Bourgon, 'Dedication,' in Canada, Canadian Centre for Management Development, *A Strong Foundation*, 4–5.
43 Canada, Privy Council Office, *Seventh Annual Report to the Prime Minister on the Public Service of Canada* (Ottawa: Author, 31 March 2000), 2.
44 Canada, Privy Council Office, *Ninth Annual Report to the Prime Minister on the Public Service of Canada* (Ottawa: Author, 29 March 2002), 11.
45 Canada, Privy Council Office, *Tenth Annual Report to the Prime Minister on the Public Service of Canada* (Ottawa: Author, 31 March 2003), 14.
46 Quoted in Canada, Office of the Auditor General, *Report of the Auditor General of Canada*, chapter 2, 'Accountability and Ethics in Government,' November 2003, 12–18.
47 Quoted in Canada, Office of the Auditor General, *Values and Ethics in the Federal Public Sector* (Ottawa: Report of the Auditor General of Canada, October 2000), chapter 12.
48 See ibid for a review of the survey, 12–10 and 12–11.
49 Langford, 'Acting on Values,' 445 and 450.
50 'Cutting Red Tape Was Part of Guité's Job Description,' www.canada.com, 23 May 2006.
51 'Ex-Health Bureaucrat Jailed for Fraud,' www.canada.com, 12 March 2005.
52 'Former Health Canada Director to Plead Guilty,' *Citizen* (Ottawa), 16 November 2005, A6.
53 'Ex-DND Bureaucrat Speaks Out,' *Globe and Mail*, 13 March 2004, A5.
54 'Former Federal Bureaucrat Pleads Guilty to Fraud,' *Globe and Mail*, 24 July 2007, A7.
55 'Charges Laid in Alleged Immigration Bribery Plot,' *Globe and Mail*, 17 December 2004, A7.
56 'Passport Officer Admits to Document Scam,' www.canada.com, 16 May 2007.
57 'Fisheries Audits Find More Abuses,' *Globe and Mail*, 24 April 2006, A10.
58 'Ex-Bureaucrat Jailed for 5½ Years in Theft of Blank Passports,' *Globe and Mail*, 18 April 2005, A9.

59 'Canadian Envoy Ran Saudi Spy Ring: Lawsuit,' *National Post*, 14 May 2004, A1 and A11.

60 '400 Million Federal Deal Bungled Twice, Auditor General,' *Globe and Mail*, 8 November 2006, A4.

61 'Feds Audit Employee Overtime,' *Times and Transcript* (Moncton), 9 October 2006, B1.

62 'Senior Civil Servant Charged in Income Trust Leak,' *Globe and Mail*, www.theglobeandmail.com, 15 February 2007.

63 'RCMP Charge Finance Official in Income Trust Investigation,' *Citizen* (Ottawa), www.canada.com/ottawacitizen, 15 February 2007.

64 'Globe Request Caused Crisis, Guité Trial Told,' *Globe and Mail*, 11 May 2006, A1.

65 'Big Spending Days Over for Ottawa,' *National Post*, 24 April 2004, RB1.

66 'Accountability Act's Five Year Lobbying Ban Sends Retiring ADMs out Early: Moore,' *Hill Times*, 16 July 2007, 1 and 7.

67 Consultation with a government of Canada official, Ottawa, May 2006. I wish to report that the official was a middle-level manager with the Department of Foreign Affairs who holds strong and rather negative views about the appointment of the last clerks to ambassadorial posts. I decided to report his views and not quote him verbatim.

68 U.K., House of Commons, Committee of Public Accounts, 'Proper Conduct of Public Business. Eighth Report from the Committee of Public Accounts' (London: HC154, 1993–4).

69 *Observer*, 16 October 1994, and *Guardian*, October 1994.

70 Retrieved 1995 from www.archive.official-documents.co.uk/document/parlment/nolan/nolan.htm.

71 Ibid.

72 U.K., Cabinet Office – Office of the Public Service, *The Civil Service Code* (London: Author, 1996).

73 U.K., Cabinet Office, *Civil Service Code* (London: Author, January 2006).

74 Baroness Usha Prashar, 'Westminster Explained Ethics and Accountability,' speech on Civil Service Code, (London: Civil Service Commissioners, 20 March 2003), 5.

75 U.K., Cabinet Office, *Summary of Responses to 2006 Consultation on New Civil Service Code* (London: Author, June 2006).

76 Ibid.

77 U.K., Cabinet Office, *Civil Service Code*, January 2006, n2.

78 U.K., Library, House of Commons, 'The Ministerial Code' (London, July 2005), 7.

79 Ibid., 5.

80 U.K., Cabinet Office, The Propriety and Ethics Teams, 'Code of Conduct for Special Advisors' (Undated), 1–7.
81 Lord Butler of Brockwell, in Amy Baker, *Prime Ministers: The Rule Book* (London: Methuen, 2000), preface.
82 Baroness Usha Prashar, 'Westminster Explained Ethics and Accountability,' 5.
83 Ibid., 9.
84 'Sir Andrew Turnbull's Valedictory Lecture,' London, 26 July 2005, mimeo.
85 See the Hutton inquiry and the Butler inquiry. Lord Hutton, *Report of the Inquiry into the Circumstances Surrounding the Death of Dr. David Kelly, C.M.G.* (London: House of Commons, Return to an Address of the Honourable the House of Commons, dated 28 January 2004); The Rt Hon. The Lord Butler of Brockwell, *Review of Intelligence on Weapons of Mass Destruction* (London: House of Commons, Report of a Committee of Privy Counsellors, Return to an Address of the Honourable the House of Commons, dated 14 July 2004).
86 See, among others, Canada, Office of the Auditor General, *Values and Ethics in the Federal Public Sector* (Ottawa: Report of the Auditor General of Canada, October 2000), 12–18.
87 Robert D. Behn, 'Management by Groping Along,' *Journal of Public Analysis and Management* 7 (Fall 1988): 643.
88 Canada, Office of the Auditor General, *Getting at Root Causes: Why Things Go Wrong in Government Programs* (Ottawa: Author, May 2004), mimeo, 6.
89 Ibid., 16, 17, 20, 23, and 24.
90 Consultations with a deputy minister, Ottawa, 10 June 2006.
91 Rafe Mair, a journalist, made this observation before Justice Gomery at the roundtable consultations, Commission of Inquiry into the Sponsorship Program and Advertising Activities, Vancouver, British Columbia, 25 October 2005, 12.
92 The former senior federal government official made the observation before Justice Gomery at the roundtable consultations, Commission of Inquiry into the Sponsorship Program and Advertising Activities, Moncton, New Brunswick, 31 August 2005.
93 Quoted in Christopher Hood and Martin Lodge, *The Politics of Public Service Bargains: Reward, Competency, Loyalty and Blame* (Oxford: Oxford University Press, 2006), 98.
94 Quoted in Donald J. Savoie, *Governing from the Centre: The Concentration of Power in Canadian Politics* (Toronto: University of Toronto Press, 1999), 156.
95 Quoted in 'Blair's Rule Full of Gaffes, Spin and Control Freakery, Says Mandarin,' www.thescotsman.scotsman.com, 10 December 2004.

96 Sir Christopher Foster, *Why Are We So Badly Governed?* (London: Public Management and Policy Association, October 2005), 11.
97 Julian LeGrand, *Motivation, Agency and Public Policy: Of Knights and Knaves, Pawns and Queens* (Oxford: Oxford University Press, 2003), 58.
98 Aucoin, 'A Profession of Public Administration? A Commentary on A Strong Foundation,' *Canadian Public Administration* 40, 1 (Spring 1997): 36.
99 Tait, 'A Strong Foundation,' 76.

7. Voices Everywhere

1 Albert O. Hirschman, *Exit, Voice and Loyalty: Responses to Decline in Firms* (Cambridge, MA: Harvard University Press, 1970).
2 Sir Andrew Turnbull quoted in Vernon Bogdanor, 'Oxford and the Mandarin Culture: The Past Is Gone,' *Oxford Review of Education* 32, 1 (February 2006): 159.
3 B. Guy Peters, *The Politics of Bureaucracy: A Comparative Perspective* (London: Longman, 1978).
4 'Sir Andrew Turnbull's Valedictory Lecture,' London, 26 July 2005, mimeo, 14.
5 Ibid., 11.
6 John Stuart Mill, *Considerations on Representative Government* (New York: Harper, 1869), 100.
7 J.R. Mallory, *The Structure of Canadian Government* (Toronto: Macmillan of Canada, 1971), 122.
8 Donald J. Savoie, *Thatcher, Reagan, Mulroney: In Search of a New Bureaucracy* (Pittsburgh: University of Pittsburgh Press, 1994), 26.
9 See Herman Finer, *The British Civil Service* (London: Allen and Unwin, 1937), 196; and Sharon Sutherland, 'Responsible Government and Ministerial Responsibility: Every Reform Is Its Own Problem,' *Canadian Journal of Political Science* 24, 1 (March 1991), 100.
10 Quoted in Henry Parris, *Constitutional Bureaucracy* (London: George Allen and Unwin, 1969), 80.
11 J.E. Hodgetts, *Pioneer Public Service: An Administrative History of the United Canadas 1841–1867* (Toronto: University of Toronto Press, 1969); and J.E. Hodgetts, *The Canadian Public Service: A Physiology of Government, 1867–1970* (Toronto: University of Toronto Press, 1973), 27.
12 Luther Gulick, 'Notes on the Theory of Organization,' in Luther Gulick and L. Urwick, eds, *Notes on the Theory of Organization* (New York: Institute of Public Administration, 1937).
13 Consultations with a former senior official with the Department of Indian and Northern Affairs, Ottawa, 22 May 2003.

14 See, among others, Christopher Pollitt, 'Joined-up Government: A Survey,' *Political Studies Review* 1 (2003): 46.

15 Edward C. Page and Bill Jenkins, *Policy Bureaucracy: Government with a Cast of Thousands* (Oxford: Oxford University Press, 2005), 121.

16 Stephen Goldsmith and William D. Eggers, *Governing by Network: The New Shape of the Public Sector* (Washington, DC: Brookings Institution Press, 2004).

17 Christopher Foster, *British Government in Crisis* (Oxford: Hart Publishing, 2005).

18 Lord Wilson of Dinton, 'The Mandarin Myth,' fourth lecture in a series on Tomorrow's Government, 1 March 2006, 16.

19 Canada, Treasury Board Secretariat, 'Management Accountability and Accountability for Horizontal Initiatives: Climate Change' (Ottawa: Author, 3 March 2004), 9.

20 Britain, *Wiring It Up: Whitehall's Management of Cross-Cutting Policies and Services* (London: Performance and Innovation Unit, 2000), 7.

21 Canada, Treasury Board Secretariat, 'Management Accountability and Accountability for Horizontal Initiatives,' 14.

22 Marcel Massé, 'Partners in the Management of Canada: The Changing Roles of Government and the Public Service,' paper presented at the 1993 John L. Manion Lecture, Canadian Centre for Management Development, Ottawa, 5 and 8.

23 Steven Rogelberg, D.J. Leach, and P.B. Warr, 'Not Another Meeting: Are Meeting Time Demands Related to Employee Well-Being?' *Journal of Applied Psychology* 91, 1 (March 2006): 86–96.

24 Pollitt, 'Joined-up Government,' 161.

25 Canada, Federal Accountability Act and Action Plan, www.faa.gc.ca, 2004.

26 OECD, *Government of the Future* (Paris: Author, 2000), 32.

27 'Ottawa Should Remove Itself from Own Fiscal Forecasting: Economist,' *Globe and Mail*, 13 October 2004, B9.

28 Canada, Federal Accountability Act and Action Plan, www.faa.gc.ca.

29 See Alan C. Cairns, *Charter versus Federalism* (Montreal and Kingston: McGill-Queen's University Press, 1992), 172.

30 Tom Parklington, 'Against Inflating Human Rights,' *Windsor Yearbook of Access to Justice* (Windsor, ON: University of Windsor, 1982), 85.

31 See, among others, L.A. Pal, *Public Policy Analysis: An Introduction* (Toronto: Methuen, 1987); G. Bruce Doern and Richard Phidd, *Canadian Public Policy: Ideas, Structure, Process* (Scarborough, ON: Nelson Canada, 1992); and John W. Langford and K. Lorne Brownsey, eds, *Think Tanks and Governance in the Asia Pacific Region* (Halifax: Institute for Research on Public Policy, 1991).

32 Lord Wilson of Dinton, 'The Mandarin Myth,' 26.
33 'British Firms Top Foreign Spending on US Lobbyists,' *The Times*, www.timesonline.co.uk., 20 January 2006.
34 See www.politicos.co.uk/category.jsp.
35 See, among others, 'How Business Pays for a Stay in Parliament,' *The Times*, www.timesonline.co.uk., 13 January 2006.
36 Quoted in Donald J. Savoie, *Governing from the Centre: The Concentration of Power in Canadian Politics* (Toronto: University of Toronto Press, 1999), 517.
37 John Major, *The Erosion of Parliamentary Government* (London: Centre for Policy Studies, 2003), 14.
38 Robin V. Sears, 'Harper vs. the Press Gallery,' *Policy Options* 27, 6 (July-August 2006): 5–8.
39 Ibid.
40 Lord Wilson of Dinton, 'The Mandarin Myth,' 17.
41 Jeffrey Simpson, 'The Brain of Our Existence: A Lot of Imitators but No Equals,' *Globe and Mail*, 16 May 2006, A13.
42 See, among others, Tom Resenstiel, *The Beat Goes On: President Clinton's First Year with the Media* (New York: The Twentieth Century Fund Press, 1994), chapter 7.
43 John Lloyd, 'The Media and Politics,' in Baroness Usha Prashar, ed., *Changing Times: Leading Perspectives on the Civil Service in the 21st Century and Its Enduring Values* (London: Office of the Civil Service Commissioners, 2005), 151–3.
44 Jeffrey Simpson, 'Shame on the Media for the Punch and Judy Sgro Show,' *Globe and Mail*, 5 February 2005, A19.
45 Douglas Fisher, 'A Celebration of 50 Great Years,' *Sun News*, www.ottsun.canoe.ca, 30 July 2006.
46 'I Was in Love and Still Am with Centre Block, Says Douglas Fisher,' *Hill Times*, newspaper online, www.thehilltimes.ca, 7 August 2006.
47 Foster, *British Government in Crisis*, 280.
48 See, among others, ibid., 13.
49 See, for example, Richard Johnson, André Blais, Henry Brady, and Jean Crête, *Letting the People Decide: Dynamics of a Canadian Election* (Montreal and Kingston: McGill-Queen's University Press, 1997).
50 Christopher Hood and Martin Lodge, *The Politics of Public Service Bargains: Reward, Competency, Loyalty and Blame* (Oxford: Oxford University Press, 2006), viii.
51 Canada, Access to Information Act, RSC, 1985, c.A-1, 39.
52 Giles Gherson, Public Opinion, *This Morning*, CBC broadcast, 3 December 1997.

53 Ibid.

54 Ibid.

55 Quoted in Donald J. Savoie, *Breaking the Bargain: Public Servants, Ministers, and Parliament* (Toronto: University of Toronto Press, 2003), 50.

56 Alasdair Roberts, 'Administrative Discretion and the Access to Information Act: An Internal Law on Open Government?' *Canadian Public Administration* 45, 2 (Summer 2002): 175.

57 'Contract Specifies That Consultant Leave No Paper Trail in Federal Offices,' www.macleans.ca, 10 October 2005.

58 Consultations with a deputy minister, Ottawa, 11 June 2006.

59 'Ottawa's $2–Billion Hit List,' *Globe and Mail*, 26 September 2006, A1.

60 'Finance at Odds over GST Cut,' *Globe and Mail*, 24 April 2006, A1, and 'Ambrose Not Yet Briefed on Science of Climate Change,' www.thehilltimes.ca, 16 October 2006.

61 The point was made by several participants at the Quebec City roundtable, 14 September 2005, Canada, Commission of Inquiry into the Sponsorship Program and Advertising Activities.

62 Hugh Winsor made these observations at the Toronto roundtable, 5 October 2005, Canada, Commission of Inquiry into the Sponsorship Program and Advertising Activities.

63 Quoted in Lord Wilson of Dinton, 'The Mandarin Myth,' 11.

64 John M. Reid made these observations in a letter to Justice Gomery that was made public in October 2005. Canada, Information Commission of Canada, Ottawa, 14 October 2005.

65 See, among others, 'MPs Lose Fight to Keep Their Travel Expenses Secret,' *Sunday Times*, 11 February 2007, 9.

66 'MPs Claims of £5 in Travel Expenses Show Big Variations,' *The Times*, 14 February 2007, 2.

67 'The Eco Minister's 11,000 Mile Car Claim,' *Sunday Times*, 18 February 2007, 8.

68 Marcia P. Miceli and Janet P. Near, *Blowing the Whistle: The Organizational and Legal Implications for Companies and Employers* (Toronto: Maxwell Macmillan Canada, 1992), 45.

69 Paul Thomas, 'Debating a Whistle-Blower Protection Act for Employees of the Government of Canada,' *Canadian Public Administration* 48, 2 (Summer 2005): 153.

70 Kenneth Kernaghan, 'Encouraging Rightdoing and Discouraging Wrong-doing: A Public Service Charter in Disclosure Legislation,' in Canada, Commission of Inquiry into the Sponsorship Program and Advertising Activities, *Restoring Accountability: Research Studies*, vol. 2, *The Public Service and Transparency* (Ottawa, 2006), 76.

71 Canada, 'Providing Real Protection for Whistleblowers,' 2005, www.faa.1fi.gc.ca.

72 Kernaghan, 'Encouraging Rightdoing and Discouraging Wrongdoing,' 94.

73 Consultation with a senior Canadian government official, Ottawa, 10 June 2006.

74 Kernaghan, 'Encouraging Rightdoing and Discouraging Wrongdoing,' 95.

75 Thomas, 'Debating a Whistle-Blower Protection Act for Employees of the Government of Canada,' 178.

76 Mark Bovens, *The Quest for Responsibility: Accountability and Citizenship in Complex Organisations* (Cambridge: Cambridge University Press, 1998), 195.

77 Ibid., 179.

78 'RCMP Poll Finds Unrest in the Ranks,' *Globe and Mail*, 30 September 2006, A14.

79 See, among others, Paul G. Thomas, 'The Past, Present and Future of Officers of Parliament,' *Canadian Public Administration* 46, 3 (Fall 2003): 288.

80 See Sharon Sutherland, 'Parliament's Unregulated Control Bureaucracy,' *Briefing Notes* (Kingston: Queen's University School of Policy Studies, 2002), 9.

81 Ibid.

82 'The Woman Who Enraged Voters,' *Citizen* (Ottawa), 9 June 2004, B1.

83 Privacy Commissioner of Canada, 'Privacy Commissioner Launches Charter Challenge,' News Release (Ottawa, 21 June 2002).

84 Ibid.

85 Quoted in Paco Francoli, 'Access Commissioner Reid: Parliament Doesn't Take Me to Task: It's Lost Interest,' *Hill Times*, 28 October 2002, 1.

86 Michelle Falardeau-Ramsay, quoted in *Parliament and Government* 15 (September 2002): 17.

87 Thomas, 'Debating a Whistle-Blower Protection Act for Employees of the Government of Canada,' 171.

88 'The Role of the National Audit Office,' www.nao.org.uk.

89 Oonagh Gay, 'Officers of Parliament – A Comparative Perspective' (London: House of Commons, Research Paper 03/77, 20 October 2003).

90 'Judicial Appointments Commission – History,' 2005, www.judicialappointments.gov.uk.

91 Baroness Usha Prashar, 'Speech at the Annual ILEX Luncheon,' Judicial Appointments Commission, Clothworkers Hall, London, 17 May 2006, 2.

92 Thomas, 'The Past, Present and Future of Officers of Parliament,' 311.

93 'The Chief Justice Gives Voice to Unwritten Principles,' *Globe and Mail*, 15 May 2006, A13.

94 See, among others, 'Supreme Court Pick Favours Restraint,' www.canada.
    com, Network, 28 February 2006.
95 See, among others, 'Thompson Set up Ottawa Office to Promote Province,'
    www.herald.ns.co, 18 January 2006.

8. Searching for Loyalty

1 Robert Armstrong, 'The Duties and Responsibilities of Civil Servants in
   Relation to Ministers,' in Geoffrey Marshall, ed., *Ministerial Responsibility*
   (Oxford: Oxford University Press, 1989), 140–1.
2 The Right Honourable Tony Blair, 'The Civil Service Reform, Delivery and Values,' Speech to the Delivery and Values Event, London, 24 February 2004, 3.
3 Ibid.
4 'Naked Ambition,' *Western Standard*, 13 June 2005, 18.
5 Quoted in www.cbc.ca/story/canada/national, 18 May 2005.
6 'Former Liberal David Emerson Defects to Tories,' www.uofaweb.
   ualberta.ca/gov, 7 February 2006.
7 'PM Picks Muslim Liberal MP as Adviser on Mideast,' *Globe and Mail*,
   9 August 2006, A1.
8 'Crossing the Floor,' *Globe and Mail*, 8 January 2007, A1.
9 Canada saw the defections of Jack Horner from the Conservatives to the
   Liberals in the 1970s, Jean Lapierre from the Liberals to the Bloc Québécois
   and then back to the Liberals under Martin, Scott Brison from the Conservatives to the Liberals in 2005, and the list goes on. In Britain, the gang of
   four (Shirley Williams, David Owen, Ray Jenkins, and Bill Rodgers) left the
   Labour party in 1981 to form the Social Democratic party, and a total of
   twenty-eight Labour MPs and one Conservative MP eventually joined.
   Alan Haworth left the Conservative party to joint Labour in 1999, Shaun
   Woodward left the Conservatives to join Labour in 1999, Paul Marsden left
   Labour to join the Liberal Democrats in 2001, and here too the list goes on.
10 Quoted in 'Political Defections in Canada Go Back to 1869,' www.ctc.ca/
    ctvnews, 17 May 2005.
11 'If He Loses, Will He Quit?' *Toronto Star*, www.thestar.com, 30 August 2006.
12 See, among others, 'Tories Quietly Seek to Hire Liberal Staffers,' *Telegraph
    Journal* (Saint John), 20 January 2006, 1.
13 See Donald J. Savoie, *Visiting Grandchildren: Economic Development in the
    Maritimes* (Toronto: University of Toronto Press, 2006).
14 James Q. Wilson, *The Politics of Regulation* (New York: Basic Books, 1980).
15 James Q. Wilson, *Bureaucracy: What Government Agencies Do and Why They
    Do It* (New York: Basic Books, 1989), 159.

16 Blair, 'The Civil Service Reform, Delivery and Values,' 4.
17 Oliver James, *The Executive Agency Revolution in Whitehall: Public Interest versus Bureau-Shaping Perspectives* (London: Palgrave Macmillan, 2003), 136–7.
18 Edward C. Page and Bill Jenkins, *Policy Bureaucracy: Government with a Cast of Thousands* (Oxford: Oxford University Press, 2005), 5.
19 Canada, Privy Council Office, 'Discussion Paper on Values and Ethics in the Public Service' (Ottawa: Author, December 1996), 57.
20 See, for example, Donald J. Savoie, *Thatcher, Reagan, Mulroney: In Search of a New Bureaucracy* (Pittsburgh: Pittsburgh University Press, 1994).
21 Canada, Privy Council Office, 'Discussion Paper on Values and Ethics in the Public Service,' 37.
22 See, for example, presentation made by Nevil Johnson to the Treasury and Civil Service subcommittee, 29 January 1986 (London: Her Majesty's Stationery Office), 170–1.
23 Quoted in Savoie, *Thatcher, Reagan, Mulroney,* 317–18.
24 The study was prepared by the Public Management Research Centre for the Treasury Board Secretariat and made public in early 1998. See 'PS Leaders Put Politics before Public Interest, Report Says,' *Citizen* (Ottawa), 11 November 1997, A3.
25 See Donald J. Savoie, *Breaking the Bargain: Public Servants, Ministers, and Parliament* (Toronto: University of Toronto Press, 2003), chapter 7.
26 J.E. Hodgetts, *The Canadian Public Service: A Physiology of Government, 1867–1970* (Toronto: University of Toronto Press, 1973), 208.
27 Canada, Privy Council Office, 'Discussion Paper on Values and Ethics in the Public Service,' 19.
28 See, among others, Savoie, *Breaking the Bargain*, and Christopher Foster, *British Government in Crisis* (Oxford: Hart Publishing, 2005).
29 Quoted in R.A.W. Rhodes, 'United Kingdom: Everybody but Us,' in Patrick Weller and R.A.W. Rhodes, eds, *The Changing World of Top Officials: Mandarins or Valets?* (Buckingham: Open University Press, 2001), 143.
30 Quoted in ibid., 150.
31 See contributions by practitioners in various issues of *Canadian Public Administration* and *Public Administration*.
32 Consultation with a senior Canadian government official, Ottawa, 21 August 2006.
33 Christopher Hood and Martin Lodge, *The Politics of Public Service Bargains: Reward, Competency, Loyalty and Blame* (Oxford: Oxford University Press, 2006), 77.
34 Ibid., 80.

35 Patrick Weller and R.A.W. Rhodes, 'Introduction: Enter Centre Stage,' in Weller and Rhodes, eds, *The Changing World of Top Officials*, 1.

36 B. Guy Peters, *Institutional Theory in Political Science* (New York: Continuum, 2005), chapter 5.

37 See, among others, Julian LeGrand, *Motivation, Agency and Public Policy: Of Knights and Knaves, Pawns and Queens* (Oxford: Oxford University Press, 2003).

38 Ibid., 141.

39 James Travers, 'Mandarins Learning to Like Harper,' *Toronto Star*, www.thestar.com, 22 August 2006.

40 'Harper Cleans House in Ottawa,' *Toronto Star*, www.thestar.com, 28 August 2006.

41 R.A.W. Rhodes and Patrick Weller, 'Conclusions: Antipodean Exceptionalism, European Traditionalism,' in Rhodes and Weller, eds, *The Changing World of Top Officials*, 238.

42 Ibid.

43 Ibid.

44 James, *The Executive Agency Revolution in Whitehall*, 141.

45 Hood and Lodge, *The Politics of Public Service Bargains*, 65.

46 Ezra Suleiman, *Dismantling Democratic States* (Princeton: Princeton University Press, 2005), 207.

47 Morley Gunderson, D. Hyatt, and C. Riddell, 'Pay Differences between the Government and Private Sector: Labour Force Survey and Census Estimates,' discussion paper (Ottawa: Canadian Policy Research Network, 2002).

48 See, for example, R.F. Ellitt and K. Duffus, 'What Has Been Happening to Pay in the Public Service Sector of the British Economy? Development over the Period 1970–1992,' *British Journal of Industrial Relations* 34, 1 (1996): 51–85.

49 Morley Gunderson and W. Craig Riddell, *Labour Market Economics: Theory, Evidence and Policy in Canada* (Toronto: McGraw-Hill Ryerson, 1993).

50 'Cost of Swelling PS Skyrockets,' www.canada.com, 30 July 2007.

51 'Expenditure Review of Federal Public Sector – Overview,' www.tbs.sct.gc.ca/spsm-rqsp. The report is dated November 2006.

52 These points were made by Jean-Guy Fleury, a senior Canadian government official in 'Performance Management Program in the Canadian Federal Public Service,' his presentation to the Governance for Performance in the Public Sector seminar, OECD, Berlin, 13–14 March 2002, 7.

53 Ibid.

54 Quoted in ibid., 8.

55 Ibid., 11.
56 Quoted in 'Don't Get a Bonus, You Should Be Fired, PS Execs Told,' News at www.canada.com, 10 May 2004.
57 Kathryn May, 'Disgraced Bureaucrat Got $7,000 Bonus,' News at www.canada.com, 1 November 2003.
58 Ibid.
59 'PS Executives Cash in as Bond Sales Fall,' www.canada.com, 13 June 2005.
60 Public Policy Forum, 'Canada's Public Service in the 21st Century, A Discussion Paper' (Ottawa: Author, April 2007), 9.
61 Ibid., 76–81.
62 See, among others, Patricia Ingraham, 'Linking Leadership to Performance in Public Organizations' (Paris: OECD – Public Management [PUMA], June 2001).
63 'Supplements to Ex-Deputy Ministers on the Rise,' Globe and Mail, 2 July 2007, A4.
64 See Frederick C. Mosher, Democracy and the Public Service, 2nd ed. (New York: Oxford University Press, 1982), 154.
65 C.E.S. Franks, The Parliament of Canada (Toronto: University of Toronto Press, 1987), 237.
66 Ekos conducted the survey in May 2001 for Canada, Public Service Commission, The Road Ahead: Perceptions of the Public Service (Ottawa: Author, 2002), 1.

9. The View from the Bottom: A Big Whale That Can't Swim

1 Consultations with a director-level Canadian government official, Moncton, New Brunswick, 6 September 2006.
2 Ekos Research, Perceptions of Government Service Delivery (Ottawa: Ekos Research Associates, 1996), 10.
3 See, among others, George Radwanski, Trudeau (Toronto: Taplinger, 1978).
4 See, among others, Donald J. Savoie, Regional Economic Development: Canada's Search for Solutions (Toronto: University of Toronto Press, 1992).
5 David Good, The Politics of Public Management: The HRDC Audit of Grants and Contributions (Toronto: University of Toronto Press, 2003).
6 Ibid.
7 Robin Clarke, New Democratic Processes: Better Decisions, Stronger Democracy (London: Institute for Public Policy Research, 2002), 4.
8 Ibid., 20 and 24.
9 Conservative Democracy Task Force, An End to Sofa Government: Better Working of Prime Minister and Cabinet (London: Author, June 2007), 2.

10 See, among others, Carey Goglianese, 'The Internet and Citizen Participation in Rulemaking,' John F. Kennedy School of Government, Harvard University, RWPO4-044, November 2004, 9.

11 Ibid.; and see also Sandford Borins, Kenneth Kernaghan, and David Brown, *Digital State at the Leading Edge: Lessons from Canada* (Toronto: University of Toronto Press, forthcoming), 4.

12 Ross Fergusson and Barry Griffiths, 'Thin Democracy? Parliamentarians, Citizens and the Influence of Blogging on Political Engagement,' *Parliamentary Affairs*, www.oxfordjournals.org/cgi/reprint, 10 February 2006.

13 Wilson Wong and Eric Welch, 'Does E-Government Promote Accountability? A Comparative Analysis of Website Openness and Government Accountability,' *Governance* 17, 2 (April 2004): 275.

14 U.K., 10 Downing Street website, www.number10.gov.uk/-epetitions, 15 February 2007.

15 '590,682 Sign Britain's Biggest Petition,' *Daily Mail*, www.dailymail.co.uk, 27 January 2007.

16 'Road Rage,' *The Times*, 14 February 2007, 16.

17 U.K., 10 Downing Street website, www.number10.gov.uk/output11050. asp, 21 February 2007.

18 Ibid.

19 Canada, Office of the Auditor General, 'Information Technology: Government On-Line,' chapter 1, *Report of the Auditor General of Canada* (Ottawa: Author, 2003), 1.

20 Wong and Welch, 'Does E-Government Promote Accountability?' 275.

21 Borins et al., 'Introduction,' *Digital State at the Leading Edge*.

22 Perri 6, 'Don't Try This at Home: Lessons from England,' in Borins et al., *Digital State at the Leading Edge*, 328.

23 See Helen Margetts, 'E-Government in Britain – A Decade On,' *Parliamentary Affairs* 59, 2 (March 2006): 257.

24 Ibid.

25 'Out-of-Control Spending Suspected at DND: Report,' www.canada.com, News, 13 July 2004, and 'Computer Revamp Costs Soar,' www.thestar.com, 22 April 2006.

26 Margetts, 'E-Government in Britain,' 254.

27 Perri 6, 'Don't Try This at Home.'

28 'The NHS's £20 Bn Computer Isn't Working,' *Daily Mail*, 13 February 2007, 2.

29 See, among others, Canada, Treasury Board Secretariat, *Quality Services Guide: Who Is the Client? A Discussion Paper* (Ottawa, June 1996).

30 Jon Pierre, 'The Marketization of the State: Citizens, Consumers, and the Emergence of the Public Market,' in B. Guy Peters and Donald J. Savoie, eds, *Governance in a Changing Environment* (Montreal and Kingston: McGill-Queen's University Press, 1993).

31 Consultations with a front-line civil servant employed with the Atlantic Canada Opportunities Agency (ACOA), an economic development agency of the Government of Canada, Moncton, 11 September 2006.

32 See, among many others, Gilles Bouchard, 'Les relations fonctionnaires-citoyens: Facteurs d'influence,' Thèse de doctorat, Département de science politique, Université de Montréal, 1986; Christopher Pollitt, 'Bringing Consumers into Performance Measurement,' *Policy and Politics* 16, 2 (1988): 77–87; Katherine A. Graham and Susan D. Phillips, 'Citizen Engagement: Beyond the Customer Revolution,' *Canadian Public Administration* 40, 2 (1997): 255–73.

33 Consultation with a Canadian government official with a social development department, Ottawa, 12 September 2006.

34 Consultations with a front-line civil servant employed with ACOA, Moncton, 11 September 2006.

35 Consultations with a U.K. government official, London, 8 February 2007.

36 See Donald J. Savoie, *Governing from the Centre: The Concentration of Power in Canadian Politics* (Toronto: University of Toronto Press, 1999).

37 Ibid., chapter 9.

38 Consultation with the Hon. Andy Scott, Sussex, New Brunswick, 9 September 2006.

39 See Donald J. Savoie, *The Politics of Public Spending in Canada* (Toronto: University of Toronto Press, 1990), 213.

40 Savoie, *Governing from the Centre*, 286.

41 J.R. Mallory, *The Structure of Canadian Government* (Toronto: Macmillan of Canada, 1971), 122.

42 Quoted in Savoie, *Governing from the Centre*, 287.

43 Ibid.

44 Barbara Wake Carroll and David Siegel, *Service in the Field: The World of Front-Line Public Servants* (Montreal and Kingston: McGill-Queen's University Press, 1999), 47.

45 Jacques Bourgault, 'De Kafka au Net: La lutte incessante du sous-ministre pour contrôler son agenda,' *Gestion* 22, 2 (Summer 1997): 21–2.

46 Ibid.

47 Quoted in Savoie, *Governing from the Centre*, 278.

48 Graham K. Wilson and Anthony Barker, 'Bureaucrats and Politicians in Britain,' *Governance* 16, 3 (July 2003): 360.

49 Ibid., 361.
50 Ekos Research, *Perceptions of Government Service Delivery,* viii, ix, and 35–8.
51 Canada, Treasury Board Secretariat, 'A Policy Framework for Service Improvement in the Government of Canada' (Ottawa: Author, undated).
52 Canada, Treasurer Board Secretariat, 'Citizen Centered Service: From Research to Results' (Ottawa: Author, undated).
53 The survey was carried out in late 2005 and early 2006. The results have not been made public. The information was provided by a senior Treasury Board Secretariat official, Ottawa, 12 September 2006.
54 'People, Service and Trust,' *Canadian Government Executive* 11, 5 (June-July 2006): 6.
55 Consultation with a line-department official, Ottawa, 13 September 2006.
56 Consultation with a senior Treasury Board Secretariat official, Ottawa, 13 September 2006.
57 Carroll and Siegel, *Service in the Field,* 200–3.
58 See, among others, Accenture, *Leadership in Customer Service: Building the Trust,* 7th report, undated, 100–1.
59 Ibid., 10.
60 Bernard Herdan, *The Customer Voice in Transforming Public Services: Independent Report from the Review of the Charter Mark Scheme and Measurement/ Customer Satisfaction with Public Services* (London: Cabinet Office, June 2006), 6.
61 Mary Tetlow, 'The Canadian Experience,' www.publicfinance.co.uk, 30 January 2004.
62 Richard Mulgan, *Holding Power to Account: Accountability in Modern Democracy* (Basingstoke: Palgrave Macmillan, 2003), 197.
63 www.servicecanada.gc.ca.
64 This information was provided by C.E.S. Franks in correspondence with the author, dated 24 April 2007.
65 Taylor Cole, *The Canadian Bureaucracy and Federalism, 1947–1965,* (Denver: University of Denver, Social Science Foundation and Graduate School of International Studies, Monograph Series in World Affairs, vol. 3, 1965–6), 19.
66 This and other information is available at www.civilservice.gov.uk/ management/statistics/publications.
67 Guy Lodge and Ben Rogers, *Whitehall's Black Box: Accountability and Performance in the Senior Civil Service* (London: Institute for Public Policy Research, 2006), 45.
68 Ibid., 47.
69 Ibid., 49–52.

70 Carroll and Siegel, *Service in the Field*, 119.
71 'Cabinet Cannot Keep All Its Secrets,' *National Post*, 12 July 2002, A1.
72 'Politician Laments Reversal of Firings Over Emails Porn,' *Globe and Mail*, 13 July 2004, A1.
73 'Civil Servants to Be Held Accountable for Ad Scam: Brison,' www.canada.com, 11 October 2005.
74 Jean-Jacques Blais, among others, made the case about the 'bureaucratic inability to impose sanctions' at the Toronto roundtable, Commission of Inquiry into the Sponsorship Program and Advertising Activities, 5 October 2005. See also 'NRCan's Institutional Inertia Impedes Renewable Energy Development in Canada: Advocates,' *Hill Times*, 10 July 2006.
75 'Ottawa Fires Dissident Scientists,' www.globeandmail.com, 15 July 2004.
76 'Liberals Unveil World Class Audit Policy,' www.canada.com, 22 October 2005.
77 Canada, Treasury Board Secretariat, *Management in the Government of Canada: A Commitment to Continuous Improvement* (Ottawa: Author, October 2005), 17. See also 1–21 and 30–9.
78 Ibid., 38.
79 Ibid. See also 'Bureaucrats Warned of Total Constipation,' *National Post*, 17 November 2005, A8.
80 Ian Clark, *Ottawa's Principal Decision-Making and Advisory Committee* (Ottawa: Privy Council Office, December 1993), 15.
81 Savoie, *The Politics of Public Spending in Canada*, 118.
82 Savoie, *Governing from the Centre*, 232.
83 Canada, Office of the Auditor General, *Report of the Auditor General of Canada: An Overview of the Federal Government's Expenditure Management System* (Ottawa: Author, 2006), 15.
84 Consultation with a Canadian government official, Ottawa, October 2005.
85 Canada, Task Force on the Coordination of Federal Activities in the Regions, *Delivering Federal Policies in the Regions: Partnership in Action*, Final Report (Ottawa, July 2002), 12.
86 See, among others, Good, *The Politics of Public Management*.
87 U.K., *Capability Reviews: The Findings of the First Four Reviews* (London: Stationery Office, 2006), 18 and Guy Lodge, 'Is Whitehall Fit for Purpose?' (London: Institute for Public Policy Research, December 2006).
88 See, for example, 'Publication of First Capability Reviews Steps Up Civil Service Reform,' www.cabinetoffice.gov.uk, news release, 19 July 2006.
89 See Michael Bichard, 'Public Sector Reform' (London: Institute for Public Policy Research, 2007), 6.

90 'Another Reason to Distrust School Rankings,' www.Canada.com, 16 June 2006.
91 Gwyn Bevan and Christopher Hood, 'Have Targets Improved Performance in the English NHS?' downloaded from www.bmj.com, February 2006, 420. See also Gwyn Bevan and Christopher Hood, 'What's Measured Is What Matters: Target and Gaming in the English Health Care System,' *Public Administration* 84, 3 (2006): 517–38.
92 See, among others, Christopher Hood, 'Control, Bargains and Cheating: The Politics of Public Service Reform,' *Journal of Public Administration Research* 12, 3 (July 2002): 309–32.
93 Ian D. Clark and Harry Swain, 'Distinguishing the Real from the Surreal in Management Reform,' paper prepared for *Canadian Public Administration*, 31 January 2005, mimeo, 6.
94 Ibid., 7.
95 Ibid., 9.
96 Sir Peter Gershon, *Releasing Resources to the Front Line* (London: Her Majesty's Treasury, 2004).
97 Perri 6, 'Don't Try This at Home,' 330.
98 Conservative Democracy Task Force, *An End to Sofa Government*, 1.
99 Jacques Bourgault, *Profile of Deputy Ministers in the Government of Canada* (Ottawa: Canada School of Public Service, 2005), 3.
100 See www.civilservice.gov.uk/archive/deliveryandreform/seniorcivilservice, 24 September 2006.
101 See, for example, 'Publication of First Capability Reviews Steps Up Civil Service Reform.'

10. The View from the Top: 'I'm Like Hank Snow, I Have Been Everywhere, Man'

1 Donald J. Savoie, *Breaking the Bargain: Public Servants, Ministers, and Parliament* (Toronto: University of Toronto Press, 2003).
2 Jean Chrétien, *Straight from the Heart* (Toronto: Key Porter Books, 1985), 18.
3 The former clerk and secretary to the cabinet made these observations at a Toronto roundtable, Commission of Inquiry into the Sponsorship Program and Advertising Activities, 5 October 2005.
4 Hugh Winsor made this observation at a Toronto roundtable, Commission of Inquiry into the Sponsorship Program and Advertising Activities, 5 October 2005.
5 Consultation with a deputy minister, Ottawa, 12 September 2006.

6 See, among others, David Richards and Martin J. Smith, 'Interpreting the World of Political Elites,' *Public Administration* 82, 4 (December 2004): 121–46.
7 See, among others, Christopher Foster, *British Government in Crisis* (Oxford: Hart Publishing, 2005).
8 Donald J. Savoie, *Governing from the Centre: The Concentration of Power in Canadian Politics* (Toronto: University of Toronto Press, 1999), and Foster, *British Government in Crisis*, chapter 12.
9 Foster, *British Government in Crisis*, 159.
10 See, Taylor Cole, *The Canadian Bureaucracy and Federalism* (Denver: University of Denver, 1966), 2.
11 Gordon Osbaldeston, *Keeping Deputy Ministers Accountable* (Toronto: McGraw-Hill Ryerson, 1989).
12 Canada, Treasury Board Secretariat, *Federal Institutional Governance Universe* (Ottawa: Author, 2004). See also 'Ottawa Boasts over 453,000 People on Payroll,' *Hill Times*, www.thehilltimes.ca, and Public Policy Forum, *Canada's Public Service in the 21st Century – A Discussion Paper* (Ottawa: Author, 2007), 6.
13 'The Machine Sends Its Thanks,' *Toronto Star*, www.thestar.com, 24 September 2006.
14 Based on correspondence with David Hill, director of communications, 10 Downing Street, 23 January 2007.
15 Edward C. Page and Bill Jenkins, *Policy Bureaucracy: Government with a Cast of Thousands* (Oxford: Oxford University Press, 2005), 167.
16 Consultations with a former senior Canadian government official, Moncton, New Brunswick, 21 November 2006.
17 C. Hood, Martin Lodge, and C. Clifford, *Civil Service Policy-Making Competencies in the German BMWi and British DTI: A Comparative Analysis Based on Six Case Studies* (London: Smith Institute, 2002), 30.
18 See, for example, James Travers, 'Mandarins Learning to Like Harper,' *Toronto Star*, www.thestar.com, 22 August 2006.
19 See, among others, Thomas Axworthy, 'Of Secretaries to Princes,' *Canadian Public Administration* 31, 2 (1988): 252.
20 Denis Smith, 'President and Parliament: The Transformation of Parliamentary Government in Canada,' in Thomas A. Hockin, ed., *Apex of Power: The Prime Minister and Political Leadership in Canada*, 2nd ed. (Scarborough: Prentice-Hall, 1977), 114.
21 Chrétien, *Straight from the Heart*, 85.
22 See, among others, Sharon Sutherland, 'Responsible Government and Ministerial Responsibility: Every Reform Is Its Own Problem,' *Canadian Journal of Political Science* 24, 1 (March 1991): 101–3.

23 Walter Bagehot, *The English Constitution* (Oxford: Oxford University Press, 1958), 4.
24 Conservative Democracy Task Force, *An End to Sofa Government: Better Working of Prime Minister and Cabinet* (London: Author, 2007), 1.
25 See, for example, Jeffrey Simpson, *The Friendly Dictatorship* (Toronto: McClelland and Stewart, 2001).
26 See Savoie, *Governing from the Centre*.
27 See, among others, M. Burch and I. Holliday, *The British Cabinet System* (London: Prentice Hall, 1996).
28 See, among others, Jeffrey Simpson, 'From Pariah to Messiah: Send in the Clerk,' *Globe and Mail*, 9 March 2005, A15.
29 Ibid.
30 U.K., Parliament, Select Committee on Public Administration, *Minutes of Evidence*, 1 April 2004, 1 and 2.
31 Ibid., 5.
32 Eddie Goldenberg, *The Way It Works: Inside Ottawa* (Toronto: McClelland and Stewart, 2006), 83.
33 'All LAV IIIs to Be Replaced within the Year,' *Globe and Mail*, 3 April 2007, A1.
34 In the case of Britain, see, among others, Conservative Democracy Task Force, *An End to Sofa Government*.
35 'Poll Crafted to Support a Certain Response,' *Globe and Mail*, 16 July 2007, A4.
36 See, for example, Peter Hennessy, 'Rulers and Servants of the State: Blair Style of Government 1997–2004,' *Parliamentary Affairs* 58, 1 (2005): 8.
37 Quoted in ibid.
38 U.K., Parliament, Select Committee on Public Administration, *Minutes of Evidence*, questions 540–56, 21 October 2004, 3.
39 Ibid., 4.
40 See, among others, Foster, *British Government in Crisis*, 161.
41 Consultation with Hon. Bernard Valcourt, Ottawa, various dates.
42 See, among others, 'Labour Party Battle Heats up in Britain,' *Globe and Mail*, 9 September 2006, A12.
43 See also Oliver H. Woskinsky, *The French Deputy* (London: Lexington Books, 1973), and James L. Payne, *Patterns of Conflict in Columbia* (New Haven: Yale University Press, 1968).
44 See Donald J. Savoie, *The Politics of Public Spending in Canada* (Toronto: University of Toronto Press, 1990), 241.
45 Quoted in Timothy W. Plumptre, *Beyond the Bottom Line: Management in Government* (Halifax: Institute for Research on Public Policy, 1988), 130. See also Savoie, *The Politics of Public Spending in Canada*, 192.

46 'Harper's Staff, Media Battle over Access Issues,' www.ctv.ca/servlet/
   CTVNews, 27 March 2006.
47 'Harper's Role as Point Man Questioned,' *Globe and Mail*, www.
   theglobeandmail.com, 27 April 2007.
48 Goldenberg, *The Way It Works*, 97–8.
49 Ibid.
50 Consultation with the Hon. Mitchell Sharp, Ottawa, March 1998. See also
   Donald J. Savoie, 'The Rise of Court Government,' *Canadian Journal of Political Science* 32, 4 (December 1999): 660–1.
51 'Harper's PR Aides Secretly Ask Cabinet Staff to Critique Bosses,' *Globe and
   Mail*, 17 November 2006, A4.
52 Quoted in 'Liberals Hire Lobbyist to Run Their War Room,' *Citizen*
   (Ottawa), 16 November 2005, A1.
53 'Lobbyist Sought $9 Million to Set Bush Meeting,' *New York Times*,
   www.nytimes.com, 10 November 2005.
54 'Top Tory Organizers Challenge Lobby Rules,' *Globe and Mail*, 12 June 2006,
   A1.
55 Harvie André made this observation on a number of occasions, including
   on 19 October 2005 at the Edmonton roundtable of the Commission of
   Inquiry into the Sponsorship Program and Advertising Activities.
56 See, for example, Foster, *British Government in Crisis*, 177.
57 Joel D. Aberbach, Robert D. Putnam, and Bert A. Rockman, *Bureaucrats and
   Politicians in Western Democracies* (Cambridge, MA: Harvard University
   Press, 1981).
58 See, among many others, Savoie, *Breaking the Bargain*, and Foster, *British
   Government in Crisis*.
59 Ezra N. Suleiman, *Politics, Power and Bureaucracy in France* (Princeton:
   Princeton University Press, 1974), 5.
60 Lawrence Martin, 'The Unwritten Bylaw of Bytown: Fall in Line or Fall out
   of Favour,' *Globe and Mail*, 9 August 2006, A1 and A6.
61 Jim Travers, 'Branding Team Harper,' www.thestar.com, 6 February 2007.
62 Canada, Commission of Inquiry into the Sponsorship Program and Advertising Activities, Ottawa, vol. 65, 28 January 2005, 11,256.
63 Ibid., vol. 72, 8 February 2005, 12,563 and 12,567.
64 Ibid., vol. 71, 7 February 2005, 12,415–16.
65 Ibid., 12,415.
66 Ibid., 12,339.
67 Ibid., vol. 62, 25 January 2005, 10,906.
68 Ibid., 11,045.
69 Ibid.

70 Ibid., vol. 60, 21 January 2005, 10,509.
71 Ibid., 10,600.
72 Ibid., 10,600, 10,603.
73 Ibid., vol. 67, 1 February 2005, 11,547.
74 Ibid., 11,548.
75 Ibid., 11,570.
76 Ibid., 11,640.
77 Ibid., vol. 68, 2 February 2005, 11,798.
78 Cited in ibid., 11,781.
79 Ibid., cited in vol. 67, 1 February 2005, 11,622.
80 Ibid., vol. 68, 2 February 2005, 11,743.
81 Ibid.
82 Ibid., vol. 70, 4 February 2005, 12,119–20.
83 Ibid., vol. 71, 7 February 2005, 12,319 and 12,326.
84 Ibid., 12,350.
85 Jacques Bourgault, *Profile of Deputy Ministers in the Government of Canada* (Ottawa: Canada School of Public Service, 2005), 11.
86 Ibid., 12.
87 Quoted in 'The Hole in Accountability,' *Citizen* (Ottawa), 18 November 2006, B4.
88 Osbaldeston, *Keeping Deputy Ministers Accountable.*
89 Bourgault, *Profile of Deputy Ministers in the Government of Canada*, 14.
90 C.E.S. Franks, 'Tenure of Canadian Deputy Ministers, 1996–2005: Notes and Comments,' Kingston, Ontario, unpublished paper, 29 June 2006, 7.
91 Quoted in 'We're Not Very Good Leaders and We Can't Make Decisions, Insecure Bureaucrats Say,' *Citizen* (Ottawa), 3 October 2006, A1.
92 'The Hole in Accountability,' B1 and B4.
93 Franks, 'Tenure of Canadian Deputy Ministers, 1996–2005,' 15.
94 Ibid., 18.
95 Canada, Public Service Commission of Canada, *Statistical Study on Priority Appointments of Ministers' Staff* (Ottawa: Author, 4 May 2006), 2.
96 Peter Aucoin, 'Influencing Public Policy and Decision-Making: Power Shifts,' notes for presentation to the APEX Symposium 2004, 'Parliament, the People and the Public Service,' Ottawa, 6–7 October 2004, 4.
97 Ibid.
98 Colin Campbell, *Executive Political Leadership in Canada* (Washington, DC: Association for Canadian Studies, 1989), 89.
99 'Accountability Bill Will Saddle PS with Political Cronies,' *Citizen* (Ottawa), 10 October 2006, A1.

100 Brian Marson, *Organizational Alzheimer's: A Quiet Crisis* (Ottawa: Treasury Board Secretariat, 2006), 7.
101 Quoted in Goldenberg, *The Way It Works*, 73.
102 U.K., Cabinet Office, *Ministerial Conduct* (London: Her Majesty's Stationery Office, 2001), 8.
103 Sir Robin Butler told me that, contrary to popular belief, it was a journalist, not he, who coined the phrase 'sofa government.'
104 Alan Doig, '45 Minutes of Infamy? Hutton, Blair and the Invasion of Iraq,' *Parliamentary Affairs* 58, 1 (2005): 109.
105 James Humphreys, 'The Iraq Dossier and the Meaning of Spin,' *Parliamentary Affairs* 58, 1 (2005): 156–70.
106 Ibid., 166.
107 Ibid., 165.
108 *Terms of Reference*, www.bnutlerreview.org.uk/.
109 The Review of Intelligence on Weapons of Mass Destruction, Press Conference, opening statement by the chairman, The Right Honourable Lord Butler of Brockwell, London, 14 July 2004, 5.
110 Quoted in Anthony Gless, 'Evidence-Based Policy or Policy-Based Evidence? Hutton and the Government's Use of Secret Intelligence,' *Parliamentary Affairs* 58, 1 (2005): 140.
111 Ibid., 141.
112 Rodric Braithwaite, a former JIC chairman and ambassador to the Soviet Union and foreign policy adviser to Prime Minister John Major, quoted in ibid., 143.
113 Memorandum from Alastair Campbell to John Scarlett, dated 17 September 2002.
114 U.K. Parliament, Select Committee on Public Administration, *Minutes of Evidence*, questions 352–9, 14 March 2002, 3.
115 Ibid., 2.
116 Ibid., 3.
117 U.K., Parliament, Select Committee on Public Administration, *Minutes of Evidence*, questions 300–19, 7 March 2002, 1.
118 Lord Wilson of Dinton, 'The Mandarin Myth,' fourth lecture in a series on Tomorrow's Government, London, Royal Society for the Encouragement of Arts Manufacturers and Commerce, 1 March 2006, 9.
119 Quoted in U.K., Parliament, Select Committee on Public Administration, *Minutes of Evidence*, questions 352–9, 14 March 2002, 2.
120 Ibid., 1.
121 U.K., Parliament, Select Committee on Public Administration, *Minutes of Evidence*, questions 300–19, 7 March 2002, 2.

122 See, among others, 'Aide Apologises for Attacks Memo,' *BBC News*, 10 October 2001, www.bbc.co.uk.

123 See, for example, 'Feuding Whitehall Aides Are Forced to Resign,' www.politics.guardian.co.uk, 16 February 2002, and 'A Good Day for No. 10 to Bury Jo Moore's Career,' www.telegraph.co.uk.

124 Quoted in 'Britain: Government and Civil Service at Loggerheads,' www.wsws.org, 8 March 2002.

125 U.K., Parliament, 'Managing Communications in DTLR,' in Select Committee on Public Administration, *Eighth Report*, chapter 2, www.publications. parliament.uk/pa.

126 C.E.S. Franks, 'The Respective Responsibilities and Accountabilities of Ministers and Public Servants: A Study of the British Accounting Officer System and Its Relevance for Canada,' in Canada, Commission of Inquiry into the Sponsorship Program and Advertising Activities, *Restoring Accountability*, vol. 3 (Ottawa, 2006), 165.

127 Various consultations with current and former senior government officials, London and Oxford, February 2007.

128 Peter Aucoin, 'The Staffing and Evaluation of Canadian Deputy Ministers in Comparative Westminster Perspective: A Proposal for Reform,' in Canada, Commission of Inquiry into the Sponsorship Program and Advertising Activities, *Restoring Accountability; Research Studies*, vol. 1, *Parliament, Ministers and Deputy Ministers*, 323. See also Peter Barberis, *The Elite of the Elite: Permanent Secretaries in the British High Civil Service* (Aldershot: Dartmouth, 1996).

129 Franks, 'The Respective Responsibilities and Accountabilities of Ministers and Public Servants,' vol. 3, 182.

130 See, among others, R.A.W. Rhodes, 'United Kingdom, Everybody but Us,' in R.A.W. Rhodes and Paul Weller, eds, *The Changing World of Top Officials* (Buckingham: Open University Press, 2001), 118.

131 Aucoin, 'The Staffing and Evaluation of Canadian Deputy Ministers in Comparative Westminster Perspective,' 326.

132 Guy Lodge and Ben Rogers, *Whitehall's Black Box: Accountability and Performance in the Senior Civil Service* (London: Institute for Public Policy Research, 2006), 40.

133 Canada, Commission of Inquiry into the Sponsorship Program and Advertising Activities, Toronto roundtable, 5 October 2005.

134 Ed Straw, *The Dead Generalist: Reforming the Civil Service and Public Service* (London: Demos, 2004), 28.

135 'Four-Year Postings Time-Limited Postings,' www.civilservice.gov.uk./ archives/deliveryandreform.

136 Sir Christopher Foster, *Why Are We So Badly Governed?* (London: Public Management and Policy Association, 2005), 76.
137 Graham K. Wilson and Anthony Parker, 'Bureaucrats and Politicians in Britain,' *Governance* 16, 3 (July 2003): 370.
138 They have gone farther and argued that deputy ministers are now acting like ministers promoting party policy positions. See, for example, 'ACOA Head Shouldn't Promote Liberal Policy, Says Conservative MP,' *Daily Gleaner* (Fredericton), 5 March 2004, 1.
139 Lodge and Rogers, *Whitehall's Black Box*, 4.

11. Accountability: 'I Take the Blame, but I Am Not to Blame'

1 Canada, Commission of Inquiry into the Sponsorship Program and Advertising Activities, Ottawa, vol. 47, 8 December 2004, 8235.
2 Canada, Privy Council Office, *Responsibility in the Constitution* (Ottawa: Author, 1993), chapter 7.
3 Ibid., chapter 1: 2.
4 This information was provided by C.E.S. Franks in correspondence with the author, dated 7 May 2007.
5 Canada, Treasury Board Secretariat, *Access to Information Review Task Force Report – 4* (Ottawa: Author, August 2001), 6.
6 Canada, Privy Council Office, *Responsibility in the Constitution*, 3.
7 Notably, plans related to the introduction of the accounting officer concept. Consultations with senior Canadian government officials, Ottawa, 12 September 2006.
8 See, among others, Christopher Kam, 'Not Just Parliamentary "Cowboys and Indians," Ministerial Responsibility and Bureaucratic Drift,' *Governance* 13, 3, (July 2000): 380.
9 See, for example, Sir K.C. Wheare, *Maladministration and Its Remedies* (London: Stevens and Sons, 1973), 94.
10 See, among others, Barry K. Winetrobe, *The Accountability Debate: Ministerial Responsibility* (London: Home Affairs Section, Research Paper 9716, 28 January 1997), 9. See also Peter Aucoin and Mark D. Jarvis, *Modernizing Government Accountability: A Framework for Reform* (Ottawa: Canada School of Public Service, 2005), 67.
11 Alex Himelfarb in testimony before House of Commons Public Accounts Committee, 3 May 2004.
12 'Guité Links PMO Official to Scandal,' *Globe and Mail*, 16 May 2006, A6.
13 See, among others, John D. Huber and Charles K. Shipan, *Deliberate Discretion? The Institutional Foundations of Bureaucratic Autonomy* (Cambridge:

Cambridge University Press, 2002), chapter 4. See also Matthew Flinders, 'MPs and Icebergs: Parliament and Delegated Governance,' *Parliamentary Affairs* 57, 4 (2004): 767.

14 Richard Mulgan, *Holding Power to Account: Accountability in Modern Democracies* (Basingstoke: Palgrave Macmillan, 2003), chapter 1.

15 Consultations with Gérard Veilleux, Montreal, Canada, various dates.

16 'Gomery Inquiry: Jean Chrétien, a Former PM Testifies,' www.cbc.ca/news, 8 February 2005.

17 'Enron Collapse Most Painful Thing in My Life, Lay Says,' *Globe and Mail*, 3 May 2006, B14.

18 'Deal Reached in Domi Divorce Battle,' *Globe and Mail*, 27 September 2006, A3.

19 'Public Works Issuing More Window Dressing,' *Citizen* (Ottawa), 13 January 1995, A2.

20 'McClung Travel of No Benefit: MPs,' *Ottawa Sun*, 9 March 2004, www.canoe.ca.

21 See, among others, 'Public Works Advisers Sent Packing,' *Globe and Mail*, 1 September 2006, www.theglobeandmail.com.

22 Consultations with a deputy minister, Canadian government, Ottawa, 12 September 2006.

23 J. Patrick Boyer, *Just Trust Us: The Erosion of Accountability in Canada* (Toronto: Dundurn Press, 2003), 68.

24 'Federal Sponsorship Scandal,' *CBC News Online*, 19 June 2006, www.cbc.ca/news/background.

25 Canada, Privy Council Office, *Crisis Management* (Ottawa: Author, nd), 5–14.

26 Robert D. Behn, *Rethinking Democratic Accountability* (Washington, DC: Brookings Institution Press, 2001), 85.

27 A deputy minister made a similar observation in Robin V. Sears, 'The Old Accountability Shuffle,' *Policy Options* 27, 5 (June 2006): 21.

28 Christopher Hood, 'A Public Management for All Seasons,' *Public Administration* 69, 1 (1991): 3–19.

29 Mulgan, *Holding Power to Account*, 14.

30 U.K., Parliament, Select Committee on Public Administration, *Eighth Report*, www.publications.parliament.uk./pa/com, 2001–2, 1.

31 See, among many others, C.E.S. Franks, *The Parliament of Canada* (Toronto: University of Toronto Press, 1987).

32 'So You've Served Your Country. So What?' *Globe and Mail*, 27 February 2007, A3.

33 H. George Frederickson, 'Research and Knowledge in Administrative

Ethics,' makes this point in T.L. Cooper, ed., *Handbook of Administrative Ethics* (New York: Marcel Dekker, 1994).

34 Hugh Segal, *The Long Road Back: The Conservative Journey 1993–2006* (Toronto: HarperCollins, 2006), 164.

35 Sears, 'The Old Accountability Shuffle,' 22.

36 Quoted in 'Coverage of TieLinda's Scandal Sign of Things to Come in Infotainment Age,' *Telegraph Journal* (Saint John), 29 September 2006, A8.

37 Eddie Goldenberg, *The Way It Works: Inside Ottawa* (Toronto: McClelland and Stewart, 2006), 5.

38 Edward Greenspon and Anthony Wilson-Smith, *Double Vision: The Inside Story of the Liberals in Power* (Toronto: Doubleday, 1996), 253.

39 Boyer, *Just Trust Us,* 30.

40 Canada, Office of the Auditor General, *Report to the House of Commons: Reflections on a Decade of Service to Parliament* (Ottawa: Author, 2002), 34–6.

41 Canada, Testimony of Brian MacAdam to the House of Commons Standing Committee on Public Accounts, 3 February 2005, quoted in Liane E. Benoit and C.E.S. Franks, 'For the Want of a Nail: The Role of Internal Audit in the Sponsorship Scandal,' in Canada, Commission of Inquiry into the Sponsorship Scandal and Advertising Activities, *Restoring Accountability: Research Studies,* vol. 2, *The Public Service and Transparency* (Ottawa, 2006), 275–6.

42 Benoit and Franks, 'For the Want of a Nail,' 276–86.

43 Canada, Treasury Board Secretariat, *Review of the Respective Responsibilities and Accountabilities of Ministers and Senior Officials* (Ottawa: Author, 2005), 42 and 46.

44 U.K., Privy Council Office, *Review of Intelligence on Weapons of Mass Destruction: Report of a Committee of Privy Councillors* (London: Stationery Office, HC 898, 14 July 2004). See also U.K., Parliament, Select Committee on Public Administration, *Minutes of Evidence,* Questions 500–19, 21 October 2004, 1.

45 U.K., Parliament, Select Committee on Public Administration, *Evidence Heard in Public,* Questions 703–915, 12 January 2005, 16, www.publications.parliament.uk/pa, and Sir Alan Budd, *An Inquiry into an Application for Indefinite Leave to Remain* (London: Stationery Office, HC 175, 21 December 2004).

46 Justice John Gomery asked this question at all five roundtable sessions held across Canada. Canada, Commission of Inquiry into the Sponsorship Program and Advertising Activities, Ottawa, 2005.

47 See, among others, Sharon Sutherland, 'The Al-Mashat Affair: Administrative Responsibility in Parliamentary Institutions,' *Canadian Public Administration,* 34, 4 (Winter 1991): 395.

48 Diana Woodhouse, 'UK Ministerial Responsibility in 2002: The Tale of Two Resignations,' *Public Administration* 82, 1 (2004): 16.

49 P. Jones, 'Reviewing the Fourth Estate: Democratic Accountability and the Media,' *Journal of Sociology* 36, 3 (2000): 239–47.

50 Diana Woodhouse, 'The Reconstruction of Constitutional Accountability,' Newcastle Law School Working Papers 2000/10, Department of Law, Oxford Brookes University, 4.

51 Boyer, *Just Trust Us*, 141.

52 Ibid., 135.

53 See, for example, 'Quebec, Ottawa Waste Tax Dollars in Budget Battle,' 23 February 1999, www.newsworld.cbc.ca, and 'Auditor General Blasts Gun Registry Mess,' www.thecanadianencyclopedia.com, undated.

54 'Since Radwanski, Ottawa's Top 99 Bureaucrats Have Spent $14,000,000 on Travel and Hospitality in a System Ripe for Abuse,' *Maclean's*, 29 May 2006, 18.

55 Ibid.

56 Fraser Institute, *Government Failure in Canada, 2005 Report*, Occasional Paper Series 86 (Vancouver: Author, October 2005), 39.

57 Andrew Cohen, 'Double Toil and Trouble, Foreign Burn and Trade Bubble,' *Globe and Mail*, 22 February 2005, A15.

58 Matthew Elliott, *The Bumper Book of Government Waste: The Scandal of the Squandered Billions from Lord Irvine's Wallpaper to EU Saunas* (London: Harriman House, 2006), 7.

59 See, among others, 'How the Wheels Came off U.K. PLC,' *Sunday Times*, 22 January 2006, 13.

60 Consultation with an official, London, 19 February 2007.

61 'Pettigrew Says Driver's $10,000 Trips Justified,' www.ctv.ca, 14 September 2005.

62 See, among others, 'The Sleaze That Won't Go Away,' www.ness.bbc.co.uk., December 1999.

63 Richard Kinsber, 'British General Election 1997: Election Manifestos, Political Science Resources,' www.psr.keele.ac.uk, 27 February 2006.

64 'Cameron: Make Me PM and I'll Let Parliament Decide on Going to War,' www.politics.guardian.co.uk, 7 May 2006.

65 'Consultations with a member of Parliament while director of research for the Commission of Inquiry. Canada, Commission of Inquiry into the Sponsorship Program and Advertising Activities, Ottawa, 8 November 2005.

66 Canada, Library on Parliament, *The Parliament We Want: Parliamentarians' Views on Parliamentary Reform*, a report prepared by the Library of

Parliament under the direction of two MPs and one senator (Ottawa: Author, December 2003), 6 and 10.

67 See, among others, David C. Docherty, *Legislatures* (Vancouver: University of British Columbia Press, 2005).

68 Patrick Borkey testifying before Canada, Standing Committee on Government Operations and Estimates (Ottawa: House of Commons, 21 November 2006).

69 Canada, Treasury Board Secretariat, *2006–2007 Estimates, Parts I and II, The Main Estimates* (Ottawa: Author, 2006), 4.

70 Commission of Inquiry into the Sponsorship Program and Advertising Activities, Testimony of Jocelyne Bourgon, Transcripts, vol. 48, 8300.

71 Consultations with senior government officials, Ottawa, various dates.

72 U.K., Treasury, 'Budget 2006 Summary' (London: Author, 2006).

73 U.K., Treasury, 'Central Government Supply Estimates 2006–07,' Vote on Account (London: Author, HC 465, November 2005).

74 Consultations with U.K. MPs and officials working with parliamentary committees, London, various dates in February 2007.

75 Peter Aucoin, 'Improving Government Accountability,' *Canadian Parliamentary Review* (Autumn 2006): 22.

76 This information was provided by C.E.S. Franks in correspondence with the author, dated 7 May 2007.

77 David Good, *The Politics of Public Money: Spenders, Guardians, Priority Settlers and Financial Watchdogs – Inside the Canadian Government* (Toronto: University of Toronto Press, 2007), 32.

78 Quoted in Donald J. Savoie, *Breaking the Bargain: Public Servants, Ministers, and Parliament* (Toronto: University of Toronto Press, 2003), 233.

79 See, among others, 'How to Be a Civil Servant,' www.civilservant.org.uk., undated, and U.K., Cabinet Office, Propriety and Ethics Team, 'Departmental Evidence and Response to Select Committees (the Osmotherly Rules),' www.cabinetoffice.gov.uk., undated.

80 'Sir Andrew Turnbull's Valedictory Lecture,' London, 26 July 2005, 15.

81 Aucoin and Jarvis, *Modernizing Government Accountability*, 67. See also Canada, Auditor General, Report to the House of Commons, *Reporting Performance to Parliament: Progress Too Slow*, December 2000, chapter 19. Canada, Auditor General, Report to the House of Commons, *Rating Departmental Performance Reports*, 2003, chapter 1. U.K., Comptroller and Auditor General, National Audit Office, *Good Practice in Performance Reporting in Executive Agencies and Non-Departmental Public Bodies*, March 2000. House of Commons, Select Committee on Public Administration, *On Target? Government by Measurement*, vol. 1, Fifth Report of Session 2002–3, 22 July 2003.

Australia, Auditor General, Report No. 11, 2003–4, Performance Audit, *Annual Performance Reporting*, 2003. New Zealand, Controller and Auditor General, *Reporting Public Sector Performance*, 2nd ed., January 2002.

82 Peter Aucoin and D.J. Savoie, *Managing Strategic Change* (Ottawa: Canadian Centre for Management Development, 1998).

83 U.K., Keith Burgess, Caroline Burton, and Greg Parston, 'Accountability for Results' (London: Treasury, undated), 1, 4, and 5.

84 David Richards and Martin Smith, 'Central Control and Policy Implementation in the U.K.: A Case Study of the Prime Minister's Delivery Unit,' Sheffield University, 8 August 2006, mimeo, 22.

85 See, among many others, 'Tories Pledge to Rein in Public Spending,' www.society.guardian.co.uk., 17 July 2006.

86 'Releasing Resources for the Frontline: Independent Review of Public Efficiency,' www.hon-treasury.gov.uk/spending.review, 12 July 2004.

87 U.K., Office of Public Service Reform, *Better Government Services: Executive Agencies in the 21st Century* (London: Stationery Office, 2007), 13, 31, and 34.

88 Canada, Commission of Inquiry into the Sponsorship Program and Advertising Activities, *Restoring Accountability: Research Studies*, vol. 1, *Parliament, Ministers and Deputy Ministers* (Ottawa, 2006).

89 See, among others, 'Even Liberals Attack Government over Gun Registry Costs,' www.cbc.ca, 4 December 2002.

90 'McLellan Censured over Gun Registry,' *Citizen* (Ottawa), 2 November 2006, A1.

91 Ibid.

92 Ibid.

93 Peter Dobell and Martin Ulrich, 'Parliament and Financial Accountability,' in Canada, Commission of Inquiry into the Sponsorship Scandal and Advertising Activities, *Restoring Accountability: Research Studies*, vol. 1, *Parliament, Ministers and Deputy Ministers* (Ottawa, 2006) 25.

94 Ibid., 37.

95 Ibid., 2–37.

96 Ibid., 37.

97 Ibid., 16–17.

98 Kevin Theakston, *The Civil Service 1945* (Oxford: Blackwell, 1995), 169.

99 Flinders, 'MPs and Icebergs,' 781.

100 Canada, Office of the Auditor General, *Report of the Auditor General of Canada to the House of Commons for Fiscal Year Ended 31 March 1976* (Ottawa: Supply and Services, 1976), 10.

101 Donald J. Savoie, *The Politics of Public Spending in Canada* (Toronto: University of Toronto Press, 1990), chapter 6.

102 David Judge, *The Parliamentary State* (London: Sage, 1993), 47.
103 Jonathan Malloy, 'The Standing Committee on Public Accounts,' in Canada, Commission of Inquiry into the Sponsorship Scandal and Advertising Activities, *Restoring Accountability: Research Studies* vol. 1, *Parliament, Ministers and Deputy Ministers* (Ottawa, 2006), 64–100.
104 Consultation with Hon. Reg Alcock, Ottawa, 8 October 2005.
105 Alasdair Roberts, 'Worrying about Misconduct: The Control Lobby and the PS 2000 Reforms,' *Canadian Public Administration* 39, 4 (1997): 518.
106 Canada, House of Commons, *Transcript of Testimony before the Public Accounts Committee* (Ottawa: Author, 4 May 2004), 5.
107 Mulgan, *Holding Power to Account*, 200, and Savoie, *Breaking the Bargain*.
108 Barry K. Winetrobe, *The Accountability Debate: Ministerial Responsibility* (London: Home Affairs Section, 1997), 81.
109 Canada, House of Commons, Standing Committee on Public Accounts, *Evidence Number 51*, Ottawa, 25 October 2005, 2.
110 Ibid.
111 Judge, *The Parliamentary State*.
112 Canada, Treasury Board Secretariat, *Estimates Part II and III* (Ottawa: Author, 2006–7), and consultations with Jean-Carol Pelletier, adviser to the minister of transport, infrastructure and communities, Ottawa, 1 November 2006.
113 Consultations with Jean-Carol Pelletier, adviser to the minister of transport, infrastructure and communities, Ottawa, 1 November 2006.
114 Quoted in Winetrobe, *The Accountability Debate*, 73.
115 Ibid., 79.
116 Alasdair S. Roberts, 'Spin Control and Freedom of Information: Lessons for the United Kingdom from Canada,' *Public Administration* 82, 2 (2005): 4.
117 Ibid., 8, 9, and 13.
118 See, among others, Alasdair Roberts, 'Two Challenges in Administration of the Access to Information Act,' in Canada, Commission of Inquiry into the Sponsorship Program and Advertising Activities, *Restoring Accountability: Research Studies*, vol. 2, *The Public Service and Transparency* (Ottawa, 2006).
119 Consultations with an MP, London, 20 February 2007.
120 Mark Bovens, *The Quest for Responsibility: Accountability and Citizenship in Complex Organizations* (Cambridge: Cambridge University Press, 1998), 85.
121 Ibid., 86.
122 Colin Turpin, *British Government and the Constitution: Texts, Cases and Materials*, 2nd ed. (London: Oxford University Press, 1994), 438.

123 Udo Pesch, *The Predicaments of Publicness* (The Netherlands: Eburon, 2005), 135.
124 John Martin, *Changing Accountability Relations: Politics, Consumers and the Market* (Paris: OECD, Public Management Service, 1997), 6.
125 M. Weber, 'Politics as a Vocation,' in H.H. Gerth and C.W. Mills, *From Max Weber: Essays in Sociology* (New York: Oxford University, 1958), 95.
126 Aucoin, 'Improving Government Accountability,' 20.
127 U.K., Select Committee on Public Administration, *Politics and Administration: Ministers and Civil Servants*, Third Report of Session 2006–7, vol. 1, 15 March 2007, 10.
128 www.homeoffice.gov.uk/about-us/organisation.
129 Ibid.
130 U.K., Select Committee on Public Administration, *Politics and Administration*, 10.
131 See, among others, Kevin Lynch, 'Remarks to Masters of Arts in Public Administration Society of Carleton University,' in which he quotes Prime Minister Harper (Ottawa: Privy Council Office, 9 March 2007), 8.
132 B. Guy Peters, *The Future of Governing: Four Emerging Models* (Lawrence: University Press of Kansas, 1996), 6.

12. Power: Locating It and Holding It to Account

1 'Inside Story,' *Globe and Mail*, 24 November 2006, A1 and A4.
2 'Nation Plan Costs Harper,' *Globe and Mail*, 28 November 2006, A1.
3 Consultation with a former senior government official, Oxford, 13 February 2007.
4 See Eddie Goldenberg, *The Way It Works: Inside Ottawa* (Toronto: McClelland and Stewart, 2006), 33.
5 Conservative Democracy Task Force, *An End to Sofa Government: Better Working of Prime Ministers and Cabinet* (London: Author, June 2007), 1.
6 Ibid., 5.
7 Max Weber, 'Politics as a Vocation,' in *From Max Weber: Essays in Sociology*, ed. and trans. H.H. Gerth and C. Wright Mills (New York: Oxford University Press, 1958), 91.
8 Donald J. Savoie, *Governing from the Centre: The Concentration of Power in Canadian Politics* (Toronto: University of Toronto Press, 1999).
9 Canada, Library of Parliament, *The Parliament We Want: Parliamentarians' Views on Parliamentary Reform*, a report prepared by the Library of Parliament under the direction of two MPs and one senator (Ottawa: Author, December 2003), 6.

10 'Retiring MP Decries Decline of Parliament,' *National Post*, 3 December 2005, A6.

11 John Major, *The Erosion of Parliamentary Government* (London: Centre for Policy Studies, 2003), 4 and 6.

12 David Docherty, *Mr. Smith Goes to Ottawa: Life in the House of Commons* (Vancouver: University of British Columbia Press, 1997), 190.

13 'PM Driven by Patronage Instincts? Or Economic Concerns,' *Globe and Mail*, 22 November 2000, A1.

14 Quoted in ibid.

15 'The Great Escape – Again and Again,' *Globe and Mail*, 3 November 2005, A8.

16 Canada, Office of the Ethics Commissioner, News Release, Ottawa, 21 November 2004.

17 Rod Love made these comments before Justice Gomery at a roundtable consultation in Edmonton, Commission of Inquiry into the Sponsorship Program and Advertising Activities, 19 October 2005, 2.

18 Arthur Kroeger made the point time and again at informal sessions where I was present and before the Public Accounts Committee of Parliament.

19 C.E.S. Franks, 'Members and Constituency Roles in the Canadian Federal System' (Kingston: Queen's University, 2007), mimeo, 6.

20 U.K., House of Commons, 'You and Your MP,' www.parliament.uk/commons, October 2005, 1.

21 Ibid., 3.

22 Ibid., 4.

23 http://www.alanmeale.co.uk/role.

24 See, among others, Philip Norton, 'The Growth of the Constituency Role of the MP,' *Parliamentary Affairs* 47, 6 (October 1994): 715.

25 Greg Power, *Representatives of the People* (London: Fabian Society, 1998), 3.

26 Ibid., 13.

27 Ibid., 3.

28 See, among others, Paul Thomas, 'The Emerging World of Accountabilities and Ethics: Parliamentary Scrutiny and Redress of Grievances,' a paper for the Canadian Study for Parliament Conference, Winnipeg, 9 December 2006, 14.

29 Stephen Coleman, 'New Media and Parliamentary Democracy,' in Philip Giddings, ed., *The Future of Parliament: Issues for a New Century* (Basingstoke: Palgrave Macmillan, 2005), 252.

30 The following MPs responded to my request: Barbara Follett, Paul Flynn, Gavin Strang, Tom Harris, Jim Sheridan, James Purnell, Derek Conway, John Randall, Adrian Sanders, Evan Harris, David Chaytor, Mark

Lazarowicz, Andrew George, John Horam, Robert Key, Keith Vaz, and Rudolph Viz. A number of MPs responded by saying that it is difficult to rank the importance of their duties because it changes over time. One wrote that the most important duty is to 'read, observe and listen to constituents' (Jill Henday). Another wrote that the five duties do not fully represent what MPs do. He argued, for example, that 'keeping in touch with constituents about what the MP is doing on their behalf' also constitutes an extremely important duty (Andrew Smith). It should be noted, however, that both observations stress the importance of their role on behalf of constituents.
31 See, among others, C.E.S. Franks, *The Parliament of Canada* (Toronto: University of Toronto Press, 1987).
32 Consultations with Robert Key, London, 7 February 2007.
33 Consultations with a government official, London, 19 February 2007.
34 Power, *Representatives of the People*, 12.
35 Ibid., 11.
36 Valence L. Ralice and V. Willis, *Member of Parliament: The Job of a Backbencher* (London: Macmillan, 1990), 5.
37 Lowell Murray, 'MPs, Political Parties and Parliamentary Democracy,' *Isuma* 1, 2 (Autumn 2000): 3.
38 C.E.S. Franks, *The Parliament of Canada*, and Christopher Foster, *British Government in Crisis* (Oxford: Hart Publishing, 2005).
39 Veteran *Globe and Mail* columnist Hugh Winsor made this observation before Justice Gomery at the Toronto roundtable consultations, Commission of Inquiry into the Sponsorship Program and Advertising Activities, Ottawa, 5 October 2005, 18.
40 See, among others, Institute for Research on Public Policy, *Parliament's Performance in the Budget Process: A Case Study*, Policy Matters, vol. 3, no. 5 (Montreal: Author, May 2002).
41 Canada, Office of the Auditor General, *Report of the Auditor General of Canada to the House of Commons* (Ottawa: Author, November 2006), chapter 1: 22, paragraph 67.
42 Canada, Library of Parliament, *The Parliament We Want*, 6–7.
43 Major, *The Erosion of Parliamentary Government*, 7.
44 Consultation with an official with the Library of Parliament, Ottawa, 17 November 2006.
45 Canada, Treasury Board Secretariat, 'Canada's Performance Report and the Broader Issue of Reporting to Parliament: A Concept Paper' (Ottawa: Author, 2005), 4.
46 Nevil Johnson, *Reshaping the British Constitution: Essays in Political Interpretation* (Basingstoke: Palgrave Macmillan, 2004).

47 Barry K. Winetrobe, 'The Accountability Debate: Ministerial Responsibility,' Research paper 97/6 (U.K., Home Affairs Section, 28 January 1997), 48.
48 David Natzler and Mark Hutton, 'Select Committees: Scrutiny à la Carte,' in Giddings, ed., *The Future of Parliament*, 75.
49 Johnson, *Reshaping the British Constitution*, 116.
50 Nevil Johnson, 'What of Parliament's Future?' in Giddings, ed., *The Future of Parliament*, 14.
51 According to National Statistics and the Cabinet Office, Personnel Statistics, the Home Office reported on 21 October 2004 that the Home Office had 67,800 employees. This number includes all employees, and only a small number of them would work on policy. U.K., Cabinet Office, Personnel Statistics, *Civil Service Staff Numbers: Media Brief* (London: Author, 21 October 2004), 9.
52 Consultations with members of Parliament and staff of parliamentary committees, Ottawa and London, various dates in September 2006 to February 2007.
53 See, for example, C.E.S. Franks, 'The Respective Responsibilities and Accountabilities of Ministers and Public Servants: A Study of the British Accounting Officer System and Its Relevance for Canada,' in Canada, Commission of Inquiry into the Sponsorship Program and Advertising Activities, *Restoring Accountability*, vol. 3 (Ottawa, 2006).
54 Consultations with U.K. MPs and staff of parliamentary committees, London, various dates in February 2007.
55 Anthony Barker, 'Political Responsibility for U.K. Prison Security – Ministers Escape Again,' in *Public Administration* 76, 1 (Spring 1998): 18.
56 Consultations with U.K. MPs and staff of parliamentary committees, London, various dates in February 2007.
57 Ibid.
58 Richard Whitaker, 'Parliament and Government, 2005–06: Reforms and Reflections,' *Parliamentary Affairs* 59, 4 (September 2006): 697.
59 See, among others, William Cross, *Political Parties* (Vancouver: University of British Columbia Press, 2004).
60 Cheryl S. King, 'Reforming American Public Administration: Public or Private Solutions,' in Mark R. Rutgers, ed., *Retracing Public Administration* (London: JAI Elsevier Science, 2003), 79–80.
61 M. Foley, *The British Presidency* (Manchester: Manchester University Press, 2000), 231.
62 Douglas Alexander and Stella Creasy, *We Can Be a Movement Capable of Making the 21st Century the Era of Progressive Change* (London: Demos, 2006), 32.

63 'Jean's Job Will Be to Prove Naysayers Wrong,' *Globe and Mail*, 4 August 2005, A4.

64 Howard R. Wilson, 'The Constantly Rising Ethics Bar,' notes for a presentation to the Canadian Centre for Ethics and Public Policy, 7 November 2002.

65 John Ibbitson, 'Suspicion Fuels Deep Scrutiny of Politicians,' *Globe and Mail*, 10 May 2006, A4.

66 Susan E. Scarrow, 'Parties without Members? Party Organizations in a Changing Electoral Environment,' in Russell J. Dalton and Martin P. Wattenberg, eds, *Parties without Partisans: Political Change in Advanced Industrial Democracies* (New York: Oxford University Press, 2000), 79–101.

67 Quoted in 'Volpé Should Quit Liberal Race,' *Toronto Star*, www.thestar.com.

68 'And They're Off,' *Chronicle Herald* (Halifax), 9 April 2006, A6. See also 'Liberal Party Run Like an Oligarchy: Grits,' *National Post*, 2 March 2006, A7.

69 See, among others, ibid; Dalton and Wattenberg, eds, *Parties without Partisans*; and various publications produced by the Institute for Research on Public Policy (Montreal) under its *Strengthening Canadian Democracy* series.

70 William Cross, 'Policy Study and Development in Canada's Political Parties,' in Laurent Dobuzinskis, Michael Howlett, and David Laycock, eds, *Policy Analysis in Canada* (Toronto: University of Toronto Press, 2007), chapter 17, 425.

71 Janine Brodie and Jane Jenson, 'Piercing the Smokescreen: Brokerage Parties and Class Politics,' in Alain Gagnon and A. Brian Tanguay, eds, *Canadian Parties in Transition* (Scarborough, ON: Nelson, 1991), 52–72.

72 Robert A. Young, 'Effecting Change: Do We Have the Political System to Get Us Where We Want to Go?' in G. Bruce Doern and B. Bryne Purchase, eds, *Canada at Risk? Canadian Public Policy in the 1990s* (Toronto: C.D. Howe Institute, 1991), 77.

73 See, among others, John Dunn, *Setting the People Free: The Story of Democracy* (London: Atlantic Books, 2005).

74 Alexander and Creasy, *We Can Be a Movement Capable of Making the 21st Century the Era of Progressive Change*, 37.

75 Canada's deputy prime minister was accused of political interference when she inquired about a specific case involving aircraft maintenance. See 'Deputy PM Accused of Interference,' *National Post*, 20 October 2005, A4.

76 See, for example, Tex Enemark, 'Ottawa's New Reality Show: Let's Make (and Keep) a Deal,' *Globe and Mail*, 22 March 2005, A19.

77 Consultation with a senior Canadian government official, Toronto, 12 October 2006.

78 David Richards and Martin Smith, 'Central Control and Policy Implementation in the U.K.: A Case Study of the Prime Minister's Delivery Unit,' *Journal of Comparative Policy Analysis* 8, 4 (December 2006): 415.
79 Richard Rose, *The Prime Minister in a Shrinking World* (Cambridge: Polity Press, 2001), 6, 10, and 24.
80 Graham K. Wilson and Anthony Barker, 'Bureaucrats and Politicians in Britain,' *Governance* 16, 3 (July 2003): 370. See also B. Guy Peters and Jon Pierre, eds, *Politicization of the Civil Service in Comparative Perspective: The Quest for Control* (London: Routledge, 2004), 40.
81 Canada, Office of the Prime Minister, 'Prime Minister Harper Establishes Advisory Committee on the Public Service,' news release (Ottawa, 21 November 2006).
82 'Mulroney's Old Top Guns to Fix PS for Harper,' *Citizen* (Ottawa), 22 November 2006, A1.
83 Canada, Privy Council Office, *Guidance for Deputy Ministers* (Ottawa: Author, 2003), 13.
84 Civil servants have, however, long held program implementation to be an important part of the responsibilities. See, for example, Joel D. Aberbach, Robert D. Putnam, and Bert A. Rockman, *Bureaucrats and Politicians in Western Democracies* (Cambridge, MA: Harvard University Press, 1981).
85 Nick D'Ombrain made these observations before Canada, *Federal Court Trial Division*, Examination no. 03–0629.6, Federal Court File No.T-1640–00, Ottawa, 7 July 2003, 17.
86 Lawrence Martin, 'Police Force or Political Force?' *Globe and Mail*, 18 March 2004, A15.
87 A senior PCO official made these comments before Justice Gomery at the Quebec roundtable, Commission of Inquiry into the Sponsorship Program and Advertising Activities, Quebec City, 14 September 2005.
88 Norman Spector, 'Public Servants Cannot Escape All the Blame,' *Globe and Mail*, 3 May 2004, A13.
89 Norman Spector, 'Above and Below the Sponsorship Radar,' *Globe and Mail*, 12 March 2004, A15.
90 Richards and Smith, 'Central Control and Policy Implementation in the U.K.,' 444. See also Steven Kelman, 'Improving Service Delivery Performance in the United Kingdom: Organization Theory Perspectives on Central Intervention Strategies,' *Journal of Comparative Policy Analysis* 8, 4 (December 2006): 393–419.
91 See 'Prime Minister's Delivery Unit (PMDU),' www.cabinetoffice.gov.uk.
92 Richards and Smith, 'Central Control and Policy Implementation in the U.K.,' 447.

93 See, for example, SES Research/Crossing Boundaries/Public Policy, www.cpac.ca/forms/index.

94 'Left, Right: You're Talking about Feet, Right?! *National Post*, 22 December 2005, A5.

95 See, among others, Cheryl Simrell King and Camilla Stivers, ' Citizens and Administrators: Roles and Relationships,' in Richard C. Box, ed., *Public Administration and Society: Critical Issues in American Governance* (London: M.E. Sharp, 2004), 276.

96 See, among others, François Simard, 'Self Interest in Public Administration: Niskanen and the Budget-Maximizing Bureaucrat,' *Canadian Public Administration* 47, 4 (Winter 2004): 406. Milton Friedman, quoted in 'Champion of the Free Market,' *National Post*, 17 November 2006, A17.

97 William A. Niskanen, Jr, *Bureaucracy and Representative Government* (Chicago: Aldine-Atherton, 1971).

98 'PM Irked as Diplomats Miss Activist's Hearing,' www.theglobeandmail.com, 6 February 2007, and 'Chinese Police Tortured Activist, Family Says,' www.theglobeandmail.com, 7 February 2007.

99 A senior minister from the Trudeau government made this observation before Justice Gomery, Commission of Inquiry into the Sponsorship Program and Advertising Activities, Quebec City, 14 September 2005.

100 A senior minister from the Mulroney government made this observation before Justice Gomery, Commission of Inquiry into the Sponsorship Program and Advertising Activities, Moncton, New Brunswick, 31 August 2005.

101 Sir Michael Bichard, 'Public Sector Reform' (London: Institute for Public Policy Research, February 2007), mimeo, 4.

102 Jonn Dunn, *Setting the People Free: The Story of Democracy* (London: Atlantic Books, 2005), and Arthur Lupia and Mathew D. McCubbins, *The Democratic Dilemma: Can Citizens Learn What They Need to Know?* (New York: Cambridge University Press, 1998), 1.

13. From Formal Processes, Rules, and a Doctrine to the Individual

1 Quoted in Charlotte Sausman and Rachel Locke, 'The British Civil Service: Examining the Question of Politicization,' in B. Guy Peters and Jon Pierre, eds, *Politicization of the Civil Service in Comparative Perspective: The Quest for Control* (London: Routledge, 2004), 115.

2 Peter Hennessy, *Cabinet* (Oxford: Blackwell, 1986), 115–16.

3 See, among others, Donald J. Savoie, *Governing from the Centre: The Concentration of Power in Canadian Politics* (Toronto: University of Toronto Press, 1999).

4 Consultations with a senior deputy minister, Ottawa, 24 November 2006.
5 See, for example, Nevil Johnson, *Reshaping the British Constitution: Essays in Political Interpretation* (Basingstoke: Palgrave Macmillan, 2004), 84.
6 See, among others, Christopher Foster, *British Government in Crisis* (Oxford: Hart Publishing, 2005) and Christopher Hood, Oliver James, and B. Guy Peters, *Controlling Modern Government: Variety, Commonality and Change* (Cheltenham: Edward Elgar, 2004), chapters 1, 2.1 and 3.9.
7 This was the main theme coming out of four extensive citizens' dialogue exercises. See Julian Abelson and François-Pierre Gauvin, *Transparency, Trust and Citizen Engagement: What Canadians Are Saying about Accountability* (Ottawa: Canadian Policy Research Network, December 2004), vi.
8 Johnson, *Reshaping the British Constitution*, 88.
9 Canada, Office of the Auditor General, *Matters of Special Importance* (Ottawa: Author, November 2006). The auditor general in Canada, for example, has made this case time and again since the late 1970s. In her 2006 annual report, the auditor general once again sounded the alarm over the government's apparent inability to manage spending. She pointed to three issues: the need to strengthen its challenge function, particularly for ongoing programs; the proper alignment of funding with program needs; and the increased use of Supplementary Estimates by departments instead of the main estimates.
10 'Sir Andrew Turnbull's Valedictory Lecture,' London, 26 July 2005, mimeo, 14.
11 'Before You Clamour for Results-Based Management in the Civil Service, Remember Chuck Guité Could Be Its Poster Boy,' www.theglobeandmail.com, 23 November 2005.
12 See, among others, Arend Lijphart, *Parliamentary versus Presidential Government* (Oxford: Oxford University Press, 1992).
13 There are many studies on principal-agent theory. See, among many others, J.J. Lamont, *Incentives and Political Economy: The Economic Theory of Incentives* (Cheltenham: Edward Elgar, 2003).
14 Richard W. Waterman and Kenneth J. Meier, 'Principal-Agent Models: An Expansion?' *Journal of Public Administration Research and Theory* 8, 2 (1998): 173–202.
15 Peter Barberis, 'The New Public Management and a New Accountability,' *Public Administration* 76, 3 (Autumn 1998): 464, and N. Lewis and D. Longley, 'Ministerial Responsibility: The Next Steps,' *Public Law* 3 (Autumn 1996): 501.
16 See, for example, Johnson, *Reshaping the British Constitution*, 134.
17 See, for example, James C. March and Johan P. Olsen, *Democratic Governance* (New York: Free Press, 1995).

18 See, among others, Jan-Erik Lane, *Public Administration and Public Management: The Principal-Agent Perspective* (London: Routledge, 2005), 52.
19 'Zafirovski Knows the Clock Is Ticking for Nortel,' *Globe and Mail*, 2 January 2007, B4.
20 See, among others, Joseph S. Nye Jr, Philip D. Zelikow, and David C. King, eds, *Why People Don't Trust Government* (Cambridge, MA: Harvard University Press, 1997).
21 See, among others, Richard Mulgan, *Holding Power to Account: Accountability in Modern Democracies* (London: Palgrave Macmillan, 2003), chapter 3.
22 See, among others, Lane, *Public Administration and Public Management*, 56.
23 Barberis, 'The New Public Management and a New Accountability,' 464.
24 Allen Schick, 'Can National Legislatures Regain an Effective Voice in Budget Policy?' *OECD Journal on Budgeting* 1, 3 (2002): 22.
25 See, among others, David Docherty, *Legislatures* (Vancouver: University of British Columbia Press, 2005).
26 Schick, 'Can National Legislatures Regain an Effective Voice in Budget Policy?' 25.
27 Joel Molinier 'Parliament's Financial Powers: A Comparison of France and Britain,' in David Coombes, ed., *The Power of the Purse: A Symposium on the Role of European Parliaments in Budgetary Decisions* (New York: Praeger Publishers, 1975), 211.
28 Schick, 'Can National Legislatures Regain an Effective Voice in Budget Policy?' 24.
29 Frank Anechiario and James B. Jacobs, *The Pursuit of Absolute Integrity: How Corruption Control Makes Government Ineffective* (Chicago: University of Chicago Press, 1998).
30 George Post, Conversations with Canadian Public Service Leaders (Ottawa: Canadian Centre for Management Development, March 1996), 13.
31 U.K., House of Commons, Select Committee on Public Administration, *Politics and Administration: Ministers and Civil Servants*, Third Report of Session 2006–7, vol. 1, 15 March 2007, 3–4.
32 Barbara Wake Carroll and David Siegel, *Service in the Field: The World of Front-Line Public Servants* (Montreal and Kingston: McGill-Queen's University Press, 1999), 119.
33 Canada, Office of the Auditor General, *Getting at the Root Causes: Why Things Go Wrong in Government Programs* (Ottawa: Author, May 2004), mimeo, 6.
34 Kate Jenkins, 'Parliament, Government and the Civil Service,' *Parliamentary Affairs* 57, 4 (2004): 801.

35 Johnson, *Reshaping the British Constitution*.
36 See, among others, Baroness Onora O'Neill, 'Question of Trust,' Reith Lectures 2002, www.bbc.co.uk/radio4.
37 'Walk with Order' is in response to Matthew Flinders, *Walking without Order: Delegated Governance and the British State* (Oxford: Oxford University Press, 2005).
38 Tony Blair said that the powers of the prime minister, 'including the exercise of power under the Royal Prerogative, have evolved over many years, drawing on convention and usage, and it is not possible to precisely define them.' Quoted in G. Allen, *The Last Prime Minister: Being Honest about the UK Presidency* (London: Politicas, 2001), vii.
39 Jean Chrétien, *Straight from the Heart* (Toronto: Key Porter Books, 1985), 85.
40 Canada, Office of the Prime Minister, 'Letter to Eminent Canadians' (Ottawa: Author, 14 December 2006).
41 Conservative Party of Canada, *Stand Up for Canada* (Ottawa: Author, 2006), 7–14.
42 See, among others, Jenkins, 'Parliament, Government and the Civil Service,' 801.
43 Johnson, *Reshaping the British Constitution*, 10.
44 Ibid., 19.
45 Jenkins, 'Parliament, Government and the Civil Service,' 811.
46 Alasdair S. Roberts, 'Spin Control and Freedom of Information: Lessons for the United Kingdom from Canada,' *Public Administration* 83, 1 (March 2005): 4.
47 See, for example, 'The Ministerial Code' (London: House of Commons Library, July 2005), 7.
48 Quoted in Guy Lodge and Ben Rogers, *Whitehall's Black Box: Accountability and Performance in the Senior Civil Service* (London: Institute for Public Policy Research, 2006), 48.
49 Ibid., 84.
50 Lodge and Rogers make the same observation in ibid., 7.
51 'Mulroney's Old Top Guns to Fix PS for Harper,' *Citizen* (Ottawa), 22 November 2006, A1.
52 Sir Michael Bichard, 'Public Sector Reform' (London: Institute for Public Policy Research, 12 February 2007), mimeo, 4.
53 Paul Appleby, *Policy and Administration* (Tuscaloosa: University of Alabama Press, 1949), 170.
54 David M. Levitan, 'Political Ends and Administration Means,' *Public Administration Review* 31, 3 (Autumn 1943): 316.

55 Arthur Kroeger, 'The Elected Should Have the Last Word,' *Globe and Mail*, 7 February 2006, A15.
56 Frederik Mosher, *Democracy and the Public Service*, 2nd ed. (New York: Oxford University Press, 1982), 6.
57 C.E.S. Franks gives a full account of the two cases in his 'The Respective Responsibilities and Accountabilities of Ministers and Public Servants: A Study of the British Accounting Officer System and Its Relevance for Canada,' in Canada, Commission of Inquiry into the Sponsorship Program and Advertising Activities, *Restoring Accountability*, vol. 3 (Ottawa, 2006), 218–27.
58 See, among others, Anthony Barker, 'Political Responsibility for U.K. Prison Security – Ministers Escape Again,' *Public Administration* 76, 1 (Spring 1998): 1–23.
59 'Secret Home Office Papers on Prison Row Fail to Clear Howard,' www.politics.guardian.co.uk, 2 March 2005.
60 Ibid.
61 Barker, 'Political Responsibility for U.K. Prison Security – Ministers Escape Again,' 3.
62 See, among others, Johnson, *Reshaping the British Constitution*, 89–90.

Index

academics, and civil service, 11, 15, 75

Accenture, 197, 198

access to information commissioner (Canada), 286–7

access to information legislation, 71; and anonymity, 65–6, 161; in Britain, 69–70, 163–4; central agencies and, 202–3; and front-line workers, 212–13; impact of, 161–3, 286–7; and media, 69–70, 160–1; ministerial code and, 137; ministers and, 202–3; opinions regarding, 45; and 'oral culture,' 161–2, 163, 287; and protection of governments/ ministers from error, 143; and public opinion surveys, 161; and scrutiny of civil servants, 134; and transparency, 328; use by MPs vs Parliament, 300; and values/ethics, 135; and whistle-blowing, 164

accountability: accounting officers and, 55–6, 57, 63; authority and, 257, 258, 284; as avoidance of mistakes, 264; under Blair, 81; and blame, 261, 268–73, 279, 283, 332; breakdowns of, 282–3; chain of, 328–31, 339, 340; citizens and, 195, 265, 316–17, 322; civil servants and, 178, 288, 332, 340, 341; deputy ministers and, 55, 56–7, 62–3, 178, 246; as election campaign commitment, 272–3; and entrepreneurship, 331; expenditure budgets and, 329–30; of formal processes, 325; for government spending, 328–9; within hierarchy, 258, 288; horizontal/joined-up government and, 153; individuals and, 322, 335–9; and 'it depends,' 339; joining of executive and legislative branches and, 324; management and, 87, 88, 89, 92, 127, 140, 218, 321; managerial vs political, 267; media and, 170–1, 279, 335; and minimization of political damage, 264, 266; and minister–civil servant relationship, 317; ministerial responsibility and, 59–60, 61–2, 257, 259, 283, 285; of ministers, 32, 56, 57; of monarchy, 26; MPs and, 330; network government and, 325; and news management, 266; officers of Parliament and, 170–1;

ethics, 335; anonymity and, 128; of civil service, 54, 125; in government, 124; image of politicians vs public servants and, 125–6; public opinion of standards, 118, 119. *See also* values

Ethics Commissioner (Canada), 296

European Commission (EC), 13

European Convention of Human Rights, 51

European Union (EU), 51, 233

European Values Survey, 97

executive agencies, 78, 88, 184–5, 258, 279. *See also* Next Steps: agencies

Exit, Voice and Loyalty (Hirschman), 147

expenditure. *See* spending

expenditure budgets, 330; accountability and, 329–30; cabinet and, 330–1; departmental, 333; and focus on individual, 345

external examiners, 338

Fabian Society, 74, 298

family ties, disruption of, 99–101

Fathers of Confederation, 36

Federal Accountability Act (Canada), 58

Federal Accountability Action Plan (Canada), 247

federal-provincial relations: and briefing material, 203; division of powers, 36, 53; prime ministers and, 233

Federalist Papers (Madison), 22

feudalism, 7

Financial Administration Act (FAA) (Canada), 64, 227, 333, 343

Financial Management Information system, 77

Finer, Samuel E., 3–4, 7, 21, 23, 37

Fisher, Douglas, 159

Fisheries Resource Conservation Council (Canada), 154

Fleury, Jean-Guy, 189

Flinders, Matthew, 282

Foley, Michael, 304

Fonberg, Rob, 271

For Want of a Nail (Benoit, Franks), 267–8

formal processes: for decision making, 325; individualism vs, 319–20; for policy making, 325; and program decisions, 326

Foster, Sir Christopher, 50, 68, 144, 152, 159, 227, 254

Fox, Graham, 175

franchise. *See* voting rights

Franks, C.E.S. (Ned), 50, 62, 246, 357n66; *For Want of a Nail*, 267–8

Fraser, John, 67, 151

Fraser, Sheila, 168. *See also* Auditor General, Office of the (Canada)

Fraser v. Public Service Staff Relations Board, 61

fraud, 132–3, 189

Freedom of Information Act (U.K.), 65, 69–70, 163

Friedman, Milton, 316

front-line managers, 222–3; authority shifted to, 321; common service agencies and, 221; and employment equity, 222; ministers and, 313; and oversight bodies, 221–2

front-line workers: and access to information legislation, 201, 212–13; citizens and, 213; and customers, 213; ministers and, 212–13; and performance evaluations,

managers: accountability of, 88; delegation of authority to, 77; empowerment of, 77, 90; government administrators as, 76–7; on information technology, 197–8; resignations of, 178–9; salaries of, 90–1; in staff positions, 203. *See also* line departments/managers; program managers

mandarinate: decline of, 11, 15; origins of, 25; postwar period of, 45; self-confidence, 71

Marshall, Geoffrey, 32–3, 42, 51

Marson, Brian, 248

Martin, Lawrence, 241, 313–14

Martin, Pat, 135

Martin, Paul: appointment of Reporter, 239; centralization of government under, 230; and Chrétien's approach, 230, 306; on Himelfarb, 65; and Martin-Alcock reforms, 217–18; public sector reforms, 82–3, 84; and sponsorship scandal, 82, 263

Mary II, Queen, 28

Massé, Marcel, 152

McClung, Lucie, 262

McLachlin, Beverly, 52–3, 170

McNaught, Kenneth, 36

'Measurement of Customer Satisfaction' (U.K.), 208

media, 157–60; and access to information legislation, 69–70, 160–1; and accountability, 170–1, 335; in Britain, 68–9, 250, 251–2; and cabinet ministers, 236; change in, 158, 159; civil servants and, 145, 157–8, 310–11; confidence in, 117, 118, 119*table*; and decline of Parliament, 50; and elections, 159–60;

'gotcha' journalism, 68, 157, 291, 331; government gaffes and, 143, 144; and individualism, 265–6; and Iraqi WMD issue, 250; ministers and, 39, 269; and political-administrative boundaries, 144; and political patronage, 304; and politician–civil servant relationship, 145; politicians and, 308; power of, 157–8, 251–2, 291; pressure, 17; prime ministers and, 231, 236; and Prime Minister's Questions (PMQs), 275; relations with government, 66–70; role of, 158; scrutiny of public sector, 262–3, 265; and spending estimates, 273; status-participant cabinet ministers and, 235; strategy for, 159; and whistle-blowing, 164. *See also* television

members of Parliament (MPs): and accountability, 275, 330; in Britain, 273, 275, 297, 298–9; challenges to governments, 303; citizens on role of, 295; and constituencies, 295–6, 297, 298–300, 308, 328; demands on, 279; duties of, 298–9; governing by, 32; gun registry and, 280–1; and HRDC affair, 195; meetings with ministers, 308–9; numbers of, 275; and parliamentary committees, 301–2; payment for questions asked in Parliament, 135; revolts of, 303; role of, 295–6, 297; spending estimates and, 273–82; turnover of, 273, 275

merit principle, 4, 25, 124, 129, 174–5, 242

Mill, John Stuart, 34; *Considerations on Representative Government*, 149

salaries. *See* remuneration
sanctions, 268–9, 270
Scarlett, John, 251
Schick, Allen, 331
Schumpeter, Joseph, 34
Scott, Andy, 202–3, 269
Scott inquiry, 59
scrutiny: of accountability, 265;
media, 262–3, 265; by Parliament,
301; and performance assessment,
339–40; of politicians, 305; of
prime ministers, 227
Sears, Robin, 157
Second World War: bureaucracy during, 10, 53; governments during,
10
Secret Intelligence Service (U.K.), 250
secretary to the cabinet (U.K.), 312
secularism, 97–9
Segal, Hugh, 265
Select Committee on Public Administration (U.K.), 126, 230, 249, 251,
265
self-interest: among senior civil servants, 309; ascendancy of, 192; loyalty to civil service vs, 175; loyalty
to political parties vs, 174; program decisions and, 326; public
opinion of, 316; rational choice
theory and, 15
Senate (Canada), 37
Senior Appointment Selection Committee (U.K.), 253
senior civil servants: and accountability, 269, 331, 340; appointment
of, 17; bosses of, 226; court insiders
and, 240; and horizontal government, 228; and joined-up government, 228; loss of institutional
memory, 248, 254, 255; mobility of,

248, 254; performance assessment
of, 339–40; and plausible deniability, 92; policy role, 228–9; and policy vs administration, 228; political
partisanship of, 183, 247–8; politicization of, 246–7; and politics,
225–6; and prime ministers, 241;
prime ministers' expectations of,
228; program managers vs, 331–2;
protective role, 255; qualities of,
226; resignations of, 225, 229; rotation of, 224–5, 229, 248; scapegoat-
ing of, 269; skills of, 228–9; and
sponsorship scandal, 323; tenure
of, 225. *See also* deputy ministers;
mandarinate; minister–senior civil
servant relationship; permanent
secretaries; prime minister–senior
civil servant relationship
Service Canada, 213
service delivery: in Britain, 207–8,
210–11; capability reviews, 219;
deputy ministers and, 207;
improvement of, 205, 209, 328;
Internet and, 196; networking and,
292; 'outside-in' citizen approach,
205–6; by private sector, 208, 210–
11; and public confidence in civil
servants, 209
Sgro, Judy, 158–9, 269
Shakespeare, William, 44
Shared Governance Organizations,
285
Sharp, Mitchell, 237
Shawinigate, 82, 127, 295–6, 313–14
Siegel, David, 204, 207, 215, 333
Simpson, Jeffrey, 49, 67, 158–9
Singh, Harjet, 158
single-issue movements, 154
Sixsmith, Martin, 252, 253

The Institute of Public Administration of Canada Series
in Public Management and Governance

Networks of Knowledge: Collaborative Innovation in International Learning,
Janice Stein, Richard Stren, Joy Fitzgibbon, and Melissa Maclean
*The National Research Council in the Innovative Policy Era: Changing
Hierarchies, Networks, and Markets*, G. Bruce Doern and Richard
Levesque
*Beyond Service: State Workers, Public Policy, and the Prospects for Demo-
cratic Administration*, Greg McElligott
*A Law Unto Itself: How the Ontario Municipal Board Has Developed and
Applied Land Use Planning Policy*, John G. Chipman
Health Care, Entitlement, and Citizenship, Candace Redden
*Between Colliding Worlds: The Ambiguous Existence of Government
Agencies for Aboriginal and Women's Policy*, Jonathan Malloy
*The Politics of Public Management: The HRDC Audit of Grants and
Contributions*, David A. Good
*Dream No Little Dreams: A Biography of the Douglas Government of
Saskatchewan, 1944–1961*, Albert W. Johnson
Governing Education, Ben Levin
*Executive Styles in Canada: Cabinet Structures and Leadership Practices
in Canadian Government*, edited by Luc Bernier, Keith Brownsey, and
Michael Howlett
The Roles of Public Opinion Research in Canadian Government,
Christopher Page
The Politics of CANDU Exports, Duane Bratt
Policy Analysis in Canada: The State of the Art, edited by Laurent
Dobuzinskis, Michael Howlett, and David Laycock
Digital State at the Leading Edge: Lessons from Canada, Sanford Borins,
Kenneth Kernaghan, David Brown, Nick Bontis, Perri 6, and Fred
Thompson
*The Politics of Public Money: Spenders, Guardians, Priority Setters, and
Financial Watchdogs inside the Canadian Government*, David A. Good
*Court Government and the Collapse of Accountability in Canada and
the United Kingdom*, Donald J. Savoie